THE GIRL IN THE GREEN DRESS

JENI HAYNES and DR GEORGE BLAIR-WEST
with ALLEY PASCOE

hachette
AUSTRALIA

hachette
AUSTRALIA

First published in Australia and New Zealand in 2022
by Hachette Australia
(an imprint of Hachette Australia Pty Limited)
Gadigal Country, Level 17, 207 Kent Street, Sydney, NSW 2000
www.hachette.com.au

This edition published in 2023

Hachette Australia acknowledges and pays our respects to the past, present and future
Traditional Owners and Custodians of Country throughout Australia and recognises the
continuation of cultural, spiritual and educational practices of Aboriginal and Torres Strait
Islander peoples. Our head office is located on the lands of the Gadigal people of the
Eora Nation.

NATIONAL
LIBRARY
OF AUSTRALIA

A catalogue record for this
work is available from the
National Library of Australia

ISBN: 978 0 7336 4487 0 (paperback)

Cover design by Christabella Designs
Cover photography courtesy of author collections; Shutterstock
Internal photography courtesy of author collections unless otherwise credited
Typeset in Adobe Garamond Pro by Kirby Jones
Printed and bound in Australia by McPherson's Printing Group

THE GIRL IN THE GREEN DRESS

From Jennifer Margaret Linda, the Original Child

This book is dedicated to my dear Symphony, without whom I would not be alive. You saved me from a monster at great risk to your body, mind and soul. You deserved so much better. You were my mother, my saviour and my friend through the worst. I thank you with all my heart and soul.

From Jeni

This book is dedicated to everyone in this world who has Multiple Personality Disorder or Dissociative Identity Disorder. My story is in many ways your story. For far too long the monsters who commit such terrible crimes as we have endured and survived have been able to get away with them. They've been safe, knowing that if we disclose their abuse and/or our coping strategy of MPD/DID they can simply claim that we are liars, insane, crazy or deluded. This ends now. For at last MPD/DID has been recognised as a legitimate coping strategy for dealing with extreme abuse and sexual torture. At last our very diagnosis is evidence against the monster and is proof we are telling the truth.

Now justice is possible.

From Symphony

This book is dedicated to my three hero cops: Rod Messer, Rachel Lawson and Paul Stamoulis.

And also to my alters: To each of you who walked out of the back of my head to help me, all 2681 of you, thank you. I would thank you all individually, but that would be a book of its own. So I will say this:

Thank you for your love, thank you for when you listened to me and did as I asked, thank you for stepping up, and standing down. I will love you forever.

From Amber

I dedicate my book to Erik, Rosemary, Cherry-Lynn, Gemma, Bobby, Carrie-Anne and Jessie. While I never got to hold you in my arms, you are forever in my heart.

From Jeni's Army

Dedicated with love to Jay Osmond. While you've never met me, your music, and that of your family, saved my life and sanity more than I can tell. At the worst of times I could always rely on you. You gave me more than you could ever imagine. Thank you.

* * *

From Dr George Blair-West

To my wife, Penny – heartfelt appreciation for your patience and considered input into my writing over the years and this book in particular. Having such an intelligent and accomplished clinical psychologist, who is always willing to assist, has been an incomparable gift. You have my deepest love.

Publisher's note: The life that is revealed in these pages is one lived through horrific, ongoing abuse. In the process of finding justice, Jeni had to give police excruciating explicit detail. Telling her story in this book means managing the details and holding back some of the trauma so the words don't harm readers. But, even so, Jeni has to share moments that are at times almost unbearable to read because she needs you to understand the words and descriptions a child might use to try to disclose abuse. They won't have the words an adult would. Looking away is not going to stop perpetrators from abusing children. Only knowing the signs, paying attention and listening when a child (or adult) tries to speak up will do that. But if you have suffered abuse or trauma, please see the warning below, and for anyone who is struggling see page 431 for some important contact details that may be useful for you. Be gentle on yourself as you read this book. But also know that, like Jeni, you can overcome.

The telling of Jeni Haynes's story is complemented and strengthened by a rare writing partnership between Jeni Haynes and the psychiatrist she started working with in 1998, Dr George Blair-West. Over the next two decades patient and therapist together evolved and pioneered a therapeutic approach that took them to the forefront of both the legal and clinical worlds. Their collaboration captures the complexity and criminal ramifications of Jeni's intriguing psychological condition. At various points throughout the text, Dr Blair-West adds a clinical perspective to help readers understand the human mind and the process of how to rise above extreme trauma.

Warning from Dr George Blair-West: Any of you reading this book who find yourselves being triggered – please seek out an experienced trauma therapist to help you if you have been abused. You can call a helpline (in Australia we have Beyond Blue and Lifeline) but the level of support this offers for people who have been abused is limited and variable. Most countries have websites, run by the registering colleges for psychiatrists, psychologists and social workers, that allow you to search for a therapist by skill sets and special interests.

The best resource that I suggest people start with is simply look for therapists who are trained in EMDR which, by definition, means they treat trauma. Start with emdr.com and also look for the registering body in your country (in Australia this is called emdraa.org). Many EMDR therapists have also completed advanced training in dissociation, which you can also add to your search criteria, ensuring that they can both understand and cope with dissociative disorders. Do not go and see just any therapist as most are not trained in dissociative disorders because it is, regrettably, not a typical part of core training.

Contents

ALL THE PARTS OF JENI WHO WILL SPEAK TO YOU IN THIS BOOK

Note: The term 'Front Runner' describes the alter you would most likely meet if you were talking to Jeni. We have had numerous Front Runners over the years. They gave us consistency and hid our condition. We would probably be dead if not for the masking they did during our life. They are phenomenal people.

Many of our key alters have multiple jobs. You'll see these as you go through the book.

The Original Birth Child

Jennifer Margaret Linda — Symphony took her place after six months of life, keeping her safe and untouched by Dad.

Executive Alters

Symphony — Our Core Personality. The girl in the green dress. She was Dad's original victim. She created all of us to help keep Jennifer Margaret Linda safe from Dad.

Erik — Symphony's first alter, the architect of our inner landscape from the 1970s to 2000s and coordinator.

Little Ricky — He gave us our jobs after initial emergence.

The Rulebook — Constructs rules of engagement to guide us and keep us safe.

The Assassin — It's all in the name, folks.

Front Runners

Jenny — The Front Runner of the 1970s. Victim, survivor, mask.

Linda — Front Runner of the 1980s; strong, competent and contemptuous, mask.

Erik — Our Front Runner of the 1990s (see above for other roles).

Protectors

Muscles — Our protector and muscle.

Captain Busby — Head of the army protecting Mum.

Janet — Head of the army protecting Sheila.

Squadron Captain — Boss of the army protecting Frank.

Speakers

Amber — Mother figure.

Judas — He who tells.

Happy — Finds joy and happiness in everything.

Zombie Girl — Little Miss Compliant.

Magsy — Terrified child victim.

The Joker — Finds something funny in everything and anything.

Maggot — Frightened, badly abused teenager.

Volcano — Our inner psychologist, supports, reassures and guides.

The Student — Our academic.

Ed the Head — Practical, no-nonsense kind of guy.

Charlotte — The soother.

Gabrielle — The girl who holds all our femininity safe.

Mr Flamboyant — Bright, colourful, extravagant but deadly witty, straightforward and sharp. Calls it as he sees it.

Jeni — The adult survivor, thriver and witness.

And

The Entity Currently Known as Jeni — Holds all the knowledge we need to get through each day. Changes every day to meet our needs.

Author's Note

Don't be fooled. The girl on the front cover of this book is not me, Jennifer Haynes. She is, in fact, Symphony, the alter who took over my body when I was six months old and created an elaborate internal world to protect me from my father's abuse. At her core, Symphony is a protector. Right now, she wants to tell you to put this book down because she doesn't want to alarm or scare you; she doesn't want you to have the same nightmares we do. But she does want to help people, and she knows this book has the power to do just that. Symphony knows silence protects abusers. That's why we have to speak up, we have to tell our story, we have to scream and shout for all the children who don't yet have the words.

This has been a hard story to tell – and a hard life to live. I know some parts of this book will be as difficult for you to read as they were for me to write. In these moments, I'd like you to do what we did every time we finished a chapter. I want you to remember that I am okay now, I am safe, and I am free.

I want you to breathe. And I want you to step away if you need to take a moment and comfort yourself.

I want you to know that my will to survive is stronger than the evil that tried to destroy me over and over again. I want you to know that there is a happy ending to this story – and the happy ending is me.

Breathe.

Prologue

SYMPHONY

It's our red-letter day: 18 February 2019. My entire life – all forty-nine years of it – has been leading to this moment: to me walking down Elizabeth Street to Sydney's Downing Centre Court. Four years of police interviews, 900,000 words in victim statements, endless therapy sessions, a lifetime of pain: it's all been working up to this walk to the Downing Centre Court. My legs shake with each step. But I don't stop. I keep going.

I know it's going to be awful; I just know it. My father is going to plead not guilty and force me to testify, to tell all the sickening details of his abuse, to relive all the trauma he put me through, to spell out his acts for his entertainment. Make no mistake, it will be entertaining for him. Since I was a baby, he's found pleasure in my suffering, my terror, my humiliation. I can see him licking his lips in delight at seeing me upset on the stand. I shudder at the thought. But I don't stop. I keep going.

I'm prepared. It's easy to testify when you are telling the truth. That doesn't make it any less scary. But this thought does: Jeni has a plan. This plan steels me as I walk through the heavy glass doors of the Downing Centre Court for the first time. My mum follows behind me. We put our mobile phones, keys and handbags on a tray to be scanned. I walk through a metal detector and am patted down by a security guard with a gun strapped to his waist. They're looking for weapons. If they're worried about bombs going off, they

should scan my tongue. What I've got to say in court is going to be explosive.

As we approach the courtroom, the shaking gets worse. My legs almost buckle underneath me. But I don't stop. I keep going. My prosecutor, Sean Hughes, and his instructing solicitor, Ellen Dando, are waiting for us. 'Are you ready for this?' they ask. I say yes. My trembling legs say, 'Hell no.'

My mum asks Sean if Dad has indicated whether he will enter a plea today. No one knows. Maybe not even Dad. He's had two years to think about it, since the charges were first laid, but Dad's always been a rogue. Just when you think you've seen the worst of him, he trumps it with an act so abhorrent you could never have seen it coming. He's blindsiding, whiplashing, utterly terrifying.

But no matter what Dad does today, Jeni has a plan.

Finally, after what seems an absolute age of waiting, the door to the courtroom opens and we're called in. I've only been in an empty courtroom before today and to see this one full of bodies is very disconcerting. I feel their eyes on me. *There she is*, I imagine they're thinking, *the victim*. They're looking at Jeni, a 49-year-old woman wearing thick glasses with a purple rim and a butterfly top embellished with jewels. They can't see me. I'm Symphony. I'm four. I like singing songs, cats and my hand puppet Sweep. I don't like Dad. I'm the girl in the green dress on the front cover of this book.

From the door of the courtroom, I can see the jury box ahead. It's empty. In the centre of the room, the tables for the prosecution are to the left and the defence on the right. I stare at the dock where Dad will soon be the sole occupant. It's a small wooden box-like affair with a door at the rear and a small window. I remember the small window in the outside toilet of my childhood home. I used to stare out of it when Dad attacked me, wishing to be anywhere else, wishing to disappear, wishing to die. I wonder if Dad will wish to die when he's staring out of the dock window today?

Straight ahead is the witness box and beside that – high above us all – are the seats for the judge and her associate. Their area seems to be on an entirely different level to the rest of the room, but it's

only a step up. I walk forward to take a seat behind the prosecution. Sean turns to me and smiles, trying to reassure my shaking legs. It's daunting for me to sit at the front of a crowded room knowing what's about to happen. I hope it's even more daunting for Dad. After all, I'm only the victim. He's the accused. No matter, Jeni has a plan.

As I settle into my seat, the door at the rear of the dock opens and Dad walks through. Oh my gosh. He needs a haircut. That's my first thought. I haven't seen him in ten years. He really needs a haircut. His grey hair is so long it's slightly curling over his collar. He's wearing an ill-fitting green tracksuit. I thought he would be wearing a suit to show the world he's a 'respectable' man. He looks haggard, but he walks into the dock with his head held high, carrying an air of arrogance with him.

'He's going to plead not guilty,' I whisper to Mum, who's sitting beside me. She looks at him, turns to me and nods her head in agreement. His arrogance swamps the room. Everyone else thinks he will plead guilty. We have a strong body of evidence against him. I am the body of evidence.

But the physical impact of my dad's abuse pales in comparison to the mental. And that's saying something. My mind is home to over 2500 different personalities I created as a coping mechanism to deal with the abuse. It's because of these personalities that I can recall the events of my childhood with perfect clarity. It's because of these personalities that I'm alive. And it's because of these personalities that I know I can take on Dad today. We've fought him thousands of times before, we'll fight him again today. And this time, Jeni has a plan.

I stare at my father. I only have eyes for him. It's like everyone else in the courtroom disappears and it's just him and me. He refuses to meet my eye. He won't – or can't – look at me.

Dad looks like he's shrunk. He used to be ten foot tall, so big and dominating. Today, he's a shell of a man. An empty void. A non-person.

All I can hear in my head are the lyrics to the Donny Osmond song 'Big Man' I listened to as a kid. The lyrics were about being a big man … and my father was no longer this in so many ways.

JENI
The plan

Judge Huggett enters the courtroom. Everyone rises. She starts proceedings for the State v Richard Haynes, and explains that because it's a rape case, the complainant will be afforded anonymity. Sean clears his throat. 'I have instructions from the complainant on this,' he says.

The defence lawyer's head whips around to look at the prosecution. This is highly unusual.

'The complainant wishes to waive her right to anonymity,' explains Sean. 'She is here in the room.'

The judge asks me to stand up. My legs are shaking so violently, I have to hold on to the chair in front of me for support. The judge addresses me directly. 'Is what the prosecution said correct?' she asks.

'Oh yes,' I reply.

'Do you understand the consequences of this decision?' she asks.

'Oh yes. I understand that there will be positive and negative consequences, and I also understand that once I waive my right to anonymity, I can't take it back,' I reply.

'Would you like some time to think about it?' she asks.

'I've had twenty-three years to think about it, I think that's more than enough. I know exactly what I'm doing,' I reply.

'Does the prosecution have any objections?' The judge looks at Sean.

'No,' he says.

'Does the defence have any objections?' the judge asks.

'No,' says my dad's lawyer without even looking at him.

'Okay, the complainant seems of sound mind and is aware of the consequences of her actions. I approve her application to waive her right to anonymity,' she says.

Dad's face drops and, for a second, the air of arrogance around him dissolves into something else. Fear? Maybe. Bewilderment? Absolutely.

JUDAS
Telling

In the courtroom, Jeni takes a seat. But in her mind, there are fireworks going off. We were all in on it, you see, this plan of hers. We took a vote and agreed. By waiving our right to anonymity, we also waived Dad's. This was our plan all along. We wanted Dad's name written in the newspaper for all to see, we wanted everyone to know what he did. If a victim chooses to remain anonymous, the defendant stays hidden in the shadows. In media reports about our case, I would be a nameless 49-year-old victim and Dad would be a faceless 74-year-old man. But he isn't an anonymous 74-year-old man. He's an evil, despicable, torturous monster, and now the whole world was going to know it.

For twenty-three long years I've bitten my tongue, afraid of the explosions that would come out if I dared to open my mouth. Even after I went to the police, they told me I had to stay silent until we went to court. I've paid the price for that silence. I bit my tongue until it bled. I swallowed my words and choked on them. No more. I want to tell the crowded courtroom exactly who my father is. I want to say it out loud for the world to hear. I want everyone to know his name. Richard Haynes. Because as long as abusers stay veiled as anonymous, nameless, faceless men, they will keep getting away with it.

Jeni has a plan and it's working.

Introduction

BY DR GEORGE BLAIR-WEST

'The first point I would like to make, Your Honour, is that Dissociative Identity Disorder is not an illness. There is nothing wrong with Jeni's brain at a pathophysiologic level. Her brain functions as well as yours or mine. Indeed, in some ways her brain functions in ways that are far superior to how our minds work. These are what I call her superpowers – which I will come back to later. Her mind is living testimony to the potential genius the human mind can bring to combat the most abhorrent of abuse experiences. Indeed, DID is the mind's response to experiences that fall under the rubric of torture, rather than the overused term of abuse. In short, the testimony she will give you will come from a mind, and a memory, that is functioning as well as anyone's, indeed – better than most.'

And so I began my expert testimony. It was Monday, 18 February 2019 and Jeni was making history. For the first time ever, Dissociative Identity Disorder (DID) was not being used as a defence in a trial. Instead, it was the basis for the prosecution. Until then DID, or Multiple Personality Disorder – as Jeni prefers to call it, had been exclusively the domain of defendants, often on trial for major crimes, particularly homicide. For a pinnacle crime you need a pinnacle defence and DID has always been atop the pinnacle of psychiatric diagnoses. It has been seen as the craziest of crazy.

No other psychiatric diagnosis has been as controversial, as hotly debated, as DID. I started my training over thirty-five years

ago when this condition was relegated to small print in textbooks. Even the small print was spectacularly unhelpful. Sadly, especially for the at least 77 million people around the world who have this condition, things have only improved a little.

There are three factors that typically cause DID: the experience of the most extreme forms of abuse, usually extending over many years; this abuse is perpetrated by caregivers, typically parents, that the child relies upon; and it begins while the child's mind is young, or plastic, enough, to employ high-level dissociative strategies.

I would argue there is no greater pain that humans can experience than the personal distress that causes DID. The torture of adults would come second but adults experiencing torture know that they are guilty, or not guilty, of what they are accused of. Fair or unfair, they at least have a framework for sense-making. This sense-making is simply not available to a four-year-old being violently raped with the explanation that this 'is punishment for being an evil child'. (Explanations like this are typical of how the perpetrators frame their abuse.) On top of the physical distress the child is experiencing, their very sense of self, their essence, their soul, is being heinously wounded.

In the face of such extremes of distress the human mind employs some surprisingly clever strategies to cope. The most sophisticated is dissociation. Jeni is going to take you into her mind and show it to you firsthand. By making sense of Jeni's case you will come to understand core facets of not just the human mind, but the human state and how it responds to extreme abuse.

One of Jeni's superpowers – as a part of her DID – is memory. Indeed, she has a form of 'Hyperthymesia' also known as Highly Superior Autobiographical Memory (HSAM). This is the ability to 'accurately and readily recall numerous details about events … including exact dates and intricate information about previous experiences.' This has particular benefits for legal proceedings.

Recent research confirms that DID is nearly always the result of extreme abuse at a young age. This is true of the almost two dozen

cases I have seen in my career. Accordingly, pretty much every case of DID means that someone has committed a crime against an innocent, young child. This has powerful legal ramifications that Jeni will elaborate.

If DID is a response to extreme trauma, then its prevalence is a result of how much a given society protects its children. For this reason, I am hopeful that DID is becoming less common in a world where children and women have rights and are protected by the justice system.

Encouragingly, in my professional lifetime I have seen an emerging investment in child protection and a new preparedness in the justice system to prosecute historical abuse. Jeni's case is a landmark of import against this landscape.

I wanted the judge to appreciate that Jeni does not, and never did, have an illness. This is a leap for a world that has made DID the craziest of crazy. What Jeni has is a genius coping strategy that we should all hold in awe.

PART ONE

BREAKING

CHAPTER ONE

Bittersweet Symphony

JENNIFER MARGARET LINDA

I can feel the wind rushing against my cheeks. A man I don't know has picked me up from my cot and lifted me in the air with his hands under my armpits. As he swings me around, he says, '*Wheeeeeeeeee*, bop.' I'm crying. My grandmother screams at the man, 'Tony, you can't do that! She's a baby.' Tony is my uncle, my father's brother. I don't know this at the time because I am six weeks old.

People tell me I can't possibly remember being a baby, but I can. The memory of being twirled through the air is as crisp as the wind was rushing against my newborn cheeks. I know this happened when I was six weeks old, because my grandmother died four months later, and this was the only time my mother remembers me being with her and Tony.

I was born in January 1970. We lived in a two-storey house in Bexleyheath in the UK: my mother, father, and older sister, Sheila.

My mother, Patricia, comes from a family of secrets. Her father was Jewish but when he met my grandmother he jettisoned his religion in order to marry outside the faith. As a result, his family said the prayers for the dead and never spoke to him again. My mum was sixteen when she found out her mother had been adopted, and she still doesn't know what her father did for work during the war. Everything in Mum's life was veiled in a layer of secrecy. Don't ask, don't tell.

My father's family is related to the De Vere family and the now dormant title the Earl of Oxford. My paternal grandfather was an

upper-class man, so my father had built-in respectability. He was from 'good people'. Dad's family taught him that he was predestined to sit at the right hand of God when he died. Nothing he did or said would change this. Dad used this notion of predestination to validate, excuse and otherwise justify his abuse of me. He was destined to be with God, he was perfect no matter what he did and there would be no consequences for his actions. He could do what he liked to me; even God was on his side. He was bulletproof. All of Dad's actions were informed and, in many ways, tainted by this belief. If God was on his side, what couldn't he do?

My mum and dad were both the eldest children in their families. They met at a dance class where the boys stood on one side of the room, the girls stood on the other, and they got together in the middle to waltz. It was called the School of Dancing, but its main aim was matching up young couples, so it could well have been called the School of Dating. A few months after meeting on the dance floor, my dad started crying because my mum wouldn't marry him. He hadn't asked her. 'I don't suppose you'll marry me?' he said through sobs, and she agreed under duress and guilt.

It snowed the day of my parents' wedding. The snow was a curse. My mum started her period sometime between the ceremony and the reception, and she told my father as much when they got home from the party. 'I've waited long enough,' he said. He forced himself on her. She bled. I don't know if she realised it at the time, but my mother's first sexual experience with my father was rape.

When they got married, Mum stopped being Patricia and started being Richard's wife. My dad chose my mother. He deliberately sought her out for her subservience and ignorance. She didn't ask questions, she couldn't read body language, and she knew her place was in the kitchen. It wasn't until my mum was in her seventies that she was diagnosed with autism.

There was very little affection in my parents' marriage. I can't remember them ever holding hands, and their goodbye kiss of a morning when Dad went to work was an official peck on the cheek.

Mum worked as a shorthand typist, and Dad was an electronics engineer. He smelt like the inside of a television, a putrid mix of burning Bakelite and sweat.

Mum told me when my older sister, Sheila, was born, she was bloody red. In comparison, Mum said I looked much more serene. Years later Sheila used to tease me that I came out 'peaches and cream' as though that was a bad thing. Perhaps the teasing was the residual twist of spite from an older sibling resenting the new baby.

When my older sister, Sheila, was born, my dad was working nights, so he didn't spend much time with her. But he was at home a lot more when I was a tiny baby. Unfortunately for me.

My mother comes from a family of secrets, and so do I.

Before my first birthday, I had created a top-secret army in my mind. It was an accident. I didn't set out to create thousands of alter personalities, I was forced to. From the moment I was born – before that, even – my dad did things that threatened my life. His abuse was unrelenting. There was no escape. I had no one to rely on, nowhere to go and no way of asking for help, so I created an army. Multiple Personality Disorder (MPD) isn't a symptom of abuse, it's a coping strategy.

It started with Symphony. It's hard to know where Jennifer Margaret Linda (the original child) ends and where Symphony starts. It's almost as though Mum gave birth to twins in the same body.

Symphony divided her world into 'Daddy' and 'distractions' – the sounds, smells, tastes and pain that made it hard to focus on what Dad needed. Symphony accidentally created alter personalities to deal with the distractions. She would identify a need, and someone would walk out of the back of our head to help her. It was an unconscious process.

The alters all had a job: to swallow Dad's semen, to block out his stench, to look after the family and to keep the secrets so they wouldn't die. Their united mission: keep Jennifer Margaret Linda alive. Each alter had a job title, but they didn't have names. The names came much later, when psychologists, detectives and lawyers asked for them. I could hardly tell a doctor that someone was called

'the dick sucker' or 'the scream muffler'. And so, we had a bucket of girl's names and a bucket of boy's names that we drew from. It was a lucky dip.

I've since learnt that MPD is developed by highly intelligent children in the worst of circumstances. As a kid, I had no way out, so I retreated inside. In many ways, MPD is the greatest act of self-love. I know I wouldn't be alive today if it wasn't for Symphony and her creative survival strategy. That might sound melodramatic, but it's true. When Dad nearly killed us physically, Symphony removed the alter who was almost dead and replaced them with a fresh alter who had the ability to keep going.

Symphony is a walking, talking miracle.

SYMPHONY

I can't ever remember being without Jennifer. She is six months old when I decide to take over and protect her. Dad is hurting us. She gets terribly upset and I start to sing to calm her down. I mimic Mum's voice and sing a nursery rhyme about a spider climbing up a waterspout. When I don't know the words, I hum the tune.

Dad puts something in our mouth, and we can't breathe. It tastes disgusting. Jennifer panics. I sing. Then Dad takes the thing out of our mouth and puts it between our legs. I don't know what 'it' is – but I know it hurts. Jennifer screams and Dad puts his hand over her mouth. That's when I take over. I lay Jennifer on her side on a beanbag and build walls around her, so she is safe, then I go out to deal with life. I make Jennifer deaf, dumb and blind so she can never be hurt again. When someone interacts with Jennifer, they are interacting with me.

I sing to Jennifer until she stops crying, which is only after Dad leaves. The music calms her down. That's why everybody calls me Symphony, because I make the music. My name is the symbol for the treble clef. I'm not alone for long. The others soon join us. We all have a job to do.

Erik is our architect. I made him so he could build a place for us to sit, but he's also our organiser and our first front runner, the

person in charge of the body. Erik is a grown-up; tall and skinny, but strong. In many ways, he looks like Dad. Except Erik always smiles, and Dad never smiles. We don't smile at Dad either, because if you smile at a crocodile, you might get eaten. That's another song we sing.

AMBER

My first memory isn't a memory. It's a subconscious feeling: I'm unwanted. Before I was even born, my dad did everything in his power to get rid of me; he poured gin down my mother's throat and threw her down the stairs. He stopped shy of bending a metal coat-hanger and dragging me out of the womb. He's lived with regret and resentment ever since.

I'm unwanted. I'm hated. I'm a non-person.

In the days leading up to my birth, my father refuses to name me. My mum throws endless suggestions at him, but he refuses to catch them. He lets them drop to the floor and smash, like he wishes I would.

In the end, I'm not given one name, I'm given three: Jennifer Margaret Linda. My mum settles on Jennifer out of sheer desperation. My dad has dismissed every other name, but he only grunts at Jennifer.

The name reminds my mum of a nursery rhyme she used to sing at school:

Poor Jenny is a-weeping
A-weeping, a-weeping
Poor Jenny is a-weeping
On a bright summer's day

And I weep, and I weep.

SYMPHONY

When I close my eyes now, I can see flashes of my childhood in full colour. I can picture the statue of a bust that sat at the bottom of my

17

grandmother's staircase. I can hear the music playing on the radio my mum always had on at home. I can feel the panic as my dad leads me to his darkroom where he develops photographs.

I don't like the darkroom. I'm two years old. My dad is over six foot. In that room, I open my jaw as wide as it will go. My dad pushes something into my mouth and the Boy Who Doesn't Breathe takes over. That's his job. He steps in when we can't breathe because he doesn't need to.

In another flash, I'm three. I've lost my toy puppet Sweep and I'm devastated. I'm determined to find Sweep, and Mum and Dad flip a coin to decide who will go with me. Dad loses, unfortunately for me. We walk the streets of Bexleyheath in search of Sweep. Dad knows full well we won't find him, I lost him on holiday at the Isle of Wight.

It's a Sunday, so the shops are closed. We're standing outside a store with leadlight windows that look like something out of a Charles Dickens book. My bladder starts to throb. I tell my dad I need to go to the toilet, but he ignores me. I ask him over and over again, until I'm gripping my hands between my legs in desperation. Dad laughs at me and tells me I'm a dirty girl. 'I know what you want,' he says, as he takes me to the public toilets in the park, ushering me into the men's stalls.

He sits me on the toilet, and I pull down my pants to wee. Dad also undoes his pants. 'You know what to do, get on with it,' he says. He's made me an expert at giving blow jobs, but he never calls it that so I don't know what I'm doing. I'm crying. After he's done Dad drags me home and throws me into the house. He tells Mum to go out the next day and get a new Sweep glove puppet. I don't know how he found room in the household budget. Money is always tight.

Mum makes all our clothes by hand. My favourite dress is a bright yellow number I call the sunshine dress. It has a Peter Pan collar and embroidery on the bodice. I love running my fingers across the stitches, feeling the patterns on my fingertips. I'm wearing the sunshine dress when my father puts me on the kitchen table. I'm

high off the floor and I'm scared of falling because my dad keeps pushing me up and up. He's trying to put 'it' in my underneath. I thrash around and try to stop him.

I remember the bust statue at my grandmother's house. It terrifies me. I can't work out why it's just a head. Where is its body? But when my dad hurts my body so badly I pass out from the pain, I realise the value of having no body. You can keep yourself safe if you have no body. And so, the boy with no body takes over. His name is Ed the Head and he turns out to be our most critical and practical thinker. When someone is hurt, the boy with no body scoops them up and gets them to dissociate from their body. Anything below the nipples no longer exists, which is incredibly helpful when Dad is being exceedingly painful. And let's face it, he is exceedingly painful a lot.

When Dad fails to enter me, 'it' eventually spews on my sunshine dress. Dad rips the dress off me and puts me in an outfit that belongs to Sheila. It's too big. When my mum gets home, he tells her that I had wet myself. I'm outraged. *I* hadn't wet my dress, *he* had. If that isn't bad enough, he throws my sunshine dress in a bucket to soak and turns it a muddy blue. There is no more sunshine.

JENNY

The first time I remember my dad successfully penetrating my vagina with 'it', I'm still two. The day stands out because Dad put a belt around my neck and tied me to a table, and that was unusual. I can still feel the cold metal of the buckle digging into my throat. The belt is so tight, my eyes go dark. All I can see is a black circle with a ring of yellow around it, like an eclipse. This is the first time I hear the voice. It's a gentle, calm American voice.

'Breathe,' it says.

This voice was nameless for years. I finally named him Jay in 1981 after my favourite musician, Jay Osmond. Jay Osmond sounded very like the voice and he made me feel so safe I found myself talking to the voice and calling him Jay. He didn't seem to mind. In fact, he talked to me more after this.

But Jay isn't one of us. He's not an alter; he's almost our subconscious, a higher being, a power above. He has saved my life more times than I want to think about.

I fight for a mouthful of air.

I'm suffocating, but Dad doesn't notice or care. The pain is extraordinary. I scream and Dad shoves a piece of fabric in my mouth so hard I almost swallow it.

'Breathe,' says Jay ...

* * *

JENNY

In the 1970s, doctors were gods and they spoke the gospel. When my brother Frank was born in 1973, he caught bronchitis and pneumonia. He was so sick, and Mum was very stressed. Mum brought her wheezing, weeping baby downstairs, and Dad told her to take him away. 'He's fine upstairs,' Dad dismissed.

At the time, under the National Health Service (NHS), you couldn't call for an ambulance in an emergency, you had to call your GP, wait for them to visit after clinic hours and get them to summon an ambulance. My mother called the GP at 9 am, worried about Frank. The GP arrived at 11 pm that night and chastised my mother: 'You should have called me sooner. The baby could have died.'

The backward NHS system also failed me. From the moment I could sit up, I rocked back and forth on my bottom. Sitting on the floor, on the lounge and on my bed, I rocked and I cried. Now, people understand that as a sign of trauma but, back in the seventies, my mother had no idea, so she took me to the doctor.

I rocked and cried sitting in the clinic. The doctor didn't do a physical examination of me. Instead, he dismissed my tears. 'Jennifer cries because she likes the sound of her voice,' he told my mother, who believed in the gospel of doctors. My mum took those words and held on to them for my entire life.

That doctor's diagnosis set the narrative for the rest of my childhood. Jennifer is an attention-seeker. Jennifer is weak. Jennifer

cries wolf. Had the doctor examined me, he might have found that I was upset because I had poor vision so everything I saw was blurry, huge and terrifying to a little child. He might have found that I rocked because my private parts were in agony and I was trying to take the pressure off them. He might have found that I cried non-stop because my dad was brutally abusing me.

The doctor also might have found that I had epilepsy. When I was somewhere around the age of two, I had a grand mal epileptic seizure. My mum remembers the day clearly, not least because it was the day our elderly neighbour died. The police were running around our house trying to get into the apartment next door when I had the seizure. My body seized and my back arched so it was impossible for me to lie down flat. I don't know how long it lasted.

Afterwards, my mum tried to get me in to see a doctor, but couldn't get an appointment until later in the day. By then the seizure had stopped and the only remnant of it was utter exhaustion. Once again, the doctor didn't examine me and dismissed my symptoms. 'Have you never seen a child have a temper tantrum, woman?' he told my mum.

Jennifer cries for attention. Jennifer throws temper tantrums. Jennifer should be ignored. My mum used to call me 'joyful' in a sarcastic way.

Nobody considered there might be a reason I cried non-stop. Nobody investigated what might have been happening behind closed doors. Nobody asked any questions. If someone had asked me why I rocked back and forth, I might have told them that I did it because it stopped everything from hurting. I may not have had the words to say, 'I rock because my dad rapes me,' but I would have said something.

The doctor's words gave my dad carte blanche to abuse me. If my mum questioned why I was upset or if I needed to go to a doctor, my dad dismissed her. 'It's just Jennifer being Jennifer,' he'd say. My abuser controlled the narrative.

When people ask how on earth my mother didn't know what was happening, it frustrates me to no end. The only other adult in

her world was my father, so when she raised concerns with him, he protected himself. It's not like he was ever going to say, 'Oh yeah, I think Jeni's rocking because I keep repeatedly raping her.' He would say, 'She's acting out. She's attention-seeking. She's selfish.' He always found a way to turn the attention away from him. My dad was remarkably clever, and my mum was ever so subservient.

My mother comes from a family of secrets, and so do I.

SYMPHONY

It looks painful. I don't know what 'it' is, but I know it must be hurting him and I figure the only way to ease his pain is to make it vomit. It looks like it splits in half, like a snake shedding its skin.

Taking my dad's pain away hurts me.

My dad calls them games, but I don't like playing with him. He tells me I'm doing him a big favour, that my mum and my sister could never help him the way that I do, and that they'd be upset with me if they knew. I'm taking care of Daddy, but no one else can know. It's private and confidential. My dad pronounces 'private' like the weed 'privet'.

I can't keep up with Dad's demands. Every time Dad hurts me, I have to create a new alter to deal with the new distraction. I need help and more alters walk out of the back of my head. I create someone to take away the sound of Dad inhaling sharply, the heat of his exhaling breath and the smell of his sweat.

I don't realise that alters aren't like toilet paper. They're more like tea towels. Once I create an alter, I can't flush them away. They stick around. They're not disposable the minute they're no longer needed. Besides, they're constantly needed because Dad keeps attacking me, again and again and again.

We don't learn that until much later on. For the first five years of our life, I create a hundred or more new alters a week, depending on how violent Dad is and how often he abuses us. I create all of the alters except for one. Erik creates Little Ricky, who is eight and wears an old grey suit.

ERIK

In the beginning, our internal landscape looks like a medieval dungeon. We each have a room to ourselves with a heavy iron door. It's an underground bunker, a rabbit hole, a prison.

Symphony created our inside world and I fill it with all the things we need to survive. In every room there are two buttons for our voting system. Everyone gets a vote. It's a democracy. There are tunnels full of alters grouped together according to their job descriptions. We call them the chunnels and we have one each for sight, smell, sound, taste and touch.

Underneath the dungeon are two rooms filled with communication equipment so we can talk to one another. It started with tin cans and rope, and became more sophisticated as we grew.

We don't grow like everyone else. Most of us stay the same age as the day we were created.

LITTLE RICKY

I hate my job. I'm the one who sends people out to face Dad, to help Symphony, to save Jennifer. I choose who takes over when the child in the body can't take it anymore. It's my fault they get hurt. We have hundreds of alters who take the pain. They each have a bucket, and if it overflows they get drenched with the full force of the agony. It's my job to monitor the buckets. I have eyes in the front and the back of my head. I'm constantly looking outward and inward at the same time. If a bucket is close to spilling over, I need to have a replacement lined up. I send the replacement in to take the abuse. I know that makes me as bad as Dad.

There's an unnamed alter who takes Dad's sounds and paints them on the wall like a mural of horror. She's always covered in paint smears.

There's an alter called Maggot who takes the daily beatings from Dad. She's always covered in bruises.

There are alters who take away our thoughts because thoughts are distractions – and they're dangerous. Dad can read our mind, so we can never think clearly or honestly or independently.

There are alters who take away the blood dripping down our legs. They're always exhausted from holding onto the blood and doing the mental gymnastics needed to convince ourselves that we're not bleeding. If Dad says there's nothing wrong with us, then there's nothing wrong with us and the blood-holders have to make sure of that. There's no arguing with Dad. So if he says we're not bleeding, we're not bleeding. End of story.

I'm the one who sends people out, but I can't bring them back. There's a death committee for that. When we think someone is close to reaching their limit – if they can no longer take the pain, if they have run out of blood to bleed, if they can't stifle their screams, if they are on the verge of death – we call a committee meeting. There's ten of us sitting at the round table: me, Erik, Symphony, the Assassin and whichever alters are most relevant to the worker at hand.

Everyone on the committee gets a vote. We decide if the child dealing with Dad can take more, or if we should send in the Assassin to tap them on the shoulder. The Assassin might sound scary, but really he's a ten-year-old boy, a child doing an adult's job, an innocent wearing a mask. If an alter says the magic words – 'Can I go now?' – we pull them out. When we send in the Assassin, he escorts the alter to the doorway and they never come back. They disappear – never to be seen again.

Then I have to decide who will take their place. And I have to train them.

Nobody knows what's on the other side of the Assassin's doorway. We're terrified of the beyond – until we dismantle the door at the age of twenty-eight and make a startling discovery. On the other side is an enormous room filled with every toy we've ever studied: Sindy dolls, jigsaw puzzles, ballerinas, teddies and cats. Every toy we've ever wanted to play with, but have been too scared to ask for, exists behind the door. There's an alter who can look at a toy, absorb it and create it inside for us to play with. He's created a toy paradise for all the alters who've been assassinated.

The Assassin is pissed. He's always thought he killed everyone he tapped on the shoulder, sentenced them to death, ended their

existence. And here they all are, whooping it up in toy paradise. I'm thrilled.

There's a reason we didn't know what's on the other side of the door. Hope is a deadly thing in our world. If we give one person hope of escaping Dad, then there will be a long line of people wanting to be tapped on the shoulder by the Assassin. If we all choose to die, the system will collapse around us. We must keep going. We must take what we get. We must stay alive. As if that isn't enough, we must also keep everyone else alive.

CAPTAIN BUSBY

Sometime in 1971 or 1972, I see a man on a horse wearing an impossibly furry hat. I want to pet it like a cat. Mum catches me admiring the tall cap and explains that it's a Busby military headdress and the man is protecting the Queen of England. In this moment, I am born: my name is Captain Busby and I'm four.

If the Queen has an army of 'Busby' men to take care of her, then Mum needs one too because she is our queen. I may be small, but I am mighty. My army is made up of soldiers aged between three and seven. We all wear Busby hats and some of us even ride horses. There are hundreds of us, and every time I need more backup I ask Symphony to create a new alter to join our ranks. It's our explicit duty to protect Mum.

What does Mum need protection from? Daddy. ·

Daddy threatens to kill Mum so often, we need to be on high alert at all times. We monitor the world for danger, we monitor Mum for signs of distress, and we monitor Dad for red flags. From the moment we wake up in the morning to the moment we fall asleep at night, we're on duty. It's an exhausting job, but someone has to do it.

Jeni's Superpower – Clarity of Memory

Jeni's memory is a force to be reckoned with. Indeed, the unexpected clarity of recall that people with DID have is one of the key reasons why the mental health profession had such a blind spot when it came to recognising this condition.

The most well-known examples are found in Autistic Savants, who have prodigious mental abilities but typically in only a couple of limited areas. Calendrical savants can quickly calculate the day of the week when given any date in time, past or future. The most common abilities after super-memory are musical abilities (nearly always with perfect pitch) and rapid calculation.

Savants are rare, making up around 1 per cent of those with autism, which translates to around one in a million of the general population. The problem for psychiatrists when confronted by a patient giving the level of recall that you have just read about, is that it seems highly unlikely that savant-level recall and gross abuse, with the latter erroneously believed to be rare, would coincide in the same person who is not a savant. Very few clinicians would have ever seen this phenomenon before – I certainly had not.

Jeni is not an Autistic Savant. As I mentioned in my introduction, Jeni is showing us her Highly Superior Autobiographical Memory (HSAM). Autobiographical memory refers to the ability to accurately and readily recall numerous details about events,

26

including exact dates and intricate information about one's previous experiences. I recall Jeni telling me early on in our work together how people disbelieved her story primarily because of her clarity of recall. Unfortunately, this phenomenon of not believing something because you have no experience of it and do not understand it, is exemplified by DID. While I had not witnessed recall to the level that Jeni demonstrated, through my work in trauma I was very familiar with related memory phenomena. Thirty years ago, I was trained in Eye Movement Desensitisation and Reprocessing (EMDR), which, put simply, takes people back to their traumatic experiences and allows them to recall them in vivid detail. I still remember my surprise, when I first started using it with my patients, at the incredible level of detail that they were able to describe around their traumatic experiences. Patients were often as surprised as I was, saying things along the lines of, 'I can't believe I was able to remember that so clearly, it felt like I was there.' Over time it became apparent that the greater the clarity the better the outcome of the therapy session in processing the traumatic memory so that it was no longer as distressing.

It rapidly became evident to early EMDR practitioners that, while our minds have a range of unconscious defences to allow us to suppress memories of painful experiences, the suppressed memories sit in their respective reinforced concrete vaults in all their vivid glory. Think of a pharaoh's tomb, buried deep under a heavy pyramid, but replete with valuable accoutrements, sacrificed slaves, and their important worldly belongings, just waiting to be discovered.

The issue of Jeni's memory goes beyond a fascination with (or a disbelief of) HSAM, it has profound implications legally. Historical sexual assault allegations, perhaps more than any other crime, rely squarely on the memory of the victim. Detectives will decide whether or not to pursue a case largely on the veracity and reliability of their victim and their witness/es – and there rarely are witnesses to this kind of crime.[1] Hundreds of hours, or thousands

in Jeni's case, of detailed work will follow for the lead detectives if they take on these cases, so they don't do it lightly. And what determines the veracity and reliability of a witness, or a victim, is the accuracy and consistency of the person's memory.

To fully appreciate the complexities at play here, and the trustworthiness of memory more specifically, we need to take a deeper dive into how the brain processes traumatic memories which, in turn, requires us to understand how our unconscious mind works. It has three main jobs after running our body, e.g. heartrate, blood pressure, temperature regulation etc. Job number one is fairly obvious, first and foremost: keep us safe. Staying alive comes before sustenance. There is no point in looking for dinner if you're about to be dinner. This means our senses are tuned to recognise a threat and our mind is always ready to identify and evaluate its seriousness.

The other part of safety is ensuring a constant supply of food and water – sustenance to survive. Once that box is ticked, our unconscious mind looks for gratification – this is job two. Nicer food, a more comfortable resting place, is a good day's work for one's unconscious mind.

Its third job is learning from important life experiences and laying down automated responses that worked the best in resolving these challenges. We build up a bank of habitual responses for reasons of efficiency and the avoidance of discomfort or pain. If eating a particular berry makes us sick, we avoid it next time. It takes a lot of energy to develop a new response to every new threat. It is so much more economical to just do what worked last time. If our parents cut us down to size if we speak about our achievements, we learn not to raise them. These automatic responses will be invoked when we come across triggers that remind us of the earlier experiences – particularly threatening ones.

It is also important to appreciate that the language of our unconscious is not logical thought; it is emotion. This is simply because logical thought is too slow when our life is at risk. Our brain is designed to recognise and to respond to fear, long before

we can work it out cognitively. As humans, when any kind of strong feeling is involved, logical thought is relegated to the back seat. In short, if it's important, we feel first and think second. No more so than if the feeling is that of fear in response to a threat. My wife tells the story of how she came home one day, opened the front door and threw herself back up against the door she had just closed. She recalls being quite perplexed by her own behaviour until she saw what her mind had already seen and acted upon – a large carpet python in front of her.

Ironically, our own emotions are also a threat. In a world relatively free of unpleasant beasts, our mind's number one threats today are our unpleasant emotions. The more likely something causes us pain or distress and the greater the negative emotion involved, the more our unconscious pays attention.

While traumatic experiences cause us pain, remembering them does too. While not quite as intense as the actual experience, it's not far behind. So, our unconscious mind's work in keeping us safe now becomes focused on repression of painful memories. Just imagine what your life would be like if your mind did not have a mechanism for dulling every painful experience you have in life. Imagine the torture of waking up every morning recalling every humiliating or distressing event in your life!

We take this process for granted. Given, as we have seen, that the mind can recall experiences with agonising detail, we need an equally powerful way of repressing these memories so that we can function and get on with life.

There are four psychological defences that the unconscious employs to deal with painful memories. They sit in a hierarchy from least powerful (for dealing with less upsetting memories) to the most powerful (for the most threatening memories).

We start with Suppression – a psychological manoeuvre that we are all familiar with. We suppress a memory when we decide to not think about a problem until a later time. An example would be deciding to not think about how to pay a large bill that arrives on Friday until the following Monday so that we can relax and enjoy

the weekend. It works for less troubling issues because we are planning to deal with it later, which helps our mind put it aside for a limited time.

Then we come to Repression, where we more completely move a memory into our unconscious such that it is not as readily accessible as a suppressed memory. Anyone who has done something that left them feeling humiliated will be familiar with this process. The next day you will awaken inwardly cringing with thoughts like, 'I can't believe I did that!' But as your mind moves it slowly but surely into your unconscious, a month or so later you will awaken blissfully free of any awareness of your humiliation. Repressed memories typically only surface if a trigger comes along that springs them from their trap in our unconscious. Triggers take a number of forms and can range from smell, to music that might have been playing at the time, to someone simply raising the humiliating event e.g. 'Hey weren't you that person who ...?' When people reassure us with that old nugget, 'Time heals', what they are really describing is how time allows repression. Our painful memories reside in their vaults but they are not lost to us, they are just waiting to be reawakened.

Next, we have Denial. This is a refusal to accept external reality because it is just too threatening. It usually only works for a limited time, largely because external reality has an annoying habit of asserting itself eventually. I first witnessed this defence when I was working as an intern on a respiratory ward for war veterans who often continued their war-time habit of smoking. I had to give one patient the news that he had lung cancer, with the added sad caveat that his cancer was too advanced for treatment and there was nothing we could do. It was estimated that he had six to nine months to live. A few days later I was there as he was preparing for discharge. As he packed his things, we discussed his future plans. It became obvious that he was not operating on the basis that he had terminal cancer at all.

I discussed this case with the ward consultant, who was very familiar with this response amongst his cancer patients. He advised

me to ensure the man's immediate next-of-kin knew the full story. As he said, 'There's no need to take away his denial, reality will do that soon enough, it will allow him to enjoy some of the precious time he has left.'

Finally, we have Dissociation. This is the most powerful defence of all. This is what Jeni's brain had to use. It involves a drastic modification of one's personal identity or character to avoid emotional distress. As Jeni describes beautifully, her mind came up with the ultimate creative solution – to create other parts of herself that would experience the abuse and then these parts, to varying degrees were 'split off' from her consciousness to allow her to function day-by-day without the system becoming overwhelmed and imploding.

There is a very simple reason why our brain keeps traumatic memories hidden. Remember the first job of our unconscious is to keep us safe and the third is to develop automatic responses for future threats. It is for these reasons that we can't afford to let these painful memories fade. It is also why locking them away in vaults is not a complete process. These vaults leak. They have to, because to avoid future threats we need to be able to learn from the old ones and this requires a degree of access to them. So, while they are relegated to their vaults, they remain connected to our unconscious. There is a conduit there that connects the memory to parts of our unconscious mind.

This conduit keeps open a channel of communication that tells the unconscious when they could be in a similarly dangerous situation and need to take evasive action.

What is particularly confusing for patients and doctors alike is that this conduit can feed information to our unconscious to take evasive action without us knowing consciously what is going on and why we are doing it. The source event remains hidden from awareness. For example, several of my patients who were orally raped as children find themselves avoiding going to the dentist, or really struggling with gag-inducing throat swabs, sometimes with no awareness of why. These avoidance behaviours are

feeling-driven and often go unquestioned by the person. They often use simple 'post-rationalisation cognitions' to explain these behaviours, for example, 'I can't afford to see a dentist', or, 'My teeth are fine.'

Feeling-driven behaviours that are then dismissed by post-rationalisation cognitions is something all of us do, to one degree or another. Anybody who has decided to eat that ice cream when trying to lose weight and falling back on a post- rationalisation like, 'I will get back on my diet on Monday,' is a slave to a feeling-driven behaviour.

When psychotherapists talk about living a more conscious life, in simple terms they are talking about understanding more of these unconscious feeling-driven behaviours. These behaviours are learnt during our formative years, and they will continue to be applied unconsciously to similar-looking situations, which in reality are quite different. A child who was repeatedly dismissed by her parents for asking questions about what they were feeling will often, as an adult, not explore their partner's emotions. We call this learnt pattern a 'psychodynamic' – 'psycho' as in a psychological learning, 'dynamic' as in being applied on an ongoing basis.

The splitting-off of dissociation sits on a spectrum. The younger the mind is, i.e. the more plastic it is, the more it can employ dissociation as a trauma defence. It is unusual to see DID develop in people who were traumatised later in their childhood. While somewhat arbitrary, as it is difficult to research, around the age of eight the mind seems to consolidate to a level that Jeni-like dissociation does not readily occur.

Fortunately, we can all dissociate from the fullness of what is happening if the trauma is extreme enough. This has been reported mostly on battlefields where soldiers can appear quite relaxed and peaceful as they die from horrific injuries, but it has also been seen in civilian settings, particularly serious car accidents.

At the less severe end of the clinical spectrum of dissociation, we have people who can talk about a horrible abuse experience without displaying any emotion at all. Somewhere in the middle,

we have those who shift into sudden states of acute distress, or who behave surprisingly irrationally, when they are triggered by something that reminds them of their trauma experiences. The parts of them that are reacting, and their traumatic origins, may not be at all well-defined. This less differentiated form of dissociation, commonly seen in the borderline personality construct, is more difficult to treat than DID because of this lack of definition.

On the severe end we have the strategy that Jeni uses, where she actually splits off a part of her mind almost entirely. What Jeni's mind does is create what are called 'amnestic barriers' between these parts of her mind. This is how she can have personalities that have no knowledge at all of her abuse.

Imagine a pizza where the cuts between the slices represent the amnestic barriers. We all have different parts to ourselves, e.g. an anxious child part, a playful child part, a part that goes to a job, a part that is a partner and so on. Our pizza parts make up our whole person. Unlike most of the population, Jeni's parts, separated by amnestic barriers of varying opacity, evolve over time into personalities of varying depth and complexity.

This evolution occurs with a surprising degree of independence from each other, in a way that does not occur for the greater population. We call these 'alters' – some of whom develop full personalities while, at the other end of the spectrum you have 'fragments', who might have only existed for a short period of time to experience extreme abuse. Nevertheless, Jeni still has her complete pizza that makes up a whole, like the rest of us. It is the presence of protective amnestic barriers which form in response to the abuse, that make up the essence of DID. DID is a spectacularly clever mental manoeuvre for three reasons. First, it allows the person to function in the outside world without showing the normal human responses to their abuse (e.g. overt anxiety and depression) that would draw unwanted attention. In short it allows them to continue to fit in and be accepted by those around them, particularly their parents. Second, they develop a

stable of alters, each bringing special interpersonal skills that will, hopefully, keep them safer in the future. Depending on who is in front of them, they can bring out the best personality to deal with the situation.

Finally, it gives the child a much-needed sense of mastery over their perpetrators. They have a place they go to in their mind when they know that they are being wronged and that they are worthy of better treatment. As Jeni illustrates, again and again, she retained this awareness, this faith, although at times it was harder to access. For all people with DID, this stronghold of self-respect is the source of their resilience and, ultimately, their salvation.

I'm often asked, 'Why go into that Pandora's Box of trauma, why not leave well enough alone?' Typically, this question comes from family or a close friend. Patients, particularly those who have taken the leap to end up in my office, know why they are there; they want control of their life back. They have had enough of living increasingly narrow lives as dictated by their unconscious mind trying to keep them safe through avoidance of anything that their unconscious decides is 'not for them'.

On top of this, they are never truly happy. This is because that necessary conduit that is open to the horrible trauma in the memory vault is leaking out very unpleasant feelings of guilt, shame and huge sadness.

In its simplest form the job of trauma therapy is to allow the patient to finally return to these memories and process them so they can let go of them once and for all. This dismantles the feeling-driven avoidance that is holding the person back. It is very difficult to author a good life when your unconscious mind is continually hijacking your actions in the service of keeping you safe.

Safe is the enemy of a great life.

What underpins this therapy is showing the patient that 'the war is over'. Convincing them of this is not easy, as they have built the equivalent of a fortified castle in their head. Until the therapist can convince the trauma patient that the war is over, they remain

understandably reluctant to start to dismantle this elaborately fortified castle. It took some years before I could convince Jeni that her war was over. There was a lot of work done to free Jeni from that trauma, but in telling her story she is showing that she did indeed win the war.

CHAPTER TWO

Give Me Time to Breathe

JENI

I didn't know anything about Australia, but I knew I was excited to go there. In 1974, Mum decided Frank needed sunshine to help with his health problems, so we prepared to move to the other side of the world. I hoped that the sunshine would help Dad as well. Maybe in Australia things would be different. Maybe he would stop hurting me. Maybe.

In April, we headed to Southampton on England's south coast and boarded the SS *Australis*. My mum bought me a new blue coat for the voyage. My grandmother wanted to buy me a new Sweep puppet because the replaced original was a little tattered. I refused; I loved my Sweep. He was the only thing I packed.

Mum held my hand as we walked on to the ship, but she didn't realise she was also holding the hand of the hundreds of people inside my head. I wasn't just Jeni. By the time I was four, Erik had built tunnels in my mind for my army to live in. Every time I needed help, Symphony created an alter to deal with the outside world.

Early on in the trip to Australia, my dad sat me on the ship railing and held me over the edge of the deck. My feet dangled beneath me. For a moment, I thought he was going to throw me over the side. I couldn't swim. I cried and I wet my pants in fear. Dad proceeded to hit me for being a 'disgusting little brat'. For the rest of the voyage, I avoided the edge of the boat at all costs, and I tried to avoid my dad as well.

We slept in a tiny cabin with bunk beds and a cot for Frank in the middle of the room. Living in such close confines, I thought I might be safe from my dad's prying hands. His fingers seemed to be everywhere, touching me, rubbing me, poking me. All the time. Fat fingers. Everywhere.

At night, I cuddled Sweep tightly. I whispered my secrets to him. 'Daddy hurts me,' I said. 'Maybe if I try harder or do it better, it won't hurt so much.' I hoped. Maybe.

On board, there was a safety briefing where the adults were given instructions on what to do if the boat went down. Afterwards, my father dismissed the advice and told my mother that if anything happened to the boat, she should abandon us kids. 'You can always have more children,' he reasoned. Mum spent the remainder of the journey planning escape routes and working out how she might grab enough lifejackets to save three kids on her own. She vomited often; I don't know if it was from seasickness or worry. Mum lived in terror for the entire five weeks we were on the boat. I did too.

When we stopped in South Africa, I was fascinated by a small train that carried freight from one side of the docks to the other. I watched it going back and forth, and the alter who absorbs things took note. Because I liked the little train, the absorber created a small train system with tracks and carriages to transport people around the dungeons of our inner world. It was the kindest gesture anyone had made for me.

While in South Africa, we took a trip to the top of Table Mountain. On the way back down, the cableway was delayed. Mum panicked – convinced the boat would leave without us. She pushed Frank in a stroller and dragged me and Sheila along beside her. Dad walked casually behind us on his own. He didn't make any effort to help. After all, you can always have more children.

* * *

Upon arrival in Sydney, the first thing my mum noticed was a flourish of trees shaped like pineapples. She'd never seen anything

37

like them before. The first thing I noticed was the warmth. In England, I was always cold. Here, I revelled in the sunshine. I took off my blue coat. After five particularly unhappy weeks on the boat, it was lovely to be on solid land.

We stayed in a hostel in Sydney at first and then moved to a house in Dulwich Hill. Our furniture took eighteen months to arrive from England, so the house echoed with emptiness. The backyard was blindingly green. From the back steps, you could see over the fence into the next-door neighbour's garden. The mum's name was Carla, and her daughter was Debbie. There was no dad. I wondered what it would be like living in a house without a dad.

I shared a bedroom with my sister Sheila. She'd started school and there was an Italian boy in her class called Gianni Rometty. He had dark, curly hair and he came to my sister's birthday party. His name felt funny in my mouth, and I said it over and over again. Gianni Rometty.

One day, I was sitting in the living room on the sofa playing with Sweep. The rest of the family was there too, my brother and sister were sitting next to each other on the floor and Mum was sewing something next to them. I was murmuring to Sweep and making him nod in agreement. When I first got Sweep, Dad had ripped the squeaker out of him, so he didn't have a voice. Much like me.

My dad sat down next to me and asked for Sweep. He slipped the puppet onto his hand, but his fingers were too big and stuck out of Sweep's paw. Fat Fingers. Everywhere. 'You're hurting Sweepie,' I said.

'Sweep knows I'm just playing. He wants to play. Do you want to play?' Dad said. I nodded my head and he smiled at me.

My father began to put Sweep behind his back to play hide and seek with me. He sat very close to me and started to stroke my legs. My mother and sister and brother might have been in the same room, but it was as if we were in different worlds. The more he played with Sweep, the further up my legs he stroked until his fingers wriggled under my skirt. I was focused on following Sweep and ignored his touch for a long time. It was only when my father picked up my legs

and slipped his body underneath my legs that I really paid attention. He kept stroking me and it was both soft and a little irritating. Like a bug walking over my skin; it tickled and made me want to brush it away.

Dad moved his hand from stroking my leg to my bottom. At first this touch was gentle and it even felt nice. I thought it was part of the game. However, after a little while Dad's fingers stopped stroking me softly and began to probe and poke at my underpants.

Dad brought Sweep up to his ear like Sweep was talking to him and said, 'Really?' He then nodded Sweep's head and took him back to his ear as if Sweep was whispering again. I wanted to know what Sweep was telling him, and I was a little frightened that Sweep might tell my father some of the things I had told him.

I had told Sweep everything my father had ever done to me and how much it hurt me. I did not know what my father was doing to me, but I did know how it felt and I had told Sweep all of that. I truly believed that Sweep could tell on me, and I began to get very scared. Dad continued to make Sweep talk, and tutted at me as if Sweep had told him that I had been naughty.

All the while my father was playing with Sweep, one of his fingers pressed against my bottom, trying to force its way into me. This hurt and I shifted position trying to get away from him. I felt a sharp pain in my lower abdomen every time my father thrust into me. It felt like Dad was stabbing into me and I opened my mouth to cry out. My father flung himself forwards and began to rub Sweep all over my face. He kept Sweep's lower body over my mouth and pressed harder into me as he rubbed Sweep's head over my cheeks, nose and eyes. He used Sweep's head to wipe away my tears. It felt like he was ripping me apart.

Dad said, 'Ohhhh, Sweepie's told me some things about you! I know all your secrets now! Oooooo, you're in trouble!' His voice was quite jolly, but it just made me cry harder. I was sure Sweep had told on me and now Dad knew just how much he hurt me and scared me. Dad talked about how he now knew that I liked cats and dollies and the colour pink. All true.

Suddenly Dad pushed his finger deep inside me. I could smell his hot burning Bakelite scent. He pulled his finger out of my bottom sharply and my undies snapped back into place.

'I want Sweepie,' I cried, and put my hands out for him.

'Oh, all right,' Dad said in a fed-up tone as he ripped Sweep off his hand. Then he got up off the sofa and walked out of the room.

I held Sweep to my chest and stroked his head. 'Sorry Daddy hurt you,' I murmured and kissed him better like my mother had taught me.

My brother, sister and mother did not notice any of what had just happened. My dad was a monster who hid in plain sight.

I truly thought that Dad had made Sweep tell him my secrets and for a while afterwards I was frightened to confide in my puppet friend. Dad had taken away the one source of comfort I had. He'd deprived me of my only confidant. I was all alone.

A while later Dad hurt me so badly I bled.

'If you tell your Mummy she will die, because she will find out what a dirty little girl you are,' Dad said.

So, I started telling Sweep again instead.

SYMPHONY

The first time Dad comes into the Dulwich Hill bedroom I share with Sheila, I instinctively squeeze my bottom as tight as I can. Dad sits beside me on my bed, pulls the bedcovers off and lifts my nightdress. He opens my legs apart ever so slightly to fit his hand in between my thighs. Fat fingers. Everywhere. All the time.

* * *

✶ *Dear Reader, the next section details high-level trauma and could cause significant distress for some readers. You can choose to skip ahead and rejoin the narrative at the star on page 45. Jeni*

Dad calls me a 'naughty, silly girl'. His face is red with anger. I'm stiff with fear. He storms out of the room with loud thumps. You

can tell what mood Dad is in by the sound of his footsteps. The louder they are, the angrier he is. The softer they are, the happier he is. Loud steps meant imminent danger, soft steps meant hidden danger.

'I didn't mean to make him angry,' I tell Sweep.

Dad has this weird thing he likes to do to me. It involves shoving things into my bottom. I don't understand it at all. But it hurts, scares and disgusts me all at once. After all, it's dirty!

Sticking things inside my bum became a ritual for him. This ritual develops over time getting more complex and violent. I didn't know what he was using on me until four years later when he started making me clean up after him. The ritual starts with Dad using a silvery stick. The objects get progressively bigger; each one is thicker than the last. The first is a crochet hook, then knitting needles of various widths, the handle of a wooden spoon, both ends of a black and yellow screwdriver, the handle of a hammer, a chisel and a burning soldering iron.

If Dad gets the order of the ritual wrong, he starts again from the beginning. After stretching me, he then anally rapes me. Between 1973 and 1981, the ritual happens hundreds of times, too many to count, especially when you're four and still use your fingers to get to the number ten.

We fight him at every opportunity. We squirm and resist and scream. We plead, 'No, Daddy! Please stop. It hurts. It hurts. It hurrrrrts.' We never lie back and think of England. We're an army, after all.

Dad can read my mind. He tells me so, and I believe him. He tells me that if I ever think of trying to get help, he will hurt me very badly, and I believe him. He tells me if I share our secret, he will kill my mum, brother and sister, and I believe him. I can't think my own thoughts safely, so I turn to my default. I sing. Song lyrics become my language. I sing to soothe Jeni and the alters, to communicate and to think. I try to reach out to Mum in song lyrics, but unfortunately there isn't a power ballad that says, *'My Daddy is raping me and it hurts, please help.'*

JENI

In Australia, Mum became a valued member of the community. She took us kids to playgroups and met with other mums. She taught English to an Arabic woman, and we all cheered when the woman learnt to say, 'Please shut the door.' She also ran a family day-care group with Carla from next door. Between them they'd wrangle eight kids. They'd take us to the shops, to the playground, for train rides. Mum collected toys for us to play with. My favourite one was a 'boy's toy'. It was a little table with shapes cut out of it that you'd hammer through the holes. There was a star, a square and a round cylinder, which went missing one day. I believe my father saw the cylinder as an opportunity and pocketed it for a later purpose.

To the best of my knowledge, my dad never abused any of the family day-care children. He wasn't an opportunist, he was calculating. He got off on wielding complete control over me. He suppressed his urges and reserved his violence for me. After all, he couldn't risk having another child run home and tell their parents about the scary man at day care.

I couldn't run home and tell anyone about the scary man because he lived there. We teach kids about stranger danger, but we don't talk about the dangers that lurk at home.

* * *

The grass in Australia was drier than England. I was sitting in the garden one afternoon, playing with my doll and running my hands over the blades of grass, when Dad came and sat down beside me. Mum was inside lying down with a migraine, and I was worried about her.

'Let's play a game, that will cheer you up,' said Dad, who started running his hands over the grass like me. I hoped we'd play with my doll together, but when Dad ran his hand from the grass to my leg, I knew it was a different kind of game.

'No,' I whispered.

'Oh, you don't love me?' said Dad with disappointment. He started to cry. I crept closer to him and put my arms around him. 'I do love you, Daddy, don't cry,' I assured him.

'If you really loved me, you'd play with me.' He pouted. I didn't have the words to explain that I loved him, but I hated his games, so I agreed to play with him. Dad grinned and immediately forced his hand into my underpants. He picked me up and carried me to the back of the garden behind the thick bushes.

Dad pushed my hand on to his penis. 'Go on, rub it. You want Daddy to feel good, don't you?' he said.

I felt sick and faint. My head nodded and sagged down towards my chest. Dad didn't notice. 'Keep going, oh yes. Nearly there. Harder, do it harder!' he said. His breathing was choppy like it was being ripped out of him. I rubbed as hard as I could until there was thick liquid over my hand.

Everything went blurry. I was still conscious because I could see and hear, but it was as though everything was shrouded in a thick fog. 'I guess I'd better check on your mother,' he said.

I opened my mouth to ask for help, but nothing came out. My eyes caught sight of a white dandelion puff and I tried to focus on that. As I put my hand out to catch it, everything went black. I lost consciousness and when I woke up, my hand was covered in ants. Tiny, itchy, sticky ants. I flew to the bathroom and put my hand under the hot tap. I scrubbed. The water was so hot it burned me, but I kept scrubbing, until my mum came into the bathroom and pulled my hand out of the stream. 'You'll burn yourself,' she said. 'You need to be careful. Why didn't you stop when it started to hurt?'

'I got ants on it. I don't like ants. They were all over my hands, Mummy, and, and …' I couldn't find the words to say Dad had ejaculated all over my hand and left me semi-conscious on the ground. But I had the word for ants.

In that moment, I thought back to the dandelion puff. I wondered what would have happened if I had caught it and made a wish before I passed out. I'd have wished to take my dad's pain away.

Pain was something I understood. In early 1975, I remember a two-week period when Dad wouldn't stop inserting objects into my bottom. He was as relentless as the agony I felt in my lower belly from constipation. During this period, I was desperate to poo, but was unable to. When Dad forced himself inside my bottom at the start of the fortnight, the pressure was insurmountable. It felt like all of my internal organs had been pushed upwards towards my head and squashed to the point of bursting. I passed out and woke up to Dad vigorously shaking me and slapping my face.

'You're such a dirty girl,' he said. 'You need me to take care of you. If you ever tell Mummy how I take care of you, she will die. You don't want Mummy to know how dirty you are, do you? Do you?'

I felt too ill to respond.

'What we do is privet and confidential. If you even think of telling anyone, I will know and I will hurt you so badly,' Dad threatened. He repeated this mantra so often, I genuinely believed he could read my mind and that my mum was in mortal danger if I thought the wrong thing.

For the next ten days, Dad 'took care of me'. Every day, I willed myself to defecate. I strained and pushed and cried, but the only thing that came out of my bottom was blood. At the same time, I wee'd almost constantly. It was like my bladder was a leaking tap I couldn't turn off. My underpants were wet all the time and I kept finding a strange glue-like substance on the crotch. The discharge went from being a sticky mucus to a dry cracked glaze on my underpants. It was a yellowish colour and smelt horrid. After a few days, the yellow turned to a green tinge, and it truly smelt like something was rotting inside me.

Eventually I was able to empty my bowels, and I hoped the discharge would resolve itself as well. It did, but not before some of the neighbourhood kids started to call me 'smelly'.

My mum gave me Dettol baths, but the smelly nickname wouldn't wash off.

Bath time was intriguing for me. I still hadn't worked out what made Dad's actions different to others, but I'd noticed one

distinction. When Mum washed my private parts in the bath, her breath stayed steady. When Dad touched my private parts, his breathing changed: he gasped for air, exhaled sharply and moaned deeply. I became excruciatingly aware of breathing patterns.

Mum touched me to clean me, and Dad touched me for his own sick sexual gratification – but as a child I had no concept of motives. So I focused on breathing patterns.

I don't tell you these details to shock or horrify you. I tell you them because they need to be told. There's a reason it's so hard for some people to believe in MPD and the extreme cases of abuse that cause it, and that's because the stories are so rarely told. More often than not, victims of such depravity don't survive to tell the tale. Their bodies are the only things that can speak for them because their abuse is overshadowed by a final act of violence: murder.

Surviving is a rare miracle, and it comes with a duty: to tell the story in the hope of helping others. I'm alive and so I have to speak out. I want people to know that MPD isn't a mental illness, it doesn't make you a serial killer and it's not fodder for entertainment. People with MPD have experienced the worst of the worst, and their mere survival should be applauded. But to understand MPD you need to know what happened to me: the relentless, the cruel, the manipulative, the depraved, the evil – all of it.

Betrayal Trauma

Jeni's story is extremely confronting. As Jeni points out at the end of the last chapter, she wants people to understand the fullness of what happened, of what created her condition. Her condition, (remembering it is not an illness) was, until relatively recently, not accepted as a valid medical diagnosis. This was largely because it was simply *too* confronting. Even experienced health professionals did not believe, or want to believe, that the kind of experiences you have just read about actually happened to innocent children.

Earlier I wrote about feeling-driven responses that we then explain through post-rationalisations. We all have our biases and our unconscious programming – collectively called our psychodynamics – they hide from conscious awareness but have an enormous influence over how we interact with the world, and in our relationships in particular. No one is immune. In the medical world the feeling-driven need to dismiss stories like Jeni's was post-rationalised around a key issue: memory. More specifically the accuracy and reliability of trauma memories and the big question – can they be implanted?

Jeni experienced a kind of abuse known as betrayal trauma.

This adds another dimension to our understanding of how the mind handles memory and is thought to be particularly relevant to why a child's mind develops DID. The story of betrayal trauma has a relevant history.

Betrayal trauma was first described in 1994 by psychologist, Dr Jennifer Freyd, a professor at the university of Oregon.[1] It occurs

when the perpetrator is a powerful figure in that child's life, one who they rely upon for their very survival and developmental growth and, hopefully, to thrive. Typically, as in Jeni's case, it is a parent, but if parents are largely or completely absent, this role can be taken on by a relative, foster parent, teacher etc.

For betrayal to occur, we first must have a relationship of weighty trust with a corresponding level of vulnerability in the victim. What is a young child to do when they are betrayed by a parent they trust and rely upon for their very survival? What was Jeni to do?

As an adult we can respond to betrayal and choose to no longer interact with the person. It is the child's absolute lack of choice that defines them as a true victim. Once we are old enough to leave home, or get away from the people who are hurting us, we can escape victimhood and save ourselves. Children cannot do this in the face of betrayal. Instead of physically moving to safety they have to do something quite complex in their mind – they *psychologically move to safety*. They achieve this by developing amnesia for the bad deeds, i.e. repressing their memories, or dissociating as Jeni did. These particular forms of forgetting allow the child to continue to relate to the perpetrator so they can maximise their chances of continuing to be cared for. The more effective the amnesia, the better their chance of being cared for. Like most challenges Jeni has taken on, she responded by learning to 'forget' at the highest level.

When the other parent is absent or their role as a nurturing protector has been undermined, the betrayal is even more acute and the need to forget is even greater. Jeni's father operated with impunity, subjugating his wife along with his children.

Consciously or not, he chose a woman to marry who would not stand up to him as he went about his dirty business and would be very likely to keep shameful secrets. As Jeni said, her mother came 'from a family of secrets' and her father 'deliberately sought her mother out for her subservience and ignorance'. This is telling, as is Jeni's mother's diagnosis of Autism. People on the spectrum

have difficulty appreciating and interpreting where others are at emotionally, i.e. with empathy. Accordingly, they have difficulty reading emotions in the faces of others. They are less likely to enquire as to what is going on for them. All this played into Jeni's father's control of his family. Jeni's reliance on her father was much greater, so the betrayal trauma was greater and therefore the need to employ more complete full-blown dissociation for her abuse was greater.

CHAPTER THREE

A Sorry Sight

SYMPHONY

My daddy tickles me. He tickles me until my sides hurt, until my eyes well with laughter, until my lungs scream silently for air.

Sometimes the tickling is a game. Other times it's a *game* – the kind Dad likes playing and I don't. He alternates between tickling my tummy and groping between my legs. He sticks a finger inside me.

It's confusing because Dad is inconsistent. He doesn't always grope me. Sometimes it is just tickling. I treasure the moments when he tickles me for fun. These are some of the rare times he's pleasant and cheerful. Dad wears so many masks, I can't keep track of them. There's nice Dad who wants to spend time with me. There's hurt Dad who needs my help to feel better. There's scary Dad who yells at me. And beneath them all, there's monster Dad who makes my insides hurt and my skin crawl. He's always there, lurking just under the surface.

I don't have the words to tell Dad I like it when he tickles me for fun, but I hate it when he touches me between my legs. If I tell him I don't want to play at all, I'll miss out on him being nice. Or worse, I'll be punished. I don't have the words. So, I sing in my head the words: 'Stop, stop, stop!'

JENI

When I turned five, two things happened: I started school and then, a bit later, I got glasses. I had enviously watched my sister Sheila

leave for school every morning and I was very excited to join her. My mum sewed me a dress to wear, and I carried a little suitcase with my lunch in it. I loved learning how to run, jump and catch balls, but I was afraid of people seeing my bottom when I did so. Girls weren't allowed to wear shorts and I was deathly scared of skirts and dresses because they allowed easy access to my private parts. I started wearing two pairs of underwear in an attempt to protect myself.

By this stage, Symphony had created the NotGirls – a group of alters that were neither girls nor boys. Dad always threatened to do the things he did to me to Sheila and Mum as well, but he never mentioned Frank. With that in mind, Symphony created a new gender to keep me safe.

I didn't think of school as an escape from my abuse, because I thought all adults were a danger.

Everyone was a threat. Nowhere was safe.

I don't remember much about my first year of school because I spent most of my time there trying to figure out what Dad was doing to me. When Dad was at work and I was at school, I figured he couldn't read my thoughts. While everybody else was learning how to count and spell their names, I tried to work out what Dad was doing to me.

Symphony made alters to deal with the distraction of school so she could focus on Dad. It was exhausting. And so Symphony created alters to deal with the distraction of the exhaustion.

I cried in class because I couldn't understand what was going on – partly because my mind was focused on other things, and also because I couldn't see the blackboard at the front of the classroom.

It wasn't until I started school that I had my eyes tested. Before then, everything was blurry and scary. When I got my first pair of prescription glasses – which were pale blue and entirely too big for my little face – I could finally see properly. The world was clear and a little less scary. A couple of kids called me four-eyes, but I snapped back, 'Four eyes are better than two.' And they were.

My teacher told my mum that after I got my glasses, I was a different kid. I participated in class, paid attention and stopped bursting into tears.

It didn't last long. My vision was only part of the problem. The other part was my dad.

* * *

✱ *Dear Reader, here again is a harrowing section that outlines severe traumatic abuse. Please pause here and start reading again at the star on page 62 if it feels too much.*

SYMPHONY

It's the day of my school fancy-dress parade. Mummy has made me a costume from *The Princess and the Pea* fairy tale. I have a very pretty dress covered in tiny seed pearls and a bag with a single pea in it. It's taken Mum weeks to make. The living-room floor has been covered in bundles of beads, buttons, pearls and fabric. Now my costume is finished and I can finally wear it. I'm so excited. At school, everyone tells me how pretty I look and I feel proud and happy. I walk around with my head held high like a princess.

I love my costume, but I don't understand the story of *The Princess and the Pea*. I can't see how having trouble sleeping made the girl a princess. I often can't sleep because I'm afraid of Daddy getting into my bed and hurting me, but I'm not a princess. I also can't fathom why someone would make up a bed of so many mattresses. Who has twenty feather mattresses lying around the house to make into one bed? I'm puzzled.

When Dad comes into my room in the night, I ask him my questions about *The Princess and the Pea*.

'Well, princesses have very soft skin. My perfect princess has beautiful long red hair. She looks just like you and has a body just like yours, only better,' he says, walking his fingers down my body.

JENI

From the day I got my glasses Dad used them as weapons. He stole my glasses from off my face every time he wanted to abuse me. He took away my eyes and held them hostage until he had finished abusing me. I became terrified of being without my glasses.

In summer, when the other kids in our street were swimming in our neighbour Carla's pool, I hesitated. I desperately wanted to jump in, but I didn't want to take my glasses off.

Eventually Carla coaxed me in and taught me how to swim by pretending to be a shark chasing me. She tugged on my feet playfully and I squealed with childish delight. I loved it.

One day I was swimming in the pool when I needed to go to the toilet. I was climbing out of the pool when I heard my dad's very angry voice. He was calling my name. I thought I was in trouble and froze, but I wet myself at the same time, accidentally peeing a little in the pool. I flew out of the water and went to see what my father wanted.

My mother, Frank and Sheila were out and he was angry that he had been unable to find me. He yelled that I should have come when he called me. He gripped me by my shoulders and forced me to bend over. He hit me across my back and bottom with his bare hand. I cried and tried to cover my bottom with my hands.

I was dripping water onto the kitchen floor and my dad yelled at me for doing so. After hitting me over and over with his bare hand, Dad let go of me and moved away. He said, 'Stay there, or else.' I froze in place. I felt my bladder let go and urine trickled down my legs. I cried, 'I'm sorry, I'm sorry,' but I had no idea why I was apologising or what I had done to deserve the beating.

My father stood with his hands on his hips. He was panting.

His cheeks were bright red, and his face looked huge. He lunged at me and dragged me alongside the table. The table was large, and it had a hard wooden top and cylindrical metal legs. My father shoved me between the table and the kitchen cupboards and turned me so my back was to the table. He opened his trousers and pulled his penis out of the gap. He jerked his body forward at me and his

penis stood out of his trousers like a sword. I only saw it for a few seconds before he moved his hands in front of it. My father gripped my hands tightly and pulled them to the front of his trousers. He thrust his hands onto his penis and forced me to grip it. He snarled, 'Get on with it. Do it fast!'

I began to roughly and quickly rub his penis. I was so upset, and in so much pain from the beating, that I was not as careful as I normally was. I was shivering with the cold and fear, and I desperately wanted it to be over. 'Hurry up,' said Dad, sounding breathless. I sped up my movements and gripped him harder. I refused to watch what I was doing, and I stared at his chest instead. He was wearing a white shirt with the sleeves rolled up a little. There were dark patches under his armpits that got bigger the more I rubbed.

As I stared at these patches, my dad began to jerk his hips forward thrusting his penis deeply into my hand. He grunted each time he jerked forwards and he sounded disgusting, like a pig rooting around in rubbish. I stared up at my dad's face and I watched as it got redder and redder and more and more bloated. He began to gasp, like the breath was being forced out of his lungs. I kept rubbing him even though my hands were beginning to throb in pain and my shoulders were getting stiffer. My dad thrust into my hands and then he seemed to hold his breath. His penis twitched against my fingertips and then my hands were wet and sticky. My father exhaled sharply.

After he pulled his trousers back up, he threw a towel at me and said, 'Clean up this mess. Just look at the mess you've made on the floor!'

It was always my fault, never his. I cleaned up the floor and then fled to the toilet. My stomach was cramping, and I had sharp pains in my right side. I ripped off my swimming costume and threw myself at the toilet. My body tensed as the toilet seat pressed into the marks on my bottom where my father had hit me, and I cried out in pain.

A few weeks later, the swimming pool next door turned green and slimy. I knew it was because I'd accidentally peed in it and was overwhelmed with guilt. I was sure that if anyone knew they would

hate me and punish me. Worse still, they would tell Dad and he would punish me.

HAPPY

Let me tell you a secret. There is happiness in every memory, you just need to know how to find it, how to separate it from the sadness and how to float it into the air like a helium balloon so it can't be tainted. That's my job; I take our happy memories and keep them safe. My name is Happy and I'm eleven years old.

I've been doing this job since the Christmas of 1976. It's not an easy job. Dad is determined to destroy everything that brings us joy, so I have to bury our happiness down deep and cover the hole with dirt. That's where our dollhouse is hidden. Mum gives us the dollhouse for Christmas and it's the most beautiful thing we've ever seen. I love it. I sit next to Daddy on the floor, and we build it together, clipping the pieces in place to create the mansion of my doll's dreams.

I play with the dollhouse all afternoon. I wonder if the roof comes off so I can look down on my dolls in their mansion. It doesn't, and we don't mind at all. It's the best gift we've ever been given.

In the morning, we wake up ready to play. But the roof of the dollhouse has been broken into little pieces overnight. Our heart sinks.

'How dare you?' Mum scolds. 'How dare you take a gift and destroy it within twenty-four hours.' But I didn't. I hadn't. I swear.

'You're not worth buying nice things for,' Mum dismisses.

And so, I take the memory from Christmas Day – the joy of unwrapping the dollhouse, the satisfaction of building it with Daddy, the fun of playing all afternoon – and I separate it from the destruction. I hold the memory tight, and I store it underground so I can pull it out when things are tough.

The dollhouse memory sits next to the love we feel for our cat Tawny, the magic of watching *One of Our Dinosaurs Is Missing* at the cinema, and the feeling of the sunshine in the garden. These are the memories that keep us going when it feels impossible to do so.

JENI

At the end of 1976, we moved from Dulwich Hill to a two- bedroom house on a nice street in Greenacre. Mum didn't want to buy the house; Dad bought it anyway.

I loved the garden at our new house, it had all my favourite flowers: hydrangeas, frangipanis and honeysuckle. I shared a room with Sheila across the hall from Mum and Dad's bedroom at the front of the house. There was a small bathroom with no toilet, a dining room with a huge chest freezer in the corner and a long kitchen that led into Frank's makeshift room at the back of the house. Dad put the TV and a bookcase in front of the back door in the living room, so there was only one way in and out. The back door leading out into the garden was heavy and had a massive bolt – I didn't know whether it was to keep people out, or in.

The house had an outside toilet and laundry with a set of big concrete sinks. Mum saw the outhouse as a nuisance, Dad saw it as an opportunity, and I soon began to see it as my personal hell. Beside the toilet was a window. My mum sewed a set of lace curtains for it, but my dad positioned them so he could still watch people going to the bathroom from outside. The toilet door also had a massive bolt, and we were told we were never allowed to lock it. Mum saw it as a safety issue – she didn't want to be locked out if one of us kids was hurt inside. Once again, Dad saw it as an opportunity – he wanted to be able to walk into the toilet at any time, regardless (or because) of who was using it.

On the other side of the yard from the outhouse was a garage, which became my dad's domain.

A few days after we moved into the Greenacre house, I was in the front garden looking across the street at the neighbour's flowers. Mrs Rice saw me admiring her roses and invited me to come over and pick a bunch for my mother. I loved the velvety texture of rose petals and would gently stroke them, careful not to pull them off. Standing in her sweet-smelling garden, Mrs Rice asked me a lot of questions about my family. I told her all about my mum, how lovely and pretty she was, how she liked sewing and cooking toffees. I told

her all about my older sister and little brother. Then Mrs Rice asked, 'And what does your father do?'

I went rigid. 'I don't know,' I said, staring at the bed of gladiolas in front of me. 'I better go home, my mum will be worried.'

'Oh, but you can't go home without some flowers for your mother,' said Mrs Rice, asking me to pick out my favourites. I pointed to a large purplish hydrangea, and Mrs Rice cut it for me. 'Don't you like your daddy? You have told me lots about your mummy, but nothing about your daddy,' she said.

'I've got to go home, Mummy will be angry,' I replied, running out of the garden with a handful of flowers for my mother. As I expected, when I got home, my parents were furious that I'd been gone so long, and that Mrs Rice had asked me so many questions.

Later that afternoon, Dad grabbed me as I passed him in the garden and pulled me into the outside toilet. He shut the door and locked the bolt with a clunk. Dad was the only person allowed to bolt the door. 'What did you tell Mrs Rice about me?' he snarled.

'Nothing, Daddy. Honest, I didn't say anything,' I said.

He didn't believe me and spun me around, so I was facing the double sink. Dad raised my skirt and smacked my bottom with his hand. He pulled my underpants down and kept hitting me again and again. Then he slipped his hand between my legs.

'You had better not have said anything about me. If I find that you have said even one word about me, I will kill your sister or your brother. You don't want to be responsible for Sheila or Frank dying, do you?' he said as he hit me harder and harder. It was the first time he threatened to hurt Frank, too.

I cried so much that I couldn't catch my breath. 'Oh stop pootering!' Dad demanded. He turned me to face him and pushed me down to my knees. I felt him remove my glasses and heard the sound of a zipper. 'Get on with it,' he said. I stretched my jaw as wide as I could. Dad thrust in and out of me, harder and harder, deeper and deeper. I thought he was going to rip out my throat. It hurt and I screamed when I could catch my breath.

Afterwards he said, 'Are you ever going to talk about me?'

'No, Daddy, I promise,' I replied.

'Good.' He walked outside, slamming the door shut behind him. I crawled across the cold concrete floor to the toilet and sat beside it. I put my fingers into my mouth and threw up, trying to get rid of the taste.

That night, I had dreadful nightmares of Sheila and Frank dying. The nightmares haunted me for my entire childhood. As did my fear of the outside toilet. I wet the bed every single night I lived at Greenacre because I was too afraid of getting up in the middle of the night and being attacked by Dad. I developed chronic constipation from the abuse and sodomy. Because I didn't want to put myself in a vulnerable position with Dad, I started wiping my bottom from the back to the front, trying to hide my private parts to avoid being watched through the lace curtains. Of course, I then developed infections, which made going to the bathroom even more painful. It was a catch 22.

SYMPHONY

The garage smells damp and musty. The concrete floor feels gritty. Every time I walk in there, I want to run back inside and wash my feet in the bathtub because they feel dirty. Not that I ever walk in there by choice; I'm usually dragged, coaxed or summoned.

The garage and the toilet are always cold; physically and emotionally. I know I can't expect a shed and an outhouse to protect me, but I still resent those rooms for not helping me. They're as cold and as unfeeling as Dad. I'm desperately trying to keep my family safe by helping Dad, but the garage and toilet don't give a toss.

Lying on the concrete floor, the cold seeps deep into my bones.

I know I'll never be warm again.

JENI

On a summer's night in the beginning of January 1977, my dad visited me in bed. He took me by the hand and led me into the living room and sat me on the sofa, which he'd lined with towels. They were a soft blue colour. Dad told me he'd thought of a fun

game we could play and put his hand on my leg. I froze up inside. The game started like all the others: with Dad running his hand over my bottom in circles and stroking towards my private parts. Then he pushed my face into a cushion and dug at me. I inhaled sharply and Dad chastised me, 'Shh, you'll wake Mummy!' I bit my tongue. I didn't want to wake Mum up because if she saw me playing Dad's game, she'd die, and it would be all my fault. As much as I hated 'playing' with Dad, I loved my mother more.

Dad whispered half sentences into my ear, 'Feels so good ... Takes me to a higher plane.'

I bit my tongue again to stop myself from howling in pain. It was so excruciating, I thought for certain that my dad had pierced the skin. Dad's body went stiff. Dad yanked the soft blue towels out from underneath me and told me to 'Go to bed.'

First, I went to the outside toilet. I sat on the toilet and put my hands between my legs. When I pulled them out, they were covered in blood. I cried and rocked back and forth on the toilet. As I blotted at the blood, I gently touched the hole again. It felt like a wound. The edges were sore and red. At the time, I didn't know the hole was my vagina, I was sure Dad had quite literally torn me a new one. I thought of it as the hole that never healed. I stuck toilet paper into the hole to stop my insides from falling out in my sleep.

The next day, I tried to remove the wad of toilet paper, but it was stuck. I knew I couldn't ask my mum for help, and I didn't dare ask Dad. When I finally pulled the wad out after a number of attempts, it was blotched with dark red dried blood and lighter fresh blood from the tears when I'd pulled it out.

I was too frightened to put more toilet paper inside me, so I lined my underpants with it instead. I spent most of the day in the toilet, checking to make sure that the blood didn't seep through. I wore undies to bed that night, even though I was forbidden from doing so by Dad. For the rest of the week, I kept checking the hole to see if it had closed up, but it never did.

This attack confirmed to me how strong and dangerous Dad was. If he was capable of ripping a new hole inside me with his fingers, I

knew he wouldn't hesitate to follow through on his threats to kill my mother and siblings.

LITTLE RICKY

Dad says we're not bleeding, so we're not bleeding. What he says goes. He's right, we're wrong. When blood drips from our underneath, I send the blood-holders in to clean up the mess. They must blur their eyes and think mind-bending thoughts to make the reality a delusion.

The blood-holders are the alters who face the death committee the most. We send in the Assassin for over one hundred of them. It's a hard job holding the blood and it's a hard job sending in the Assassin, but someone has to do it. At least that's what I tell myself.

JENI

The night of my seventh birthday, my dad woke me up and whispered that he had a surprise for me. Sitting on the sofa in the living room, Dad explained that birthdays were not a celebration of my birth, but rather a day to give birth. He laid me down and pulled my legs apart, shoving his fingers inside me. Dad ripped his fingers out and bent down to grab something from the floor. With his hands between my legs again, he pushed a hard, cylinder-shaped object inside me. 'You are going to have a baby. Bear down and give birth,' he said. I had no idea what he was talking about. I went to grab the object with my hands, but Dad hit them away and told me to push.

'I'm frightened,' I said.

'It's all right, Daddy's here,' he replied.

This did not make me feel any less frightened.

I tried to push down like I was going to the toilet, but I was afraid of making a mess on the sofa. I clenched with all my might, but the object didn't move at all. Dad stroked my vagina with his fingers and traced the edge of the object. I was afraid I would never get it out of me. I thought I was going to faint with the pain of it. The world started to spin, and I could feel my heart beating between my legs. I focused on the heartbeat. As long as I felt the thumping, I knew I was still alive.

'It hurts, Daddy,' I said.

'It's painful to be beautiful,' he replied.

MUSCLES

When I look down, I see a flat chest and a six pack. That's not why they call me Muscles. They call me Muscles because I create muscles to fight Dad. When he pushes his penis into our bottom, I flex my muscle and try to push him out. When he inserts the cylinder into our vagina in the birthday ritual, I flex my muscle and try to squeeze it out. I push and I squeeze, and I push and I squeeze.

I do the impossible. The body of a seven-year-old girl isn't made to give birth – to cylinders or anything else. It's impossible. So I take over. I wrap myself around the object and flex my muscles until I get it out. I was born to give birth.

I'm a seventeen-year-old boy and I'll always be a seventeen-year-old boy. When you turn eighteen, you can get a gun licence. If I turn eighteen, I'll blow the fucker away.

JENI

'Bear down, you're nearly there,' Dad said, after I clenched so hard I wet myself. I gulped for air. A wave of pins and needles washed over my head. It felt like all my hair was trying to stand up on its own. I tried to shake the feeling away, but I'd used up all of my energy tensing.

With another almighty push, I felt the object move out of me. It was hard and rigid, but also slimy. I was surprised when Dad handed me a small doll covered in bubbly wet slime. The doll had no clothes on and looked like a naked Kewpie doll you'd get on a cane from the Royal Easter Show. Dad used the canes to beat me and Sheila when he was punishing us.

Dad made out that I'd just given birth to the doll, but the shape he shoved inside me felt different. It didn't have arms and legs to grip on to, just smooth edges, like a battery, but much bigger.

'You have done well! Good girl!' Dad said as he wiped down between my legs. 'Happy birthday.'

I felt woozy as I stood up and my private parts felt raw and battered. I hadn't realised I'd been lying on a towel until that moment. I saw it was stained, but couldn't tell if the marks were blood or shit. Or both.

I staggered to bed and hugged Sweep to my face. The pain between my legs felt distant. I was aware of it, but it seemed so far away from me. I felt like my body didn't belong to me. I focused on hugging Sweep, who got very wet from my tears as I cried into him. The following morning when I went to the toilet, I found flakes of dried blood between my legs.

I did not understand what Dad had made me do – or even how he had done it. From the age of seven to eleven, my dad forced me to give birth on my birthday. Each time, he produced a naked Kewpie doll covered in slime, which was equally confusing and distressing. I was certain the object he inserted inside me was not doll-shaped. It was a hard cylinder, just like the piece that went missing from the wooden 'boy's toy' I played with during family day care.

When people talk about ritualised abuse, they often picture satanic cults, pentagrams and ceremonial daggers. The reality is darker: knitting needles, wooden spoons and kewpie dolls. Ritualistic abuse doesn't happen in candle-lit covens adorned with skulls. For me, it happened on my family sofa or in my parents' bed on carefully laid towels, and in the outhouse and my bedroom. It happened anywhere my father wanted. Nowhere was safe.

My survival strategy to cope with the ritualised abuse was led by Symphony, who created armies of alters. The Backroom Boiler Boys, Girls and NotGirls – which is what we called our working bees behind the scenes – were as important to my existence as my lungs, kidney and liver. They were always there, doing their jobs, but I only became aware of them when something went wrong. You never take much notice of your kidneys until you get a UTI.

At any one time, there could be twenty-four alters in the body at once. They would be front runners from each of the different internal branches who worked together simultaneously. The alters didn't just look after me and Dad, they looked after the whole family. As well as Captain Busby, who was in charge of protecting Mum, there was Squadron Captain, who looked after everything to do with Frank; and Janet, who took care of Sheila.

Squadron Captain had an army of forty-odd teenage soldiers, mostly boys because Frank didn't play very well with girls. The soldiers worked to shield Frank from Dad's physical abuse and to keep him happy at all times. It was as much a physical job – stepping in to take the blows Dad would otherwise inflict on Frank – as it was a mental one: learning how to cheer Frank up with dinosaur questions when he was upset.

Because Frank was the youngest and a boy, he didn't need as much protecting as Mum and Sheila; that's why his army was significantly smaller. Squadron Captain didn't know why Dad didn't hurt Frank like he hurt us. But now we know: Frank didn't have the anatomy that appealed to Dad, and Frank also had the charm needed to stay on Dad's good side. Frank didn't, however, have the emotional capacity to cope with Dad's mind games and cruelty. He needed protection from those. In those moments, Squadron Captain and his soldiers were ready with a tissue and a kind word.

Janet's team was far larger and more complicated. She didn't describe it as an army like the others; it was a universe. Janet created a world that revolved entirely around Sheila. She was fifteen and thought so much of Sheila that she took her name from one of her middle names. The alters were all NotGirls and they were divided into teams who monitored Sheila's interactions with Dad, Mum, Frank, her friends, teachers and strangers. At the hint of upset, they would jump in and try to help Sheila. They were prepared to do anything for her. In the Meatloaf song, he sings he'd do anything for love, but he won't do *that*. Janet and her NotGirls would do *that* for Sheila. There were no bounds when it came to keeping her safe. They

would take punishments, offer encouragement, and stand between Sheila and Dad. Janet and her team lived on tenterhooks. They didn't have an off switch.

* * *

My schoolbooks were clear evidence of my MPD in action. Inside the pages, there were marked differences in the handwriting, language, drawings, colours, and personality. The schoolbooks looked like they'd been written by a whole class of different students – because they had. If a person with knowledge of MPD had read my schoolbooks, they might have been able to count the number of different alters who sat in my classes. But, unfortunately for me, there wasn't much known about MPD during the seventies. There still isn't much knowledge in the general public today. Hopefully this book will change that.

My childhood could be a checklist for symptoms of MPD; a scavenger hunt of clues, a treasure map to discovery. The signs were all there: imaginary friends, speaking as 'we' instead of 'I', inconsistency of likes and dislikes, forgetting meeting people, losing time, different voices and ways of speaking.

The signs may have been all there, but no one was looking for them. Nobody saw anything. And that meant no one could save us.

Solving Torture – the Sleeping Power of Dream Resolution

Jeni's father's motivation was power. The sex acts obviously had some sexual pleasure involved, but this was secondary. As with men who rape adult women, it is firstly about overcoming their sense of deficient masculinity and establishing dominance. But this power then needs to be protected. Secrecy is everything, but how to enforce it?

When you torture someone, you inevitably take them to a point where the pain no longer makes a difference. They may abandon the desire to live. Jeni reached this point more than once. Rather obviously, why would you want to live if there is more interminable pain coming your way? It's an unusual but comprehensible point where offering to kill someone more quickly becomes an offer of value. I suspect that the earliest torturers worked out, within the first few days of getting their feet under the torture table, that what motivated people to accede to the torturer's wishes was not the threat of pain to themselves, it was the threat of pain to those they cared about.

This was the case with Jeni. In Jeni's interaction with Mrs Rice, we see the fullness of a critical issue that needs to be covered off from the playbook of a sexual predator – stopping their victim from telling. It is unlikely that anything occupies the mind of a predator more than being caught, especially when they are repeatedly offending (as opposed to a one-off opportunistic assault). Jeni's

father, like torturers from time immemorial, worked out that Jeni would not be overly intimidated by her own pain. He couldn't help but notice that Jeni had already developed a surprising pain tolerance as she employed the fullness of her dissociative powers. Indeed, it is as he was beating her, recognising that this pain was not threat enough, that he said, 'If I find that you have said even one word about me, I will kill your sister or your brother.' He follows this with the killer line, 'You don't want to be responsible for Sheila or Frank dying, do you?'

All predators need to deal with this issue, especially if the child can readily identify them – which is the norm. The USA Centers for Disease Control's Adverse Childhood Experiences Study, which has been ongoing since 1995, found that a family member, close family friend, or other trusted family acquaintance is responsible for 80 to 90 per cent of sexual assaults perpetrated against children.[1] Threatening those who a child cares about is the usual starting point for enforcing silence. To add power to the threat of harming family, hurting, or even killing, pets is another common strategy. This too happened to Jeni.

Jeni's father had to invest an enormous amount of energy to enforce Jeni's secrecy. And so Jeni entered a strange and enduring battle with herself to try to kill the secrecy, but not her family. This was the beginning of recurrent nightmares that haunted Jeni for her entire childhood.

Dreams – the window to the unconscious

It is worth spending some time on understanding dreams and nightmares as they are a key part of the trauma picture. They are also informative in understanding the primary treatment for trauma – Eye Movement Desensitisation and Reprocessing (EMDR). Dreaming is affected by trauma and gives us an insight into key elements of a person's trauma and where they are at in dealing with it.

Dreams are the window into what our unconscious mind is dealing with, while, by definition, our conscious mind sleeps. By

understanding our dreams, even at an elementary level, we can work out what our unconscious mind is concerned about. At the very least, without too much difficulty, we can work out how troubled, or relaxed it is, at any given point in time.

Why should we care what our unconscious mind is concerned with? Our unconscious mind is running our lives in more ways than you might realise. To start with, the unconscious mind is way more powerful than our conscious mind. For these reasons, before we dive into the intriguing world of dreams, and what they represent, we need to understand the power of our unconscious mind.

Your unconscious mind is the part of your mind that does everything else except the things that you consciously think about and make decisions around. And that is a lot for our unconscious to do. It runs our body's systems while allowing us to walk (a surprisingly complex activity – ask any 12-month-old) and chew gum at the same time (not so complex).

Indeed, it makes many more decisions, in a given day, than we do consciously. Researchers have suggested that only around 5 to 10 per cent, or even less, of the decisions we make in a day are actually made with our conscious mind.

By making so many decisions for us, our unconscious mind frees us to make conscious decisions throughout our day. And while we might like to think that these are the most important decisions, I have some bad news. Decisions we make consciously are the ones that we would *like to make* – the ones we are most comfortable with, rather than the most important ones.

The greater power of our unconscious mind is perhaps best illustrated by how it can do multiple complex tasks at the same time. In contrast, our conscious mind can only do one thing at a time.

While people look like they are multitasking with their conscious mind, the truth is they are quickly switching between tasks. This has been tested by looking at the brain wave attentional patterns of people who appear to be able to do two complex tasks at the same time. For example, doing mathematics at the same time as

playing piano. What they found was that the mind jumps quickly from one task back to the other with the unconscious mind doing most of the previously learnt piano playing. On the other hand, your unconscious mind is quite able to do several complex tasks at the same time.

Scientists estimate that our five senses send up to 11,000,000 bits per second of information to the unconscious mind for processing. Our conscious mind can only process around 50 bits per second. Stop and think about that for a moment – that is not a little difference.

To use a computer analogy, our conscious mind is like the keyboard on a computer. It is nowhere near as powerful as the CPU (the brain in a computer) which equates to our unconscious. The good news is that while the keyboard is relatively under-powered, it has the ability to ultimately control what the brain of the computer does. Moreover, while we might like to think that our unconscious mind can only make simple decisions, in fact they can be decisions that require quite a lot of complex calculation and judgement.

If you doubt this, think about the experience of driving a car. I could spend many hours in an office setting giving you a conscious, intellectual understanding of driving a car. We could go over and over it until you have it completely clear in your head. Then, I could put you in a car for the first time, and give you the following instructions; 'Drive up to that five-way intersection, take the second right, while you sing along to the song on the radio, chew gum and wave to your friend on the opposite corner as you turn.'

It would be a rare person who could do that on their first drive. Our conscious mind is simply not able to attend to these different tasks at the same time. But after only a few years of driving we can all do that – literally 'without thinking about it'. The difference is that over time, our unconscious takes over more and more of these tasks, leaving our comparably puny, conscious mind to do a simple task, like wave at our friend.

Now think about the challenge of turning in front of oncoming traffic, particularly two lanes of it. It is quite a complex calculation

to work out the speed of oncoming cars and your own speed as you turn in front of them. Your unconscious mind processes this data and takes a decision for you, without any difficulty, after it has had some practice. I remember being late for work one day and thinking, 'I will drive through this particular intersection on the yellow light, as it is such a long wait on the red.' I was distracted and my unconscious mind, very annoyingly, stopped me on the yellow light, because I was not consciously in control. This was when I realised that my unconscious mind was a better driver than I am. The point I want to highlight here is that, my unconscious mind was *actually making a decision – without my awareness*.

I outlined in the previous section how our unconscious mind controls our access to memory. Now add to this the capacity for our unconscious mind to process the more complex information and make decisions for us, and you start to appreciate the power of your unconscious mind.

Dreaming is problem solving

Ongoing trauma like Jeni's becomes a central focus for the unconscious mind. More so when she realised very early on that no one was coming to save her. And because of her father's threats, she couldn't safely reach out for help. No, her mind had to solve this on its lonesome. Problems that we can't solve quickly are held over until when we sleep, until we dream. Now, you can see how any windows into the unconscious through interpreting dreams are highly informative.

Interpreting dreams is not as difficult as many people think. Dream content is symbolised, which is what can make dreams so confusing. Our unconscious mind does this so that it can work away on a problem without bothering us. We can wake up and think, 'that was a weird dream' and then get on with our day. We would not be able to function so well if we awoke with the awareness that we had spent night after night concerned about our biggest problems. The symbolism allows our unconscious to worry about a problem, while consciously we can dismiss our silly dream and

focus on getting to work on time. It is a clever trick of working on a problem on one hand and allowing it to be suppressed from awareness on the other.

Unconscious workings during sleep do not have to be about upsetting problems. There are many examples of humans throughout history who have solved complex problems while asleep. Einstein said that his dreams helped him to both invent and solve problems. Isaac Newton was very probably the first person to talk of 'sleeping on a problem.' Very specifically René Descartes wrote that the basis of the Scientific Method came to him in dreams he had on 10 November 1619.

Through dreaming we don't just solve problems, we do something more profound, we learn and assimilate the events of life into 'experience'. One cannot underestimate the importance of this process. Any wisdom that we might acquire over time is built on our experiences and dreaming is the process by which we integrate and make sense of these learnings.

While dreams are symbolised so that we dismiss them as weird, there is, however, a simple trick to making sense of dreams, and nightmares are the key to unlocking this insight. Jeni's nightmares were clearly about her father's threats. It is through understanding nightmares that we can gain clarity over dreams and the informative role they play in our lives.

What are not symbolised in dreams are feelings. They can't be. This is because the very language of the unconscious is emotion. Remember our discussion of emotion-driven decisions that we post-rationalise? We are in the same space. Our unconscious, rather than using rational logic, uses emotional pattern recognition and then starts separating out the various emotions so they can be understood and processed.

In simple terms, as a therapist the way that I interpret my patient's dreams is not from concentrating on the narrative of events but, rather, I focus on the emotional evolution of the dream. It is not who is in the dream that is important, but how the person feels towards them or each point at which there is an emotional

shift. By looking at what emotions come up in a dream, we can then match these emotions to day-to-day experiences to work out what the dream is playing out.

If there is a particular emotion coming up in a dream, typically in an interaction with someone else, e.g. jealousy, anger, fear, we just need to look at who we have had similar reactions to in the day or two prior to the dream, to work out who the dream is about. From there it is not hard to work out what particular issues a mind is concerned about. By understanding the emotional narrative, we gain other specific insights. For example, when two people you know appear in a dream and one merges into the other, you know that you feel similarly towards them both on a significant emotional level. For instance, if the merge is with someone you distrust, you can see that your mind has worked out this other person has certain traits in common with them and maybe should not be trusted either. Our unconscious is much better at this pattern recognition than we can ever hope to be at a conscious level. (Just as with intuition, I don't suggest people take these messages as gospel, but as a warning that needs to be checked out by further interaction and evaluation of the other person.)

The good news is that if we are having dreams that are relatively benign and happy, we can be assured that at both conscious and unconscious levels we are travelling okay. Troubling dreams mean that we may have something that we need to come back to, when we have the time, to sort things out.

The importance of sleep was documented as early as 1896. Three Americans were kept awake for ninety hours until one of them started to hallucinate. A colleague of mine told me the story of how many years before he was the support person for a friend of his who entered a competition to win a car by seeing who could stay awake the longest. He recalled how around day three his friend became acutely paranoid, asking him why he was there and what he was doing to him? Competitions like this were later banned for this reason, but it was not until the development of sleep laboratories that we understood what was going on.

While dreaming is a time to process the day's events, we need to dream for our very sanity. We dream primarily during the rapid eye movement (REM) phase of sleep. REM sleep is not actually the deepest of the sleep cycles – that is deep or 'slow wave' sleep. While slow wave sleep appears to be more important for our physical health, e.g. tissue repair and strengthening immunity, REM sleep appears to be important for mental health. Humans deprived of REM sleep do not become any sleepier during the day, but they do inevitably become crazier with each night without sleep. Typically, they start to experience hallucinations around night four and by night six they often have full blown 'sleep deprivation psychosis'.[2]

What this tells us is that something special is happening during REM sleep. Something beyond problem solving, something that keeps us balanced. Earlier when I spoke about repression, I noted that through this mechanism, humiliating experiences, over time, no longer bother us. Let's add to this understanding.

Less troubling experiences are fully processed to resolution when we dream. We make sense of what happened, accepting that to err is human, learn what we need to from them, and move on. I wholeheartedly agree with Pema Chödrön's idea that, 'Nothing ever goes away until it has taught us what we need to know.' If a feeling, thought, or memory continues to haunt us, chances are there is something that we need to learn. Conversely, learning what we need to know from an experience, *allows it to go away*. This is what we are doing when we dream. Okay, so less troubling experiences we learn from and process while dreaming, greater ones we repress, what about bigger ones again? What about trauma like Jeni's? As you might guess, they turn into recurrent nightmares. This is simply a result of the unconscious mind trying to process something that is too overwhelming for it. The dream processing machine gets fired up as a person enters REM sleep, the trauma material gets fed into it, the dream begins ... and it is too much for the system. In Jeni's case, the terror of what she's dealing with kicks in, the demon, in this case her father, becomes variably

symbolised, but it ends without resolution, often with the person waking up. A night or two later the unconscious mind makes another futile attempt ... and so it repeats. Recurrent nightmares are one of the core symptoms of a post-trauma syndrome and herald the exposure to something that the normal mind cannot process.

Because we dream during REM sleep, this is the phase where our body enters a degree of paralysis simply so that we don't do anything too dangerous while we sleep. This is a problem in nightmares, as we can sometimes sense our paralysis, which in turn increases our fear when we feel we are under threat but can't run away. When it comes to nightmares, our protective sleep paralysis makes the dream even worse. Dream resolution completely fails.

So, could dreaming have something to tell us about treatment? Could dream resolution somehow be empowered to cope with paralysing nightmares or more ... The answer is, yes.

Dreaming meets therapy

I have specialised in treating trauma for three decades now. I have been trained in and/or trialled every major therapy touted as a treatment for PTSD. Indeed, in my very first term as an intern working in a ward with veterans, I ran a research programme that involved emotionally flooding war veterans with images from the front line while getting them to exercise. Later, in my psychiatric training, I treated patients with the gold standard of the time; a Cognitive Behaviour Therapy protocol that involved imaginal exposure and flooding.

Over the last three decades I have, amongst other things, trained in Body Tapping therapies, Narrative Therapy, Solution Focused Therapy, Acceptance & Commitment Therapy, Compassion Focused Therapy, Internal Family Systems (particularly useful) and even travelled to the Amazon jungle to explore the use of psychedelics in therapy.

Of all these therapies the standout for me has been Eye Movement Desensitisation and Reprocessing (EMDR) therapy.

I returned from the EMDR workshop in the early 1990s, run by the founder of this therapy, Francine Shapiro, to find that my patients, who had not responded to any other therapy, responded dramatically to EMDR. For the first time ever, I even had some patients who were completely cured after only a handful of EMDR sessions. Most patients at least improved to a significant degree.

It was a mind-blowing experience for me. Indeed, it was because of the thrill of curing people – not something you see much of in psychiatry – that I decided to give up general psychiatry to focus on just a couple of areas, one of which being treating posttrauma syndromes. Jeni arrived a few years later because of this transition.

What does this have to do with dreams? You will have undoubtedly noticed the words 'eye movement' in EMDR. To do this therapy, after the preparatory sessions, we ask the patient to follow our finger as we move it from side-to-side while they think of their trauma. We are emulating the rapid eye movement of REM sleep. What typically followed was the patient would then work through their trauma and spontaneously come to a pivotal realisation, like 'it was not my fault', 'I did nothing wrong', 'there was nothing more I could have done,' or 'given the circumstance I was surprisingly brave.' These insights were arrived at without the patient being led to them by the therapist. Importantly, these insights were accompanied by powerful emotional, cathartic reactions that heralded an enduring shift in the meaning the trauma held for the person. Most importantly, their distress around the event would reduce from ten out of ten down to a negligible number – zero, one or two. And the distress stayed down days, weeks or even years later.

Why is EMDR so effective, so potent? As you might guess, what EMDR seems to be is an auxiliary pump to the natural process of dream resolution. It is perhaps this aspect of EMDR that engages me the most – that it seems to tap into a natural resolution process, fortifying it to take on the greatest traumas of all. Not only is it at the opposite end of the spectrum from using drugs, but it's also as natural a therapy as there could possibly be. It taps into a process

that we humans have developed over millennia – the best the mind otherwise has at its disposal: dream resolution.

The most fascinating aspect of treating patients with EMDR is when they move into an actual dream sequence. In this you see the total overlap between EMDR and dream resolution processes. I still recall the first time this happened twenty-five years ago. I was working with a doctor who had been abused as a child. As we were working through the abuse, she said, 'That's odd, I'm deep underwater holding a child who has drowned ... there's the anchor line going up ... I can see a boat up there ... somehow I can breathe here, underwater.' At this point I recognised we had left her trauma narrative and she was experiencing a dream in which normal laws of physics are overlooked in the service of dealing with a problem. For an unconscious mind focused on solving a dilemma of some magnitude, normal planetary laws are irrelevant and just get in the way. As the dream progressed, she brought the drowned child up into the boat and resuscitated it. Of course, the drowned child represented her innocent child who 'died' as the abuse commenced. By bringing that child back to life, she was re-owning this lost part of herself and becoming whole.

The most magical part of a patient moving into dreaming mode during EMDR is that they resolve more issues more quickly. Instead of just reducing the distress around a particular incident, patients in this dream mode typically resolve other, similar traumas, and have major shifts towards getting their lives back on track.

Latest therapeutic developments

Even with the benefits of EMDR, the treatment of DID requires further skill and training in understanding, negotiating and treating dissociation and its underlying trauma. There is way too much dissociation-related trauma and way too few appropriately trained therapists. Fortunately, there is one other way to enter a dream state with promising therapeutic benefit and that is with psychedelics.

In 2021 the respected journal *Nature Medicine* published a peer-reviewed, placebo-controlled trial on psychedelic assisted

treatment of trauma. The results were impressive. With just three, medically supervised sessions using MDMA, 67 per cent no longer had PTSD – more than double the placebo group. There was no increased risk of abuse and, crucially, those with dissociation responded as well as those without.[3] Given the special skills otherwise required to navigate dissociation, this latter finding was a big deal.

There are currently over a hundred psychedelic-assisted therapy trials being conducted worldwide. It would appear that these drugs allow a resetting of a part of the brain known as the 'Default Mode Network' (DMN) that otherwise holds on to recurring, distressing thoughts – especially around guilt and shame. During REM/dreaming sleep the DMN fires up, but the normal resetting process fails with overwhelming trauma.

Between the understanding we have developed of DID and the effective therapies available now, with more coming in the future, the prospects for treating this complex condition have never looked better.

CHAPTER FOUR

The Pact

JENI

I remember the first time I heard my dad say 'shit'. It was 1977 and I was seven years old. At first, I didn't know he was referring to poo, and I was quite confused. Dad had taken me by the hand and led me to my bedroom. 'I'm going to help you, so you don't have the same problems going to the toilet as your mother,' he said, shutting the door behind him.

Dad pulled my underpants down and guided me to sit on the side of the bed. He sat beside me and pushed a finger into my bottom. I whimpered in pain. I desperately tried to move away from Dad, but instead I fell backwards so I was laying on the bed with my legs spread wide and Dad sitting in between them. As I lay there, I could see the shadows the leaves from the tree by the window cast on the floor. Then Dad hooked my glasses off my face with a finger and I couldn't see anything. With his other finger – the one that was deeply embedded in my bottom, Dad made a violent pulling movement.

'Please stop, Daddy, it hurts,' I cried.

'No, you need this. It's going to help you,' he said, with a chirpiness in his voice. 'If you put a finger into your bottom when you are constipated and bend your finger, you can remove shit and it feels good.'

Dad did just that: oh god it hurt!

Without my glasses, everything looked blurry. Dad had two burning black holes for eyes and a gaping hole for a mouth. He was grinning.

'Now you can control your bowels. Try it, you'll see. It will make life much easier when you can't go to the bathroom,' he declared, victoriously.

I didn't see how. What Dad had done to my bottom hurt more than constipation did. Nevertheless, I nodded my head and agreed with him. In that second, I would have said anything to stop him from hurting me.

My agreement only bought me a momentary reprieve.

I didn't feel Dad remove his fingers from inside me. I couldn't feel between my legs; I couldn't even feel my bottom against the bed. It was as if my body had switched off.

Dad used my underpants to wipe my genitals and hopped off the bed. 'Now you won't have a problem like Mummy, that's good, isn't it?' he said, happily.

I just stared at him.

Dad walked to the door quite cheerfully, as if he had just said hello to me and hadn't savagely penetrated me. His footsteps were light and soft.

I felt sick to my stomach and was afraid to move. My underpants were lying on my stomach – wet and dirty – but I didn't have the strength to move them. I turned onto my side and cried into my pillow. I must have fallen asleep because when I put my glasses on later, the room was dark and cold. My body was stiff. I remember wandering through the house on shaky legs and hearing my mother say, 'Hello, sleepyhead.'

In the following years, I was forced to use Dad's 'shit' technique to hide bloodstains on my underpants – so my mother wouldn't find out what Dad was doing to me and die. The fact that I had to take Dad's advice was humiliating and I felt an enormous sense of horror and shame every time I had to remove shit from my anus to cover his abuse.

SYMPHONY

Underneath the house is dark, dirty and full of cobwebs. It's a spider's heaven, an arachnophobe's hell, and – for me – a safe space. I reserve

my hiding spot under the house for the most desperate of situations. I know I can't risk Dad finding me and blowing my cover, so I only escape there when there is no other option. Over the years, I only use this bolthole twice. This is one of those times.

I'm playing with Lego in the backyard when a figure appears in front of me and blocks out the sun. I look up. Dad's face is cold and stern. His lips are pressed together into a thin white line. I open my mouth to speak, but before I can get a syllable out, Mum opens the back door and asks for a hand from Dad. 'I'll deal with you later,' he says to me.

I don't wait around to be dealt with. I shoot under the house and scramble further into the darkness. I make my way to a room-like space under the kitchen and Frank's bedroom, between the stumps holding the house up. I sit still. I hear Dad calling me. I sit still. I hear Dad bend down and push his head under the house. I sit still. I hear Dad yell my name. I flinch.

I can't tell if Dad can see me in my hiding spot, so I hold my breath until I hear him walk away in a huff. I don't dare move in case it's a trick. It *is* a trick. Dad pokes his head under the other side of the house and bellows my name. I can tell from the sound of his voice that I'm in deep trouble. I sit still.

I hear the back door slam shut and Dad's heavy footsteps stomping above me. It's only when I hear his chair creak as he sits down inside that I exhale. I stay in my safe space until I hear my mother call me for tea. I creep out from underneath the house, careful not to be spotted. I shake my dress free of dirt, careful not to give away hints about my hiding place. I walk into the dining room, careful not to make eye contact with Dad.

I avoid making eye contact with Dad again later in the outside toilet where he makes good on his promise to 'deal with me'.

JANET

In the middle of 1977, Dad said what was possibly the most terrifying sentence I'd ever heard. He was lying behind me in my single bed after attacking me. 'Do you think Sheila would play these games as well as you do?' he whispered.

I didn't have a chance to answer before Dad got out of bed and walked across the room towards Sheila's bed. I flung myself off the bed and threw myself at his feet. I begged him not to touch her. 'You can do anything to me, but please don't touch my sister,' I pleaded. I thought Sheila was awake, but she made no noise.

My bargaining deal took immediate effect. Dad dragged me back to my bed and pushed me onto my side. As he attacked me he said, 'Stay still! I always knew you wanted this.' I wanted to deny it, but I was afraid Dad would go to Sheila and hurt her, so I said nothing.

In the morning, I stayed silent. I didn't speak to Sheila or Mum about what had happened the night before. I didn't say anything because I was sure it would get Sheila killed. Of course, I'd wondered if Sheila was being abused by Dad as well, but she never confided anything like that to me or anyone else, then or later.

From that night on, Dad increased the frequency and violence of his attacks on me. I had told him that he could do anything he wanted to me if he left Sheila alone, and that's exactly what he did. Dad took my attempt to protect Sheila at face value. He acted as though I had said I wanted it, I needed it, I loved it. I felt as though I had lost the right to complain, to fight him off or to tell him to stop. I thought I had to be quiet, to stifle my cries and swallow my screams. I believed if I complied with all of Dad's demands, I would be able to protect my sister. I was at Dad's mercy. I took the abuse because I knew Sheila couldn't. She wasn't strong enough. She didn't have an army on her side.

Sheila was my reason for living. She was the first thing I thought about when I woke up in the morning, and the person I saw in my dreams at night. Whatever torture Dad put me through, I had to put up with it, for Sheila. Keeping Sheila safe was my purpose in life.

I learnt to scream silently, but often I couldn't hold back my tears. 'Stop pootering or I'll give you something to really cry about,' Dad growled. Even though he told me to stop crying, I don't think he actually wanted me to. I'm sure Dad was aroused by my tears, pain and suffering. I tried not to give him the satisfaction of seeing me upset. I repeated Sheila's name over and over again in my head

like a mantra. 'Stop crying, he'll go to Sheila. Do it for Sheila,' I thought.

In my mind, the pact was about more than words. It wasn't just that I had to obey Dad's every whim and not tell a soul about it, I also couldn't scream out loud, I couldn't look at him like *that*, I couldn't move away, and I couldn't think about what he was doing to me. And so, Symphony accidentally created hundreds of alters to keep the pact. There were alters who removed our eyes so we couldn't look at Dad the wrong way, alters who remained perfectly still so we didn't move the wrong way, alters who performed cognitive dissonance so we didn't think the wrong thing. In the year 1977, over a thousand alters walked out of the back of our mind. All of them with one goal – keep Sheila safe no matter the cost.

SYMPHONY

I know all the words to 'Any Dream Will Do'. I've been chosen to be part of the combined children's choir. It's an honour. Only a few students from each school are recruited for the choir and I'm one of them. We've been practising for weeks, and on the day of our first show we take a minibus to Bankstown Square. The teachers tidy our uniforms and tie red ribbons in our hair. A girl from a different school throws a tantrum because red isn't her school colour. I'm sure she remembers this as the day the choir instructor tied the wrong-coloured ribbons in her hair. What an outrage.

Before we walk on stage, the choir leader gathers us together and gives a stirring speech. 'It's a great privilege to have you in my choir,' she says. 'You're all the best in your year at singing and you should be proud of yourselves for representing your school with your talent.' The choir leader looks like my mum, and when she says I'm talented, I believe her, despite being told differently by my father all my life.

It's show time. The choir lines up in two rows in the shape of a V. In the middle of the V, sitting in the audience, I spot a woman dressed all in green – green hat, green coat, green shoes, even a green purse sat perfectly on her lap. She claps gently when we finish singing. After she leaves, the teachers explain that we've just sung for

the Queen. The significance goes over my head. My lasting memory of the day is having ice cream after the performance.

I tell Mummy about the girl with the wrong-coloured ribbons and the after-show ice cream. It's not until I see the Queen on TV that night that I tell Mum she was the woman I had sung for. I had sung for the Queen, but I didn't know it was an accomplishment. I tell my mum and she is unimpressed because she's a staunch anti-monarchist. I tell my dad. He calls me a dirty little liar.

JENI

For months, I did as I was told to keep the pact. And it almost cost me my life. One night in September 1977, I woke up to find my dad's penis in my mouth. It was like a slug touching the back of my tongue. My heart started to pound as I felt Dad's hand on the back of my head, pressing my face forward and pushing his penis further towards the back of my throat. I tried to pretend I was asleep.

'I know you're awake, there's no point pretending. Now you can make Daddy feel really good,' he said. 'Open your chinny chops.'

He filled my mouth and I couldn't breathe.

I thought I was going to die. I heard whistling in my ears and saw stars in my eyes. I was conscious of the pain in my chest, the erratic beat of my heart and heaving in my lungs. I felt a hot liquid smash against the back of my throat.

Everything went silent and still. I don't know how long the nothingness lasted before I heard a voice from far away. I was too tired to make out who it was. I closed my eyes and the darkness laid over me like a thick blanket. I let myself be wrapped up in it. I couldn't hear the whistling, see the stars or feel my heart beating. The stillness was broken by a screaming voice. It seemed to rush at me and, as it got closer, the words began to make sense. I heard a voice that sounded just like mine screaming, 'Sheila! Sheila! Sheila!'

A second voice spoke up. This voice didn't sound like mine, it was Jay. It wasn't screaming, it was calmly instructing. 'Breathe,' Jay said. 'Just take one deep breath and it will be fine. Just breathe.'

I did as I was told. I sucked in a mouthful of air and suddenly I was back in my body, in my bed, in agony. My heartbeat pounded in my ears, and I felt it thudding through my entire body. It all hurt: the breathing, the pounding, the thudding. 'I know it hurts, but you must keep going. Don't give up now,' Jay insisted.

I took slow, shallow breaths, but I longed for the thick blanket of darkness to cover me again. It didn't hurt under the weight of the blackness. When I opened my eyes to face my reality, it felt like there were razorblades under my eyelids. I turned my head to see who had been speaking to me, but I could see no one. Dad was gone. Sheila was asleep. And, somehow, I was still alive.

SYMPHONY

It's a hot summer night and I've swapped beds with my brother Frank because I'm unwell. The sheet underneath me is damp with sweat. I'm not wearing a nightdress and only have a thin sheet covering me, but I'm boiling. My dad comes into the room to check on me. 'Are you all right?' he asks. Before I have time to answer, Dad has forgotten I'm a person. I'm nothing more than a naked body to him.

Dad lifts the thin sheet off me and stares at me. His eyes are dark, and they don't seem to recognise me. He refuses to look at my face and is intently focused on my chest. Frank's single bed sags as Dad gets on top of me and forces my legs to open. I feel the tip of 'it' pressing at my private parts and pushing into me. In and out, in and out.

The more I cry, the further he drills into me. I open my mouth to scream, and to my surprise, and his, noise comes out. The scream is long and piercing, and it makes Dad pull back sharply, dragging 'it' out of me. Dad jumps up and throws the sheet over me. He must have heard my mother coming to check on why I was screaming.

When Mum opens the door, I'm crying hysterically. Under the thin sheet, my private parts feel like they're on fire. I'm sobbing so hard, I can't correct Dad when he tells Mum I had a bad dream and that he's taking care of me.

Mum goes back to bed. Dad takes care of me. He forces 'it' into my mouth to muffle my screams. Frank's bed groans with every thrust. I start hitting Dad's inner thighs as hard as I can. I swing my arm with all my force and it lands near his groin. Dad gasps and rips 'it' out of my mouth. He sits on the side of the bed and cups between his legs. His face had been red, but now it's pale. He stumbles out of the room and slams Frank's door behind him.

I grab the pillow from the bed and hide in the corner as far away from the door as I can get. I curl myself into a ball on the floor and rock to soothe myself. Back and forth, back and forth.

JENI

In many ways, 1977 was the best year of my childhood. I loved to sing and my voice was noticed. I was asked to join the district's combined children's choir. I thrived in that choir, where I was praised and felt like part of a team. We started practising for our big performance, the end-of-year District Music Festival. The weekend before that, I practised non-stop. I sung in the garden, I sung to myself, I sung while I did my chores. I sung until my dad told me to 'shut up'. But even then, I kept singing, just quieter.

Sunday afternoon, Dad stood over me and demanded I 'stop caterwauling'. I tried to explain that the dress rehearsal for the music festival was the next day, but he wouldn't hear it. 'Stop your noise. I don't care about the performance; I don't care about your singing. What do I have to do to get some peace and quiet around here?' he said, dragging me to the outside toilet.

'I won't sing anymore, Daddy, I promise,' I assured.

'Too late,' he muttered.

Dad stopped me from singing and forced me to use my mouth for something else. 'This is your own fault. You should have stopped when I told you to,' he reasoned.

Eventually I tasted metal, I was sure my mouth was filled with blood. I gagged. Dad grunted. When he finally pulled out of my mouth, I fell forward and gasped for air. Liquid dribbled out of my mouth. It wasn't blood. My jaw hurt as I tried to close it and I was

sure I'd broken my mouth. I crawled over to the toilet and spat into it. My mum's words rang in my head, 'Animals spit, people don't.' My dad had turned me into an animal.

My throat burned and felt like it had been scraped with a harsh brush. The next morning, my throat still felt terribly sore. I opened my mouth wide to show my mum and she said it was 'red raw'. She said I was probably getting a cold; I didn't tell her otherwise. Mum gave me a packet of Butter Menthols and sent me off to join the choir for the dress rehearsal. Singing hurt, but I pushed myself to hit all the notes.

The day of the big performance, I gave it my all. Mum and Dad sat in the audience. In the intermission, I rushed to the bathroom backstage and spat into the toilet – like an animal. When I wiped my mouth, the toilet paper turned red with blood. I knew I'd busted open the hole Dad had created in the back of my throat, and I kept spitting until my mouth was clean. Before we went back on stage, a teacher told me I was singing really well, and I was so surprised; I was sure I sounded terrible because of my throat. I sucked another Butter Menthol and finished the show with a bow.

The choir performance should have been a happy childhood memory – and it was – but it was spoiled by having to spit blood into the toilet at intermission because of my father. Dad had a way of destroying my joy, taking away my talents and ruining my self-confidence. Even though I loved it, the choir was a distraction from taking care of Dad, so Symphony created an alter to deal with it. There was an alter who swam, one who drew and another who ran. The good distractions became jobs like the bad distractions, and I became a withdrawn and joyless child. They say it takes a village to raise a kid, but I needed entire armies to survive my upbringing at the hands of my dad.

HAPPY

Daddy spoils everything, so I need to get creative. We could sit in the devastation of what he does to us, and we do, but we also keep pockets of happiness hidden. When the body freezes, we could

chastise ourselves for not fighting hard enough, or we could realise the body does whatever is needed to stay alive. When Dad hurts us so badly that we fall unconscious, we could fear the darkness, or we could let the big, black, warm velvet blanket wrap us up and take us away from the pain. When we choke for air, we could submit to the suffocating, or we could cheer on the Boy Who Doesn't Breathe for rebelling against Dad and keeping us alive. It's all about perspective. And it's my job to sift through the cookie crumbs and find the chocolate chips.

Undermining Dad is a unique kind of happiness. When he loses in controlling us, we win. And so, our happiness becomes an act of rebellion, a power play, a survival plan built entirely out of spite. Finding happiness is a fight, and I was made for fighting.

JENI

In 1977, I made two pacts. One with my father and the other with my siblings. Dad had been punishing all three of us for things we swore we hadn't done. He found a finger hole in a tray of jelly in the fridge, we all got the blame, and we were all flogged for it. Frank's shoes went missing, we all got the blame, and we were all flogged for it. Sheila, Frank and I all proclaimed our innocence, but Dad wouldn't listen. So, one day, we made a pact with each other that we'd always tell each other the truth. So, when Sheila and Frank insisted they hadn't broken the thing Dad was flogging us for, I believed them. Interestingly, the finger hole in the tray of jelly in the fridge was the size of an adult's finger and Dad was the one who eventually found Frank's shoes after they went missing. Funny that.

Understanding DID

It is both inspiring and utterly intriguing the way in which Jeni's mind, or more specifically Symphony, creates her personalities – technically known as 'alters'. This capability is the very essence of DID. It's a condition I think of as a gloriously creative solution to extreme abuse, which, as we have seen, means a heinous crime has been committed. I also want to look at one personality in particular, who you met briefly back in the first chapter and then again in the chapter you have just read – Jay. Jay is not a typical alter, indeed Jeni makes a point of how he is not an alter at all. This is quite odd as Jeni obviously knows what an alter is, yet she makes a point of separating Jay out. Who and what is Jay?

But before we do this we need to back up and look at the diagnosis of DID itself. I have spent some time in previous chapters looking at how the mind manages memory from repression to dissociation and the controversy around this. The history of DID is no less controversial.

The evolution of DID as a diagnosis is remarkably brief in terms of medical history, let alone the specialty of psychiatry, and I have seen the bulk of its history unfold in my professional lifetime. Having graduated medicine in 1983 at the University of Queensland, I began my training in psychiatry eighteen months later, when I was twenty-five. For the first five years of my six years at medical school I had no idea why I was there and what I was going to do. It was not until my fifth year that I did my first psychiatry term and I finally realised why I was there. Then and

now I find the human mind challenging and intriguing, but I have also come to see that it is less complex and more knowable than it first appears.

The most daunting textbook I had ever seen was to become my closest frenemy for the next five years of my fellowship training. Kaplan & Sadock's *General Psychiatry* (1985 Ed) had pages that were so thin that you could almost see through them. Tissue paper was way thicker. This was how they could fit 2129 pages between the covers (not much later they moved to two volumes). My point is that this was the definitive textbook that any trainee psychiatrist in the English-speaking world had to learn. It shaped us.

And how did they introduce Jeni's diagnosis? This is how the entry begins, word for word:

Multiple personality: Morton Prince's 'Sally Beauchamp'—
'The Saint, the Devil, the Woman', as he hesitantly christens her—is the most renowned of the some 200 patients known to have developed multiple personalities.

In an exceedingly traditional and dutifully dry medical textbook I believe I can argue, without fear of contradiction, that this sentence was the most engaging and entertaining of the hundreds of thousands in this text. It is quite revealing at several levels.

First, it reads like a book review for the *New York Times*, not as an introduction to a medical diagnosis in a respected medical specialty training textbook. The way the authors have abandoned a traditionally dry, medical description heralds the sensationalism, mystique and the scientific irreverence that so often defines this condition. If I were to write the opening words in the style of the rest of this psychiatry textbook, even allowing for their limited knowledge of the time, I would suggest it would have read something like this:

This condition, thought to be rare, is a complex, poorly understood condition that is related to Psychogenic Fugue

in which behaviour occurs for which there is amnesia and where a new alternate identity is in evidence, that is not due to an organic mental disorder.

Second, the juxtaposition of the words Saint/Devil/Woman (further amplified with the word 'renowned') was the earliest version of clickbait, that served to immediately position this condition as an installation in *Ripley's Believe it or Not* and a topic of conversation for trainees of the weird and wonderful end of psychiatry. As the definitive English language textbook, it dictated how aspiring psychiatrists would have come to know DID. Equally, it accurately reflected the sideshow-alley nature of the condition as seen by the psychiatric establishment of the time.

It is also a great example of an old and clever trick for writers who do not want to own an opinion that they hold, knowing it would be considered unscientific and biased. By quoting another source, you can claim innocence of the view while presenting it as authoritative. I am particularly taken by how the text launches immediately into characterising the diagnosis through Prince's work without qualification, thus allowing the title of his book to define this entity. It is a disingenuous writing artifice that betrays how the authors saw this condition. I doubt that any of my junior compatriots of the time appreciated this bias. I certainly did not.

The third point is the supposed rarity of this condition. '... the most renowned of the some 200 patients known' is problematic in its emphasis. The word 'known' has particular import. In this context it means: in the entirety of recorded history ... ever! The authors fail to point out that 'known cases' typically grossly under-represent a much greater number of unknown cases in the wider community.

As presented, this would make this condition perhaps the rarest psychiatric condition ever reported scientifically. The implication is profound. I have not been able to find the population of the English-speaking western world around 1985, but that of just the USA and the UK was 282 million people. As a percentage of these

populations, 200 cases would have been 0.0000007 per cent, i.e. zero, ergo no psychiatrist would ever expect to see a case.

So, how likely is a psychiatrist to come across DID in their practice in reality? Recent studies of patients admitted to psychiatric wards find that around five per cent of this population have DID. This means that roughly every twentieth patient a psychiatrist will find arriving on their ward has the condition. In a busy, acute admissions ward this would equate to the staff psychiatrist meeting a person with DID every couple of weeks. The rates are even higher if the unit sees psychiatric emergencies (typically self-harm), where rates were six per cent in New York and a staggering 14 per cent in Istanbul. What about outpatient clinics? A psychiatrist (or psychologist) working in office practices in the western world is going to meet someone with DID every fifty patients or so, i.e. two per cent of this population.

So, how good are these health professionals at recognising and diagnosing the people with DID that they come across? Abysmal. Thanks to unhelpful textbooks, and even more limited training in diagnosis, historically we have been failing these patients miserably. It takes six to twelve years of repeated presentations to mental health professionals before the correct diagnosis is made.[1] As Jeni will relay in her experience of trying to get help, she had to work much harder than she should have had to, over many years, before she finally found me and was correctly diagnosed.

More problematically, while awaiting the correct diagnosis, those with DID, on average, received three to four incorrect diagnoses. Diagnoses exist to inform treatment. When the wrong diagnosis is made the wrong treatments are given. Unfortunately, the drugs with the most problematic side-effects that psychiatry uses are for the conditions that DID is often mis-diagnosed as, i.e. schizophrenia and bipolar disorder.

Bipolar

Bipolar is primarily a disorder of mood. In bipolar disorder patients are either depressed, elevated (manic) or sometimes

a mixed picture, with people quickly bouncing between states with irritability in between. In extreme cases bipolar patients can present with beliefs of being some form of messiah. Since it is a disorder of mood, feelings of being up and elevated, or down and depressed, accompany the personality changes. Only rarely do bipolar patients hear voices, but if they do the voices are also reflective of the mood state, e.g. telling them to kill themselves when down, or that they are Jesus incarnate when up.

Schizophrenia

Schizophrenia, on the other hand, is a disorder of thinking and perceiving. Schizophrenia is the closest condition to DID, as patients with schizophrenia often hear voices. There is a particular quality about them though that Jeni did not describe, when she told me about hers. In schizophrenia the voices reflect the delusions that are the primary feature of this condition. Most commonly the delusions are about some form of paranoia or persecution by people or CIA-type entities. Accordingly, the voices will mirror these concerns, e.g. telling them how or why the CIA has an interest in them. The deeper you go into their world the more apparent it becomes that, while it may be intricate, there are no foundations in reality.

It is such a travesty when someone with DID is prescribed powerful drugs that, while helpful for people with mental illness, are a horrible experience for those with normal brain physiology. Most DID patients I have seen have come to me on a cocktail of these powerful drugs as more were added and doses increased when, not at all surprisingly, they were never going to help.

DID by any other name

There are a large group with DID who receive the non-clinical diagnosis of demonic possession. In many countries where DID is seen as possession, it then becomes a matter for the Church, rather than for psychiatric care. In India when they studied all

presentations over ten years to a psychiatric service: 'Unlike in the West, dissociative identity disorders were rarely diagnosed; instead, possession states were commonly seen in the Indian population.'[2] Similar results have been found from studies in Japan, Oman, China and Iran.

It is not hard to see how switching into certain personalities would invoke possession as an explanation. It is very confronting, the first time you experience it, to find a more masculine voice (complete with male mannerisms) with a completely different accent coming out of the body of a woman who, moments before, was speaking with a typical female voice and intonation. Jeni's Muscles is a perfect example. When he comes through, often the first thing he does is check to make sure he's not wearing a dress, as he leans back and puts one leg up on the other, like a typical bloke and then often opens with a couple of choice words.

And then you have some DID patient's personalities who have an obvious demonic quality to them. They often arrive suddenly, snarling, growling, apoplectic with anger and threatening you physically if you come close. While Jeni did not have any personalities who were like this, by the time I did see this for the first time in other patients I had fortunately attended a workshop with Dr Colin Ross. Dr Ross was, and remains, one of only a handful of authorities in the world on this condition. 'The average age of the devil is six years old,' he intoned offhandedly as he spoke about the people, brought to him, who had been unsuccessfully treated with exorcism.

These 'demonic personalities' were horribly abused at a very young age and were inevitably told by their abusers that they were pure evil, or, at least, they had the devil in them. This is from perpetrator school, Lesson 101 – the brainwashing begins to ensure the child never reports them. After all, you can't report someone for being evil if you are evil too – it would be an exercise in self-incrimination. Some abused child personalities may whole-heartedly adopt this suggestion, as their experiences did, indeed, look a lot like those of a demon. When you appreciate that

they are only a gullible, confused six-year-old as you work with them in therapy, it changes everything. As both therapist and patient understand this and offer compassion to the 'devil' they respond accordingly, and the healing begins. What defines these personalities in their 'devilhood' is no more than they were on the receiving end of a living hell. They are only demonic by association, not by definition.

Coming under the 'care' of the Church, they might dodge the antipsychotic drugs of the western world, but I'm not sure what's worse. The misconceptualisation of DID as possession means they are treated as pariahs at best, and incarcerated and punished as demons, at worst. The accounts that I have been given of patients who have come to me who have been treated with exorcisms here in Australia, while not as barbaric are still disturbing. The central tenant is, of course, that you have a demon inside you that needs to be cast out – it is worse than bad, it is evil. When this fails, as it does, the patient is left with the scary prospect of having a demon inside them. Contrast this with the central tenant of the treatment of DID which is that 'all parts are welcome'. The 'demons' are recognised for what they are, which is very traumatised young children who have been tortured and scared to their wits' end. Add to this that they have been in 'dissociative hibernation', they arrive with an expectation that they are about to be abused again. They can be forgiven for being snarling and aggressive.

While I respect the rights of religions generally, specifically, possession should always be treated as DID until proven otherwise. The first case of possession that proves to not be DID, but is that of genuine possession by a demonic force, will make world news both in the lay press and the scientific community. The fact that to date this has not happened after tens of thousands of cases have been identified, leads me to be confident that possession is DID by any other name.

We have looked at the prevalence and presentation of DID in clinical populations, which now brings us to the question: How common is DID in the general, non-clinical population? These

are very expensive studies to do. Large samples of people, often entire communities, have to be individually interviewed to get reliable data. There are only a handful available. Prevalence ranges from 1.1 per cent in Turkey, through 1.5 per cent in New York State and 1.3 per cent in Canada.[3] While we can assert, with high level confidence, that at least one per cent of the general population suffer from DID, 1.3 per cent is probably a defensible and more accurate estimate.

As the world population is approximately 7.7 billion people, 77 million at least have the condition, while 1.3 per cent gives us 100 million. If you want to argue that because these studies are done in the West, which is largely true, they are not representative of the world – that is probably true. As I discussed in the introduction, DID nearly always results from extreme abuse to young children. Accordingly, its prevalence will be a function of the extent to which a given society protects the rights of its children. In older, more traditional cultures, children's rights are even less recognised and respected than in the West. Accordingly, we would expect to find a higher prevalence of child abuse and DID in these cultures.

DID finally understood and recognised

Over time, DID has become both better understood and recognised. Those with DID have Vietnam veterans to thank for this as it was this population that put PTSD on the clinical map. The war in Vietnam caused much higher rates of PTSD than any war before it because of its guerrilla nature. The two world wars had frontlines and a clearer sense of when you were safe or in danger. This was not the case in Vietnam where you could be attacked anywhere, anytime even while on leave in Saigon. Even the frontline was ill-defined and changeable. Unpredictable but recurring threats cause a chronic state of hyperarousal that dramatically increase the risk of developing a posttrauma syndrome. (You can see how I have just described Jeni's childhood.)

PTSD, then called 'shell shock', was not uncommon in the two world wars, but all governments of the time decided, in their self-

interest, and rather barbarically, to define it instead as 'human weakness'. Fortunately, Vietnam veterans were returning with an undeniable number of cases at a time when psychiatry was embracing more useful forms of psychotherapy as it abandoned the limited dogma of traditional Freudian analysis. The new kid on the block, psychodynamic psychotherapy, was much more interested in how symptoms arose from traumatic experiences. At the same time psychologists were developing Cognitive Behaviour Therapy with consideration to treating posttrauma syndromes with various forms of exposure. In the early 1990s EMDR arrived as a therapy entirely focused on treating trauma in rape victims as well as Vietnam veterans.

Society was changing too. As we approached the end of the twentieth century, women's rights gained even more traction and they thankfully dragged children's rights along at the same time. From this crucible of aligned forces, a new understanding of trauma and an awareness of the reality of childhood abuse helped move DID from the sideshow alley to centre stage as we began the twenty-first century. As it became obvious it was a response to trauma in a young, plastic brain, DID began to make sense in a way it never had before. Without the trauma link, DID was just a weird spectacle. With this link, it now made sense as a legitimate mental condition because it had a coherent and understandable cause. Finally, as much as the professional world did not want to believe that horrible abuse stories like Jeni's were true, the alignment of all these forces were too overwhelming to deny.

The most widely accepted psychiatric diagnostic system in the world are the various iterations of the Diagnostic and Statistical Manual of Mental Disorders (DSM). The DSM included Multiple Personality Disorder (MPD) in 1980 and the diagnosis was refined with every new edition. It was in the DSM-IV that came out in 1994 that MPD was replaced with DID. This change in name was largely due to a concern that it was potentially misleading to call all alters, 'personalities' as many of them were created without the full depth and breadth of what we know as a personality. As you

know, Jeni has around 2500 alters that all have different functions; from dealing with bodily functions when being abused; through coping with parts of a larger trauma experience; to full-blown personalities that you have met narrating in this book. Dissociative Identity Disorder better represents this diversity and reflects the psychological defence mechanism by which it occurs. Finally, with the current DSM-5 of 2013, as the research into DID grew, things like recognising that amnesia may be for day-to-day events, not just traumatic ones, were included.

To be included in the DSM, conditions have to be recognised and accepted by the experts of international standing in psychiatry in any given diagnostic category. Qualifying for DSM status is not easy. If a diagnosis is debatable, it will only be given tentative, conditional standing and designated as a 'condition for further study' and only later accepted once there is general agreement by the authorities in that field. Accordingly, those who now do not accept DID as a genuine condition are on the outside of mainstream knowledge and not up to date with current research and thinking.

Guidance from on high – meet Jay

I want to close this section by returning to Jay, named after Jay Osmond, the drummer and vocalist in the Osmond Brothers. Jeni says, he is very different from her other alters and, as you know, she has a lot of them to compare him with. In her words, 'Jay isn't one of us. He's not an alter; he's almost our subconscious, a higher being, a power above.' Jay helps Jeni by calming her as she experiences the horrifying combination of rape and suffocation.

Most of my DID patients have a Jay. For me they are perhaps the most fascinating of the fascinating condition that DID is. They all point out that these personalities are not an alter like the rest are and they are equally as definitive about this as Jeni is. What they all share is this sense of being 'above' the system[4] of alters, a word that often comes up when I have asked about them. My patients who are more spiritual will say that these personalities

are their spiritual guides. My non-spiritual patients will say they are their 'higher self'. By this they seem to be describing the most mature and wise part of themselves. The second attribute they all share is a quality of peaceful wisdom that my patients find very calming – just as Jeni describes Jay. This quality gets them through the worst of their abuse experiences. As Jeni said, 'He has saved my life more times than I want to think about.'

As I started to come across my patients' 'Jay-equivalents' I would start to ask them about themselves and their roles in the system. What struck me time and time again, was the calmness and sagacity they emanated. They all seemed to have a wisdom beyond their years, but it was an ethereal serenity that defined them more than anything. I could see how this soothing presence was even more reassuring than any words they might have said. I would ask them how they saw themselves as relative to the system. Their answers tended to respect the comfort their hosts had with spirituality and vary from outright spiritual guide to the person's higher self. I sensed this latter description was out of a concern not to create a conflict for hosts who were less spiritually inclined.

When I started working with this population, I was a dyed in the wool, worms-eat-your-body-after-you-die-and-that's-it atheist. My conversations with these entities who bring a special, calming love, have forced me to question my previous absolute position.

These entities are so powerfully calming I now routinely go looking for them before I commence trauma work in my DID patients. As I undertook Internal Family Systems (IFS) training, I was intrigued to see that they saw this as a key, indeed a necessary step in setting up for trauma work. They posit that most adults will have a wise, higher self that has gained a degree of compassionate wisdom as the person has grown into adulthood that needs to be enlisted in therapy. (Interestingly, IFS sees this as one's highest spiritual self or soul.) Their ability to soothe and settle a patient as we do the demanding work of revisiting traumas makes them invaluable allies to a trauma therapist. Perhaps the greatest point of alignment with therapy is that their core desire is to help their

host to rise above the trauma and get back onto the track of how to make the most of this life. Moreover, once they rise above, they will be able to go forth knowing they have the proof, the confidence that they know how to overcome adversity at the highest level.

While we can explain a calming, higher self that brings the wisdom of the years to soothing an adult patient dealing with traumatic events, it is much more difficult to explain a Jay that arrives in early childhood that has so much serenity and maturity to bring to bear. Psychiatry cannot explain it.

It does not matter a hoot if the therapist is religious, spiritual or neither, if we bring an open mind, these entities, whatever they are – higher self or guide – are valuable co-therapists. Often when I have been stuck on where to go in therapy, I will have a conversation with a Jay and between us we can work out where to go next. Interestingly, like my early psychotherapy supervisors, they rarely tell me what to do next, but they guide me to varying degrees as to where we *could* go next. I then discuss this with the system and we then make a final decision together – as it should be.

It could be asked, if these entities are spiritual beings why don't they just heal the person from their pain there and then? Early on I asked this exact question, but the answer was always the same. In effect the message was that the rising above process, while it can be sped up with therapy, is a journey of soul-saving momentousness. At the same time the journey is a human one. Rising above one's trauma is not done at the end of the story through a sudden realisation, it is fought for from the outset. The journey is the destination and Jeni's story could not illustrate this better. Jeni began her journey to rise above at the moment her abuse began.

Understanding MPD/DID: One Step Further – Recognising People with MPD/DID as Victims of Crime

MR FLAMBOYANT
Response to the numbers

Wow, that last chapter was heavy! Those numbers are scary. Reading them was super triggering for us. Given most of us work our butts off to protect folks in danger, the proposed prevalences discussed by George were hard to deal with. To read 77 to 100 million people are estimated to have MPD/DID distresses and horrifies us. That means 77 to 100 million people are suffering or have suffered extreme, unavoidable, inescapable, life-threatening sexual, physical and emotional abuse regularly during their early childhood with no one to help them. We can't help them, we can't make it stop, we can't protect them. We are so triggered it's not funny.

But at the same time the horror keeps hitting us, that's 77 to 100 million victims of crime! And god knows how many predatory sex offenders. Worse still, these monsters get away with their crimes!

Can you imagine?

Abuse your child so badly, and in circumstances where they can't escape or get help so that they are forced to create alter personalities simply to survive you, and up until now you've been bulletproof.

Justice hasn't even been a dream for us with MPD. Abusers cause us to fragment to survive their horrific crimes, and then they use that fragmentation to avoid justice claiming we are mentally ill and not credible.

And if we are misdiagnosed into one of the groups George mentions, well, who's going to believe us when we are diagnosed as having delusions, hallucinations, and believing things that aren't real?

And when our disclosures of abuse are seen as fantasies no one seems to question why people would fantasise about the kind of sexual torture I experienced. They don't seem to be accused of being a fantasist if they disclose other crimes. You don't see articles or literature on people fantasising about being a victim of road rage, or theft, or vandalism. No, disclosures of these crimes are taken at face value. It is only the sexual abuse and torture of tiny babies and children where so much effort is put into denial, dismissing the victim, and taking sides.

Being triggered is only the beginning. How are victims to deal with this?

Are you triggered too? Take a break and settle. The words won't go away but it might help to recognise you are safe.

ERIK
George's prevalence estimates: the implications

Looking at numbers there seems to have been an enormous boom in cases of DID. Going from an estimate of .0000007 per cent in 1985 to the estimate of 1.3 per cent in 2022 is a spike of epic proportions.

What does this mean? Has there been a spike in the number of predators committing such horrific crimes that the victim can only survive through the utilisation of DID? I think not.

What I feel explains this huge change is the rise of psychiatrists like George. Psychiatrists willing to accept the evidence of the patient in front of them instead of dismissing their accounts of abuse and torture as the imaginings of particularly perverted minds, or the mentally ill. It has, historically, been easy to view accounts of the sexual abuse of children as evidence of severe mental illness

in the alleged victim. But now with the rise of effective therapies, empathetic psychiatrists and psychologists and legal remedies DID is stepping out of the shadows and patients are asking for help. Now all we have to do is provide it.

Diagnosing MPD/DID

JENI
Diagnostic features of DID
The current DSM-5 has the following diagnostic criteria for DID.

Two or more distinct identities or personality states, each with its own relatively enduring pattern of perceiving, relating to, and thinking about the environment and self.

This criteria gives no guidance to the features of DID that help to diagnose it and it completely misses the point of DID: it is a response to serious criminal acts. While DID could be seen as a post trauma response, it is more of a response to trauma happening during the development of the child's brain, mostly before the ages of 5 or 8 years. DID doesn't develop after trauma, it develops in the immediacy of abuse, right in the middle of the trauma being inflicted upon the child. Symphony did not create alters to deal with Dad's stench after he had abused her. She created us to take the stench away NOW, so she could continue to do what he was demanding of her in that moment.

If I were amending the diagnostic criteria for MPD/DID I would add the following:

DID is a coping strategy used by highly intelligent children to deal with significant, extensive, extreme, unavoidable, inescapable, and life threatening sexual, physical and/or emotional abuse as it is happening to them. Moreover, these criminal acts of abuse occurs in settings where the victim has no one to turn to for help. It develops when the sense of identity is most fluid and the brain is most plastic, usually under the age of eight.

DID is a highly flexible and functional response to childhood abuse. DID has many defining features including, but not limited

to; a significant history of sexual, physical and emotional abuse in childhood, abrupt changes in emotions, opinions and ways of communication, the loss of time, amnesia for important personal information; two or more separate personality or identity states, identity states expressing themselves through different names, genders, sexual identities and ages, trauma responses to triggers, and variable trauma awareness and knowledge.

Each case will present differently as the abuse which causes the creation of alter personalities is unique. The response of each child to that abuse will be equally unique.

The protective strategies at the heart of DID only tend to become dysfunctional and distressing once the abuse has ceased, normally when the child becomes an adult. Intrusive flashbacks, body memories and trauma responses are common, as are uncontrolled switches between personality states.

ERIK
Lost opportunities

I had to go find my own diagnosis and work out what was going on for myself. I knew there was something strange going on, but I had to go to university and study to work it out. Having diagnosed myself with Multiple Personality Disorder the mental health professionals I turned to for help failed me at every turn. They should be ashamed and devastated by this. I was disbelieved and mistreated because I did not fit their preconceived ideas. It took me from 1985 to 1998 until I got the help I needed. Nearly every psychiatrist, psychologist, counsellor and occupational therapist I saw before George dismissed me and implied that I was a liar or a roaring fantasist. Their assumptions about me unintentionally supported and protected my dad, allowing him to abuse my sister. Had the occupational therapists acted in 1985 they could have saved my sister years of abuse by my dad. Thus, the beliefs of those I approached for help had significant implications for me, my sister and our abuser.

JENI
Protective invisibility

Psychiatrists, psychologists, therapists and counsellors need to be more like George, willing to look for DID among the competent, the over achievers. Above all, they should recognise that DID hides in plain sight. The central core of DID is hiddenness. My invisibility to the psychiatrist community is the norm not the exception when it comes to DID. The central core of DID is what I call 'protective invisibility.' I had to hide my alters from Dad and the rest of the world simply to survive. Being seen equalled being abused and I could not face that again. As an adult, away from my monstrous father, I struggled to let myself be seen. It was extremely hard to let George see my alters. I was not going to let myself fall apart so badly that I ended up in a psychiatric ward. It is important then to consider that the vast majority of people with DID do not present to psychiatrists in either the office or the hospital emergency room. DID is also a disorder of the highly intelligent, so you can expect to find it in the over achievers and the extremely capable: the very groups whose competency precludes them from being viewed as in need of help. If we could fall apart we might get more help, or more abuse. But I was unwilling to take the risk of being seen. Unfortunately, this protective invisibility strategy hurts more than it helps once the abuse has ended. It is one of the most important features of DID that becomes dysfunctional and causes significant issues once the abuse is over. Unchecked protective invisibility will deny people with DID almost all of what little help is available.

JENI
Legal implications of delay in diagnosis

As George mentions above, it takes a long time to get a diagnosis of DID. His estimates mean that the patient suffers a further six to twelve years where the trauma of their childhood sexual abuse is not addressed, or is treated inappropriately. Worse of all, that is a huge amount of time that the offender is free to do this to more children. Even if the victim is willing or able to seek legal remedies against the

offender, they are denied justice for years. When we consider that DID is our response to criminal behaviour, that these factors impact our right to justice is disappointing at best, horrifying at worse.

ERIK
Legal implications of misdiagnosis

The disastrous implications of treating victims of serious sexual assaults with anti-psychotic drugs or as if the victim is possessed are profound. Reading George's account of how people defined as possessed are treated, I am struck by how much their 'treatment' replicates and prolongs the physical abuse and emotional blackmail they have experienced. The treatment of these individuals is also far worse than any punishment which might be handed down to their abuser.

Importantly, adult abusers know this and use all of their society's resources to protect themselves. If that means making their victim a pariah in society, they won't hesitate. What matters to the abuser is to allow them to continue the abusive behaviours that they enjoy and get gratification from. Their behaviour meets a need for them, and the consequences for the victim don't matter.

Dismissing disclosures as lies, fantasies, delusions or possession and failing to believe victims of crime can have the effect of allowing serious and violent sexual predators to continue to prey on the patient and other possible victims. At the same time the treatment of victims of crime with DID can validate and reinforce the lies and manipulations of the abuser/s. Dad threatened us with horrific treatment by mental health professionals, making me terrified of going to them for help. He promised us that if we told 'no one will believe you. You'll be taken into a mental home, tied down and electrocuted.' Looking back he was threatening us with electric shock therapy, but at the time it was terrifying to us. It seemed like he was promising to hand us over to others to hurt us too.

Perpetrators are very good at victim blaming and manipulating the system to their advantage. So how can a patient who has been misdiagnosed as schizophrenic, bipolar or as having been

demonically possessed, hope to be believed if they go to the police. Their diagnosis is not struck off their record and labelled as a misdiagnosis. The damage is done to victim's reputation and their chances of being believed when they go to the police to report their abuser. Now remember, the first thing an alleged abuser says to rebut the allegations is that the victim is a liar or is crazy. Their lawyers will always use the complainants' mental health history against them.

ERIK
MPD/DID equals victim of crime

What we want to do with this book is change the dialogue around the real meaning of a diagnosis of Multiple Personality Disorder or Dissociative Identity Disorder. We want to make it so that anyone who hears about a person having MPD/DID understands immediately that they are a victim of crime and treats them with compassion and empathy. At present we can be treated a bit like a circus act. But every time we have to disclose our abuse to someone we get just that little bit more traumatised. If we can make the connection MPD/DID = Victim of Crime it will make a huge difference.

Over the past decades MPD/DID have been fodder for entertainment. People with MPD/DID are usually portrayed as the most bonkers of all, serial killers, liars and criminals of every possible colour. This could not be further from the truth. We are the VICTIMS OF CRIME not the criminals. After all, having endured the abuse that caused my condition specifically to protect my family from my dad, I'm hardly going to go out and inflict the same type of traumas on random people.

If our portrayal wasn't so damaging it would be laughable. It's like the efforts of criminals, like Billy Milligan, John Wayne Gacy and Kenneth Bianchi to avoid criminal liability for their crimes by attempting to claim split personalities or MPD, have become representative of the whole of those of us with MPD/DID. This could not be further from reality. The vast majority of us are struggling to cope with being victims of horrific crimes inflicted by family

members, close family friends or persons in a position of authority over us. We are not acting out our own abuse on others, abusing children or committing other crimes. We are attempting to survive quietly in the world.

An interesting point to raise here as well is that when MPD/DID is portrayed in movies it occurs in men who become rapists, serial killers and monsters. As George points out, females are more likely to develop DID and MPD. Surely if the movies are taking their inspiration from the real world of DID research we should be seeing female serial killers, rapists and murderers with MPD/DID. But we are not. Let's stop allowing the fictional depiction of MPD/ DID to dominate the discourse, and let reality shine through. MPD/DID is synonymous with being a victim of crime. So let's put justice back into the picture. How about we start thinking about putting the abusers, the paedophiles, the rapists and torturers in prison where they belong.

What is missing from the debate is the key feature of our diagnosis. MPD/DID is a response to being a victim of extreme criminal acts. While a tiny percentage of victims may become offenders, believing the lies of their abuser that this is normal, they want it and they are evil, the vast majority of survivors do not. We are invisible. But we must stop being invisible. In order to get the best outcome for ourselves, and the next victim along the therapy or justice journey they deserve we must stop being invisible in the debate about our condition. These crimes were inflicted on us. We survived it through a super creative coping strategy. The criminals did not prevail. We did. Now all we need is support to lock our abusers away in prison where they can't do it again. We need justice and so do our abusers.

When talking with George he makes it very clear that psychiatrists see their role as distress reduction for the patient, not seeking legal remedies. While I deeply respect George and his opinion, in this I must vigorously disagree. I believe that we need to change the dialogue around MPD/DID and put the fact that it is a response to extremely traumatic crimes of physical and/or sexual violence within a context of emotional manipulation and blackmail. These crimes have had

significant impact on the victim both at the time they occurred and later. The aftermath of the torture these children survived is enormous. One way in which we can address the distress of the adult survivor is to ensure the offender has to face consequences for their actions. George has indicated that he feels criminal proceedings are not necessary for the patient to get therapeutic resolution. But what of the next victim? What of the 'unknown children'? Do we not have a moral responsibility to try to stop these horrific criminals? Would we let them off if they had attempted to kill someone? Would we let them off if the crime was different? Could I live with myself if I had let Dad hurt another child? No, I really couldn't. Putting the offender in prison is the greatest distress reduction strategy you can get. Yes, going through court is hard, but the more victims are supported to do this, the less offenders will get away with their crimes, the less others will be willing to follow in their footsteps. This horrific crime has consequences for the victims, consequences that last for decades. And the mental health community have a significant role to play in helping in this.

Perhaps more patients would be willing to investigate legal remedies if they think they will be believed, and their allegations will be taken seriously. Now I have opened the door for them justice *is* possible.

One of the biggest challenges facing the police and psychiatric communities is how they will address this situation. As more patients consider their options going forward how can police, prosecutors, the legal system as well as psychiatrists, psychologists and other therapists help them to get justice or a therapeutic resolution? How they address this will have a significant impact on the future success of the attempts of people with MPD/DID to report these crimes.

Detective Stamoulis and the Bankstown Police did an extensive investigation of MPD as part of their investigation of my allegations. Perhaps the information they obtained can be used by the police to assist the next victims to get justice far faster than the ten years I had to wait. They can use this material to show that MPD/DID has been accepted in law and is not only a valid response to extreme abuse but also the more extreme the alleged abuse the more the police can

expect to find evidence of MPD/DID. Working together, the legal world and psychiatric community can make a huge difference to these child survivors of torture.

It is my greatest wish that this book changes how people with MPD/DID are seen and recognises the reality of their situation as victims of crime. If the psychiatric and legal communities can start a conversation about how best to meet the justice needs as well as therapeutic needs of this community I will be thrilled.

CHAPTER FIVE

The Girl Without a Name

JENI

I had a recurring dream as a child. In the dream, I was dead, and my family was celebrating. They threw a big party because they didn't have to see me anymore. The first night I had the dream, I was eight. Before I went to bed, my dad had tried to brush my hair. It was all knotted and he called it a 'rat's nest'. Dad gave up brushing and dragged me into the bathroom. He pushed me in front of the mirror and chastised me. 'Look at you, you're ugly, ugly, ugly! So ugly that you could break the glass,' he said.

I looked away from the mirror in disgust. From that day forward, I avoided my reflection at all costs. I didn't brush my teeth, get dressed or comb my hair in front of the mirror. Dad's insult affected me for years.

'You're a disgusting, dirty little girl and no one will ever love you,' he said.

I cried. He rubbed my crotch.

'You're too ugly for words,' he said.

I apologised. He ejaculated into his pants.

That night, my dad made me feel absolutely worthless. I believed everything he said and truly felt that no one cared if I lived or died. I cried myself to sleep hugging Sweep. 'Oh, stop pootering!' said Dad.

My dad never called me by my name. He'd call me 'dirty girl', his 'floozy', 'trollop' and sometimes 'Tatiana', which confused me

to no end. I didn't know anyone called Tatiana. For some reason, Dad seemed to have a soft spot for the name. To Dad, I was never a person except when I was Tatiana. And I was only Tatiana when he was abusing me.

One day when we were sitting in the garden, I worked up the confidence to ask Dad about Tatiana. 'Daddy, can you answer a question?' I said. 'Who is Tatiana?'

'Where did you hear that name?' he replied.

'You called me Tatiana last week,' I said.

'I did not! You must be mistaken.'

'But you did, Daddy, when we were in the living room, and you got me to touch –'

'We don't talk about that! I didn't call you Tatiana.'

Dad looked around the garden as if he was scared someone was going to overhear us. 'If you are very, very good, perhaps one day you will be my perfect little girl. She looks like you, but has long red hair. You have a long way to go to be my perfect little Tatiana because you're such a dirty girl,' he continued. 'Maybe if you try hard enough, you'll be my Princess Tatiana.'

'But who is Tatiana?' I was desperate to know.

'That's for me to know, and you to find out. Someday, maybe when you're good enough,' he said.

I never did find out. I never was good enough.

Later, my mum told me that Dad had wanted to call my sister Sheila 'Tatiana' after watching the James Bond film *From Russia with Love*. Mum vetoed the name because she thought my sister would be called 'Tits' for short.

ZOMBIE GIRL

It's my job to tell Dad what he wants to hear. He asks the questions and I parrot back the answer – like an echo song at a school camp, only more sinister. 'What are you?'

'I'm Daddy's dirty little girl.'

'And what do you want?'

'I want it, I need it, I love it. I like it when you hurt me. I need to be punished.'

And so on, and so forth.

JENI

Because of my dad, I had zero self-confidence and was often surprised when someone paid me a compliment. At the school sports day in February 1978, my class was sitting on the grass and watching the races. We were told there were prizes up for grabs; if we heard our names called over the megaphone, we had to run as fast as we could to Mr Teller and if we arrived in time, we'd win something. When I heard my name called later in the day, I ran so quick I fell over and scraped my knee. I could hear Mr Teller and the other kids calling out encouragement as I went. When I finally made it to Mr Teller, he bent down to speak to me. 'You run like the wind!' he said. 'Do you like to run?'

I was so breathless, I just nodded and smiled. He handed me a packet of salt and vinegar chips and picked up the megaphone to say, 'Congratulations to Jennifer Haynes on picking up her prize, and doesn't she run like the wind!'

If only I could have run like the wind away from my father.

I remember an incident a few months after my eighth birthday. Like the year before, Dad had made me 'give birth' to the kewpie doll in the birthday ritual on my eighth birthday in January.

In May, nine months before my next birthday, I was reading under the lemon tree in the back garden when Dad sat down beside me and put his hand on my leg.

'No, don't,' I said.

He ignored me and dragged me to a patch of grass behind the garage.

It hurt so much I couldn't even cry. After, Dad lifted his head to look up at me and smiled. 'That was good, wasn't it?' he said. I just stared at him.

'You're pregnant now and you'll have a baby in due course,' he said. The next year, on my birthday, he completed the birthday ritual

once more. I went on to have seven 'in due courses' in my childhood, but never got to have the babies. Amber will come back to this later.

* * *

My teacher's name was Mrs Sully. One morning during art class, she taught us how to draw circles using a compass. I loved how the circles intersected and I tried to draw a flower with overlapping petals using the compass. I wanted to get the colours to blend so blue and yellow made green.

When Mrs Sully saw my drawing, she was impressed. 'Jeni, that's very good,' she said. 'You are very talented.'

Mrs Sully walked to the front of the classroom and brought me back a box of pastel pencils, which were better for blending. 'Try these,' she said, encouraging me to do more drawing at home. 'If you do more pictures, I would love to see them. You should ask your mum to buy you some paints too.'

At the end of the lesson, I left Mrs Sully's box of pencils on my desk, but before I could leave, she called after me. 'Don't forget your coloured pencils, Jeni,' she said, holding out the box for me.

I thought she was lending them to me for the weekend, so I promised her I would take good care of them. I didn't realise they were a gift.

When I got home that afternoon, I rushed outside with the box of pencils to keep drawing under the kitchen window. It was a warm afternoon and I could hear someone mowing their lawn in the distance. I focused on shading between the lines of my compass-drawn flowers and using the pencils evenly so that I didn't wear any down too much. I treated each pencil as a precious item and was so engrossed in my drawing that I didn't notice Dad storming towards me until he was standing over me.

Dad grabbed my picture out of my hands and ripped it to shreds. The colourful flower petals I'd spent so much time shading were torn into confetti. I felt nothing but sadness when the confetti showered down over me.

'Look at it! It's rubbish, just rubbish,' Dad hissed. 'There's no way I'd waste money on paints for a filthy girl like you. You're not worth it. Don't you ever waste time on rubbish like this again.'

Dad stomped down hard on Mrs Sully's box of pencils, and kept stamping until they broke. I tried to save them, but he just trod on my hand and refused to stop. 'No! Don't, Daddy, they're not mine,' I screamed.

Dad smiled and stomped harder.

SYMPHONY

My face is hot with fury. My hands are clenched in tight fists. My teeth are gritted. I'm so angry it feels like I'm floating above my body. My temper takes on a life of its own. I lose control of my hands and hit out at Daddy. I scream with such venom it comes out as a snarl.

Every thought I've swallowed down in the last year erupts from my mouth. Ever since I made the pact to protect Sheila from Daddy, he's hurt me, and I've been powerless to stop him. In this moment, I'm making up for every time I bit my tongue, blinked away tears and forced myself to scream silently. I'm angry about the pencils, but my resentment runs deeper than that. My hatred for Daddy bursts like a water-bomb on the concrete. I yell and I scream and I sob. My words are tinged with bits of spit, like poison.

Daddy hits me across the face, and I taste the metal of blood in my mouth. I don't feel it as pain, that comes later. My anger has turned my body to ice and my fear has been frozen away. I'm numb.

'How dare you!' Daddy yells as he drags me into the outside toilet. He slams the door and bolts it shut. My hands are still clenched into fists. Daddy takes off his belt and hits me across my back, stomach, legs and bottom. I scream until he shoves my underpants into my mouth. My words die and my anger turns to fear. I'm sure he's going to beat me to death, and I try to run away.

Daddy grabs me and throws me over the open toilet. I scream and my underpants fall forward in my mouth. The smell of the toilet and Daddy's sweat makes me sick. I throw up and my underpants are

pushed out of my mouth. Daddy doesn't stop slamming into me. In fact, he gets faster and harder.

I know I'm being punished for my outburst, but the punishment proves my outburst true. My daddy is a mean, bad man and I do hate him.

'Get out of my sight!' Daddy roars, and I try to crawl away. 'If you ever speak to me like that again, I will kill you. And no one will help you. No one loves you.' The world goes black.

JENI

The next thing I remember is my mum drawing me a Dettol bath. The water was a milky white colour as I lowered myself into it. My body was covered in dull red stripes that stung with the Dettol. I clung to the sides of the bath as my body twitched in pain. I was on fire both inside and out. I felt so weak it took me an eternity to pick up the sponge and soap to wash myself. I wiped myself as gently as I could, but it hurt so much, I gave up.

I held on to the wall as I shakily got out of the bath and attempted to dry myself. I was still damp when I slipped my nightdress on and asked my mum if I could go to bed early. Dad climbed into my bed during the night. The bed sagged under his weight and woke me up. Dad laid down behind me and held me tightly. I knew he was going to hurt me.

'So you hate me and wish I were dead, do you? How dare you say such terrible things to me? To me! I'm going to make you wish you'd never been born,' he said, and he did. 'I can do what I like to you, no one cares. No one gives a damn about you. You're nothing.'

I begged for my mother.

'Your mother doesn't care about you! She hates you. She wishes you were dead,' Dad said. 'If she loved you, don't you think she'd come to help you? Where is she? She isn't here because she doesn't love you. She knows you need punishment and she's glad I'm doing it. You deserve it.'

His words burned as much as my open wounds in the Dettol bath.

Later, my mum told me the Dettol bath happened on the Sunday night, not the Friday after my dad destroyed the pencils – and me. Dad had belted me so hard, I lost two days. I retreated into myself completely and have no recollection of what happened during those two days. There wasn't a front runner in my body. We were on autopilot, going about our business like a zombie, except even Zombie Girl was in hiding.

SYMPHONY

'Let's play a game,' says Dad, who's been teaching me checkers and card games. I'm sitting outside reading my book in the garden, but I follow Dad inside to play. Mum, Sheila and Frank are shopping in Bankstown so Daddy and I are home alone. Instead of taking me to the kitchen table where we play card games, Dad leads me to his bedroom. There are towels on the bed. No! Towels mean I'm going to be hurt. *No!* I pull my hand out of Dad's grasp and try to wriggle away from him.

'Behave,' he snarls, slapping my face and pushing me onto the end of the bed. He shoves my face into the mattress. A minute ago, I thought I was going to be playing a fun game of checkers with my dad. Now he's a different man. His movements are sharp and hard.

'You'll like this game,' he assures me, picking up a silvery stick. I don't like this game; it's the ritual, but I don't know that word yet.

'Botheration!' he spits. I can hear the anger in his voice and feel it in his movements.

'I'm sorry, Dad,' I whisper.

'So you should be.'

We're back to the beginning. He must have made a mistake in his ritual, and now he has to start all over again. Dad's the one who made the mistake in his game, but I'm the one who loses.

The last object is always the worst. The pain is so enormous, my back arches uncontrollably. I scream. Dad slaps my bottom.

'Oh, don't be silly, you know you love it really,' he demands.

I shake my head. No!

'Tell me you love it. I know you do, you're humping it,' he says.

I stay silent. I don't know what humping is.

'You want it, don't you? DON'T YOU?' he pushes.

'Yes,' I cry.

'Don't, please, Daddy, it hurts,' I beg.

'But you want it, you just said so! You love it.'

He replaces the object with himself and when he pulls out of me, the contents of my bowels come out with him. I poo all over the bed uncontrollably.

'You filthy creature! How dare you?' Dad roars. 'I play a nice game with you, and this is how you repay me. Stay there, do not move.'

I stay frozen in the stench. I couldn't move if I wanted to. I'm weak with pain and sick with worry. Dad storms back into the room and wipes my bottom with rough newspaper.

'Oh, you are just disgusting. Get out of my sight, you filthy creature,' he spits, pushing me out of the room and slamming the door in my face.

I run to the outside toilet to clean myself up. I'm mortified. I can't believe I pooped on Mummy's bed. I don't want her to hate me when she finds out. I decide it's better if I own up to it and tell her before Dad does. I try to find the words to tell her what I've done, but they're out of my grasp.

That's when I hear his voice. It's definitely a boy. I turn my head and see him. He's small and vulnerable, but when he opens his mouth, he's big and tough.

JUDAS

Judas is my name and blabbing is my game. I have the words, the magic words.

I can tell Mummy what happened. I can explain it wasn't our fault. We didn't mean to poo on her bed, it was an accident. While Symphony can only communicate in song lyrics, I can use words. I can think in words. Dad can't read my mind like he can Symphony's. I'm compos mentis.

The words dance through my mind and settle on the tip of my tongue. When Mum gets home from shopping, I'm ready. I fly

through the house, past Dad and meet Mum outside the living room. I open my mouth and the words I've prepared fly out.

'I don't like Daddy's games,' I say, confidently, because the games made me shit on Mummy's bed.

As if by magic – dark magic – Dad appears beside me, and my confidence shrinks.

'That's because you don't play fair,' he says, cutting me off.

I open my mouth to tell Mum more about Dad's games, but the words die in my throat. Dad is standing so close to me, I know I can't tell. He's glaring at me so evilly, I know I can't tell. His hands are clenched into such tight fists, I know I can't tell.

I let it go. The dark magic wins – this time. I let it go, but I don't forget. My job is to tell, and I will do my job to the best of my ability. I will look for the right opportunity, the right moment, and the right person to be honest about Dad. I know the rules. I can't tell Mum about what Dad does, but I can tell her why I shit on her bed. There's a difference.

The stakes are high. If I say the wrong thing, Mum will drop down dead. But there has to be a way.

I know I need to tell, but what am I telling? What is it that Dad is doing to us? Why is he so scared of us telling?

I think. I watch. I listen. I work it out. The time for telling is coming.

JENI

After Judas told Mum about Dad's games, the name changed. Dad never called them 'games' again. From that moment on, they were 'punishments'. He told me I deserved to be punished because I'd been naughty. I must have been the naughtiest girl on the planet; the punishments occurred almost every day. I couldn't work out what I'd done so wrong, but I knew I must have been evil to deserve the pain Dad inflicted upon me.

I remember an incident in 1978. It was a gloomy day outside, and I rubbed my arms to warm them up. I was inside sitting on my parents' bed, and I was completely naked. Dad angrily prodded me

and ran his hands along my throat and under my chin. I felt a thick piece of leather being laid across my throat and pulled tight. It was Dad's belt. The cold metal of the buckle scraped against the side of my jaw. The leather rubbed behind my right ear as Dad secured the belt to something above my head out of sight.

I couldn't move my head without putting pressure onto my throat. I moved my left hand up to my neck to try to ease the tension, but Dad's hand flashed across my face. 'Don't you dare,' he said, slapping me again.

'Stay put,' he said, pointing a finger at me.

Don't point, Mummy says pointing is rude, I thought, but didn't dare say out loud.

Dad got on the bed. I felt his weight on top of me. Then I felt his penis plunge into me. The pain was huge. I bucked, and screamed, and jerked my head from side to side. The buckle dug deep into my neck. A stream of tears trickled down the sides of my face. Drip, drip, drip.

The choking around my throat hurt more than the stabbing between my legs. I struggled for air and thrashed my arms up and down, trying to get Dad's attention. I tried to scream with my eyes, 'I can't breathe, I can't breathe.' Pressure built in my ears until everything went black. I was falling, but I never hit the ground.

The next thing I remember was my dad holding me upright on the side of the bed. My head was so heavy it sagged down towards my chest. Everything felt fuzzy and thick. I could see my knees, but they seemed to be miles away. I saw faint shapes in front of my eyes like those in my bead kaleidoscope. The belt had been taken off and the pressure was gone, but the pain in my neck was worse than ever. There was also pain in my bottom and genitals, so I believe Dad raped me while I was unconscious. When I breathed, the pain travelled from my neck to my lungs and ribs. The air burned my throat.

'Breathe,' said Dad, but his voice was so far away. I tried to turn to look at him, but my dizziness turned to darkness once again. When the darkness cleared a little, I heard Dad speak again. 'You're back.

Thank God,' he said. I believe my dad thought he had nearly killed me – and he had.

I moaned involuntarily and the sound that came out of me shocked me so much, I lost control of my bladder. Pee ran down my legs onto the floor. Drip, drip, drip.

I tried to speak, but I couldn't get my mouth to work. I kept trying. '... sorry, I'm sorry, I'm sorry,' my voice cracked.

'Yes, well don't do it again. It would have only taken a little more to kill you,' Dad replied. I was struck by these words. He could have killed me. It would have only taken a little more. Just a little more.

Dad dressed me, held me up and walked me across the hall to my bedroom. I couldn't lift my feet, so they dragged along underneath me. Dad lifted me into my bed and sat down beside me. 'You were naughty and you deserved your punishment. Naughty girls get punished. Do you understand?' he said. 'We don't need to bother Mum with this because I've dealt with it. Do you understand?'

I tried to nod my head, but I felt a savage pain in my throat. I lifted my hand to rub my neck, but Dad grabbed it before I could. 'Don't do that! Just tell me you understand,' he demanded.

'Yes,' I replied, but my voice was faint.

Dad clapped his hands together, got off the bed and put my glasses on the bed beside me. 'Good!' he said.

I have a mark on my neck from this incident. It's like a crease line on my neck with a dot that looked like a blob of dirt in the centre. The marks came from the edge of the belt and the pin of the belt buckle. Mum kept trying to wash it away in the bath. No matter how much soap she used, it didn't budge. It took decades to fade. The dot on my neck is a permanent reminder of how easily my dad could kill me. It would have only taken a little more. Just a little more.

After this attack, Dad never tied his belt around my throat again. I believe this was because he was frightened that he'd nearly killed me. It certainly was not because he felt any compassion for me, but because he was scared of what would happen to him if his dead daughter was found with his belt around her neck and her

underpants on the floor. He might have been too afraid to tie his belt around my neck after the incident, but it didn't stop him from using his belt to beat me. Dad would thrash me with it until his arm grew sore.

Dad punished Frank and Sheila with his belt too when they misbehaved, but their lashings were never as brutal as mine. Still, I hated seeing my siblings in trouble and would have happily traded places with them to save them from a beating.

I had a close relationship with my little brother Frank. He was a warm spot in my cold life. We played in the laundry together, using the double sink as a swimming pool for Lego people and other toys. One day I was filling up the sink while Frank ran inside to get the toys. I heard the laundry door open and was surprised to see Dad instead of Frank. He closed the door and smiled at me, but his lips were pursed thin and white.

Silently, Dad took my hand from the sink and pressed it to the front of his trousers. He opened his trousers, pushed me onto the floor and pulled down my pants. He grabbed my legs and positioned me so my bottom was on his lap, his erect penis digging into my crotch and eventually pushing into my vagina. Dad began to saw in and out of me. 'You are so good at this,' he said into my ear.

I heard the door open, and Frank walked into the laundry. He was five and a half. Dad told him to sit on the floor beside him and watch what he was doing to me. 'One day you'll be old enough to do this,' Dad told Frank, as he continued thrusting inside me. Frank said nothing. What could a five-and-a-half-year-old say?

'No, Daddy, please,' I begged, trying to escape. I couldn't get away, but I kept saying no, no, NO! When Dad finally pulled out of me, he took Frank's hand and walked out of the room. I was convinced Dad had taken Frank away to tell him how he could sexually abuse me too. I was terrified he had made me a girl without a name for Frank, freeing him to hurt and hate me when he was 'old enough'. During my childhood, I was worried that Dad would get my brother to attack me. That day Dad took an ice pick to my warm relationship with my brother, and for me it never really recovered.

Thank god Frank was too young to understand what was going on. But later, I knew that if our father ever returned to the matter when he was older, Frank was strong enough never to take the road his father had shown him. Frank has never abused anybody and I have no concerns he ever would. My brother is not like that.

The Importance of Zombies and Deservedness

When you are being abused by someone who controls your day-to-day care and survival, you have to do some powerful mental gymnastics to keep them onside and stay sane. This is the essence of betrayal trauma that I discussed earlier. When you then mix in coping with unrelenting trauma that exceeds the levels of torture, you need some specialist alters like a Zombie Girl. This alter illustrates the fullness of Jennifer Freyd's Betrayal Trauma that we reviewed earlier. It is only in movies that the tortured victim heroically holds out, no matter what happens, and never spills the beans, but then, sexual assault is rarely employed.

In reality, torture gets people to say what they think the torturer wants to hear, to stop the pain. This, however, may have little to do with the truth.

It was a Tuesday, 7 August 2012, when Mexican Marines smashed their way into the house and life of Claudia Medina and took her to their naval base. Over the course of 36 hours, she was subjected to strangling, electric shocks and sexual assaults to get her to admit she was part of an international crime gang. In the end she signed a confession to this effect. She remained in prison for 23 days until she was released to face the subsequent charges.[1] There was one small problem. None of it was true. In 2014 Amnesty International launched its global *Stop Torture* campaign based on cases like, and including, that of Claudia Medina. In February 2016, after

complaining to the National Human Rights Commission in Mexico, all charges against her were dropped. The point is that torture achieves compliance but, often, not much more.

Let's review the few words that Zombie Girl gave us that so clearly capture her job and why she has to do it:

> It's my job to tell Dad what he wants to hear. He asks the questions and I parrot back the answer – like an echo song at a school camp, only more sinister.
>   'What are you?'
>   'I'm Daddy's dirty little girl.'
>   'And what do you want?'
>   'I want it, I need it, I love it. I like it when you hurt me. I need to be punished.'

Jeni was a quick study. Like all victims of recurring sexual abuse, they work out one simple fact – resistance prolongs the inevitable pain. Jeni knows that no one is coming to save her. What does resisting achieve? More pain. More distress. What would be the point of that? Pretty much every perpetrator who has attacked the hundreds of people I have treated for repeated childhood sexual abuse, gets to this at some point. They want their victim to 'admit' that they want, welcome or enjoy the abuse. I believe this is driven by three things.

First, it is to create a sense of complicity, a sense that 'I'm not doing this to hurt you, I'm doing this because you want it.' The perpetrator wants to shift the child from victim status to accomplice status. A child is much more likely to keep the secret if they are an accomplice. Second, often perpetrators are abusing children to connect. They usually struggle with relationships and have few real friends. They are unable to have an intimate, complete relationship with adult women. In the face of this isolation, 'I'm Daddy's dirty little girl,' is a statement of connection, as fake as it was.

Third, the perpetrator knows that they are responsible for bad deeds. They know if they get caught they are in serious trouble. The perpetrator wants to be told that they are doing something

of benefit to the child to counter this guilt, as embryonic as it is. 'I want it, I need it, I love it,' serves this purpose. 'I need to be punished,' further validates their acts.

It is a huge testament to Jeni's inner fortitude and her sense of justice that she continues to fight back. When she screams at her father after he broke Mrs Sully's box of pencils, the predictable physical abuse and rape followed to the point that she passed out. Not long after this we have the event where her father insists, *'"You want it, don't you? DON'T YOU?" he pushes. "Yes," I cry.'* We can all understand Jeni's compliance at these times.

The other thing some children who are repeatedly sexually abused work out is that once the perpetrator orgasms, the pain stops. As well as being compliant with the perpetrator's wishes, the next job is to get them to orgasm as quickly as possible. This can look to the abuser's twisted mind like the child is an active, agreeable participant. To help the abuser to finish quickly is logical, but it can look like the child is not just compliant, but a willing participant. This is so far from the truth, but a perpetrator's mind is so far from caring about truth.

To make matters worse, with repeated sexual assaults, victim's bodies, sooner or later, especially when no immediate pain is inflicted, often respond with some degree of arousal. This is just the human body doing what it was built to do. These are direct neural pathways that cause physical arousal from certain kinds of stimulation especially of the clitoris and penis. These direct pathways are not connected to the parts of our brain that are aware of who the partner is and if the act is morally right or wrong, wanted or unwanted. It's pure cause and effect.

While it makes absolute sense why Jeni needed to create a compliant Zombie Girl, there is a big cost to this kind of compliance – guilt and shame. This guilt and shame is experienced as being owned solely by the victim. Jeni has been less troubled by this guilt than many of my other patients, who see it as evidence that they were complicit. This is because her core personalities were able to recognise that Zombie Girl was not representative of

their core sense of self and who they were. They knew they were not willing participants.

Unfortunately, people who are not able to dissociate, who are victims of repeated childhood sexual abuse, do not get the benefit of this separation of powers. In the course of trauma therapy, it is common to find that my patients hold onto the shameful secrets of actively trying to get their perpetrator to orgasm and/or, at times, experiencing some sexual arousal.

It is important for the therapist to be very matter of fact about how these two issues are 'normal', unwitting (in every sense of the word) bodily responses and just go with the territory of childhood sexual abuse. Equally, it is important to highlight that it is just as normal for them to feel so much guilt and shame and that nearly every sexual abuse victim beats themselves up for this. The art at this point in therapy is reacting as if it is to be expected and no big deal, while coming across as not being dismissive of how big a deal it has actually been for them.

Add to this the common belief that they should have done more, fought back more, tried harder to get help, and we can see why guilt and shame haunts the minds of entirely innocent victims.

It is such a pity they typically hold onto this until the very end of therapy as it is relatively easy to treat. Often, during the re-experiencing of EMDR it becomes overwhelmingly convincing that as a young child they absolutely did the best they could have. When this does not fall out of the therapy, I have another approach. Nearly always the problem is an adult part judging their fellow child part, from the perspective of what they would do now they are older. Under my desk I have the shoe of a five-year-old and the shoe of an adult male. When my patient still believes they should have done things differently, I pull out the two shoes and put them side-by-side. 'So, you think the wearer of that shoe could have done something to stop the wearer of that shoe?' Rarely do I need to say much more to finally shift these big cogs in their mind. This self-forgiveness work is a critical part of therapy. (I can't recall who taught this to me, but I thank you.)

Acceptance of the self

Inevitably in therapy, self-forgiveness work brings us to address acceptance versus forgiveness. In my work, the goal in therapy is never to forgive the perpetrator. Nevertheless, some patients come to forgive their abusers, but this is because this works for them at some level. Instead, we work to achieve acceptance. Acceptance says nothing more than, I have learnt what I needed to learn, no more, and I can now get back on track with my life. I say 'no more' to deal with the problem where victims have learnt things that are unhelpful. Perhaps the best example is learning a version of, 'I need to stay small to be safe'. This has to be unlearnt. A related belief we need to unlearn is that the world is a dangerous place. Nothing holds people back from getting their life on track more than this. Reaching for a better life involves taking calculated risks. A global belief that the world is a dangerous place kills the motivating force that we need to reach into the world to 'follow our bliss', as the influential writer Joseph Campbell put it.

My job is to help my patients remember that although there are dangerous people in the world, they are part of a bell curve. At one end of the curve, you have people who will never hurt you and at the other end you have people who will. In between, you have most people who are law abiding and safe, provided you do not provoke them too much, as can occur in wartime or home invasions. The job then is to structure one's life to be among the people at the safer end of the bell curve. When you grow up without any choice in the kind of people around you, it can be hard to accept that you can choose, to a large extent, who is around you most of the time, that you can create a 'safe enough' world. Yes, there are dangerous people out there, but we don't want to give them the power to stop us living a full and meaningful life.

There is a role for forgiveness in therapy, but first and foremost it is of oneself. Not forgiving ourselves stops us from feeling we deserve to have a full, meaningful life. While therapy is about relieving distress, for me the greater work is helping people to move on to live a deeply rewarding life – this, to me, is the most healing of

all. Pain is not always a bad thing as it can motivate us to re-evaluate our life, to really ask the question, 'How do I want to spend the most valuable thing I have – my time?' There is never a quick solution to this existential question, but pursuing it seems to take people to a place where the pain of their abuse fades as it is used in the service of driving them to a more rewarding life. (How to do this is a book in its own right and the basis for my novel, *The Way of The Quest*.)

If we don't feel we deserve forgiveness then our mind, at both conscious and unconscious levels, will hold us back, even sabotaging opportunities that come our way, to keep us small. This is not a little problem. I do not believe that anything holds us back more in life than lacking a sense of 'deservedness'. And nothing damages deservedness more than not forgiving ourselves. As we forgive ourselves, we allow ourselves to deserve more and thereby to step up to life and live larger.

Trying to be a compliant, small target does serve us when abuse is ongoing. It does not serve us later. To stay small to avoid potential risks in life means large chunks of valuable opportunities in life are passed over. In particular, it limits developing life-enriching relationships, denying both sides the opportunity for wonderment and growth. Jeni could have stayed small by not writing this book, but that would not have served you, dear reader.

Small may be safer but safe equals sad over time. Safe is dangerous to living fully.

Marianne Williamson has written beautifully about this (atheists can just overlook the word God – it's not central to the message) and puts it better than I can:

> We ask ourselves, Who am I to be brilliant, gorgeous,
> talented & fabulous? Actually, who are you not to be? You
> are a child of God. Your playing small does not serve the
> world ... We were born to make manifest the glory of God
> that is within us. It's not just in some of us; it's in everyone.
> And as we let our own light shine, we unconsciously give
> other people permission to do the same.[2]

VOLCANO
Unlearning dysfunctional core beliefs

Thanks George. But whenever the thorny issue of forgiveness would come up in therapy it would trigger us badly. As Muscles declared 'I don't have anything to forgive myself for. I didn't do anything wrong!' I completely hear that.

Over time my understanding of this has changed. I feel it is necessary to take a step back and look at the self-perceptions and core beliefs we took away from what happened to us. Abusers look for ways to control and keep their abuse secret and to do this they call into question anything in their victim that they can manipulate. It can be your sexuality, your appearance, your intelligence, your place in a family or the world, they weaponise and distort to protect themselves. Dad forced me to believe that no one would believe me if I told and the abuse was okay anyway because it was happening to me and no one cared about me. These dreadful words became central to my sense of self and defined how I saw myself. They became my core beliefs and I acted accordingly.

However, these core beliefs come out of the sense-making efforts of a child. They are informed by and a product of the perpetrator's victim-blaming strategy. They come from powerful adults attempting to reduce their own culpability and responsibility for the crimes they have committed and wish to continue to commit. The force they bring to bear on young minds is intense. By adopting a core belief imposed upon them by their abuser the victim changes their self-perception and their sense of self, taking into themselves at least part of the world view of their perpetrator. I believe one goal of therapy is to unpick and unlearn the dysfunctional core beliefs imposed upon the child by their abuser. This can be done by getting the patient to internalise their ages at the time they internalised these beliefs; helping them to understand that they made the best judgements they could for their age, with the information they had at the time; learning that their behaviour and reactions were completely reasonable given their circumstances; and accepting that abusers impose views and perceptions upon their victims to protect

themselves. As George has outlined, EMDR has a significant role to play in this process. And it is here that I believe forgiveness has a part to play. Victims need to learn to forgive themselves for *being taken in by the abuser;* for *blaming themselves* for what was not their fault and for *taking responsibility* for aspects of the abuse or of the abuser that were nothing to do with them. After all, abusers don't rape because of anything a child does, it is all about the power and control a criminal has over his or her victim.

We all need to remember that the sexual abuse of a child is never about something in the child that causes the abuse. It is always about something in the abuser. This is their crime of choice. That says more about them than it ever will about their victim. Victims of childhood sexual abuse are never ever responsible for what is inflicted upon them. Responsibility must always lay at the feet of the adult no matter who that adult is.

CHAPTER SIX

The Magic Words

JENI

Every year I looked forward to the school sports day. I was in the Waratah (red) house with Sheila and even though we weren't participating in any of the events in 1979, we sat in our house group with our friends and happily watched on. We were chatting amongst ourselves when we noticed a male teacher rushing around. 'Looking for Jennifer Haynes, has anyone seen Jennifer Haynes?' he asked.

'Here!' I shouted out.

'We have a problem, and you may just be able to help,' he told me, saying that he'd seen me playing ball at school. He explained that the bowler for the cricket team had hurt himself and asked if I would like to bowl for them in his place. Of course I would.

I was the only girl on the oval when I took to the pitch. All the boys on the team were much bigger and older than me, but when the teacher explained I would be bowling, they nodded and took their places. 'Just do your best,' the teacher said, leaving me with the ball in my hand.

I'd watched the team play before and I knew I had to do a run-up and throw with an overarm swing. I bowled my first ball and the opposing batter hit it with an almighty whack. I bowled again and again. The boys from both teams applauded and yelled out supportive comments when I bowled someone out. My arm began to ache, but I was enjoying myself immensely. I can't remember who won the match, but it didn't matter much to me, I was on a

high. When the game ended and I walked off the pitch, the teacher who had fetched me told me I'd done really well and had made the school proud.

Sheila was screaming my name and jumping up and down. 'That's my sister!' she squealed, pushing her way towards me for a hug. 'Just wait till Mum hears!'

Sheila was puffed up like a peacock with pride and I revelled in the moment. A lot of people talked to me about the game, but I only cared about Sheila. She made me feel so good and raved about me to anyone who would listen. She kept saying how small I was in comparison to the boys, but how well I had bowled against them. When we got home, Sheila burst inside to tell Mum how I had 'shown the boys!'

'Your dad will be so pleased with you,' Mum said with a smile.

When he got home from work, Dad did say he was pleased with me, but the tone in his voice told me differently. His flat response put a dampener on my joy and made me feel a little scared.

After tea, Mum drew me a warm bath to help my 'sore bowling arm', then I went to the toilet outside. I was sitting on the toilet when Dad came in. My heart sank. I flushed the toilet and stood up to leave, but before I could, he grabbed my arm.

'What have you done to be seen by your teacher? I suppose you were showing off to them too. You've let me down. I don't like show-offs. I don't like you at all,' he spat.

'I'm sorry, Daddy. I didn't mean it,' I said, devastated.

'You've let me down, you've let your mother down and you've let yourself down. I am really angry with you,' he continued.

As I sobbed, Dad hugged me to him. His embrace didn't make me feel any better. I knew he wasn't comforting me; he was preparing to punish me. I tried not to breathe because he smelt of sweat and it was making me feel sick. 'Let me go, please let me go!' I wailed.

To my surprise, he did. Dad took his hands off me and, because I wasn't expecting it, I fell backwards. I landed on the floor and tried to catch my breath. Dad grabbed my legs and yanked me towards

him. My bottom slid across the cold concrete floor. The smell of Dad's body filled the room and overwhelmed me. 'You've been a naughty girl, and what happens to naughty girls?' he said.

I was too terrified to answer him. I knew what he wanted me to say, and I knew if I said it, he'd use it against me.

'I'm waiting! Tell me, what happens to naughty girls?' he pushed.

'... They get punished,' I whispered. And that's exactly what happened. I was punished and left lying on the ground with blood running down the inside of my legs.

Every joyful memory I have has been soiled by my father – literally and figuratively. Dad totally ruined sports for me. I loved to run, skip and swim, and was invited on a variety of teams after I bowled for the school. Dad was violently opposed to me doing any activities and refused to give me permission to join any team. 'Daddy won't let me play,' I told the teachers.

I had to ask Dad for permission to do anything, and often my question was answered with an attack and then a hard no. Or I was told I had to be a very, very, *very* good girl. I knew that meant being tortured and submitting to it.

Strangely enough, there were some things I was almost always allowed to do. One of those things was sleeping over at my friend Jasmine's house. My brother was friends with Jasmine's little sister Grace, and if I stayed at Jasmine's house, Grace would usually stay at our house. It was a child swap of sorts. Dad had a soft spot for Grace, and I always worried that he might hurt her in the same way he hurt me.

My guilt was overshadowed by my delight at spending time with Jasmine. We were good friends and I loved staying at her house, least of all because it was a small reprieve from the abuse I faced at home. One morning at school, after a particularly awful weekend at home, Jasmine found me passed out on the floor of the girls' toilet. I'd fainted and had to drag myself up to vomit into the toilet when I came around. I was shaky and weak. Jasmine was worried and asked me what was wrong.

Without thinking, I told her.

JUDAS

I can tell! Jasmine has asked a question, and I can answer.

'What's wrong?' she asks.

'My dad hurts me,' I explain.

I tell Jasmine everything Dad has done to me over the weekend. I spew the magic words out like the vomit in the toilet. I tell her every excruciating detail. I tell her about the pain, about the blood, about the hole in between my legs. The words tumble out of me and land like punches on Jasmine. She listens and flinches as I speak.

Jasmine grabs my hand and drags me outside to where Mr Teller is standing. She opens her mouth to repeat what I've told her and promptly has the most amazing asthma attack. She can't breathe and dramatically gasps for air. Mr Teller pushes me out of the way and I fall backwards onto the ground. The teachers in the hallway rush to help Jasmine and she's taken to hospital in an ambulance. I'm left alone.

I'm sure Jasmine is going to die. All I can think is that I told my friend and now she's in hospital; I've killed her. Dad has drummed it into me that if I tell, people will die. Now I know he's telling the truth. I can't tell anyone!

I swallow the words down hard but they burn.

Jasmine makes a full recovery. But the conversation we had dies. I refuse to put Jasmine's health at risk again, so I never bring up my disclosure – neither does she. Maybe Jasmine forgot our conversation after the flurry of her asthma attack, or maybe she didn't know what to say or do. Either way, that day was pushed away, with my secret still hidden.

MAGSY

The hammer! No, not the hammer please.

I could see nothing beyond it.

When Dad pushed me onto the bed, I was completely naked and I did not have my glasses on, and yet when I first laid eyes on the hammer, I had been fully dressed and was wearing my glasses. As soon as I saw it I knew Dad was going to hurt me and my body

switched off. As an adult I understand that Ed the Head and Muscles had joined me and took over. But at the time I felt nothing below my bust. I couldn't feel the bed beneath my body or the weight of my father above me. My body lay there like a lump of meat, unable to move or struggle. I could still smell the stench of burning Bakelite and sweat and hear the sounds of Dad grunting.

'Let's try this,' he said. 'You're bigger now, it'll be better.'

'No, please don't. It's too big, it hurts,' I said, but speaking was exhausting, and I did not have the strength to fight him.

Pain crept up my spine and spread throughout my body.

'That was good, wasn't it?' he asked.

I couldn't respond.

'Answer me!' he demanded.

I couldn't move.

'Come on! Snap out of it!' he snarled.

I felt boneless as Dad dressed me. I was limp as he dragged me to my feet and tossed my body over his shoulder like he was a fireman and I was a corpse. I lost consciousness as he dumped me under the lemon tree in the back garden and walked away. I remained slumped there for the rest of the afternoon until my mother called me from the back door. I don't remember getting up or going inside.

JENI

There was something unnerving about the way my eyes fixated on the hammer. Reflecting on it now, it's similar to a type of epileptic seizure I've experienced throughout my life. During these seizures, my eyes become focused on a particular object or a mark on the wall, and I stare at it until something disrupts my vision. As I stare, the object seems to glow and become much larger so it blocks my view of everything else. I've learned to break the fixation by bringing my right hand up in front of my eyes so I can focus on something else.

MAGSY

The only thing that scared me more than the hammer was a red and blue plastic toy rolling pin.

'Clean up this mess,' he said, throwing my glasses at me and walking out of the room. I knew if I didn't get up and pack away the implements, he would eventually come back and do his ritual again.

I staggered to the outside laundry, threw the towels and implements on the ground, and sat on the toilet. After wiping myself, I began wiping the implements. I rubbed them hard under the water in the laundry sink and dried them with the towel from the floor. It was covered in red and brown stains. Once the implements were dry, I took them back into the house, with the exception of the rolling pin, which I left in the laundry.

SYMPHONY

I call my heavy black school shoes 'clodhoppers'. They're regulation lace-up school shoes, but when I put them on today, they're steel-capped boots. Wearing my clodhoppers, I collect the rolling pin from the laundry and take it to the patch of concrete near the lemon tree. I drop the rolling pin on the ground and jump on it with all my force. I keep jumping and crying, jumping and crying, until the plastic rolling pin is destroyed.

My clodhoppers smash the rolling pin into splintered pieces of plastic, which I sweep up with my hands. As I bend down, I feel liquid oozing into the wad of toilet paper in my underpants. The pain in my bottom is dulled with the satisfaction of destroying Dad's torture device. I know if I don't get rid of the rolling pin, Dad will use it on me again. And next time it will be worse. It always gets worse.

I wrap the splintered pieces of plastic in the two bloody towels and throw them in the outside rubbish bin. Good riddance, I think, clodhopping back inside.

JENI

In late 1979, an American series called *Project UFO* aired on TV. It portrayed the US Air Force's involvement in UFO research under the name 'Project Blue Book'. Dad loved anything to do with unexplainable mysteries. He regularly bought a magazine called *The*

Unexplained which explored aliens, UFOs, Big Foot, ghosts, psychic photography and the like. He read it from cover to cover. I attempted to build a bond with Dad over these things, expressing interest in the Loch Ness monster, UFOs and the mystery of the ghosts of the Petit Trianon in Paris. Dad and I were fascinated by Project Blue Book. After watching an episode with Dad, he gave me and Frank the task of drawing a UFO. I took it very seriously and carefully drew curved rooms, an engine and control station. When I showed Dad my work, he paid me a lot of attention and we spoke at length about UFOs. We talked about whether aliens would look like humans and how their spaceships would work. I was delighted that my drawing pleased him and I spent the afternoon working on more pictures.

I specifically remember this day because it was one of the rare times Dad didn't intimidate or abuse me. That night, he didn't come to my bed and hurt me. I took the UFO interaction as a sign that Dad *did* love me. He never told me he loved me, so I was desperate for any sort of positive attention. I've cherished this memory all my life. Whenever people ask about my memories of Dad, it is this afternoon that I remember first.

For the rest of the week, I drew endless diagrams of UFOs and their internal layouts, considering all the details Dad and I had discussed. I was proud of my efforts and excited to show Dad on Friday afternoon when he got home from work. 'I've worked on these all week. I thought you'd like them. They're for you,' I said, passing him the pile of drawings.

I knew straightaway I'd made a mistake. Dad looked at my work with scorn. 'Why would I want anything you drew? You're useless. You can't draw for toffee,' he said, screwing up the paper and throwing it on the living room floor. 'These are rubbish. Clean up this mess!'

I bent down in tears and scrambled to pick up my crumpled pictures. I was heartbroken that he hated me again. Dad started to speak and when I looked up at him, I saw a huge bulge in the front of his trousers. 'Get here,' he beckoned. 'Get it out, you know you want to.'

Dad forced my hand onto his zipper and made me undo it. I could hear Mum and Frank's voices through the wall in the next room and I desperately wanted them to come in and save me. They didn't. 'You have been so naughty, giving me rubbish like that. Wasting my time! You should know better by now. Get on with it,' he said.

I did as I was told – and never drew another UFO again.

Once more, joy turned to dirt at the hands of my father.

JANET

From the age of nine, I fantasised about killing myself. I knew I couldn't kill Dad – he was indestructible – so I decided I would have to be the one to die. My mum had a giant bottle of liquid TCP antiseptic under the sink in the bathroom. I clocked the poison mark on the bottle and hatched my plan. All I had to do was make sure Sheila was safe, then I would drink the TCP and end my suffering once and for all. But Sheila would never be safe, and my suffering would never be over.

CHAPTER SEVEN

Outside the Vacuum

JENI

My abuse didn't happen inside a vacuum. No abuse does. It happens in a world where children are seen as lesser, where red flags are ignored, and where families aren't questioned if they're deemed respectable. Dad had a respectable family history, a good job, wasn't an alcoholic and didn't wear a flashing paedophile badge, so in the eyes of society he was a decent bloke. Sometimes I wished my father had been a raging drunk so someone might have paid attention to the darkness within him.

In our family, Mum built the respectable reputation and Dad then used it as a shield. Most of the people in my life only ever met my mother; they didn't interact with my father, so they didn't pick up on any clues about his behaviour. They didn't see my shudder at his touch. They didn't see the fear in my eyes. They didn't see his cold manipulation of me. Because all of it happened behind closed doors. You have to see the monster to recognise it as monstrous.

Likewise, we never met any of Dad's work colleagues. So, if they ever had a suspicion about him and his odd behaviour, they could never confirm it because they never saw his damaged daughter. The people who might have been able to help me couldn't because they never had the opportunity to put two and two together. Dad's life was compartmentalised so that everything looked prim and proper on the outside, and Mum unwittingly helped him to maintain the façade.

Mum was actively involved in the lives of her children. At Greenacre, she was the secretary of the school's Mothers Club and then the P&C (Parents and Citizens). She attended all the meetings that happened during school hours – because Dad would forbid her from going to things after hours – and took notes in shorthand. In 1979, Mum spearheaded the organising of the school fete. It was an undertaking that took months, and Dad resented it immensely and complained about it relentlessly.

Mum bravely asked local businesses – like the butcher shop, real estate agents and banks – for donations and received a positive response from people wanting to support the school. Dad told her she was disgusting for begging.

Mum made beautiful Victorian dolls to sell at the fete and people complimented her about them endlessly. Dad refused to let her sell them in a local shop when the store owner approached her to do so. Mum enlisted the help of us kids to pack mystery sample bags up and stored them in a pile at the foot of her bed until the big day. Dad fumed that the sample bags were in the way of the foot of the bed – the place he practised his ritual on me – and so he took out his fury on my body.

Dad didn't want Mum to be seen. He didn't want her to gain confidence. And, most of all, he didn't want her to make friends who might pop around unannounced. That's exactly what happened one day in the lead-up to the fete. Another mother on the P&C knocked on our door to ask Mum if she had any spare teddy-bear eyes because she'd run out. Mum had to dig around in her craft supplies to find a packet, but Dad wouldn't let the woman inside. He made her wait on the porch.

After months of hard work, Mum set off early to the fete on the morning of 6 October 1979. Dad was meant to follow her half an hour later, once he'd helped us kids get ready. All the husbands of the wives on the P&C had been wrangled into helping set up. Us kids were waiting by the door at 7.30 am, excited to help Mum, but Dad dragged his feet. He faffed around the house for hours, pretending to be busy shuffling papers, going out to the shed and

moving things around. I was anxious to get going but didn't dare rush Dad.

After a few hours of deliberate delays, it looked as though Dad was finally getting ready to go. I ducked outside to go to the toilet before we left. Dad followed me. I got the usual. Dad walked out of the toilet like nothing happened. I stayed back to wash my face, clean myself up and force a smile onto my lips. My underpants were wet and my private parts were in agony, but you wouldn't know it to look at me. Captain Busby and her army took over because we weren't going to let Dad ruin Mum's big day.

CAPTAIN BUSBY

I'm in pain, but I'm laughing. It hurts to move, but I'm running. My body wants to curl up into a little ball, but Mum needs change for a customer, so I dash off to grab it for her.

My army is in full force on the day of the fete. We stick close by Mum in case she needs us to run an errand. We avoid Dad, in case he clips us around the ears. Again. Dad spends the day sulking and we spend the day pretending he hasn't just raped us.

We jump on the bouncy castle. We admire the grandma-knitted soap covers. We strategically line up to get the bag of samples we had been eyeing off all morning.

We don't tell Mum about what Dad did to us the day of the fete until 2019. We shield her from the knowledge for forty years. We keep the secret to keep her safe. We do our job.

HAPPY

Even in the blur of excruciating pain, there are happy memories to be found.

Look, there's one ... It's the fluffy gonk toy I joyously find in my bag of samples.

And another ... It's the smile on Mum's face when she sells one of her Victorian dolls to a chuffed customer.

We can't forget this one ... It's a set of three painted tiles hanging on the wall in the parents' art show. There's one of Miss Piggy, Fozzie

Bear and Kermit the Frog. There's one for each of Mum's three children. Sheila, Frank and I all fall deeply in love with the painted tiles and I can see Mum trying to move money around in her budget to be able to afford them. A gift for us helping her today.

At the end of the day, we are especially happy when Mum lets Dad have it for being late, unhelpful and sulking in the corner. Mum forces Dad to stay back and pack up the stalls because he wasn't there to help set them up.

Best of all, Mum insists that Dad buys the painted tiles for us.

That is a happy memory indeed.

JENI

The fete was a roaring success. It raised a thousand dollars for the school, which at the time was a huge amount of money. Mum became a new woman. She gained a confidence she'd never known, she felt valued by the community, and she relished in her own competence. To celebrate the glory of the fete, everyone involved in organising it was invited to a special meal at the St George Leagues Club. Mum was overjoyed. Dad was outraged. Their argument went a little something like this …

'No wife of mine is going to such a den of iniquity,' ruled Dad, turning up his nose at the idea of Mum being surrounded by men drinking and gambling.

'It's a lady's lunch, Richard. Only mothers from the P&C are going and I don't drink or gamble,' replied Mum, dismissing his unwarranted concern.

'We can't afford it,' he argued.

'It's being paid for by the P&C,' she countered.

'You have to stay home to make dinner for the kids,' he said.

'The lunch is during the day, the children will be at school, I'll be home with plenty of time to make dinner,' she said.

With a new strength, she added sarcastically that it would be fine to have a lunch to celebrate the success of the fete without actually having the organiser of the fete present. But that she preferred to go.

'You are not leaving this house!' screamed Dad, standing over Mum. His fists were clenched so tight his knuckles were white. He was so angry I was sure he was going to hit Mum until she died. I'd been on the receiving end of Dad's anger more than enough times to know he was capable of killing her.

The argument was over. Dad's ruling was final. Mum didn't attend the lady's lunch.

Dad stormed out of the house and dragged me into the toilet. He snarled, 'I'll teach her to talk to me like that,' as he viciously raped me. He kept saying things like this as he attacked me until the lunch date day had come and gone.

Dad may have won the battle of the lady's lunch, but he was yet to win the war.

With her newfound sense of confidence, Mum started standing up to Dad more. On several occasions, I heard my parents arguing after I went to bed, and I distinctly remember my father shouting about Mum's desire to get a job. 'No wife of mine is going out to work,' he yelled.

For months, my father walked around the house with an air of barely suppressed rage. The more my parents argued, the more violent my dad became. As Dad's attacks on me escalated, they became harder to hide. One afternoon in early 1980, the army that looked after Frank sprang into action.

SQUADRON CAPTAIN

Dad calls Frank his 'sun and air'. It took me many years to work out he means 'son and heir'. Both versions make sense to me because Frank is my reason for being. I give him protection and he gives me purpose.

I'm playing Lego in the garden with Frank when Dad comes for me. Dad drags me into the outside toilet and does what Dad does. When he's finished with me, I creep out of the toilet and back to the patch of concrete where my brother is still building our Lego shopping centre around a multi-storey carpark. I wipe my eyes and try to smile at Frank as I sit down ever so gently, trying not to put pressure on my bottom.

'Did Daddy hurt you?' he whispers.

I try to lie and say he didn't hurt me, but my eyes tell a different story. 'I deserved it,' I assure him.

'No, you didn't,' he says. 'No one deserves that.'

I shake as I cry. Frank presses his favourite toy car into my hand, as if it will fix all my troubles.

'Do you want me to kiss it better?' he asks, mimicking Mum's cure for a grazed knee.

I shake my head and force a laugh. Instead of kissing it better, Frank runs inside and grabs me a pillow to sit on. We stay outside playing with his cars for the rest of the afternoon. The pillow didn't make the pain in my bottom go away, but it did make me feel loved and cared about.

This is the memory I come back to when my job feels thankless, when I need to put Frank's needs before my own, when my brother is being an annoying little brother and I need strength and patience. This is the memory that defines my purpose.

JENI

After the school fete, it took Dad months to hang up the painted tiles Mum had made him buy us. To him, they were a sign of Mum's disobedience, a reminder of her strength, a crack in his control over her. To me, they were a happy memory of a day my mum shined bright.

My abuse didn't happen in a vacuum. It happened before a school fete, behind the closed doors of my father's respectability.

CHAPTER EIGHT

The Year of the Lodger

JENI

In the Haynes household, 1980 was 'The Year of the Lodger'. This was the year when Sheila started staying over at friends' houses, and with her church group, every weekend, and only sleeping at home Sunday to Thursday. Dad made nasty comments to her – and the rest of the family – calling her a 'lodger' and referring to her church group as 'The Cult'. Sheila spent most of her weekends at the fellowship centre she had joined, leaving me to sleep alone in our room – and giving Dad full access to abuse me. For the entire Year of the Lodger, Dad would attack me every weekend, either in my bed or out in the garage where he performed his ritual. It was a year of relentless rapes, assaults and buggery. I hated every second of it.

The only thing that gave me the tiniest bit of comfort was knowing that Sheila was happy and safe. She was getting out in the world, meeting new people, making friends and finding the structure we lacked at home. Living with Dad was chaos. He was like a thunderstorm, always on the verge of striking lightning. Meanwhile, Sheila's church was stable and warm, and the members showered her with gifts and praise. The people there were quite touchy-feely, unlike Mum who was never a 'huggy' person, and Dad who was to be avoided at all costs. Of course, Sheila loved church. I didn't blame her. The church was an escape for her. She started quoting bible verses, praying often and constantly reminding us that Jesus loved her. Sheila was a sponge and soaked up the perspective of the church.

I knew Sheila was upset that the family didn't show an interest in her faith – and that Dad openly mocked her for it – so in February I agreed to join her for the Saturday night service. Sheila told me she was thrilled I was coming along, and I welcomed any time I could spend with my sister. That's the only reason I went. But when a kombivan picked us up from home, Sheila promptly started talking to her friends and ignored me. I felt alone and totally out of place.

The church itself was intimidating – a long building with a low roof that felt more like a school hall than a place of worship. There weren't any stained-glass windows, statues of Christ or even pews. Instead, there were rows of the kind of metal fold-up chairs you'd find at a conference centre. The compound included two bunk houses: one where the men slept and another for the women.

The men and women, and girls and boys, were separated into groups on arrival. The men wore suit pants and long-sleeved shirts, and the women wore dresses that grazed their shins. I spent most of the service looking at the people instead of listening to what the priest was saying. The one sentiment I remember the church drumming into me was that children were perfect until the age of twelve. They didn't explain what happened after kids turned twelve, but I remember hearing someone say the only way to touch perfection again was to 'be' with a child under the age of twelve. I didn't understand what the words meant but, looking back, they are chilling.

After the service, I was introduced to the matriarch of the group, a woman Sheila called Aunty. She had beautiful skin and piercing eyes. I was ten, and to me she seemed impossibly old, but she was probably only in her sixties.

Aunty took an interest in me and ushered me into a private room at the side of the church. It's here where she asked me a question I'd never been asked before. 'I've never seen you smile or heard you laugh, child. Why are you so unhappy?'

JUDAS

I'm up. Finally, a direct question! It's my time to tell. I run so fast to become the front runner that I have to skid to stop myself from

tripping over. I sit beside Aunty and look into her caring eyes. I pour it all out; I tell her all the things Dad does to confuse, scare and hurt me. I tell her about the games and the punishments, the threats and the terror, the blood and the tears. And the pain, oh the pain. Our body shakes as I speak, but I don't stop.

I'm a young boy. I don't realise I'm telling a tale of horrific abuse; I'm just explaining my unhappiness. I don't know the words for rape, buggery or incest, so I try to describe how Dad puts things inside our body – the silvery sticks, the hammer, the thing between his legs.

The words burn as they pour out of me, but it's a necessary singe and I welcome it. Burn, baby, burn.

Aunty holds me tightly and listens while I tell the story I've been longing to tell. Then she stands up and takes my hand, pulling me to my feet. 'I can help,' she says. I feel dizzy with relief.

But Aunty didn't help. She put me in more danger. She handed me over to a man I knew as Brother Simon, telling him I was 'already broken in'. He took me to his room and did the same thing Dad does to me. The same thing I told Aunty about. The same thing she said she could help me with.

My words fell on silent ears. Aunty lied.

JENI

After I disclosed my abuse to Aunty, I tried once more to get help in 1980. It was a Monday and I shakingly walked into my class with Mr Teller, aching from a particularly brutal weekend with my father. I'd had enough. I couldn't focus on the work in front of me. Instead, I was fixated on a screwdriver the groundsman must have left on a table next to me. It was just sitting there, like it was a normal tool, not a torture device. I knew better. My eyes were glued to the screwdriver all lesson.

When the bell rang, I grabbed the screwdriver from the table. I hung back until all the other children had left the room. Mr Teller was putting things into his briefcase when I approached him. 'Sir,' I said, and he turned to look at me.

'My dad does this to me,' I said, flipping my school skirt up, pulling my underpants down and thrusting the handle of the screwdriver into my bottom.

I'll never forget the look on Mr Teller's face. It was an expression of pure horror and disgust, but that horror and disgust was directed at me – not my dad. 'You dirty, despicable child. How dare you say such a disgusting thing about your dad,' he said.

I took the screwdriver out of my pants and dropped it on the table with a clunk. Mr Teller didn't say anything else. He didn't ask me if I was okay. He didn't send me to the school nurse to be checked over. His words ran over in my head, 'dirty', 'despicable', 'disgusting'. Mr Teller's response to my admission confirmed everything my dad had told me. I was nothing.

From that day on, Mr Teller turned me into his punishment child. Every time a student was naughty in class, he would tell them to go and sit next to me. They'd hit and kick me under the table. Mr Teller didn't intervene. Why would he? I didn't matter.

JUDAS

It's my fault. If only I were clearer, if only I demonstrated better, if only, if only. I blame myself for not being able to get help. That's my job and I failed. I don't know if I can try again. I want to resign, but that's not an option. There's no escape.

Dad's net wraps itself around me and, the more I struggle, the tighter it gets. I can't find a way out. I'm drowning, and no one is coming to save me. I wave my hand in the air and scream for help.

The words, they burn, but I can't get people to hear them.

JENI

Later on in 1980, I very reluctantly returned to the church with Sheila. The kombivan arrived at our house on a Saturday, and I tried to protest, but for some reason no one ever heard me when I said no. Sheila wanted me to go, and my mother didn't argue, so that was that. We were spending the night at the compound, and I hadn't even had a chance to pack a change of clothes.

I spent the entire time at the church on high alert. I was hyper-aware of every adult who came near me and steered well clear of Brother Simon and Aunty. I still had no words or voice to speak out, and Judas had given up.

I had breakfast in the concrete courtyard and played a ball game with the kids in my age bracket. I was ten, so still considered 'perfect'. Sheila was two years older, at twelve, and had been since she joined the church group, so she was above the threshold.

I was standing outside the kitchen when I first saw this woman. She had long blonde hair down to her waist and she was hysterical. Her hair shook as she cried. I knew the woman was somehow involved with Brother Simon, but I didn't know who she was. The other ladies were hugging her and stroking her hair, but she was inconsolable. 'My little girl is gone. They went too far and now my little girl is gone,' she sobbed. I somehow knew she was talking about her six-year-old daughter. Something in her voice told me that her little girl hadn't wandered off. This wasn't a passing loss; it was a permanent one. I instinctively knew the little girl was dead. She was gone and she was never coming back.

'You can have another one,' someone tried to reassure the woman. The remark only made her cry harder. While the women crowded around the grieving mother, the men surrounded Brother Simon. They weren't comforting him in the same way; it was almost as if they were reassuring him. That moment stood out to me because I could see two people were upset, but they weren't allowed to be upset together.

I went home that afternoon and confided in my mum about the little girl who'd gone from the church. Mum tried to tell me that the little girl had moved away, but that's not the kind of 'gone' I was talking about.

* * *

I never wanted to go to the church again. I was terrified of Brother Simon and couldn't stop thinking about what had happened to the little girl – and what could happen to me. But Sheila told me

people wanted her to bring me and Frank with her. Every Sunday, Sheila would come home with gifts – clothes, toys and an eyeshadow palette that I thought made her look like a clown – and, of course, I was jealous. While Sheila was having fun and being showered in presents, I was being brutally raped and sodomised in the garage, the toilet, my own bed.

So, when Sheila cried and begged me to come back to the church with her one particular weekend, I gave in. The kombivan picked us up on Friday night, and, like clockwork, Sheila started talking to her friends and ignored me as soon as we put our seatbelts on. For the rest of the weekend, I ceased to be Jeni; I was Sheila's little sister.

We stayed in the last bedroom at the front of the women's block. A lady gave me a full-length petticoat nightie to wear to bed. It was made of the softest silk I'd ever felt, and I immediately began to twirl around in it. The woman told me not to swing about, but that was like putting a piece of candy in front of me and telling me not to eat it. The woman got annoyed, pulled the dress off me and sent me to bed naked for being naughty.

Lying in the foreign single bed, I fell asleep. When I woke up later in the night, I felt like I was in a weird trance. I could hear music playing in the distance and I was drawn to it, like a robot programmed to seek out sound. I walked through the back door of the church and hid behind the metal chairs. I crouched down, listening to the singing, until one of the adults found me.

The church was meant to be a place of healing and peace, but for me it was the opposite: a nightmare of hurt and distress. The next morning, I was taken to a sitting room of sorts and left on my own. It was then that Brother Simon came for me. I tried to fight him, but it was no use.

I'm convinced I was targeted because I was already, as Aunty put it, 'broken in'. Brother Simon knew I was being assaulted at home, and that my dad was getting away with it, so he thought he could too. And he did.

I wanted to go home. The saddest thing is, I knew my dad would rape me at home, but at least I knew I could cope with that. I had a

system in place, I had an army of workers on standby, I had Symphony singing to me. I could survive Dad's attacks because I knew I was protecting my family. What happened at the church didn't make any sense to me. And so, I swept it under the carpet and tried not to think about it. I focused on what really mattered: protecting Sheila from Dad and keeping everyone alive. As ridiculous as it seems, being raped at the church felt like small stuff compared to what I was dealing with at the hands of my father.

The hardest part of thinking back on that night is worrying if my sister knew anything about it. As a kid, I tried so hard to protect Sheila from harm, and she was so happy with the church. I truly believe that Sheila wasn't abused at the church because at twelve years old, she was too old.

* * *

✳ *I know it has been hard to read up to now. I wish I could say the worst is over, that things get better from here on in, but I can't. All I can do is remind you that I'm okay and you're okay. What happened is awful – beyond that – but in this moment, right now, I'm safe and I hope you are too. Take a deep breath and look after yourself. The next sections are tough, so if you have any sort of abuse trauma and have struggled up to this point, please stop and pick up my story at the star on page 161. – Jeni*

CHAPTER NINE

The Breakdown

JENI

The Year of the Lodger – 1980 – was also the year that my MPD failed. It didn't go away, but the system broke down in an unexpected way and we didn't know how to fix it.

It was a kink in the chain, a shortcut in the circuit, and – for Symphony – it was the worst year of her life.

SYMPHONY

My favourite cat Tawny is buried under the honeysuckle bush at the back of the garden. It had been her favourite place to sleep, so it seemed fitting that it should be her final resting place. Sometimes I like to hide in the bush and talk to Tawny, even though she never answers back. I feel safe under the honeysuckle bush because it's so large and dense. I'm invisible to the outside world and – most importantly – to Dad.

Because the honeysuckle bush is a safe space, we take our guard down and a little girl becomes the front runner. She loves the feel of the honeysuckle petals and the scent of the flowers. The little girl is reading a book in the afternoon sun. Her legs are crossed and she's gently rocking back and forth. She's so engrossed in the story, she doesn't notice when Dad comes and sits down next us.

Before she has a chance to react, Dad forces us backwards and pushes his hand into our underneath. When she hears Dad undoing his zipper, she fights and struggles and pushes him away.

'Not on Tawny's grave, please don't hurt me on Tawny's grave,' she begs.

Dad laughs as though we've said the funniest joke in the world. 'Tawny wouldn't have died if you hadn't been such a dirty little girl. You killed Tawny by being a naughty, disobedient child,' he says, smiling wide and pushing 'it' inside our body.

None of my usual tactics work. I try listing all the boys' names I know in alphabetical order. I try thinking of all the colours I know that start with the letter 'P'. I try to count numbers in the inchworm game I learnt in maths class. I sing, and I sing, and I sing. But nothing works. Each alter has a different coping strategy that works for them, but no matter how hard I try, I can't get the little girl to calm down.

I'm waiting for the little girl to say the magic words and tell us that she can't take anymore. We have dozens of alters lined up in the tunnels ready to replace her. It's like that game you play in school where you pass the ball over your head to the person behind you and then run to the back of the line. When the front runner reaches their limit, we tap someone else on the shoulder and send them in to take over. Of course, no one ever volunteers to take the abuse. They are all drafted by Little Ricky, depending on what the job requires.

The little girl wouldn't have been the front runner if we knew Dad was lurking around. He's attacking her and she's begging, screaming, crying for him to stop. Not on Tawny's grave. She's distraught and we realise she can't cope. I'm sitting beside her and singing to her, and there's yelling coming from behind me. Little Ricky is having a loud discussion about pulling her out. I tell the little girl to hang on, someone's coming. But she can't hang on. The terror takes over and she turns to run towards the door. With the force of her leaving, I am pushed into the body. The little girl slams the door behind her.

I'm stuck. I know the magic words to open the door, but I don't realise the same rules apply to me. I'm usually the one sitting beside the front runner in the control room, comforting them and singing to them. I'm usually in the head, not the body. To tolerate the abuse I've faced, I had to make myself blind. I don't have eyes, so I don't have to look at Dad. I don't have a nose, so I don't have to smell his

sweat. I don't have tastebuds, so I don't have to taste his skin. I'm essentially disabled for my own sake.

There are sixty steps from the honeysuckle bush to the outside toilet. When Dad leaves me lying in agony on Tawny's grave, I know I need to make my way to the toilet to clean myself up and go inside. Between the honeysuckle bush and the back door, I grow a pair of eyes. In the space of sixty steps, I learn how to see and interact with the world again.

For the next year, I'm trapped in the body. I talk to the alters through a closed door. They sit on the other side of the door and feed me information to keep me alive. They tell me what to do and try to help as best as they can. When Dad rapes me, they comfort me, and I sing to myself. Except now that I'm in the body, I'm actually singing out loud. For the first time, people can hear me singing, 'Stop, stop, stop.' They see the bruises I can no longer hide. They smell the soiled underwear I'm forced to wear because I'm too afraid to use the toilet at home. They look at me quizzically when I start listing boys' names in alphabetical order. But no one questions my odd behaviour. No one asks me if I'm okay. No one steps in to save me. I'm all alone.

Normally, there would be fifty people lined up every night, ready to step in when Dad rapes us. But I'm on my own now. I go to bed at 8 pm and get an hour's sleep before Mum goes to bed and Dad sneaks into my room to begin his nightly ritual. He takes me outside to his garage and forces me to lie on a table. He then rapes and sodomised me for hours. When it's over, around 3 am, he dismisses me with 'get out of my sight'. I stagger back to my bed only to have him come to bed with me. It starts all over again, over and over, night after night with no let up. Dad leaves my bed at 6 am and if I'm lucky I go back to sleep until I have to get up for school at 8 am.

The alters are still being triggered. When Dad forces us to tell him how dirty we are, Zombie Girl comes to the door, but she can't come into the body. She can't take away the pain, or the exhaustion, or the humiliation.

I'm lonely. I can talk to the alters through the door, but I can't play with them or read a book together. Even if I could, I'd be too

exhausted. I'm hyper-aware every second of the day; trying to deal with Daddy, trying to make sense of the real world, trying to stay awake and alert at school. I try, and I try, and I try.

* * *

I start to crave weird things. I can't stop thinking about eating a smartie sandwich. I think about it so much, I can taste it. Two slices of white bread with a thick layer of butter and a handful of smarties lined up in perfect, pristine rows. I ask Mum to make me one, but she won't. For the whole of 1980, Mum doesn't buy a single packet of smarties.

I love the smell of navel oranges, but when I actually bite into one, it tastes like dirty dishwater. I'm craving weird things, but I'm also being sick all the time. I can't eat breakfast, lunch or dinner because I feel so nauseous. When I do eat, I throw up immediately. There's nothing in my stomach, so I throw up acidic bubbles. I can't work out how the bubbles are getting inside of me for me to vomit them up. It's a mystery.

Mum puts her hand on my stomach where my appendix is and asks if it hurts there. It doesn't. And so, I'm sent to school. If it's not appendicitis, it must be nothing. If Mum actually asked me where the pain was in my stomach, I would tell her it was quite low, between my hips and behind my belly button. I'd tell her it felt like my tummy was getting heavy. I'd tell her the two lumps on my chest hurt as well, that they've grown and have started to feel funny when they rub against my school shirt. I'd tell her that I think there is a worm inside me. I don't know how the worm got there, but every so often I feel it move against my tummy from the inside. Sometimes, when I'm lying on my back, I see the worm lift up parts of my belly. I'm scared. I imagine they'll need to stick a large hook down my throat to catch the worm and pull it out of me.

I'm lying on my side when my dad comes into my bedroom to rape me. He bends down to get on top of me, but he stops when he sees the worm move inside my tummy. He stares at my stomach,

unflinching. Then he puts all of his weight on my belly and presses down with all of his might. He pushes so hard I'm sure the worm inside me will burst under the pressure. But in the morning, I feel the worm wriggling inside me again and I know it's still alive.

The next Saturday, Dad pulls me into the kitchen late at night. He hands me a drink and I shake my head to refuse it. The glass has fume lines coming out of it, like a bottle of poison in a cartoon. It smells and I don't want to drink it. Dad puts his hand over my nose and forces the drink down my throat. I can't do anything but swallow it. My eyes water and my throats burns, but the worm still wriggles the next day.

On Sunday, Dad grabs a knitting needle from Mum's sewing bag and forces me to lay back as he shoves it inside me. He pushes it hard into the hole that doesn't heal between my legs. I cry and beg him to stop, but the crying and begging makes him push deeper. I can't tell if he's angry or excited. When he stops stabbing me with the knitting needle, he replaces it with himself and thrusts so hard into me I'm sure he's going to tunnel through my stomach and pierce my throat.

On Tuesday, Dad grabs his belt and lashes my stomach with the metal buckle. He puts on his lace-up black shoes and kicks my stomach. He folds his hand into a fist and hits my stomach. He's vicious. I faint from the pain.

On Thursday, I feel a grinding pressure in my tummy. It rumbles into the night and the following day, like a washing machine stuck on tumble dry. I start to bleed from my underneath. On Saturday, we go to the school so Mum and Dad can vote in the 1980 election. Across the road, the church is having a cake stall. I can smell the orange and poppyseed cake from a mile away and it makes my tummy churn. I try to get away from it, but the smell chases me up the street. Then Mum buys it, so the smell follows me home. I'm sick all afternoon. I escape to the garden, but it hurts to sit down. My private parts feel hard, like something on the inside is pushing down on them. I'm sure my insides are going to fall out, so I tense every part of my body to keep myself whole.

On Sunday, I wake up in total agony. The washing machine in my stomach has become a corkscrew, twisting its sharp tip inside me. It's terrifying. I don't know what's happening to me and I feel dizzy with confusion and pain. The only thing I know is that I've got to do whatever I can to keep my insides from falling out. I hide in the long grass behind the garage so I can focus on staying alive.

Dad comes outside to mow, and by mow, I mean, he pulls the ripcord on the mower a few times until the motor splutters and he swears under his breath. There's a horrible sensation in my underpants, like they're full and wet, so I try to stand up. When I do, I see the grass beneath me is black. I'm bleeding through my underpants and all over the ground. There's so much blood. But it's not just blood, it's wee and poo too. My insides are forcing themselves out of me and dragging everything else with them.

I see my dad in the corner still swearing at the mower and I call to him to help me. 'Don't come crying to me when you brought this on yourself,' he yells back.

A realisation flashes in my mind. For the first time, I put two and two together. I wonder if what is happening to me – the worm, the blood, the corkscrew – has something to do with Dad's punishments. As quick as the thought enters my mind, it leaves and is replaced once more with terror.

It seems to take Dad an age to get to me. He's walking in slow motion. When he finally reaches me, I show him the blood. It's everywhere. My underpants are soaked in different colours of red, with layers of blood staining the fabric like surf lines in the sand. Blood on top of blood on top of blood. I'm sitting with my legs crossed and Dad kneels down in front of me. I'm desperate for him to do something to help me. He assaults me instead. 'I always knew you were a filthy, dirty thing,' he says, walking away.

I sit in the same spot, frozen in shock for the rest of the afternoon. I become a rock and float above my body. As the sun begins to dim, Dad opens the back door and yells at me to come inside for dinner. It sounds like he's a thousand miles away.

I don't know where I am. All I know is that I'm in excruciating pain and that I'm cold. So cold.

The next thing I feel is Dad's hand slapping me across the face. 'Go to the toilet and clean yourself up,' he spits. 'Look at the mess you've made.'

The blood feels warm running down my leg as I stumble to the outside toilet. When I get there, I can't find a cloth and don't have the strength to turn the tap on. I have to clean myself using the water in the toilet and toilet paper. Dad opens the door and throws something at me. He slams the door shut before I realise what it is. He's thrown me a pair of clean underpants.

I'm desperately trying to clean myself – especially Dad's fingermarks on my thigh – but I'm so weak and I'm still bleeding. I keep rubbing at the bloodstain on my thigh. The fingermarks are a sign of Dad's cruelty and callousness, and I can't stand them being on me. Nothing else matters, except getting rid of the fingermarks. Fat fingers, everywhere.

I sit on the toilet. The corkscrewing gets faster and the pressure gets harder. I stuff my mouth with toilet paper to stop myself from screaming. I feel the muscles of my private parts rip open. My insides force themselves out of me and land with a plop in the toilet. Minutes later, there's more ripping and another plop. The corkscrewing stops and the cramping starts. I'm too scared to look in the toilet, too terrified to flush it. I'm in so much shock, I can barely breathe. I'm hyperventilating.

When I try to climb the stairs to get inside, I'm so faint, I almost have to crawl. I've cleaned myself as best as I can, but I'm still dirty. My private parts are sticky. Dad is standing at the back door so I have to squeeze past him to get inside. He grabs at my crotch as I do, and I feel even dirtier.

I force myself to eat a mouthful of dinner and put myself to bed. I desperately want to have a bath, but Dad forbids me. I curl into a little ball and fall asleep, until Dad comes into my bedroom. He attacks me over and over again. I'm too weak to fight him off. It feels like every ounce of blood has poured out of me and my body is

struggling to replace it. Dad hits me and tells me to put some effort into it. I realise that he enjoys it when I push back, when I cry, when I beg him to stop.

For the next few weeks, I live in a thick fog. People talk to me, but it's like they're at the end of a long tunnel. There's no light at the end of this tunnel, just more darkness.

JENI

If there's anything I could go back and change in my life, I would have looked in the toilet that Sunday night in 1980. I wish with all my might that I had looked. Maybe I could have saved my baby. Maybe I could have saved myself.

I didn't realise I had given birth to a baby until decades later. During my interviews with the police in 2010, the detective pieced everything together and told me that my insides hadn't fallen out, I'd had a baby. That Sunday night in 1980, I was eight months pregnant. I had a gynaecological examination that showed I had given birth at least once, and the detective found that I had fallen pregnant five times before I turned eleven. If we add those between eleven and fourteen, I'd had seven pregnancies before my dad was finished with me.

Four pregnancies ended in miscarriages. Of course, I didn't know any of this then. I remember four occasions when a lump of jelly came out of me. It was as wide as a one-dollar coin and as thick as four one-dollar coins stacked on top of each other. Inside the jelly was what looked like a coiled-up piece of paper: a foetus. I also went through another birth process – with the same corkscrewing sensation – when I was eight, but it was much earlier on in the pregnancy. And Dad beat another baby out of me in 1982.

When I reflect on what happened that Sunday night in 1980, I feel sick, and sad, and horrified at my father's actions. My dad knew very well I was giving birth to his baby and he didn't do a thing, he didn't take me to hospital, he didn't help me. Instead, he raped me hours after I'd given birth.

I desperately wanted to have Dad charged for the murder of my 1980 baby, but the gynaecologist who examined me refused to give

evidence that I had been pregnant and given birth. And without the baby's body, there wasn't much in the way of evidence. When I made my statement to the police, I had to recount every single rape individually. I couldn't just say my dad raped and buggered me every Saturday and Sunday night during 1980. I had to pinpoint the dates and details, which was difficult when they all blurred into one long nightmare, a never-ending ritual of suffering. We couldn't identify exactly which of his rapes during early 1980 resulted in my pregnancy.

When I realised Dad wouldn't be held accountable for the murder of my baby, I wanted to at least have him charged with raping me on the Sunday night in 1980 after I'd just given birth. And I did. My statement read:

> Later that night Dad came and lay in my bed. I was vaguely aware of hands pulling at my underpants and removing them and then I felt something sausage shaped rubbing along my genitals. I could smell my dad, and his stench of burning Bakelite seemed to choke me. He pulled his arms around my upper body and held me tightly. I felt too weak and ill to make any attempt to pull away from him. I felt heavy and yet limp at the same time. As Dad moved, my body was moved by him and I could feel myself being rocked and I could feel thrusting over my genitals. I felt my body sinking and I was unable to do anything to stop it. When I woke up the next morning, my underpants were gone and my genitals were throbbing.

Looking back, it's hard for me to understand how no one knew I was pregnant. My tummy was swollen and hard, I was vomiting all the time and I was craving a smartie sandwich, for goodness sake. Why didn't my mum notice when she felt my appendix? Why didn't the teachers at school notice when my uniform became visibly tighter? I imagine it had something to do with the consciousness of the time: hear no evil, see no evil, stay out of other people's business, children should be seen and not heard. But at the time it confirmed

everything my dad had told me: I was worthless, no one cared about me, I deserved everything I got.

Dad knew. I know he did because in the September of 1980, when I would have been seven months pregnant, Dad decided to sell the house and move back to England. He gave Mum every excuse under the sun for why he wanted to leave Australia: he was sick of the heat, he didn't like his job, he hated the people, he missed his family. But really, the walls were closing in on him and the only choice he had was to run. He must have been sure someone would notice I was pregnant, and that he would be found out for the monster he was. If only they did.

As my belly grew bigger, Dad became more stressed and panicked to leave. He took his frustrations out on me. Every time someone came to look at the house and decided not to buy it, he attacked me because it was my fault we had to move. It was my fault he raped me and got me pregnant.

Decades later in 2015, I was drawn to walk into a Catholic Church I was passing by in Brisbane. I sat in a pew and talked to Jay. God had let me down more times than I wanted to remember, and Jay had saved my life more times than I can remember. Naturally, I wasn't interested in talking to God, but I was happy to talk to Jay in my head. I was having a hard day and had been thinking a lot about the baby I'd lost. Specifically, I'd been thinking about the fact that I pooed on the baby after it was born in the toilet. I didn't know whether my baby was alive or dead, but the thought that I'd pooed on her was horrifying. I was sure the baby was a girl. I was telling Jay about how distraught I was about this thought, and he spoke to me, in his calm, clear American accent. 'I've got Gemma, she's all right, she's with me,' he said, giving the baby I never knew a name she never had.

In that moment, sitting in the church pew, Jay gave me more peace than I'd ever had before in a place of worship. My baby's name was Gemma, and she was okay, she was with Jay. He told me so.

It sounds unbelievable, but after my silent conversation with Jay, the priest came to check on me because I looked so distressed.

I told him I was okay, and he said something so profound, I've never forgotten it. 'God gave you a gem and, whatever's happened, you still have that gem. It's still a part of you.' It was as though the priest was confirming I'd had a baby and that her name was Gemma.

AMBER

Recognising my pregnancies, miscarriages and the murder of my babies was the first step towards healing from my losses. I've always wanted a huge Osmond-style family, and Dad stole that from me. He murdered, in one way or another, my babies; Erik, Rosemary, Cherry-Lynn, Gemma, Bobby, Carrie-Anne and Jessie. Thank god the girls never grew to be abused by him, 'cos I would have killed him. My dad murdered my motherhood, and I only got to reclaim it by naming my babies in 2022. But make no mistake I am a mother and I cherish my babies.

MUSCLES

Symphony has the key. She's the only one who can open the door. For a year, we've sat on the other side, whispering words of encouragement and telling her what to do. No matter how hard we try, we can't break down the door. We try to take off the hinges. We kick it. We try to start a fire. But we can't get through to her.

Then, Christmas comes early in 1980. It's a day in December. Dad finds us sitting on the toilet. It's the same story. Usually, the Boy Who Doesn't Breathe would take over, but our MPD is broken. Symphony chokes and splutters and passes out, falling off the toilet, onto the concrete floor. Dad picks her up and sticks it back in her mouth, thrusting in and out until hot liquid burns the back of her throat.

Symphony wipes her mouth with the back of her hand. 'Can I go now?' she says.

The world stops. She's said the magic words: *Can I go now.* In a split second, I fling open the door and run out to replace Symphony. Erik grabs her and drags her inside to safety.

Dad is oblivious to the mayhem going on inside. He doesn't respond to Symphony's question, but the answer is no. We can't go. Dad shoves his dick back in our mouth and I respond accordingly. This is my moment of glory. I bite down with all my might and refuse to let go, channelling a year's worth of anger and frustration into my jaw. I chew, and I growl, and I gnaw on his dick like a bone. I do everything short of ripping it off. His dick doesn't taste great but the small victory is sweet. While it lasts.

Dad squawks, shakes and hits me, but I keep clenching. He throws me to the ground and spits hatred. It's the same story: 'You are worthless. You are nothing. How dare you bite me?'

The attack that follows is as stinging as his words. Dad smashes my head into the wall underneath the window. I pass out and come to with my head being crunched into the concrete floor. As much as my resistance hurt him, it also turned him on, unfortunately.

But I don't care, I got to unleash my anger and hurt him the way he hurt Symphony. Hearing him howl in pain warms my heart.

SYMPHONY

It all happens so quickly. Before I know it, Erik has his arms around my waist and is carrying me to the other side. Everyone takes their rightful places. Muscles jumps in to fight the good fight. The Boy Who Doesn't Breathe stands by. Zombie Girl recites her lines. All the alters who've been waiting by the door fly out and help me. MPD is working again – hallelujah!

I'm weak. Erik tells me I feel like a paper doll. I'm as thin, vulnerable and fragile as a tissue. All the colour has drained from me and I'm a deathly translucent grey. Erik has built a new room for me. He's filled it with all my favourite things: a picture of Miss Piggy from *The Muppets*, Victorian dolls and Sweep, of course.

Erik lays me on my side in my room and tells me to rest. So I sleep, and I sleep, and I sleep.

CHAPTER TEN

The Apple Pie

JENI

Symphony indefinitely handed over control to Erik, Muscles and Linda. Linda was an incredibly rebellious teenager who hated Dad and thought any man who had to hurt his daughter to make himself feel good was a piece of shit. Linda was, as Sheila would say, hoity-toity. She was blessed with the task of contempt and became a master of eye-rolls and snarky stares. Together, Erik, Muscles and Linda became the front runners and shot-callers, while Symphony worked in the background. They kept her far away from the door.

While Erik, Muscles and Linda were busy taking charge inside my mind, my parents were busy organising our move back to England. In February 1981, we started packing items to ship back. I remember Sheila and Frank were fighting over a blue toy dog they both wanted to play with. They were yelling and screaming at each other and pulling the toy dog back and forth, snatching it out of each other's hands. Dad stormed over, grabbed the toy dog and ripped its head off. He handed one piece to Sheila, and another to Frank. 'Now can we have some peace and quiet?' he snarled, as Sheila and Frank burst into tears. They made more noise crying than they had fighting.

Mum came over to investigate the commotion and found the beheaded toy dog and her distraught kids. 'Richard, how could you? Was that really necessary?' she questioned.

Dad didn't answer. He was blind to the distress he'd caused. I sat rigidly still throughout the whole ordeal, praying Dad wouldn't

notice me and take his frustrations out on me. I looked at the beheaded dog and felt nothing but sympathy. Dad hurt me as easily and with as little care as he destroyed the dog. We were both defenceless victims of Dad's brutality, ripped apart by his violence and tossed to the ground.

HAPPY

Our favourite childhood book is *The Tiny, Tawny Kitten*. We loved it so much we named our cat after it. Our cat looked just like the kitten in the book: ginger and cream and oh-so sweet. The book is a happy memory of Tawny, so it's my job to keep it safe.

I try to argue when Dad says the small Golden Book is too heavy to pack for England, but he rips out a picture of Tawny the tiny kitten and throws the rest of the book in the bin. The other alters cry. The book is destroyed and they're heartbroken! I'm not upset because I know the story lives within us. We can recite the book word for word and imagine every picture of Tawny in our mind. Daddy only took away the physical book, he didn't steal our memories. The joke is on him; he can't throw our happiness in the bin.

JENI

I read a lot of Enid Blyton books growing up, so naturally I believed that all children in England went to boarding school. As you would expect, I was beside myself with excitement to move back to England and be able to escape Dad. I imagined myself making friends, sleeping soundly in a dorm and frolicking in the countryside. It was a very nasty shock when I realised this wasn't the case. In May 1981, we moved to a rented three-bedroom house in Andover, in the county of Hampshire. Instead of the boarding school in the countryside I'd dreamed of, I was enrolled in the local junior school.

With the travelling and the move things seemed better for a while, but monsters don't stop. I was eleven and Dad started raping me again within weeks of our move to Andover. The first time it happened, I unwittingly put myself in the direct path of danger.

Sheila and I were once again sharing a room, and our new beds had wooden bedheads with gaps between the bars that were wide enough for a child's head to push between, but tight enough that it was a struggle to get out. Of course, I tested the limits of physics and got myself stuck. I turned and twisted my body every way possible, but I could not for the life of me get my head out.

I was crying by the time Dad came into the room and found me. 'You have got yourself into a pickle,' he said.

'Can you please help?' I begged.

'I might,' he answered, sticking his hand under my skirt and wriggling his fingers into my underpants.

'No, Daddy, don't.' That wasn't the kind of help I was asking for.

'You are really stuck, aren't you?' he said, convincing me to turn over so he could help me get out.

Once again, his definition of helping was different to mine. Afterwards he said, 'There, all better.'

When I went to the toilet, I was bleeding heavily, and I continued to bleed for days. Not all better. Not all better at all.

From that first new rape in Andover, Dad took any and every opportunity to attack me. When my parents bought a house in the same area – a terraced home at the end of a cul-de-sac on Walnut Tree Road – we moved out of our rental, and I went from my head-trapping single bed to a bunk bed. Sheila chose the top bunk and I accepted the bottom. The bunk beds made a rhythmic thumping sound as they slammed into the wall when Dad attacked me.

One night while abusing me, Dad got his hair caught in the springs of the top bunk. He squawked in pain and took his hand off my mouth to rub the back of his head where his hair had been ripped out. I smiled in the darkness. There was a vicious pleasure in Dad being hurt while he was hurting me so badly.

Losing a chunk of hair didn't stop Dad from attacking me though. He kept thrusting into me until he froze in place and let out an enormous huffing sound. When Dad eventually rolled off me, he switched the light on and examined his head. There was a little bit of blood, which Dad wiped with his fingers and then smeared on

my inner thigh. 'Go to sleep, you filthy thing,' he said, snapping the light off.

Without the luxury of an outside toilet and a garage to keep his secrets, Dad developed a new ritual in England. Each night after dinner, he would send me into the living room and push me into the space between the rolltop desk and the door. Mum, Sheila and Frank weren't permitted into the room. No one could see what he was doing to me because the desk blocked the view. With the confidence of a man who had successfully abused me for eleven years without getting caught, Dad would start his nightly ritual by tucking my school skirt into the top of my underpants. He would remove his leather belt and hit me with the buckle across my back, bottom and genitals. I used to count the number of hits to take my mind off the pain. He never hit me less than six times, usually it was well over thirty. It was only after I began to cry that Dad would push his hand into my underpants and stick his fingers inside me. My tears seemed to signify it was time to rip my underpants off. Dad alternated between raping my bottom and my vagina, but the ritual always ended the same way: with him hitting me on the genitals with his belt buckle, presumably in an attempt to belt away the evidence. After the attack, Dad would send me into the kitchen to dry the washing up and put all of the dishes away. I had to complete the task on my own and no one was allowed in the kitchen until I had finished.

LINDA

Over time, Dad became more violent and more confident that no one would stop him. In the same way, my reaction to the ritual also changed. At first, I cried, whimpered and begged Dad to stop. But once I started to understand that my distress encouraged him, I began to hide my hurt. I refused to cry, beg or apologise (for whatever thing I did wrong to deserve this 'punishment'). As I choked back my tears, Dad turned up his torment. He would beat me over and over again until I finally gave in and cried. Then he would tell me to 'stop pootering'. It was all very confusing.

Confusing and relentless. Dad attacked me every school night – five nights a week – for over two years. That's more than 550 rapes, not including the abuse I endured over the weekends. Being raped and buggered in the living room after dinner became as routine for me as putting my glasses on of a morning.

It's amazing how much damage can be done in a matter of seconds. A nipple twist here. A grope there. A slap in between. The assaults were constant and often came from nowhere. I learned to expect them at any given moment. When they came, it was almost a relief, because I could stop tensing my body in anticipation of pain.

LITTLE RICKY

Is there anything more boring than walking in the countryside? Oh look, some grass. A gate. More grass! Dad used to enjoy taking long country walks in England when he was a teenager, so when we move back there, he starts to force them on us like a trekking tyrant.

Every Sunday morning, we head off as a family and amble along country lanes for hours. There's more traffic than when Dad was a teenager. But Dad isn't in it for the serenity, he enjoys making me suffer. Dad bans me from wearing trousers and refuses to buy me proper walking shoes, so I'm constantly in fear of tripping over. I get cow shit on my school shoes. He makes me walk in front of him, he steps on my heels and kicks me in the back of the legs. He alternates between pushing me onto the road and the verge of grass on the side of the road.

If I die on the side of the road after being hit by a Volvo, I want my gravestone to say, 'Died doing something they loathed.' Surprisingly, Sheila loves walking in the country with Dad. Finally they begin to build a bond.

JENI

It's almost comical how the smallest of things can have the biggest impacts. In mid-1981, an apple pie changed the course of my family's life. It was the summer holidays, and my mum was in bed with a

migraine. She asked Sheila to duck down to the local co-op shop to get something for dinner. Sheila bought some ham, and also the ingredients for an apple pie, having learnt the recipe at school.

When Mum came downstairs in the early evening to make dinner, she discovered that Sheila had beat her to it – and made the apple pie of her own volition. Mum was delighted at Sheila's grown-up initiative and made a fuss over her when Dad got home from work. The apple pie seemed to flick a switch in Dad. He saw Sheila in a completely different light from that moment on. She was no longer just his eldest daughter, who he criticised and belittled for being a 'lodger', she was a human being – and she was becoming a woman. Sheila was thirteen.

I watched as Dad began to build an unhealthy relationship with my sister. At first, when he started to shower Sheila in positive attention, she embraced it and encouraged it.

Part of me is desperate to speak about my complicated relationship with my sister, but the rest of me knows it's not possible. For one, there could be legal ramifications. But more than anything, I'm still fighting to protect my sister. I love Sheila – always have, always will – and I still hope that one day we'll be able to have a relationship as adults.

Dad took pleasure in creating a greater divide between us. One day, Dad started calling me Maggot, which devastated me and delighted him. It started when Sheila found a dead animal covered in white wriggling maggots in our garden.

She screamed and Dad and I came running. She showed the corpse to me and Dad, and then Dad said it reminded him of me. He thought this was hilarious and laughed. 'Oh yes, she really is a dirty maggot,' Sheila said.

I tried to protest the comparison, but my words were drowned out by Dad's laughter. 'Get out of my sight, Maggot,' Dad added, shoving me away from him and smiling at Sheila. There was a look on his face that I didn't recognise. It took me a while, but I realised Dad was seeking Sheila's approval. A grown man was looking at his young teenage daughter for validation. It was repulsive. That same

man, my father, used his other daughter for sexual gratification. He was a monster.

I stared at the flesh-eating maggots on the ground in front of me. I watched them devouring the dead animal and tried to work out how they could remind anyone of me.

From that day on, Dad called me Maggot instead of Jeni, and told Frank and my friends at school to do the same. Later, Frank told me he thought it was a nickname from my middle name, Margaret, but it was really a barbed insult designed to maim me.

That day, an alter called Maggot walked out from the back of our head. She was eleven years old, and every time Dad called us the nickname, she was called to the forefront. When Dad called us Maggot during a beating, she took the punches. When Dad summoned Maggot to his bedroom to be raped, she took the assault. Being Maggot was an awful job.

ERIK

Symphony is on an eighteen-month leave of absence. Other than Maggot, no new alters are created during this time. Instead, people take up new jobs, re-train in different areas and switch roles as needed. I'm in charge. But the game has changed, we're on a whole new level, and none of us know how to defeat the monster.

JANET

In Australia, we had one monster to deal with and three people to protect. In England, we have the same monster and we still have three people to protect – Mum, Frank and Sheila. Still Sheila, always Sheila. I tie myself in knots working to protect the person who Dad was trying to recruit to his side. I desperately try to get in between Dad and Sheila, I make up excuses to keep her from going on walks alone with Dad, and look for bruises when she gets back to see if Dad has broken the pact we made.

Erik and I form a committee. It's called the twenty-four, because there are twenty-four of us. Original, I know. We work around the clock trying to answer one question: 'What the hell do we do with

Sheila?' Our sole mission is to figure out how to keep Sheila safe.

Sheila accuses me of spoiling her fun, of getting in the way of her walks with Dad, of being jealous of the time they spend together.

I'm not jealous of her, I'm terrified for her.

LINDA

Things change under Erik's rule. I developed a rebellious streak. Mum chalked it up to ordinary objectionable pre-teen behaviour, but the truth was far from ordinary. I'd hit a wall. Dad had been raping me for eleven years, non-stop. I'd done the maths. In the first eleven years of my life, there were just three weeks when he didn't rape me. Any wonder I was being objectionable!

JENNY

I started my first term at John Hanson School in September 1981. It was autumn in Andover, but autumn in Andover was very different to autumn in Australia. I felt the cold burrow into my bones. It didn't help that my parents refused to buy me the school blazer. I shivered through my lessons with blotchy purple skin. Not only did my parents' refusal leave me cold, it also marked me as different by my peers and landed me in trouble with my teachers for not being in the full school uniform. I was told I was untidy, given detentions and forced to write lines about the correct uniform policy. I tried to explain to my form tutor that my dad wouldn't buy me a blazer, but they told me to go home and demand one. Ha! When I'd asked Dad to get me a pair of sports shorts to wear under my very short sports skirt, he brutally raped me and then declined anyway. Instead, Dad brought home a pair of scarlet slinky undies and insisted I wear them to my sports lesson. Inevitably I flashed my scarlet undies in front of my classmates and my face turned the same shade as them. I took the detention from my form tutor and didn't ask Dad about the blazer.

Although Dad said he couldn't afford my blazer, he went out of his way to buy Frank a pair of tailored long trousers for school. It was a Saturday and we travelled as a family to Burton's – the local men's

outfitter. On the way we stopped in at Woolworths and Sheila started to feel unwell. She turned pale and fainted under the fluorescent lights of the supermarket. We got Sheila a seat and some water, and I rubbed her hands to try to make her feel better. Dad shoved me out of the way.

When Mum asked Dad to take Frank to get his trousers so she could take Sheila home, Dad refused and insisted on taking Sheila home himself. I helped Sheila up and held her as we walked out of the store. I remember her leaning on me, and Dad rousing at me for not going with Mum. I wanted to be there for Sheila and said so.

We walked home slowly, and I tried to cheer Sheila up with a joke. She began to laugh and then burst into tears. Dad hit me on the head for upsetting her. Once home, Dad took Sheila upstairs to bed and I went to the kitchen to make her a cup of tea with sugar. I headed to our bedroom, but Dad intercepted me in the living room and hit the cup of tea out of my hands. 'I'm looking after Sheila!' he said, leaving me to clean up the spilt tea.

When he came back, Dad dragged me by the hair up the stairs to the bedroom he shared with Mum. There were towels draped across the bottom of the double bed. I trembled in fear. Towels were never a good sign. I begged him to stop and apologised for upsetting Sheila, but my words were wasted on him.

After drawing blood with his belt, Dad flung me onto the bed and positioned me face down so my bum was in the air and my legs were spread. The rape ended with the usual monologue. Dad threatened to kill Mum if I told anyone what a filthy, dirty girl I was.

Dad began to attack me on his towel-covered bed each weekend. He always positioned me so that my genitals were on the towels. I imagine he didn't want to stain the sheets with my blood or faeces. The towels hid the stains – and the sound of water running in the bathroom hid the noise. Dad would turn the tap on in the bathroom before he came to get me, to mask the sounds of the abuse. I came to associate towels and running water with pain and suffering.

LINDA

From the minute I discover the Osmonds' music in October 1981 they became my sanity. I focused on their songs as instructions on how to survive Dad. When I found their album *The Plan* and the amazing lyrics that told me to hang on, to be strong, that I could do it, I heard this as advice on my situation. I used their songs to save my life and sanity. I finally had something in my life to hang on to. The Osmonds were mine and the more my family hated my music, and they did, the more I played their records. Of course, I had a very limited collection so I played them over and over.

Poor Frank has an aversion to Donny Osmond and 'Too Young' to this day. It didn't help Frank when I discovered that if I put the speaker by the grate in the chimney my music could be clearly heard downstairs. Oops. I pressed a speaker by that grate every night and blasted the Osmonds into the ears of the rest of my family. Revenge was sweet. I played my records every night, rocking and telling myself Jay stories. I love the Osmonds and their music. I owe them my life. And so does Dad!

THE JOKER

I rock back and forth in a hypnotic rhythm until my mind leaves my body. If you rock at a certain speed for a certain amount of time, you can fly. It's only outside of me that I can think properly, out of my body Dad can't read my mind so I start to tell the story under my breath. In the story, I tell everything that Dad has done to me, is doing to me. I don't have the right words, but I can tell in my own words and describe the abuse that I've experienced. So night after night I would play my music and tell my story.

In the story, everything that Dad has ever done to me is being done to a combination of Jay Osmond and my Jay, the higher being with an American accent. Poor Jay. I know the story I'm telling is an ugly one, but Jay is beautiful, he can take it.

I know what I'm doing is risky because Dad has convinced me that people will die if I tell. But I'm not *telling*, I'm narrating a story. I'm desperate to work out what the hell is happening to me, so I say

the words out loud to try to make sense of them. We look at the words closely and explore them. We pick them apart and dissect their insides. My dad pushes, and pokes, and stabs, and licks, and burns, and hurts me. But in my story, it's Jay Osmond who gets pushed, and poked, and stabbed, and licked, and burned, and hurt. Poor Jay.

It's an uncomfortable job, telling these stories, but I'm the best at it. I'm the Joker and I can laugh at anything. If we are caught, I can find a way to laugh and pretend I'm not telling. I can turn pain into a joke. I can turn tears into laughter. I spend hours every night rocking back and forth and telling stories to myself. I will continue to tell these stories until 1997.

JENNY

In early 1982, it was clear the relationship between Dad and Sheila was deepening. By this time, Mum had excused the rest of us from the Sunday morning walks. She said walking together as a family of five was dangerous, so if Frank and I didn't want to participate, we didn't have to. And so, the jaunts became a private affair. No one else was welcome to comment, ask questions or talk about the walks. When someone did try to make conversation about their hours-long treks, they couldn't tell us where they'd been or what they'd seen. Sheila claimed to have seen one fox, one rabbit and one squirrel on practically every trip they took. Like the cast of an animated Disney movie.

I was only twelve but I was worried. Sheila had swapped her chorus from 'Jesus loves me' to 'Daddy loves me' and took her status as the favourite child very seriously. Dad purchased treats for Sheila, which he deliberately gave to her in front of me and Frank, who weren't given anything. Mum was disturbed, but like everything in her marriage, she felt powerless to speak up.

Our family was divided down the middle. On one side was Dad and Sheila, on the other was Mum, Frank and me. While Dad spent his Sunday mornings walking with Sheila, the rest of us joined Mum at church.

Mum had walked away from her Catholic faith at Dad's insistence after they got married. But in Andover, Mum joined the St John

Baptist Catholic Church and found the community she so desperately needed. She made friends, developed interests and stepped out of her role as downtrodden wife. It was lovely to watch Mum come out of her shell and return to the capable woman she'd once been. Dad hated it. But he was too busy gallivanting with Sheila to put a stop to it.

Despite my negative experience with the church in Australia, I shared Mum's curiosity about theology and enjoyed learning about Catholicism with Frank. For one morning a week, we had a moment of peace away from Dad's manipulating and menacing.When we set off to a holiday camp on the Isle of Wight during the school break in the middle of 1982, I thought I'd have a two week break from Dad's abuse. Surely, he couldn't attack me in such close confines?

I was terribly wrong.

However, the most terrifying part of the trip wasn't in the bedroom at the holiday camp, it was at the waxwork museum, which documented the history of the Isle of Wight. Here, on a day trip, Dad led me into a 'chamber of horrors' featuring local criminals. In one display, a woman was bent forward with her legs spread wide open and her underpants pushed down. A man stood between her open legs with his zipper open and a pinkish tube sticking out the front of his trousers. The scene depicted the woman being raped from behind by the man. The image electrified and terrified me.

I recognised what was happening as the same thing Dad was doing to me. Like the wax woman, I had been bent over and prodded with a man's pinkish tube. Like the wax woman, I couldn't scream or run away. Like the wax woman, I was a victim of a crime. But I wasn't made of wax. I was a little girl.

Above the display was a sign with words that have stayed with me ever since: 'rape', a 'terrible crime', and an 'outrage'. I was teetering on the edge of understanding what Dad had been doing to me for years, and the realisation was distressing. My head roared with thoughts, possible conclusions and unanswered questions.

I rushed back to the display of Queen Victoria to calm myself down. The wax royal tapped her foot and I tried to match my racing heartbeat with the soothing rhythm.

On the way out of the museum, I pulled on Dad's arm and tried to get him to talk to me. 'What do you want, Maggot?' he said.

I asked him why the display had a sign saying 'terrible crime,' when Dad told me it was punishment for being naughty. Dad socked me in the mouth so hard he split my lip open. He never did answer my question. Instead, when we got back to the holiday camp, Dad took me into my parents' bedroom and beat me with his belt until he was breathless. Then he gasped, 'Assume the position!' I did as I was told.

He replicated the scene perfectly.

When Dad was finished, I questioned him again.

'What we do is between you and me,' he said. 'If you tell anyone, I will kill you. I will beat you until you're dead. Do you understand me, Maggot?'

I nodded.

'Besides, no one would ever believe you, they would put you in a mental home, tie you down and stick electrodes inside you to electrocute you. It'll be your word against mine, and no one will side with you,' he concluded, before leaving me alone with my injuries and thoughts.

I believe I came very close to putting it all together that day at the waxwork museum. Dad's threats silenced my voice, but they didn't silence my mind. Although I was close to making a breakthrough, I still didn't recognise Dad's actions as sex, so I didn't have the words to explain what he was doing to me.

In the waxwork museum's display, the rapist was caught and executed for his crime. In my life, the rapist walked free, and I had to call him Dad.

CHAPTER ELEVEN

To Run Away

JENI

I couldn't tell you when I got my first period because I was almost constantly bleeding from my vagina throughout my childhood as a result of Dad's attacks. When I was taught about menstruation at school I finally had an explanation for some of the bleeding I experienced in my genitals. In the class, I was told that I could not do sports or swim if I had my period. Because I was bleeding almost all the time, I was devastated that I could no longer swim during sports classes. The pool was one of the very few places where I felt I excelled. I was free. I was weightless. After my third week in a row of sitting on the sidelines because of my 'period', the sports teacher pulled me aside and told me to ask my mother to buy me some Tampax tampons so I could use them and still swim.

MUSCLES

There's no way that's going to fit inside me. The Tampax looks like a cotton pinky finger with a plastic applicator that's meant to help with insertion. Yeah, right. I try to insert the tampon, the way Mum told me to, but I have a flashback to the birthday ritual performed by my father. My muscles contract and my body tenses. It's impossible to get the tampon even a centimetre inside me. I try and try, but ultimately fail.

MAGGOT

Mum must tell Dad about my teacher's suggestion because on Saturday he sends Mum, Frank and Sheila into town. Acting completely out of character he draws me a bath with bubbles. I splash about and the water lands on Dad's trousers. He takes them off and his underpants as well. Dad washes me with a cloth and then thrusts his fingers inside me. He tells me that Mum has asked him to do this, to ensure my 'hymen' is broken so I can use tampons.

Dad lifts me out of the bath and shoves me against the wall. He thrusts so savagely; I'm propelled up onto my tiptoes by the force. He thrusts until he goes stiff. At that moment, I push him with all my force, and he falls backwards into the bath. I'm shocked at the success of my idea and then struck by how funny he looks splayed in the bath with his legs in the air. I laugh at him. Then I run out of the bathroom to my bedroom. He chases me and hits me, but I focus on my memory of him scrambling to get up out of the bath.

Later, Dad tells me I should be able to use Tampax from now on, as though I should be grateful, as though he's done me a service, as though he's helped me. Yeah, right.

JENI

When I was menstruating – and also when I wasn't – I could only use sanitary towels, and the blood would sometimes seep through my underpants. One day during the school holidays a girl called Emily invited me out to play. I was wearing a skirt, and Emily lent me one of her tracksuits to wear so I didn't get my clothes dirty.

After playing for hours outside, we went back to Emily's house, and I changed out of the tracksuit. The crotch was stained with blood and my legs were streaked red. I tried to clean up the mess I'd made, but there was simply too much blood. Emily and her mother told me I was filthy. They yelled at me for ruining the tracksuit and being disgusting. 'Get out and never come back,' said Emily's mum.

I did as I was told and walked home crying with bloodstains on my legs. Mum tried to comfort me when I told her what happened.

She explained that sometimes girls can have extremely heavy periods and that I wasn't filthy or disgusting.

The kids at school weren't as kind. Emily released the story and it spread like wildfire through the playground. I was teased, tormented and called 'stinky' for the rest of the year.

The sex ed classes at school didn't help to dispel the myth that periods were dirty. In fact, they didn't teach us much at all. The lessons should have been named 'Procreation 101'. We were taught about the physical process – by cellular division – of making a baby, but we weren't taught anything about the act of sex. We weren't shown any images of penises or vaginas, or given any information that would have helped me understand what my dad was doing to me at home.

While I was learning about menstruation and procreation, I was developing boobs like my peers. The first time I asked my dad for a bra, he stared at my breasts through my school blouse and ran his fingers over my nipples. It felt repulsive – and even worse when he undid the buttons of my shirt and exposed my breasts. He groped me with his clammy hands and then bent his head towards my chest and bit my right breast. He bit it! I was so shocked I couldn't speak. Then he started to suck the breast he just bit. After a while, Dad stiffened and exhaled deeply. His hot breath felt sickly on my bare skin. It was only then that he answered my question about getting a bra. 'We'll see,' he said.

For months, Dad gouged at my breasts every time he passed me in the hall. Other times he would weigh them in his hands and tell me they weren't big enough for a bra yet. When I told him all my friends had bras, he snorted that I didn't have any friends. After months of me begging, and him groping, I bought two bras for myself at a church jumble sale. Dad was furious; he whipped me with one of the bras, scratched my face with the clasps, and raped me as punishment.

The bras became my body armour. They were more like corsets than a regular training bra, and I wore them to bed as an extra layer of protection from Dad.

I tried hard to make friends at school in England. There was a girl called Zoe who I shared many classes and similarities with. We were

both quiet, studious and targets for bullies. Zoe was the only person who didn't call me Maggot, and I was eternally grateful to her for that. I was also grateful when she invited me to sleep over at her house one Friday after school. Her mum, Helen, served fish and chips for dinner, and I devoured my plate with vigour and delight because at home Dad would make sure I always had the smallest portions of food, and anything Sheila liked he would take off my plate for her. Helen served me another plate, and another, and some bread with butter. I ate and ate and ate. I was so very hungry and Helen fed me without making me feel uncomfortable or like a greedy pig. 'Growing girls need lots of food,' she told me. Every time I slept over at Zoe's house, Helen went out of her way to give me lots of snacks and treats. She also sent Zoe to school with extra fruit, cakes and biscuits to share with me.

Zoe invited me to her house at least once a month, and I accepted as many invitations as I could without being labelled a 'lodger' by Dad. One afternoon, Dad banned me from going home with Zoe, claiming that her dad had called him at work and complained that I was a 'nuisance' and 'not welcome' in his home. I told Zoe I couldn't stay over at her house anymore because I didn't want to be a nuisance, but she insisted and issued me a formal invitation.

When I arrived at Zoe's home that Friday afternoon, I apologised to her dad for being a nuisance. He stared at me and then burst into a booming laugh. 'Any friend of Zoe's is more than welcome in this house,' he said, with a warm smile.

After months of sleepovers at Zoe's house, I asked Mum if she could stay at our place for the weekend. Mum agreed and Zoe accepted the invitation.

We were giggling in my bedroom after dinner when my dad pushed his head through the door and told us to go to bed. It was 7.30 pm. We obediently changed into our nighties and Dad came back to watch us take our clothes off. I was naked and Zoe had removed her top and bra. When she saw Dad leering in the doorway, she screamed and wrapped her arms around her breasts. 'Get out!' she shouted at Dad, who stood still and kept staring, before snapping the light off and walking away.

I was more stunned by Zoe's reaction than Dad's behaviour. In a matter of seconds, I learned that breasts were something to cover and protect from Dad. It was a revelation. I just wish Zoe hadn't had to go through the distress of my dad ogling her naked chest.

In bed that night, Zoe told me her dad never came into her bedroom without knocking. She whispered, so my dad wouldn't come back and yell at us.

Our slumber party was cut short when Zoe called her dad the next morning and asked him to come and collect her.

When Zoe left early, she asked her dad if I could stay over at their home the next weekend. 'It's my turn next week. You must come and stay, mustn't she, Daddy?' she said, to nodding agreement.

In the safety of Zoe's house, she told me she couldn't stay another minute in my house. She was terrified of my dad. She called him the 'terrible ogre' and 'the beast'.

The sentiment that Dad was a monster was shared by my other childhood friend Jessica.

Jessica was obsessed with horses, and one Saturday she rode her horse to my home to ask if I could come riding with her. 'Hello, can Jeni come and play please? Can she come riding with me? I've got jodhpurs and a hat for her, so she won't get her clothes dirty, I promise,' she pleaded from atop her horse in the middle of our street where I'd been walking with Dad, Sheila and Frank.

Dad gripped me by the neck and threw a tantrum on the footpath. 'I'm sick of you trying to get around me, you're going nowhere!' he hissed at me. 'And you can get lost!' he spat at Jessica, who turned her horse around and rode away.

Dad dragged me inside by my neck and called me a 'sneaky, manipulative bitch'. He kicked and hit me until I was cowering in the space between the rolltop desk and the door. He slammed me into the wall and struck me again and again.

'Stop, you're hurting her!' Frank cried out. 'Please stop, Daddy, please.'

Dad kept beating me with his fists and his belt until the buckle smacked my face just under my right eye and Frank screamed in

shock. 'Go to your room. I'll deal with you later,' he said to me. It was a promise and a threat.

I didn't wait to be told again. I fled upstairs and hid under my bed. Frank followed me and helped me out of the fetal position. 'Don't worry, Jeni, I won't let him hit you again. I love you,' he tried to comfort me.

'Please don't, Frank. He'll hit you too, I don't want you to get hit,' I said.

Jessica never rode her horse down my street again.

Not long after this, Dad started to tell me that I should kill myself. He said no one in the family wanted me or would miss me, and that he'd be happier if I was dead. 'Do the decent thing and kill yourself,' Dad insisted.

If only he knew how much I wanted to die.

SYMPHONY

My break is over. For eighteen months, I've been sitting on the sidelines with Erik acting as my gatekeeper. I've still been aware of what's happening and I've been having a say in decisions, but I haven't been the front runner. Instead, I've spent my time listening to records and falling deeply in love with the Osmonds and their music.

I've also created an alter named Gabrielle, named after the Osmonds' song of the same name. Gabrielle is like sunshine; warm and otherworldly beautiful. I hand over to her all the traits that make up a lovable girl according to the Osmonds. She gets every bit of my femaleness, my femininity and my sexuality and she takes care of them for me. I stop being a girl and a NotGirl, and I become a boy. It's safer.

Now, I'm back in the body doing my job, and I don't like what I see.

I've had enough. I can't take it anymore. Dad is right; I should kill myself.

The plan is simple. I'll throw myself under the bus Dad catches home. I work out the exact bus, its arrival time, how fast I should

be running and the exact moment I should throw myself under the wheels.

It's the day of the deed and I'm preparing for the end. I put on Donny Osmond's album *Too Young* and steel myself. The song 'To Run Away' is playing and I'm waiting for it to finish so I can lift the needle, stop the record, and kill myself. I can't die in good conscience if I end the song prematurely.

Because of Donny Osmond, I'm late for Dad's bus. I kick myself for screwing up the plan. And I curse Donny Osmond for saving my life. But the lyrics of 'To Run Away' stay stuck in my head. Whenever Dad tells me to go away, to kill myself, to get lost, I repeat Donny's lyrics like a mantra, a rally cry, a prayer. Running away is not a good thing to do.

* * *

By early 1983 things between Dad and Sheila were causing a huge rift in the family. Sheila was the only person who mattered to Dad and he made this obvious in a multitude of cruel and spiteful ways. Dad abandoned the marital bed, sleeping on the sofa in the living room.

Mum was so often away in her own world, I wondered if she even noticed his absence. Maybe she was relieved not to have Dad's sticky, stinky body snoring next to her.

Mum, Frank and I came home one Sunday morning to find Dad ripping the bedroom I shared with Sheila to pieces. The furniture was in disarray and all of Frank's possessions were strewn outside in the hallway. Dad had decided that Sheila should have the small single room and Frank should move in with me. Sheila needed her privacy, he reasoned. Mum was horrified and protested that Frank and I were too old to share a room. It wasn't right.

I don't know what Mum thought was going on. I do know that something changed in Mum after she went to see a new doctor who put her on a different antidepressant medication.

Mum had been medicated for years and described the feeling as like living in a haze. She was always tired; she could have slept

twenty hours a day and still have needed a nap. Doing anything at all – the shopping, cooking, cleaning – exhausted her. She spent most of the day sitting down, staring into space. One day in mid-1983 her doctor changed the medication she was on for depression. The haze cleared almost overnight. The fog lifted. Mum later told me it felt like she'd woken up. Suddenly, she was acutely aware of the tension in her home, the strange actions of Dad towards Sheila, and of the emotional and physical abuse Dad was inflicting on me. Mum remained oblivious to the sexual abuse, though. Dad hid it oh so well through threats, manipulation, and being very careful to ensure my school uniform covered the evidence.

In modern campaigns against child sexual abuse, they always say to look out for changes in your kids, like if they come home from school camp sullen and withdrawn. There was no such campaign for Mum to refer to. But even if there had been, I had been abused for my entire life, so there wasn't a dramatic change for Mum to notice in me. Dad had manipulated Mum into thinking I was a lying hypochondriac, so there was still a veil over her eyes.

And now Dad was behaving so blatantly inappropriately with Sheila, it was like there was a rodeo clown distracting Mum from my abuse. It was heartening for me to see Mum notice the changes in Sheila and begin to try to help and protect her. My physical, sexual and emotional torture at the hands of my dad was obscured by the song and dance that was my dad's interactions with Sheila. This was heartbreaking and soul destroying.

In every other way, Mum became an active participant in the world. I swear she grew taller with her newfound confidence and clarity. Most surprisingly, Mum became affectionate and emotional. She'd never been a 'huggy' person, but I remember a Friday afternoon after she'd started the new medication when Mum tried to stroke Dad's arm and give him a hug. He pushed her away.

'I don't love you and I haven't loved you for a very long time,' Dad declared, before telling Mum that she could remain in the home as his housekeeper. Apparently, she wasn't fit to be his wife or receive any companionship or affection, but Mum could still clean Dad's toilet.

As you would expect, the rejection cut Mum to the core. She cried all weekend. I tried to comfort her and shower her in love. Meanwhile, Dad seemed to enjoy Mum's distress.

LINDA

It's been two days of tears, and Mum's still crying. I spend all weekend validating and reassuring her, trying to calm her down. Nothing works. On the Sunday afternoon I go downstairs to make her a cup of tea. As I'm boiling the kettle, Dad and Sheila are sitting on the sofa together, talking quietly to each other. I snap.

'You disgust me,' I tell Dad to his face. 'Your wife is upstairs crying her heart out and here you are ignoring her. It's disgusting.' Predictably, Dad slaps me.

'And you don't like the truth,' I rebut.

I can see Dad for who he really is – a pathetic excuse for a man, husband and father. I give him a look that tells him as much and take Mum her tea upstairs. She's changed overnight, and so have I.

I've recognised that the things Dad does to me as punishments happen despite my actions, not because of them. The abuse comes thick and fast, regardless of what I do. If I fight, I get hit. If I apologise, I get hit. If I cry, I get hit and Dad gets hard. The attacks aren't punishment, they're entertainment. Dad enjoys every second of it. And for the first time, I realise I don't deserve what he does to me. Unfortunately, this realisation does not permeate the system. It, and my contempt for Dad, become my defining features.

The next day, Dad comes home from work with a huge bouquet of flowers. Finally! An apology and an affectionate gesture for Mum, I think. When Dad walks past Mum and hands the flowers to Sheila, I vomit a little bit in my mouth. 'Here you are Sheila, dear,' says Dad, scanning my face for a reaction.

'P-I-G,' I mouth at him.

JENI

If you ask my mum the reason she divorced my dad, she'll tell you it was over a baked bean and a Ronald McDonald ruler. Now

seeing clearly on her new medication, Mum realised that Dad was intentionally starving me at dinner. During a meal of fish and chips and baked beans, Mum made up her mind about leaving Dad. Before I could take a mouthful of fish, Sheila told Dad how much she liked it. He scraped my portion onto her plate. Then Sheila complimented the chips. Scrape. Lastly, she commented on how nice the baked beans were. Scrape.

I was left with a single baked bean on my plate in a pool of bean juice. It looked as sad and lonely as I felt. Mum noticed the interaction and was appalled. 'What are you doing, Richard? Grow up,' she said, passing me her plate of food. The baked bean was the second last straw.

The final straw was a McDonald's ruler. In the last week of August in 1983, we travelled to London as a family of five. We'd planned to do some shopping and have dinner at a restaurant called Garfunkel's, which was an elaborate salad buffet. The plan was interrupted when Sheila came down with a headache that started after she'd gotten all of the things on her shopping list. Dad insisted we go home immediately, so we made our way to Oxford Circus tube station. At the station, Dad and Sheila walked ahead of us. A man helped Mum carry the heavy shopping trolley down the steep platform stairs. She thanked the man, but didn't point out her husband was just there, failing to help his wife.

At Charing Cross station, Dad decided we were all going to go to the McDonald's restaurant on Villiers Street. He sat at a table for four with Mum, Sheila and Frank, and I sat alone at the table behind them. At the time, McDonald's was selling branded toys with their meals, a bit like Happy Meals today. The toy of the moment was a McDonald's stationery set, including a pencil case, pencil, pen, pencil sharpener, eraser and ruler. Frank asked Dad to buy him a Ronald McDonald ruler. Dad refused. Instead, he went to the counter to order our food and bought the entire stationery set for Sheila. Mum tried to give Frank the ruler from Sheila's set, but she clutched it to her chest.

Frank cried all the way home. Mum tried to console him by telling him it would all be okay. 'It's not going to be much longer, I'm going to get a divorce,' she said. Frank cried harder.

The rift in our family grew and grew until it engulfed us all. When Frank and I went on a retreat to Ascot with the church, Mum came to pick us up on her own. Dad and Sheila were meant to come, but Dad decided he and Sheila would go to Madame Tussauds in London instead.

The plan was for all of us to meet at Waterloo and catch the 5 pm train home to Andover. The 5 pm train came and went, and Dad and Sheila were nowhere to be found. We waited and waited, and Mum got more and more worried. She started to think Dad and Sheila had been injured or killed in London and decided to take the 7 pm train home so we could phone the police and hospitals.

When we finally arrived home after 9.30 pm, the house was dark and silent. There were no lights on inside. Mum opened the front door, walked into the living room and flicked the light switch. Dad and Sheila weren't injured or killed; they were on the sofa in the dark.

Mum went nuclear. I'd never seen anything like it. She screamed and yelled and unleashed a torrent of fury. When Dad stood up, she lunged across the room and clawed his face in rage, leaving deep gouge marks on his cheek.

I smiled with pride.

Dad swore that he and Sheila had just arrived home, and Mum swore back. 'You're a liar,' she roared. We'd watched the 5 pm and 6 pm trains and had been on the 7 pm train. They weren't there. We would have seen them. What we did see, standing in the living room, were two nearly empty cups of cold tea on the table by the television. Dad and Sheila had been home long enough to make tea, drink it and let the dregs go cold.

I still didn't understand what Dad was doing to Sheila was sexual. In the same way, I didn't know what he was doing to me was sexual. I was being punished and Sheila was seemingly being rewarded. He hurt me and loved her. It wasn't the same. But, of course, it was; it was rape, incest and manipulation, just delivered in different packaging. Mine was wrapped in mouldy old newspaper and Sheila's was tied with a neat red ribbon. Either way, they were unwanted

gifts. Symphony tried so hard to understand this. She says Sheila got 'candy and flowers and bears and I got blood, guts and gore'. It seemed so unfair.

Not long after the nuclear explosion in our living room, Mum phoned her mother. I heard Mum say that she had 'come to the end'. It was over. She wanted a divorce. On the other end of the line, Grandma offered support and advice. She told Mum not to leave the family house, and to go to a solicitor. In September 1983, Dad was served divorce papers. I could see some sort of light at the end of the tunnel – a life free from my dad – but it was such a long way in the distance.

From the moment the divorce papers arrived in the letterbox, Dad increased his abuse of me and became even less covert about it. Dad told me that the family was being split up because they wanted to get away from me. He said it was my fault because I wouldn't kill myself. He also forbade me from coming downstairs to the living room or kitchen except for meals. At all other times, I was forced to stay in the bedroom I shared with Frank. Every time Dad went upstairs to go to the bathroom, he attacked me. Because I couldn't go downstairs, I couldn't escape. Not that I really wanted to be in the living room either. The tension hung heavy in the air like smoke from burnt toast.

Mum became increasingly aware of the physical and emotional abuse Dad was putting me through, and the tension between me and Sheila. In Australia, she'd seen that it was common to rely on your extended family if you were having problems so she tried to protect me by seeking help from her family. She wanted to send me to her mother, but Grandma Dixon didn't want me. It seems in England, asking your family to help is not 'the done thing', as Grandma Dixon said. But my extended family agreed to have me. I packed my bag, thinking I was staying for months until the divorce was finalised, and headed to safety. But the safety only lasted a long weekend. On arrival I was told I could only stay the weekend because they didn't want me to have to change schools. After those few days, I was driven back to my very own house of horrors. My mum had

tried to keep me safe but, with no one else aware of the truth of how my father treated me, her plan didn't work.

Mum says the reason she divorced Dad was because of a baked bean and a Ronald McDonald ruler, but really it was so much more than that. Dad's overt favouritism towards Sheila was unfathomable and painful to Mum. It also pissed her off no end.

Disfavouritism

The alignment and division between siblings into parental camps is unfortunately way too common. This favouritism is also highly destructive. Back in 1931, psychiatrist Alfred Adler, a grandfather of modern psychiatry, wrote:

> It is of the utmost importance that neither the father nor the mother should show any favouritism among their children. The danger of favouritism can hardly be too dramatically put. Almost every discouragement in childhood springs from the feeling that someone else is preferred. Sometimes the feeling is not at all justified; but where there is real equality there should not be an occasion for it to develop ... Children are very sensitive and even a very good child can take an entirely wrong direction in life through the suspicion that others are preferred.

Despite Adler's warning favouritism is rife in modern families. The incidence of favouritism, depending on the study, ranges from 48 per cent to 67 per cent i.e. over half of families allow this insidious force to wreak its havoc.

No one wins, not even the favourite – although it might seem like they do for a period of time. Favouritism is the worst form of spoiling a child. It is one thing to feel loved unconditionally, just for being, as all children should be. It is entirely another to be preferentially treated on an ongoing basis, for no good reason. This

sends a different message entirely. This message is, 'you are better than other people and they do not deserve your consideration or respect.' The second part of this message is particularly problematic as these children may grow up to feel entitled at the cost of the rights of others.

Disfavouritism, as it is called, which Jeni experienced an extreme version of, caused different, additional damage from her sexual abuse. You might think that disfavouritism and abuse go together, but not necessarily. I have not infrequently treated children who were abused *and* were the favourite. While the opposite of Jeni's story, these victims, confusingly, often have a better relationship, in other respects, with the abuser than they have with their other parent. The other parent not only fails to protect their child, but is completely disengaged such that they have no real connection to the child. Worst of all, the other parent is not only aware of the abuse, but welcomes it, as it takes their partner's unwanted attention off them. At the same time, they are often jealous of the attention their child is getting from the abuser. Yes, very screwed up, but that is the fullness of the dysfunction one typically sees in these families.

The main casualty of favouritism, that is a loss for the favourite as much as any sibling, is the loss of the relationship between the siblings. They compete rather than collaborate. Siblings do this to a degree anyway, but favouritism brings a mean edge to it as the disfavoured children fight desperately for parental recognition. As I will come to in a moment, self-esteem is built on parental recognition and children need it like they need oxygen.

Siblings in families where favouritism is obvious have greater conflict with each other as the favourite lords their status over the others. This is a perfectly normal thing for children to do, without parents who teach them otherwise. This in turn results in anger towards the favoured sibling that is amplified by the anger the child has for the parent for favouring, unfairly, their sibling. Rather than express this anger to the parent, and risk further alienating them, this anger is directed at the favoured sibling. The favoured

sibling, acutely aware of the protection provided by their superior status, responds in kind and things deteriorate further. This is not happening because these are bad children, this is how perfectly normal children will respond. Some favourites, with surprising maturity, recognise this danger and work hard to rebuild the relationship with their siblings. This is less likely, however, when the favouring parent makes it clear the child is to treated as persona non grata by all.

Parents allowing favouritism fail to appreciate just how much they are destroying the very essence of what makes a family … family. As parents age and die, it is the bond between the siblings that will determine the strength of the family. Perhaps the best reason I can give parents to aggressively combat favouritism is that as they age, and illness weighs in on their life, they will rely on their children more and more for care. In my experience the favourites tend to see the menial care of the ill parent as below them. They leave the work to their lesser siblings to do the care-related chores. The other siblings, not unreasonably, feel that this is the time the favourite should be there for their parent and repay their debt. Too often the other siblings, not held to the family by stronger bonds, have moved away and are not around for parental care. The chickens come home to roost on favouritism. Unfortunately, by this time, the children of favouritism have already replicated this with their own children, and it is too late for all concerned. Contrast this with families where parents prevented favouritism and all siblings work well together in coordinating care for their parents in need.

Why does favouritism flourish in more families than not? Parents are not immune from insecurities. Far from it. The quickest salve to the pain of insecurity is to have someone on our team, someone who likes and connects with us. Parents, by virtue of nothing more than the act of procreation, wield enormous power over children. All they have to do is shine the 'you're special' light on a child and any normal child will lap it up. Parent and child now bask in the shared spotlight of grateful admiration. It is very seductive, but only the parent has the power to use it judiciously. Children will

rarely ask to turn this spotlight off. It should be used to recognise genuine achievement, but always against the backlight of *I love you just as much win, lose or draw, just as I love all my children just for being*. We love children as human beings, not human doings.

True love and self-esteem

When you think about Jeni's story here, what you are seeing is that she received complicated love from her mother and none from her father. I see true love as having two core elements: acceptance and nurturance. The definition I have developed to help my patients work out whether love is indisputably present or not is: *True love is the feeling of being fully accepted by another, who knows you intimately, and who is committed to nurturing both your personal growth and their own*. True love is not about feelings, they come and go, it is about how one acts *despite* one's feelings.

While her father failed on both counts, what saved Jeni was the love that she gave herself. Symphony and Jay in particular, brought love and care to an internal world that was not being nurtured externally. It is quite extraordinary if you stop and think about it, just how much love Jeni was able to muster up *between her parts*. I have come to believe that this internal love could well be the essence of Jeni's salvation. The period when Symphony was 'stuck' in the body during Jeni's almost-to-term pregnancy was particularly difficult, I might suggest, because Symphony was too overwhelmed to provide love to the rest of the system.

In the late 1950s US psychologist Stanley Coopersmith's research led him to understanding self-esteem around three pillars and I can see no need to improve on them. The first is being accepted for who you are (as opposed to what you do) despite your shortcomings and any bad behaviour from time to time. This relates closely to how I defined true love above. This acceptance can be conveyed in a number of ways but is best conveyed to a child by spending time with them. For this to be effective, the parent needs to spend time doing something the child enjoys doing, i.e. it is not about tagging along while the parent pursues

their own interests. Nothing says a parent accepts a child more than giving them the most valuable thing that busy parents have – their time. Regular, weekly, special time with a child is perhaps the simplest thing we can do to improve a child's sagging self-esteem. Note how Jeni reacts to her father spending time on walks with Sheila.

The second of Coopersmith's findings is the importance of parents enforcing clear boundaries. Boundaries are the backbone of recognising that we all have certain inalienable rights. A sense of rights gives us the foundations from which springs hope. If we understand interpersonal boundaries, while they might be trampled on from time to time, knowing that they exist gives a degree of safety and predictability to life. The absence of rights removes these, and fear and hopelessness thrive. Jeni describes what it's like to grow up without boundaries. Indeed, her trip to the wax works and appreciating that rape is a crime is all about her beginning to understand her body's boundaries and that violating them is a crime. She describes nicely how this opens her up to the crucial appreciation that what's happening to her is not 'punishment' but not about her at all. It is about her father committing a crime, no less. She has an emerging sense of what is happening to her as unjust and, critically, she not only does not deserve this, but deserves to be treated with respect.

The final arm of Coopersmith's triad is the need to respect what a child finds of interest and that they have the right to find their own way. This is the nurturance of personal growth that is the other key element of true love. This is about encouraging both autonomy and skill building. It is about letting them make mistakes, albeit, not standing by as children make a life-threatening or cataclysmic mistake. Most of all it is about helping one's child to find their meaning and purpose in life, especially when this may not align with their parent's values.

Favouritism can masquerade as parental acceptance but is very different. When you see your sibling being disfavoured for who they seem to be, their boundaries not being respected,

and no nurturance of their interests, a child knows that both the favouritism and the disfavouritism is a lie.

Despite all three pillars being destroyed by Jeni's father, it is a testament to her internal workings that she maintained a degree of self-esteem through her heart-rending experiences.

Favouritism on steroids

The other phenomenon that their father's relationship with Sheila raises is that of alignment with the perpetrator. It is a form of 'Stockholm syndrome' where a relationship is built between perpetrator and captive. The difference here is that they have two choices that have been played out for them by another, giving them a clear insight into what each path looks like.

As her father took an interest in her, Sheila faced a choice. She could no doubt fight back and join Jeni in the battle. She knew exactly how hard this would be as Jeni had shone a particularly bright light on how that would unfold. This would take her down the path of unrelenting sexual and emotional abuse, which included being ostracised and outcast. Alternatively, she could fall into line and embrace the relationship with the abuser and submit. With this would come a range of rewards both material, and in terms of family status. Her father's actions meant that Sheila was placed in the position of joint head of the family. Favouritism on steroids.

I see this in families of sexual abuse to varying degrees as the siblings choose where they will stand. Sheila's choice is perhaps the best human example of 'doing a deal with the devil'. In this way Sheila was a victim too. While Jeni's life growing up was horrific, life for Sheila and Frank was not good, with rampant physical abuse and a family world run by a psychopathic paedophile. In this family, rather than a currency of love and care, the currency was hurt and anger. It is a converse currency in that people do not want to accumulate it. Remember, this is a family where all children get beaten regularly irrespective of their guilt, i.e. personal rights did not exist. As their father was incapable of love, the best one could hope for was favouritism.

Nevertheless, Jeni would feel it as a betrayal that was even greater than her father's. Jeni had sacrificed so much to protect her sister, indeed, she almost lost her life doing so.

Making sense of how parental dysfunction impacts on all siblings and, in particular, their relationship with each other is part of a therapist's job. But exploring this with Jeni caused a disconnect between us. I was highlighting that in reality there are no dysfunctional families – only dysfunctional parents, as they take total responsibility for how their family operates. Children alone cannot make a family dysfunctional. In raising this it seemed to Jeni that I was ignoring her pain.

These issues destroyed the relationship between Jeni and Sheila. As they say about alcoholism in parents, 'it's never a spectator sport, eventually everyone gets to play'. It is the same with sexual abuse by a parent – everyone in the family is touched by it in one way or another. With the magnitude of Jeni's trauma we can lose track of the trauma her siblings shared.

I did appreciate what this meant for Jeni as I made the point that Sheila was a victim too and we needed to consider this factor. The point I was trying to make was that Sheila was siding with her father *not because Jeni deserved to be treated badly, but out of a primary need to align with her father for her own emotional survival*. Most importantly, I wanted Jeni to appreciate that Sheila's treatment of her was not driven by her lack of worth. It was driven by Sheila's need for her father's approval and protection.

While I tried a few different ways to deliver this key point, I failed dismally. Jeni saw me as making excuses for what she saw as Sheila's betrayal. One key mistake I made was to raise these issues with Jeni as a singular person rather than work through how each of the key alters felt about it. In the end I could not get past the alters, who carried a lot of anger at Sheila. Because of what Jeni taught me, I do it differently now when I am working with my patients with DID.

The hard part of psychiatry and psychotherapy is not in understanding the human mind. That is not as complex as one

might think. No, the hardest part, indeed the very art of therapy, is in how best to deliver healing insights, so they land effectively, and timing when to do so. The time at which I raised this delicate issue was after I had completed the bulk of trauma therapy involving Jeni's father and this had gone well. Not only was her distress greatly diminished with her self-esteem on the rise, but she had selectively integrated nearly all of her alters (more on this later) as a sign of deep resolution. With this significant progress in mind I thought we had reached a point where I could raise this issue of Sheila's victimhood, while recognising it was very, very different from Jeni's experiences. I read it wrong and screwed it up.

Only when Jeni came back to see me a few years later did I understand just how abandoned and misunderstood by me she had felt. Unfortunately, this was during the time that she allowed her father back to Australia to visit and I was not there to support her through this traumatic experience.

CHAPTER TWELVE

Welcome to the Revolution

MAGGOT

I can feel myself tripping. Dad has been pushing me and pushing me, and I'm about to cross the line of no return. I'm in the kitchen peeling potatoes for dinner. Dad's in the living room calling for me, 'Maggot, Maggot, Maggot.' When I go to see what he wants, he pretends he hasn't said anything.

I return to peeling potatoes.

It happens again and again.

'Go away, Maggot, what makes you think I want you?' he snarls when I go into the living room.

My upset turns to anger. I lose my temper. The next time Dad calls me, I bring the potato peeling knife with me. It has two serrated blades and two spikes at the tip. I say nothing as I press the knife to Dad's throat. The two spikes threaten to make a pin cushion out of his Adam's apple. I have every intention to stab him. I want to kill him. It's not planned, it's reactionary.

Inside, there's a raging debate going on. We're a democracy after all. Some alters cheer me on; others beg me not to stoop to Dad's level. Jay tells me that I'm better than that. He says if I slit Dad's throat, I'll be as bad as him. The decision is being hit about like a tennis ball.

Inside I'm getting whiplash; outside I'm immobile. Dad is frozen still too. Sheila is screaming. Mum and Frank come running. Eventually, morality wins the internal argument. I lower the knife.

There are two deep indentations in Dad's neck. 'Don't call me Maggot!' I say, as I walk back to the potatoes.

Dad grabs me before I get to them. He drags me upstairs and throws me onto my parents' bed. He takes off his belt to beat me, but his hands are shaking. The belt doesn't land with its usual force. 'How dare you?' he says.

'I've told you not to call me Maggot. That's not my name,' I reply.

Dad stops hitting me and looks at me in shock. It's as if he's heard me speak for the first time. He physically shakes the shock away – like a wet dog – then pushes my legs apart and rapes me. I lay still. When he finishes, I sit up. 'My name is not Maggot. I will not come if you call me Maggot. I mean it, Dad,' I say very coldly.

'Get out of my sight,' he says, even colder.

I return to the potatoes. No one asks me why I pulled a knife on my father. They already know the answer: he deserved it.

Years later, I see a comedy sketch that gives me comfort about not killing my dad that day. In a tongue-in-cheek song, the comedian jokes about how history gets rewritten with rose-coloured glasses after someone dies. Even tosspots turn into great blokes after they die.

And Dad is the biggest tosspot of them all.

JENI

We're still living as a family of five for Christmas in 1983. Frank had been chosen to be a server at the Christmas Day service at our church and it was a great honour. Mum and I went to watch him; Dad and Sheila refused to come. I remember thinking Frank did a beautiful job. I remember going up for communion and I remember sitting back down in the pew for the rest of the service.

I don't remember what happened next.

According to Mum, I had a 'funny faint' and slid off the pew onto the ground. It took several people to get me out from under the pews and into the foyer of the church, where I fainted again. A lady rushed to my side and told Mum she was a nurse. Mum explained

that I'd had the funny faints on and off over the years. 'They're not funny faints,' the nurse explained. 'She has epilepsy and needs to go to a doctor as soon as possible.'

When I fell to the ground a third time on our way out of the church foyer, the nurse diagnosed that I'd had a grand mal epileptic seizure and stressed once again that I needed to go to a doctor. Mum organised for a doctor to come to our house that day. When we got home, she put me on her bed until they arrived, and went to tell Dad what had happened. He didn't come to check on me.

The doctor arrived and Mum explained that I'd had my first 'funny faint' before I was two, and that our GP at the time diagnosed it as a temper tantrum. If only. The doctor examined me and hit my knees and ankles with a little hammer. My reflexes didn't respond. The doctor confirmed the grand mal epilepsy theory and said that if it wasn't Christmas Day, he'd send me to hospital. Instead, he referred me to Southampton Hospital for an EEG and wrote a prescription for medication. He told me it would be okay, and I desperately wanted to believe him.

On his way out, the doctor commented how hard it must be for Mum with her husband away. He'd assumed Dad was in the military and on duty over the holidays. 'Oh no, he's in the living room,' Mum explained. The doctor furrowed his brow and reiterated how serious my condition was.

As soon as the door shut behind the doctor, Dad yelled out.

'Are you finished yet? Sheila wants to open her presents.'

* * *

On Boxing Day, Dad and Sheila went to visit the Haynes side of the family: Dad's father, brother and nephews. Mum stayed at home with me and Frank. We weren't invited. I don't know what was said on the day, but I never heard from Granddad Haynes or my Uncle Tony ever again. When Mum divorced Dad, she also divorced his entire family. They didn't want anything to do with us.

Dad had started building a narrative that I was a liar, a thief and a slut who was jealous of Sheila. He was building his defence before I even knew he had a case to answer to.

LINDA

The frying pan is kept in the cupboard above the oven. I can't reach it. I have to stand on my tiptoes and hold the frying pan by the very end of its handle to shove it in there and slam the door shut before it falls out and hits me on the head. I escape gravity. Dad doesn't. When he opens the cupboard later in the afternoon, the frying pan smashes him in the face and clunks to the kitchen floor. 'Maggot!' Dad yells.

I find him in the kitchen, rubbing his forehead, and erupt into a fit of giggles. I picture the frying pan hitting him in the face and the image is deliciously funny. I laugh until tears run down my cheeks and cramps pull at my stomach. Dad yells, but I can't stop. Mum, Frank and Sheila come to see what's so funny.

'I've been hurt,' Dad explains. Sheila goes to hug him. Mum and Frank join me in laughter. The gulf between the family is highlighted by a falling frying pan.

'That's a stupid place to have put the frying pan, Richard, what did you expect?' says Mum.

But Dad doesn't take any of the blame because the blame is all mine. He shoves me into the usual space between the living room door and the rolltop desk ready to beat me.

'Don't be silly, Richard, it was an accident,' Mum says, releasing me from Dad's grasp and sending me to my bedroom.

Dad follows me a few moments later, with his leather belt in his hand. He hits me from behind until I turn around to face him. I grab at the belt and catch the buckle end, pulling it tight.

The belt is a straight line between me and Dad.

'Dad, it isn't fair you hitting me for the frying pan. I've told you I can't reach that cupboard. If you'd let me leave the frying pan on the sink, it wouldn't have hit you in the face,' I say, down the straight line.

Dad tries to pull the belt from my hands. I hold on tight. 'You don't hit Frank or Sheila for accidents, why do you hit me?' I continue.

Dad roars, but he doesn't answer me. I keep hold of the belt as I walk out of the room. I drop my end when I reach the door and turn to face him. 'I think you're just a mean bastard and you like hitting me, any excuse will do. You disgust me,' I deadpan.

There's silence. Then screaming. 'How dare you! Get back here right now!' he yells over and over again, until he realises I'm not coming back. I'm sitting next to Mum on the sofa when Dad walks in with a purple face and foamy spit in the corners of his mouth. He snarls. I smile.

JENNY

Dad and Sheila decided to move to Wales. Why Wales? Because Dad got a job there and they agreed to pay for his moving costs. Scrooge had struck again. Mum pleaded with Sheila to stay with us, but she refused point blank. 'Even if you get custody of me, the day I turn sixteen, I will leave you and go to live with my daddy,' said Sheila, who was days away from turning sixteen.

Mum cried and spent the next few weeks ensuring that Sheila knew she always had a home with us. No matter what.

Packing up the house was like a free-for-all game of Hungry Hungry Hippos. Things got nasty. There were arguments, and 'accidents', and underhanded tactics.

HAPPY

I will admit I too engaged in these tactics. The one thing Dad and I had bonded over was his love of the unexplained. Mysteries like Big Foot, Easter Island, aliens, the Oak Island treasure pits, and ghosts thrilled both Dad and me. During our time in Australia Dad had bought that magazine, *The Unexplained*, and he and I read every word. It was great. It was a tiny bond between us. So, as the dismantling of our family took place I slowly and carefully removed all of the magazines from Dad's box and hid them. It took weeks

but I was able to 'steal' them all. I still have them; they are a physical reminder of happier times with Dad.

JENNY
Dad and Sheila did a lot of sorting at night after everyone else had gone to bed and sealed up boxes marked for Wales. They took many precious family photos, but they left every single photo of me. Mum lost a number of family mementos, ornaments and books. I lost a lot more: pieces of myself.

We took a break from packing to celebrate Sheila's sixteenth birthday. My fourteenth birthday had passed eight days earlier with minimal fanfare. Hers, in contrast, was an elaborate affair. Dad insisted on taking Sheila shopping on the Saturday before her birthday. Sheila dragged us from store to store, pointing at items and demanding Dad buy them for her. 'I want it, Daddy, I want it now,' she ordered, and he obliged. Her voice reminded me of Veruca Salt from *Charlie and the Chocolate Factory*. The thought tickled me and I burst into a fit of giggles in the middle of a shop. I shared the joke with Frank and we both laughed out loud. We were in stitches and Dad was furious.

'What's so funny?' Dad demanded to know. 'Stop laughing or I'll knock you into next week. What have YOU got to be happy about?'

HAPPY
What have we got to be happy about? I'm glad you asked. Here is a list I prepared earlier.

Firstly, I'm happy that Mum is divorcing Dad and soon I'll be free of him. This is a thought that makes me smile. It sits on a shelf beside other thoughts: the feeling of patting a cat's soft fur, the joy of reading a good book, the freedom of being alone for more than five minutes, Frank's laugh, a nice moment with Sheila, when Mum touched my hands, eating salt and vinegar chips, wearing my fluffy coat from the op shop, listening to the Osmonds, the fact that we're still alive …

JENNY

Happy was still listing happy things, thoughts and memories when we got to dinner at the chain restaurant Poppins. For a child who's suffered enormous torture, it was extraordinary to hear Happy's list being read out in the background of my mind. And by the end of dinner, she had another entry to add to the list.

Dad forced me into the corner of a booth and touched me under the table. When the waiter came to take our order, Dad said I would have the kid's fish and chips, without giving me a choice. Sheila ordered from the adult menu. While we were waiting for our meals, Dad pinched and groped me under the table. I was horrified he would attack me in public and I gasped in shock and pain.

'Are you okay?' Mum asked.

I nodded my head very slightly, surprised – but relieved – that she'd noticed my discomfort.

When dinner was served, Sheila commented that my fish and chips looked good. I was prepared for Dad to scrape my meal onto Sheila's plate, as he usually did, but quick as a flash, Mum reached across the table and swapped my plate with Sheila's adult meal.

Mum grinned at me.

Sheila scowled. 'That's mine!' she whined.

'Oh, I thought you wanted Jeni's meal. Jeni's already started eating; it's too late now. Eat up,' Mum replied, cheerily.

I ate with my arm cupped around my plate, protecting it from being taken. I was so full, but I was determined to finish the whole meal, and I did. When Mum ordered three knickerbocker glory ice-cream sundaes for us kids, I thought I might explode. Frank and I enjoyed the rare treat and we kept cracking Willy Wonka jokes for the rest of the night.

The fact that Frank had laughed at Sheila, and Mum had protected me from her food envy, was significant. The revolution had begun, and my mother and brother were on my side.

Dad had called me revolting my entire life, but now I was revolting in a different way. Welcome to the revolution!

* * *

In the lead-up to Dad's departure, he beat me every day and raped me at night. It was as though he recognised his time was running out and was determined to attack me at every opportunity. By this point, I was a mass of bruises, with new purple marks blooming over old yellow ones. Layer on layer on layer. I was hanging on by a thread.

LINDA

On a night in early February 1984, Dad raped me on my parents' bed. It was violent and quick. As he assaulted me, I stared up at him in disgust. I realised I didn't love or respect him. When he rolled off me, panting and gasping, I pushed him away and got off the bed. I turned to look at him from the doorway.

'Get that look off your face,' he said, raising a fist to hit me.

'Go on, hit me. Get it over with. Hit me, hit me!' I dared him.

Dad dropped his fist and shoved me out of the room. He could've hit me, but he didn't. I raised my voice and he heard it.

When Dad raped me in my bedroom the next night, I was even more contemptuous of him. 'Oh, here we go again. Hurry up and get it over with,' I thought, full of resentment.

MUSCLES

After he finished, I raised my voice again. 'I hope you enjoyed that, because if you do it again, I will kill you,' I said.

JENNY

Dad moved to Wales with Sheila on the morning of 12 February 1984. Dad's last words to me were a threat. He told me that, even though he wouldn't be near me, he could still hear my thoughts. If I ever even thought of telling, he would send someone to kill me. There would be a knock at the door and when I opened it, the person – it could be a man, woman or child – would kill me.

I'd be dead and disbelieved. No one would ever believe me so I shouldn't even bother, Dad said, before he walked down the road carrying his suitcase to the train station.

We stood in the doorway watching Dad and Sheila leave. I had tears in my eyes. I couldn't tell if I was crying with sorrow, joy or relief. Part of me still didn't believe it was real, I thought it was a trick. I didn't trust that I would ever be free from Dad's abuse. Sheila turned around to take one last look at her family. Mum saw it as a moment of vulnerability, of Sheila second-guessing her decision.

I didn't wave goodbye to my father or my sister.

PART TWO

SURVIVING

CHAPTER THIRTEEN

Dry Nights

JENI

The first night without Dad, I slept through without wetting the bed. For the first time in my life, I woke up with dry sheets. It was a miracle, a triumph.

But I kept waiting for Dad to come and attack me. He may not have been there physically, but he was still in my head.

Mum and Dad's divorce officially went through on 26 April 1984. Mum, Frank and I moved into our new terrace house in Peterborough the very next day. We'd spent months searching for the cheapest house in the country, and we'd found it. Even though it was cheap, it was beautiful, with cladding on the outside to keep it warm inside and a conservatory out the back. There were two huge bedrooms upstairs and a tiny add-on built above the kitchen. The add-on became my bedroom. I shared it with the water heater, so there was often condensation dripping down the walls and from the ceiling. It felt like it was raining inside.

Dad paid for the house in cash as a part of the divorce, but refused to pay the maintenance as agreed. Mum had twenty pounds to her name. She worked very hard and got a job as a medical secretary. I babysat every week and Frank had a paper round (which Mum and I usually ended up doing). All of my money went into the household kitty. We lived hand-to-mouth, but I was eating more than I ever had in Andover, where Dad had starved me.

ERIK

It's time for a renovation. We've moved into a new house on the outside and we should have a new house on the inside, too. I get to work and transform the medieval dungeon we've called home for fourteen years into a pristine white office building. The dungeon was created by Dad. It took the shape of his actions. He kept us in the darkness and made us feel like we didn't deserve beds, or blankets. We weren't worth comfort. We were only good for raping on cold, dusty concrete floors. And so, we lived underground. Hidden; hurting.

I know different to Dad, so I build the office high into the sky. There's a window in every room looking out to the sunshine. We admire the view. We deserve it. Let there be light!

I replace our old train communication system with an elevator that travels between the floors of the office. Each army has a different floor, and the alters can travel to visit other floors that are related to their work. I can travel everywhere because I'm the architect. I built the bloody building.

VOLCANO

Unfortunately, while Erik could renovate our internal landscape we were unable to do the same for our body and mind. We would need to wait till 2012 for that. Dad may have physically left the family home, but the army believed it was a trick and he would soon return. The battle may have ended, but the war continued. The army did not stand down. How could they? He was still in our head, taunting us and undermining us. They continued to do their jobs regardless. He would be back, best to be ready!

While our body was irrevocably damaged by Dad's torture, we were, for the most part, oblivious to the real extent of the damage. We were still experiencing extreme pain, especially in our lower back, neck, throat and knees. We had constipation, constant bleeding from the anus and ongoing bladder infections. These had been so much a part of our life it did not cross my mind to talk about them. They were our normal. Had I talked, things might have changed dramatically for us and our health.

Dad had destroyed our bowels so much that defecating was nigh on impossible without pain and blood. He broke many of our ribs and dislocated our coccyx. He left us with nerve damage, calcified ligaments in the jaw and a clicking jaw.

We had psychological challenges also. These had implications for our health too. The girls and NotGirls had a terror of males. We had a terror of people putting things in our mouth, so we had poor dental hygiene, and our personal hygiene was appalling. Bathrooms terrorised all of us.

We remained oblivious to the importance of all of these physical ailments and injuries for years. Most of them continued to cause us significant pain and ill-health until a doctor examined Symphony in 2011. What she saw within our anus and rectum was shocking and resulted in emergency surgery.

JENI

The alters were still doing their jobs. We lived in fear. We had a quiet nervous breakdown. No one noticed. Mum was too busy getting settled as a single mother, looking for work and rebuilding her life to notice me falling apart. No one saw anything. That's okay, we are used to it. Physician, heal thyself.

I believed Dad when he said he'd told every man in Peterborough that they could do anything they wanted to me. Dad's warning came true one night when I was babysitting a little boy. I was looking forward to playing cars with the kid, but before I could, the father pulled me into his bedroom to show me their new waterbed.

'Do you want to try it out with me?' the father said, standing inappropriately close to me and touching me where I didn't want to be touched. I panicked and pushed him away. When the mother of the little boy returned home and paid me for babysitting, I told her that her husband had been a bit of a sleaze and tried to get it on with me. She instantly believed me and was horrified.

It was interesting that I was able to defend myself and disclose the sexual assault when the perpetrator was a stranger, but I was unable to do so when it was my own father. Funnily enough, the only person

who didn't believe me about the waterbed incident was my mother, who told me I must have misinterpreted what the man had meant.

Meanwhile, I started at the local Catholic school in Peterborough and got my first-ever school blazer. There was such a mix of people with different ethnicities and backgrounds at the school. And they offered every sport you could imagine – swimming, badminton, netball and chess. I did them all. I thrived at the school and went from being in the lowest English class in Andover to the very highest. I went from barely eating to being given a hot lunch every day. I went from only being able to give my education two per cent of my focus, to giving it forty per cent. School was no longer designated a distraction and we revelled in our newfound freedom. We were still spending a lot of time trying to understand what Dad had done, but we could finally focus on things outside of his torture of us. For the first time, we actually felt we could accomplish something.

At my new school, I could have been shunned for being the daughter of a single mum, but I wasn't. I was welcomed. I wasn't bullied. I made friends and I kept them. On my first day at school, I met a boy named Jack and we spoke every day until the weekend. On Monday morning, Jack ran up to me and asked why I hadn't been at the school dance. He said he had wanted to dance with me. He had a friendly smile on his face, but I was terrified. I was deathly afraid of any kind of male attention, even from a cute boy my age with the most beautiful dark skin I'd ever seen. I didn't know how I was going to survive my teenage years.

SYMPHONY

At home, I indulged my love of music. I discovered the pirate radio station Laser 558, which played all the songs that had been banned in England. I had the radio on all the time. I listened to all the songs of the early 1980s as well as the new songs. I loved Wham, Duran Duran and Spandau Ballet. And when Depeche Mode sang 'Blasphemous Rumours', talking of God's sick sense of humour, they were speaking my language. But it was Frankie Goes to Hollywood's song 'Relax' that struck the biggest chord with me. Finally, an adult told me I

didn't have to do what I didn't want to do. It took me decades to see the video and work out what they were actually singing about. Oops! I blame that on how vigorously it was banned in the UK.

CAPTAIN BUSBY

Mum is the quickest typist we know. Her fingers dance across the keyboard. We don't know what she's typing, but we know she's good at it.

Mum is so good, in fact, that she goes to college to upskill. She learns how to do audio typing and how to use the newest word processing programs on the market. She goes from typing on an old-fashioned typewriter to a computer. She's one of the first women in the area to attend college as a mature age student.

I'm so proud of Mum and I tell her that, loudly and often. She is trailblazing, tenacious and, still, the quickest typist we know.

In the wake of the divorce, Mum's mettle took a battering. But she's clawing it back and we're cheering her on from the sidelines. She doesn't know she has an army backing her, but we do.

JENI

I was happy to never see Dad ever again. But Frank was torn in two by the divorce and desperately wanted to keep a relationship with his father and eldest sister. At first, we had a telephone in Peterborough and we called them often, but the contact was one-sided and Dad made it clear they didn't want anything to do with any of us.

When we had to get the phone line disconnected because we could no longer afford it, we tried to stay in touch with letters. I wrote to Sheila asking about her new friends, school, and what Wales was like. I tried to keep a pleasant, amiable relationship with her, sharing my news and seeking hers. Her replies came months later and she never answered any of my questions.

More than a year after the divorce – and many failed attempts by Mum to organise a visit – Dad brought Sheila with him to see us in Peterborough. There were rules: Sheila wasn't allowed to share a bedroom with me and we were not to be left alone together.

We met Dad and Sheila at the train station. Dad hadn't changed. At one point during the visit, he forced me out of the house and onto the footpath outside. He pushed me up against the wall with hands wrapped so tightly around my neck that my eyes bulged. He repeated his threats: if I told anyone, he'd kill me. I'd heard it all before. When he finally dropped his hand from my throat, I bent over coughing for air.

Even though I knew the rules, I managed to steal a moment alone with Sheila on the second day of their visit. She was playing with our cat Patches, who Mum had claimed in the divorce, and I asked Sheila if she was happy with Dad. Subtly, I tried to see if Dad was hurting or scaring her.

Sheila screamed at me and cried to Dad that I was 'poking' my nose in and asking intrusive questions. Dad coddled her and told me to get lost.

I couldn't see any signs that Sheila was experiencing physical violence. She didn't have any bruises and, as far as I could tell, she seemed to wield the power in her relationship with Dad. She was confident, even bossy, towards him.

THE JOKER

The monster is gone, but I'm still trying to work out how and why he hurt me. I rock back and forth on my bed every night and tell the tale of Jay under my breath. I chain Jay to a pillar in a cave and recount the story of him being hit, licked, gnawed, prodded and pushed by Dad. Every hole in his body is sore. Every ounce of self-confidence is gone.

I tell the story over and over, and one night, Mum hears me. She thinks I've found a dirty magazine and am repeating what I saw in the pages. She doesn't think to ask me about it. If she'd asked me, I could have told her. I didn't find filth in the pages of a dirty magazine. Rather the filth found me, and the filth was my father. If only she'd asked. But not only did she not ask, she didn't tell me what was worrying her. I had no clue she'd heard me at all.

JENI

Mum became worried about me. She thought I'd developed a mental illness. I was talking to people who were not there. I told her I was talking to Jay, but my explanation didn't do much to ease her worry. Mum got a referral for me to see two specialists at the Peterborough Hospital – she assumed they would be experts in childhood mental health, psychologists or psychiatrists.

Mum and Frank came with me to the appointment. We sat behind a huge two-way mirror, and I immediately felt uneasy. It reminded me of the mirror in the newsagency in Greenacre where Sheila was once caught stealing. The therapist and his colleague asked why we were there. Mum told him about Jay. They asked Frank what he thought about Jay. 'If Jay makes her feel better, what's the problem?' he said.

They didn't ask me about Jay. I tried to tell them how Jay helped me, the things he said and what was going on in my mind. At the time, my alters were using Jay as a shield. This was a strategy introduced by Erik after the divorce to allow me to be as normal as possible at school. When the alters talked to me, they spoke in Jay's voice, much as, later, they would use the Student's voice during our studies, and that of 'the Entity Currently Known as Jeni' during the legal cases. The goal was to keep me as consistent as possible. This worked so well that no one ever guessed I had serious issues. Sometimes I would wish that I was a tad less competent; I might have got help much earlier if I could have let go and let people see me.

I had a lot to unpack, but the therapist didn't seem at all interested in what I had to say. It was as though everyone else in the room had a voice except for me. For the umpteenth time in my life, I felt silenced.

When the doctor left the room with his colleague to confer, I was sure they were going to have a good laugh at me and Jay. After what I imagined was a raucous giggle fit, they returned with the diagnosis. I had an imaginary friend, they told my mum. I would grow out of it. Mum should stop fretting. Was there anything else she was worried

about? Mum unloaded about Dad's inappropriate relationship with Sheila, and so, for the next six months, once a month, we would spend an hour talking about Mum's concerns.

JENI

I tried to talk about Jay and the other voices I heard in my head. I wanted them to know the voices never stopped; they told me what to do, commented on my behaviour, my thoughts and my worries. I attempted to explain how I lost time; how I could be in one place one minute and somewhere completely different a minute later, but days had passed in between without me being aware. I described the feeling of not being in control of my body. I was disclosing the key features of MPD without realising it. Unfortunately the doctor didn't realise it either.

I didn't get a chance to explain how all the voices had jobs and how they worked hard to keep me alive. I wasn't able to admit that the voices were created to help me survive the abuse my father had inflicted on me. I didn't get to tell my story, because they never asked. I never got to even hint at the issues around Jay, my surrogate sex abuse victim. I never got the opportunity to explore that story. If Mum had said this was what was worrying her, I would have happily discussed it. After all, I had no idea that what I was talking about was horrific child abuse. Only an adult could have known that, but the adults around me were deaf and mute.

After we stopped seeing the doctor, Mum realised we'd been referred to an occupational therapist instead of a psychologist. Once again, I'd been let down by the medical profession. Had the doctor and his colleague listened to what I was saying, asked me questions and tried to understand, I would have been able to disclose the abuse back in 1985, and I could have sought justice and help so much earlier.

* * *

JENI

The complicated thing about intrafamilial abuse is that the perpetrator doesn't stop being your family. My dad was still my dad. When I passed all of my end of school examinations in 1986 and discovered I'd earned some of the highest results in history and English literature in the country, I wanted to tell my dad. I was proud of my results, and even prouder when I was offered a place in the highly competitive City and Guilds Family and Community Care course at the Peterborough Technical College. We still didn't have a phone-line, so I tried to call Dad by reversing the charges in the phone booth down the road. A female operator put the call through. 'This is the operator, will you accept a reverse charge call from Jennifer Haynes?' she said.

'No, I bloody won't,' Dad replied, slamming the phone down.

I apologised to the operator for Dad's language and stood motionless in the phone booth. I don't know why I was shocked. The call confirmed everything I knew to be true about my father: he didn't give a shit about me.

Dad wasn't the only member of our family to cut ties with me, or with Mum and Frank. The entire Haynes family cut ties with us. I never saw them again. By 1987, we recognised how utterly alone we were in England. Both sides of our extended family weren't interested in having us in their lives. They'd actively discouraged us from moving back to England, and they had been right. We longed for Australia.

I could count on my hand the number of times my mum's mother Grandma Dixon visited us in Peterborough. On one of the rare occasions she did visit, she alleges that I lost my temper with her. Grandma had been incredibly rude to Mum the entire visit and I admit that I was very angry at her. However, she claims that I came down the stairs and looked her in the eye and said, 'You're a fucking old hag.'

The thing is, it wasn't me! I have no recollection of voicing the insult. To this day, no one has ever owned up to it. Regardless of who said it, I was the one who had to apologise. I mustered all of

the grace I had and said sorry to my grandmother the night we were meant to watch the Osmonds perform live on a TV show.

She didn't accept my apology, and her refusal made me very uncomfortable. As I watched the Osmonds perform I worried about being punished by my grandmother.

It was the first time I saw Jay Osmond perform and, dear lord, he was amazing. The whole Osmond family was there, but Jay was the only one I had eyes for. The show was almost like a spiritual experience for me, and I enjoyed every moment of it. Well, almost. Grandma talked through the entire performance. She really was a fucking old hag.

In 1988, Mum put in the application for us to return to Australia. Of course, the first thing she did was ask Sheila if she wanted to join us. The reply was blunt: she hated Australia, hated us, and would never return there – not now, not ever. Mum tried again a few times, but the response from Sheila was always the same.

The response from the Australian immigration department was delightful. We received a package with our passports, visas and permanent residency paperwork, welcoming us to Australia and wishing us well on our journey. Finally, it felt like we were wanted. We put the house up for sale and started packing to go home. My home was dry grass, sunny skies and the scent of honey blossom. We landed just in time for summer in November 1988.

LINDA

Before we leave, Mum insists we need to say goodbye to Dad and Sheila. I roll my eyes. The plan is to meet in London and bid them farewell like normal family members. Except, we're far from normal. To play along with the charade, Mum buys us all new outfits. I wear a knee-length black silk skirt, a blue silk blouse with a cowl neckline and long sleeves, and a black silk jacket, from Dorothy Perkins. I look fabulous. However Granddad Haynes is told that I 'looked like a slut'. Not the nicest review I've ever had!

Dad and Sheila look the opposite. It's been almost three years since we've seen them. Sheila is twenty years old but you wouldn't

know it to look at her. She and Dad look like they've aged a decade. Dad is wearing an old anorak that'd seen better days twenty years ago, and Sheila is in a tattered long skirt that grazes her calves.

We spend the day together in London and Dad makes a big show of buying Sheila new stationery. I almost say he should buy her a new skirt as well, but that would be objectionable of me. Dad makes a big thing of buying Frank something but avoids me. Mum convinces him to buy me a gift. Granddad Haynes is told that I 'conned' Dad into buying me a purple bear. This time, it's Dad and Sheila who don't say goodbye as they push us aside to board their train home to Wales.

I don't know this then, but I won't see my dad for nearly a decade. I don't mind one bit.

CHAPTER FOURTEEN

New Beginnings

JENI

No one came to send us off at Heathrow Airport. But to our surprise, Jane, the mother of my childhood friend Jasmine, the friend I disclosed everything to at school before her asthma attack, came to greet us when we landed in Sydney. We had sent her a letter about our return but didn't expect her to show up at the airport. It instantly felt like we'd made the right decision to return to Australia.

We moved into a house in Blacktown and I started working as a nurse's aide at a nursing home. After I was promoted to the resident diversional therapist, the matron encouraged me to pursue a university degree in nursing, social work or medicine. She said I had the intelligence and skills to do very well. Having someone believe in me was an unusual feeling, and I wasn't quite sure how to accept her support and kindness. I had always dreamed of furthering my studies, but back in England we were too poor for university to be a possibility. As Matron continued to encourage me, I began to seriously contemplate going to university. It was at once terrifying and strangely exhilarating. When we moved to Queensland in 1989, I began to explore what I would have to do to go to university and study.

Working with elderly and disabled people was hugely fun and fulfilling for me. I loved it and I was good at it. I found a world where I could make a difference and I threw myself into it, giving my all for the residents of the nursing home. The only trouble I had

was when people asked me about my family and my father, I told them my parents had divorced and we'd cut off the deadwood and left it in England. Most people were happy with that.

JENI
Keeping silent

Out of a misplaced sense of obligation, or an attempt to do the right thing, Mum forced us to maintain contact with Dad and Sheila, with regular letters and phone calls every couple of months. It was contact that they neither appreciated nor wanted. And for me, it was difficult and upsetting to keep putting in the effort to have a relationship with my abuser, only to have it thrown back in my face. Mum insisted I was better at talking to Sheila than she was, so she made me check in and make small talk. It took me an enormous amount of courage just to dial Dad's phone number and speak to him. I had nightmares and flashbacks just thinking about talking to him.

Unfortunately, a side effect of Mum's determination to keep contact with Sheila was that she continued the emotional manipulation and abuse from my father that had been a huge part of my childhood. It was utterly unintentional, but by insisting that I be the one to contact Dad despite my objections, Mum continued the abusive dismissal of my rights and my boundaries. She walked over my feeble attempts to assert myself and ignored the emotional distress this caused me. Unfortunately, by trying to avoid losing Sheila, Mum missed the distress of the daughter she still had.

One of the greatest difficulties I had after the divorce was that Mum believed removing Dad had fixed everything for Frank and me. In her view we were 'safe' and therefore everything was fine with us. But she did not examine her thoughts and beliefs about me or Frank to see if they were appropriate or even real. She didn't build a new view of me free from Dad's lies. So his view of me remained and informed how I was treated by her and by Frank. It was so entrenched in the family dynamic that this meant my physical and medical needs were mostly dismissed, my emotional needs were invisible, and I felt like a slave, doing the housework, the shopping,

the cleaning and washing. I felt unappreciated. It was assumed and expected, and Mum didn't stop to question any of it. It also meant that I continued to be called Maggot instead of Jeni.

Note from Jeni's mum

Reading this is difficult for me. I love my daughter and appreciate everything she did and does. The most challenging thing for me was being able to say it. I didn't have the words. Complicating this was undiagnosed Asperger's and autism. I never knew how my daughter felt. I feel like a failure. I never knew what that bastard did. I am so sorry, Jeni.

JENI

In the 1980s, divorce was seen as a solution in and of itself. Divorcing and/or leaving an abusive partner was the solution. Now we realise it is only the beginning, and we take steps to understand the impact of the abusive partner's coercive control and unpick it for both the abused partner and the children. But back in the 1980s and 1990s, when I was needing help, this element of abuse was unrecognised. My mum and brother were so impacted by Dad's coercive control of us all that they continued to use elements of Dad's attitude towards me, and every contact with Sheila or Dad, by phone or letter, reinforced and re-entrenched these attitudes and behaviours.

It had been four years since the divorce, and I hadn't uttered a single word about what Dad had done to me. I was still terrified of killing my family by speaking out, so I stayed silent. That was my default. Also, I still didn't have the words to explain what I had been through. When Dad changed his telephone number and refused to give us the new one, I took that as a glaring sign he didn't want to hear from us.

The only time Dad ever contacted us was in 1989 to tell us that his father John Henry Haynes had passed away. I answered the phone and was surprised to hear Dad's voice on the other end of the line. He wasn't as pleased to hear mine and demanded I hand the phone to Mum. Once Dad told her that Granddad was dead, he hung up. He never called back.

The phone call left me and Frank devastated, not because Granddad was dead – we hardly knew the bloke – but because our own father didn't want to speak to us. This wasn't just a glaring sign, it was a blatant refusal.

* * *

JENI
Moving on

And so, I tried to get on with my life. We moved from Sydney to Brisbane because we could no longer afford the rent in Sydney, and I started an adult matriculation course as a precursor to attending university. It was on this course that I met Mitchell. He had tight curly hair and a gorgeous smile. I was twenty and he became my first ever boyfriend.

Having a boyfriend when you're a survivor of childhood abuse isn't like it is in the movies. It's not romance and butterflies in your tummy, it's fear and apologies at the ready. Mitchell attempted to get intimate with me multiple times. He wanted our first time to be special, so he booked a hotel room for the night. There, he invited me to join him in the shower. I had a vivid flashback of being raped by my father in the bathroom in Andover, and ended up under the double bed scared shitless. Poor Mitchell didn't get lucky that night, or any other night with me. We tried, but my body was too frightened to let it happen. The closest we got was an afternoon making out in his car. If we'd kept going, I think I could have made love to him that day in that car. But it was lucky we didn't because a band broke in the engine and Mitchell used the condom we hadn't used as a temporary fix to get us home. We found that hilarious; it was a silver lining to my sexual difficulties.

I explained to Mitchell that I had trouble with intimacy, and he was lovely about it. After nine months together, I asked him to give me more time, but he didn't have any left. I understood and took it on the chin. I told myself I didn't really mind anyway because going to university was my priority. And it was.

I decided to study psychology, but I needed to get a tertiary entrance score of at least 800 from my adult matriculation course exam results to be offered a place at the University of Queensland. I ambitiously chose to do the required five subjects over one year instead of two and did remarkably well. I had the score to study law or medicine, but stuck with psychology because I couldn't afford to do such expensive courses. Also, I thought by studying psychology, I might be able to figure out what was wrong with me. By this point, I knew my mind was different, but I didn't know how – or why.

In 1990, Symphony created her very last alter: the Student. It was the Student who aced the tertiary entrance application, and who was accepted to attend university. It was the Student who walked through the sandstone arches of the University of Queensland, who took notes in lectures and who interacted with tutors. It was the Student who absorbed all the knowledge. Meanwhile, the rest of us kept the internal machine running.

JUDAS
Reconciliation

We've made a friend, his name is Ross. I start to tell him bits and pieces about what Dad did to us. I don't go into details, and I describe the attacks as 'extreme punishments'. Ross preaches forgiveness. He tells me I need to put the abuse behind me and get on with my life. He says I'm letting what happened to me hold me back. He warns I'll never be able to have a proper relationship with anyone if I'm still hung up on what Dad did. Ross repeats the same mantra over and over during our friendship: 'Forgive and forget'.

Maybe he's right. In 1993 I try to reconcile with Dad by writing him a letter. In it, I suggest we put the past behind us and try again. Dad replies saying the reason he hasn't stayed in touch with me was because I didn't want him to. That's untrue, but in the name of reconciliation, I don't point it out.

I telephone Dad and we have a cordial and polite conversation. I tell him I don't want to 'hash over the past' and instead focus on all the positives in my life. I'm doing well at university and working

towards a career in politics. I ask about his life and his interest in photography. It's small talk, but at least it's talk.

I can hear Sheila in the background, she's demanding to speak to me. My heart jumps with joy. For the first time in my life, my sister wants to talk to me! When she gets on the phone, Sheila insists I tell her exactly what caused my problems with Dad. I refuse. She pushes for details. I refuse. She hangs up the phone.

My attempt at reconciliation lasts precisely one phone call. The fool is me.

JENNY
Alone no more

It happened when I was hanging washing out on the line, one day in late 1993. It felt like a blown fuse, a strike of lightning, a burst tap – and it brought me to my knees. In an instant, I heard every single conversation going on between the alters – all 2500 of them. I could hear different accents, arguments and children crying. It was like waking up from a deep sleep in the middle of a Westfield shopping centre on Boxing Day. Instead of mild murmurings of quiet conversations; I was suddenly aware of every conversation, every argument, every debate, and every vote. The sound was deafening. I could hear it all. And I couldn't unhear it. I couldn't stop the voices. I was stunned when I realised that lots of the voices were asking questions, for information, for advice, and other voices were replying. I felt like I was eavesdropping on my own mind. It was terrifying.

Six weeks earlier, I'd started taking the antidepressant medication Prozac after telling my GP I felt 'emotionally dead'. It took those six weeks for the Prozac to kick in and, when it did, it ripped the veil off my MPD and tore it to shreds. I found myself sitting on the grass under the clothesline, sobbing, with no idea how I got there or what was happening. I stopped taking Prozac immediately, but I remained grateful to it for ripping the veil off and helping me to begin to understand the true extent of my condition. The moment under the clothesline was part of a bigger awakening, assisted by my psychology degree.

After becoming aware of all the many, many conversations happening in my head, I slowly learnt how to communicate directly with everyone and how to tune in and out of the chatter. This was no mean feat. I had to learn so much and very quickly it became apparent just how much my alters wanted to know me and help me. I found my busy life left little time for this, which was highly frustrating. Three am became the preferred time for the others to talk with me. I was back to having disturbed sleep, but I felt the benefits far outweighed the difficulties.

Over time I met so many of my alters and learned what they did to help me function. I also realised how much they had done to keep me safe. I learned about the chunnels and how they could be used to stop me from hearing and seeing distressing things, how they could stop me feeling pain, injuries, damage, and intimate touch. I also met the NotGirls and the BackRoom Boiler Boys and Girls. These amazing children formed the backbone of the system and kept picking me up ready to battle another day regardless of the abuse I had just suffered at the hands of my dad.

I was introduced to the concept of the Front Runner. This was the person who most frequently interacted in the world as Jeni. Most people in my life had only ever met the Front Runner and had never met Jeni; they were none the wiser. Most people take another person at face value, believing that the version of a person they meet is that person. But every human is different, depending on the role they are playing at the time: parent, child, sibling, lover, partner, student, teacher, worker, boss, colleague to name just a few of the faces 'normal' people wear. In my case, my faces were more extreme but just as variable. Each of my friends had a friendship with a different Jeni and keeping track was sometimes difficult. The Front Runner kept track of this and kept track of the highly complicated 'rules of engagement' we had for each person. I met The Rulebook, who wrote these rules and ensured we followed them. He was fascinating. I hadn't understood up until that moment just how tightly structured and controlled my inner world was.

Ultimately I was shown that I, too, was an alter of Symphony's.

She had created me just as she had created the rest of us. It was hard to wrap my head around this concept. I struggled with the notion I was an alter and not 'the real Jenny'. It took some time to accept that there was no 'real Jenny' but there was the one and only real Symphony. It took years before Symphony felt safe to reveal the original child, Jennifer Margaret Linda, and show us her hiding place, where she had lain protected for forty years. I am delighted I got to meet the child we were all desperate to protect from Dad.

Over time, my understanding of the role of the Front Runner became more sophisticated and my ability to explain it to others grew. The Jeni that everyone met began to refer to herself as 'the Entity Currently Known as Jeni', so as to clearly define herself as an alter. She was rebuilt daily as we needed her. She describes herself as the outer shell of a suitcase. She explains that every night we fill that suitcase with the alters who have the skills, abilities and information we anticipate we will need for the next day. Thus every day we made a new Jeni in accordance with what we needed for the day. Everything was fine until we were confronted with new people, new tasks, or unexpected visitors or telephone calls. Then we had to fly in extra information to help the Front Runner function.

I was shown by Erik how to tune in and tune out the ongoing internal chatter. He showed me a doorway where I could sit. Here I could face outwards and I could tune out the inner world, or turn inwards and block out the outside world and much of the conversations and chatter around me. I could sit in silence for a while and then I had to return my attention to the world again. This was a magical process and it helped a lot.

Finally, I got to meet Jay, my cold, calm American friend. He was very clearly not an inner person, an alter, and yet he didn't belong to the outside world either. His nature revealed itself to me very slowly over many years. But, as far as I was concerned, Jay was my personal spirit guide, my own version of Jesus. His help wasn't hammers to smite my dad, it was kind guiding words advising me throughout the difficult parts of my life.

The *Diagnostic and Statistical Manual of Mental Disorders* (DSM-3 revised edition) was every psychology student's bible. I read it cover to cover with fascination. In 1994, at the age of twenty-four, I diagnosed myself with MPD. As soon as I read the description of the disorder, all the chunnels, characters and conversations in my brain made perfect sense. Jay, Symphony, Erik, Little Ricky, Muscles and Linda weren't my imaginary friends, they were a part of me, they were real, and they mattered. It was a beautiful revelation, but not everyone agreed with it. There were alters who immediately embraced the diagnosis, others who didn't understand it, and some who flat-out rejected that MPD existed. Ed the Head was one of the latter; he simply refused to believe that anybody else lived in his head.

The revelation started to sink in for everyone after a lecture at university. A person with schizophrenia came to speak to the class, and at the end of their talk I asked a pile of questions. 'Do the voices ever say nice things to you?' I wondered.

'Do the voices talk to each other?'

'Do you talk back to them?'

'Does it take you all morning to get dressed because there are so many opposing opinions weighing in on the options?'

After the talk, the psychology lecturer invited me back to his office and very gently asked me if I heard voices in my head. 'Voices? Nuh huh, no way, not me! Sorry, gotta go,' I spluttered before racing out of the room. He accepted this and didn't question me again, but he looked at me strangely for the rest of the semester.

I'd found an explanation for how my head worked, but I still didn't understand why. In 1995, I started to join the dots about Dad. I was twenty-five, and I had only just begun to understand that the nature of Dad's abuse was sexual. I realised what Dad called a punishment was in fact sexual abuse. I still didn't have the words for sadistic rape, buggery and incest, but the puzzle pieces were there and they made a terrifying picture.

* * *

JENNY
Helping Sheila

When Sheila phoned the following year in 1996 and said she wanted out, I knew I had to help her. Talking to me and Mum on a two-way call, she admitted that Dad was getting violent and had been abusing her. When Sheila said the words 'getting violent' she immediately reactivated the army of protector alters who had cared for her previously. Those words had special meaning for me. I had flashbacks of the rituals Dad inflicted upon me – the beatings, the soldering iron and his other implements of torture – everything crashed down on me and I knew I had to get her to safety. All of this took mere seconds in real time, but for me there are still alters reeling from the notion that Dad was violently attacking Sheila. Whatever he was doing it had to stop. I am going to protect her from him any way I can.

Mum was crying so hard I had to tell her to get off her line so I could hear Sheila. I asked Sheila what Dad had done to her and she said he had raped her. I told her that Dad had also raped me.

Sheila broke down on that call and said that she should have protected me. I didn't comment. I didn't know what to say. Her comment was so out of character. I assured her I would do whatever I could to help. She said she wanted to come to Australia to be with me and Mum. In the meantime, I suggested she stay with Grandma. Sheila asked if I could organise it and tell Grandma about her abuse. I agreed.

Hearing Sheila disclose Dad's violence triggered a tsunami of memories about my own abuse – and reignited my mission to protect her. The disclosure also broke the pact I had made with Dad under duress in 1977. I told him he could do anything to me if he left Sheila alone. But he hadn't. And so, I was no longer bound by the promise I had made to him. It was game on.

After Mum and I hung up the phone to Sheila, we called Grandma Dixon straightaway. Mum told Grandma about Sheila wanting to leave Dad and move to Australia with us, and then she passed the phone to me to explain. I told Grandma that Dad

had abused both Sheila and me, that he had violently raped me as a child, and I was worried he was doing the same to Sheila, that's why we hoped Sheila could stay with her until we organised her travel to Australia. Grandma instantly agreed to help. She talked of how Dad had betrayed us all. She believed me without me having to give details and immediately started to plan Sheila's escape.

The next day, I phoned the Australian Department of Immigration, who explained that if Sheila had a domestic violence order against Dad, she could apply for an emergency visa to return to Australia on compassionate grounds to be with her family. I spent most of the day telling the department about Sheila's situation and disclosing my own abuse. They took notes and said it would help to support Sheila's application.

I also called the Sexual Assault Support Services group in Brisbane, who advised me to talk to the Australian Federal Police (AFP) and ask a 'hypothetical question' about helping a victim of abuse overseas escape her abuser. I made an appointment to attend the Brisbane AFP office the next week. I was keeping Sheila updated on the mission and she seemed grateful for the help. Part of me was thrilled to feel needed and appreciated by the sister I loved so dearly. Another part was waiting cynically for the other shoe to drop. These alters were some of the oldest and wisest I have. I was blinded by the fact that Sheila wanted me, needed me and had use for me as her sister. I ignored all the red flags and waded into the fray. I was ready to fight for Sheila no matter what.

When Sheila revealed that Dad had started to work from home to keep an eye on her, I knew she was potentially in great danger if Dad discovered she was planning to leave him. I had visions of him killing her. Remembering how Dad choked me with his belt and beat me until I lost consciousness, I had no doubt he was capable of killing Sheila.

We made a plan: Sheila would leave Dad on Anzac Day, 25 April 1996, and stay with Grandma in West Yorkshire. Until then, she would carry a large but discreet handbag to her job every day

containing essential documents and personal items, and store them at the office.

At my meeting with the AFP, I made a statement outlining what Sheila had told me of Dad's abuse of her and briefly revealed my own abuse as supplementary evidence to support Sheila. The officer cut me off. 'We don't extradite for sex crimes,' she said. I didn't give the comment much thought because I was focused on getting Sheila to safety. My story didn't matter to me, all that mattered was Sheila. She was the priority.

When the AFP asked me to return to give more details of the abuse Dad inflicted on me, I was still focused on Sheila as Dad's victim and couldn't reveal the true extent of what he'd put me through. The AFP told me I could not talk to Sheila or Mum about my abuse because it could jeopardise Sheila's application for a domestic violence order and the integrity of their investigation.

After my first appointment with the Australian Federal Police officers, I was told to go into counselling. I had been talking to AFP officer Kim Whitman about what Dad had done to me in Andover on the day I pushed him into the bath, and she said that I needed support to tell my story because she knew what I was telling her was 'only the tip of the iceberg'. This was true, but then I was only telling enough of my story to get Sheila help. I knew no one was going to help me with what Dad had done to me. Dad's assertion that as long as it was happening to me, no one would care had been validated so many times before, why would now be any different?

The AFP referred me to counsellors at a sexual assault service, but in my weekly counselling sessions with them, I only disclosed my abuse to help Sheila. Not me. Sadly, a lot of my recollections were dismissed by the counsellors – as was my self-diagnosis of MPD. When I shared an account of abuse, I wasn't counselled or given coping strategies; I was asked, 'Then what happened?' As though what I'd just revealed wasn't enough. It became harder and harder for me to open up.

The day of Sheila's escape, everything went according to plan. Sheila left Dad's house, collected her things from her work and took the train to Grandma's home in West Yorkshire.

Mum and I thought Dad might call us looking for Sheila. He didn't. We imagined he'd report her missing to the police. He didn't.

Six weeks after her escape, Sheila made a formal statement to West Yorkshire Police about Dad's abuse of her. She didn't detail any of the abuse I'd suffered. Abuse is abuse, and while Dad sexualised both his female children and saw us as playthings and sex toys that could be used for his perverted desires, he attacked me in a very different way to how he attacked Sheila.

The AFP forbade me from discussing anything to do with the abuse with Sheila, and I abided by that mandate. After disclosing her abuse when she first sought help from me, Sheila and I never discussed the ways Dad abused us. Our abuse was compressed into the comment 'Dad raped me', and no further details were provided by either of us.

One morning about two months after Sheila had escaped from Dad, the AFP called to tell me that Dad was going to be arrested that morning. All I was worried about was Sheila, and I asked the AFP to make sure she had support. When the English police raided Dad's house, the neighbours asked if he'd killed Sheila because they hadn't seen her in a while.

I continued to see Kim Whitman, disclosing my abuse and torture at the hands of my father as best I could. Unfortunately, much of what I discussed was dismissed as 'that happened in Australia, we can't talk about that'. Kim encouraged me to keep seeing the counsellors and told me that she had arranged with the head of the sexual assault centre that the counsellors would document my disclosures and that this documentation would form part of the evidence sent to the UK.

I learned later this was not done, and so the record of my first-ever disclosures of my abuse was lost. An opportunity to help me deal with my abuse and get justice was also lost.

It is my personal opinion that the counsellors could not cope with the nature of Dad's crimes against me. They were so traumatised by my disclosures that they could not believe me. I found myself trapped in a no-win situation. I have MPD which is caused by

extreme, unavoidable and inescapable abuse, but no one believed my story of abuse because I have MPD.

In mid-February 1997 the AFP called me to let me know that Dad was about to be charged with sexual offences against Sheila and me. I was shocked. I hadn't been told that Dad was being investigated for what I had disclosed. I thought I was just helping Sheila to obtain a domestic violence order. No one had bothered to look into what Dad was doing to me before, despite the fact I had disclosed my abuse to Aunty at the church, Mr Teller at school and my friend Jasmine before her asthma attack. Every time I had told my story, I'd been met with either further abuse, disbelief or a medical emergency. No one had cared before.

Over time, Dad was charged with eleven offences relating to Sheila and four relating to me. The number four seemed like a miscalculation, an insult, a drop in the ocean. I told Kim Whitman that I had only revealed a tiny fraction of what had really happened and asked if I could tell the whole story. She said she'd be happy to take a statement from me, but it might be too late. She implied the police didn't have the time to investigate the entirety of my life, but they might be able to deal with a small part before Dad came up for trial.

JUDAS
Trying to tell

If I had known the police would investigate Dad for his abuse of me, I would have made a full statement about the torture I endured at his hands in England from 1970 to 1974 and 1981 to 1984. I thought that if they were going to investigate him, they would have come back to me with requests for proof. But they didn't, and I remained blind to my chance to blab for over a year. Muscles calls an 'All In': a democratic process in which every alter gets to have input on an issue before we vote on it. I hate All Ins. The hubbub and chatter makes it hard to keep track of the little folk I look after and I spend the whole time explaining stuff I'd rather not. This is not my idea of fun. Then Muscles throws a curve ball. He wants an All In where we discuss and vote on what I'm going to tell the police. Say what?

Incidents, attacks, rapes, objects and implements are all tossed around as each alter has a say on what we might tell the police. Rituals are picked up and examined before being tossed aside. The hubbub is worse than normal. There are alters crying 'cos their abuse incident has been set aside, others argue furiously for a particular type of attack to be discarded. I have this horrible feeling as I hear murmurings about 'The Dirty'. Oh god please no, anything but that! We go to a vote, and I know the result before it's announced by Muscles.

I don't want to talk about 'The Dirty', but I know it has to be done. I muster all of my courage and book in a meeting with Kim. I still don't have the word for 'sodomy' so I describe The Dirty by saying if Jeni was a boy, it would have been homosexual rape. She recognises that I'm speaking about buggery, but she doesn't say the word out loud. Instead, she asks me why I waited so long to tell her. I explain that I didn't realise what Dad had done was sexual abuse. She says she probably can't do anything about it now.

I cry. We all cry. It was so hard to talk about The Dirty out loud – saying those words was humiliating, embarrassing and painful – and it seems it was for nothing.

JENI
Truth denied

What I did not know was that while I was desperately trying to tell the truth of his abuse of me, Dad was off trying to find someone to declare me a liar. In June 1997, he wrote to his solicitor to draw attention to an article series in *The Daily Telegraph* about the British False Memory Society. He stated that the 'society may be of use to us'. His solicitor replied swiftly to agree with him and told my father that they'd been in touch with the society. She then told him that she had spoken to a woman there, and this lady was now 'looking at the statements, particularly those of Jennifer and will give us a view on including an argument of False Memory in your defence … as she has been involved in cases where a False Memory argument has been presented before a Judge and Jury.'

Now this woman may well have looked at my statements, but she most certainly did not speak with me. I was not contacted or interviewed by anyone from the UK after early 1997; that's at least four months prior to her being approached.

The British False Memory Society appears to have been comfortable going into court to argue that my recollections of abuse were false, implanted by counsellors, or just plain lies. However, their testimony would have been based solely on the claims of innocence and lies of my father.

If members of this society were willing to go into court and declare victims liars without ever hearing them talk of what happened to them, it must call into doubt every case in which they have testified. Clearly, their testimony could not have been founded on how my therapy was being conducted; they didn't talk to my counsellors either, so it can only be founded on my dad's contention that my allegations were false. They were willing to declare me a liar despite having no evidence other than from my abuser. Of course, my father knew damned well I was telling the truth. He was looking for a way out. But this society made no effort to assess the veracity of his protestations of innocence; they took his word for it just as he had predicted when I was a child, everyone believed him, not me.

JENNY
Going back

Dad's trial was scheduled for September 1997. Mum and I were subpoenaed to appear at Winchester County Court. We flew into England the day of Princess Diana's funeral. The flight was full of mourners; I'm surprised it wasn't waterlogged with tears. Symphony spent the long-haul flight quietly singing the death songs including 'Don't Cry for Me Argentina' and 'Stars' to herself. The final lines of 'Stars' became our battle cry, our statement of intent, our promise or prophecy.

There was a person missing from the flight: apparently, there wasn't enough money in the budget to send Kim Whitman with us,

so we had to go on our own. When we landed in London, the whole country was in mourning for the people's princess.

On arrival, we were consumed with nerves and jet-lag, but the UK detective on the case picked us up from the airport and took us to Andover in search of a witness, one of my old schoolmates who lived near us at the time.

Returning to the scene of the crime was horrific. We parked down the street from our old house. In my mind, I could hear the Osmonds playing in the background, see the spot where I planned to throw myself under the bus and feel the terror of my childhood. In reality, the detective was playing Princess Diana's funeral on the radio. How morbid.

All the while, I was having vivid flashbacks and experiencing the pain of every single attack Dad inflicted on us. From the moment I landed in England, I was in physical agony. I developed phantom bruises that mirrored the marks Dad had left on me as a kid. I had a cut in the same spot on my hand where I'd been hit with a ruler. I craved salt and vinegar chips because that's what my friend Zoe would buy me from the school canteen when her mum gave her extra coins to get a treat for me. My MPD was in fine form. All the alters were present and they were all on guard, trying to protect us from the monsters we knew in our homeland.

It felt like I was being flooded with memories, but I didn't show any emotion. Erik took over and we wore our stoic face like a mask. The alters were in a state of turmoil inside. For the first time in twelve years, that night I had a nightmare about sitting on the toilet, and only barely woke up before I wet the bed.

On the Sunday before the trial, the UK detective on the case phoned me and Mum at our hotel. He explained that Dad had submitted a plea offer, and the detective insisted it was in my best interests to take it. He also said he was bringing Sheila and Grandma over to see us that night.

It was an odd family reunion. The detective stretched out on one of the hotel beds, while we made small talk, avoiding the topic of the trial on his orders. Sheila looked exactly the same as she had the

day she left our home in Andover; she was long and lanky, thin and clanky, her hair went down to her bottom, and she wore a scowl on her face.

Sheila was an iceberg. I was so pleased to see she was safe, but I was hurt that she didn't seem to want anything to do with me. I chatted to Grandma about our flight and the weather, and Mum talked to Sheila about her life and hobbies. Grandma said I was just like Granddad Dixon (her late husband), only with a sense of humour. I didn't know whether it was a compliment or not.

After an hour, Sheila declared she wanted to go back to her hotel, and they began to leave. I wished her a good night and said we'd see her in the morning. Sheila didn't respond.

The Winchester County Court was an ugly concrete building with sharp square features. On Google, it has an anonymous one-star review, 'Corrupt family court … needs to be stopped now!' But Google didn't exist in 1997, so I had no idea what I was walking into.

In the busy waiting room, the prosecutor explained that there was a plea deal on the table, but he didn't give us any details. He said Dad had agreed to plead guilty to some things, but not others. He told me that Sheila had agreed to the deal, and he encouraged me to do the same.

When I asked the prosecutor what charges Dad was going to plead guilty to, he wouldn't tell me. When I pushed to know whether the charges were related to me or Sheila, he got frustrated. When I said I was willing to testify in court and tell the truth, the whole truth and nothing but the truth, he snapped at me. 'You're putting the entire prosecution at risk and, quite frankly, being selfish. This isn't just about you, think of your sister. She's been through hell, and she doesn't want to testify.'

For the past eighteen months, all I'd done was think about Sheila and try to help her.

I felt backed into a corner, trapped by the prosecutor's demands and my loyalty to Sheila. And so I agreed to the plea deal, despite never seeing the offer or receiving legal advice about my options. Dad

was already in the dock when Mum and I entered the courtroom. His face was emotionless as the judge read out the charges, and it stayed so when he pleaded guilty to nine out of eleven of the charges relating to Sheila, including rape, the creation of child pornography and sexual assaults.

However, Dad pleaded not guilty to the four charges relating to me. I gasped out loud. The wind was knocked out of me. The judge then said the words I have never forgotten or forgiven: 'You have pled not guilty to your daughter Jennifer Haynes and I find you not guilty.' The charges for the crimes committed against me were dismissed, and I was devastated.

Dad had always said no one would believe me, and it turned out he was right. A line of alters were ready to testify, but they weren't given a chance. Dad pled not guilty, and so he was deemed innocent. What Dad said, went. All my childhood fears were confirmed: he was invincible.

In an instant, twenty-five alters threw themselves out of the glass windows of the Winchester County Court onto the concrete below and committed suicide. My body jerked in my seat. Mum told me later she had to hold on to me, because she thought I might jump out the window. Little did she know so many of my alters already had. Some swallowed razorblades and others jumped off cliffs. They were never seen again. The holes never disappeared.

It was like a bomb had gone off inside me. Muscles called Dad a coward and goaded him to hit us. Linda said Dad was lower than a bat's bogeys. Symphony cried. I heard all their voices and I felt all their pain.

Dad was sentenced to nine years in prison for his crimes against Sheila. Of course, I was pleased he had been convicted, but I also felt ripped off that I didn't get my day in court or any justice for myself. It was a kick in the guts, a low blow, a regular weekday night in the old Haynes household between the rolltop desk and the door in the living room.

After the trial was over, I went to lunch with Mum, Sheila and Grandma. I couldn't eat because I felt so nauseous.

The day after the trial I had a meeting with the detective in charge of the case. He told me bluntly that the police had not believed me. He said that he had intended to drive me to a hospital and force me to undergo a forensic medical examination to prove I was lying. I argued that I would have done one had they asked. I had been asking for them to do one for over eighteen months. He went on to tell me how the police and prosecution had planned to put me on the stand, force me to tell my story and then charge me with contempt of court, perjury, conspiracy to pervert the course of justice and perverting the course of justice. So they intended to send me to prison for being honest, for telling the truth. Had they done that forensic examination they would have found enough proof to send Dad to prison for the rest of his life. They would have been faced with clear and indisputable proof of long-term severe and violent rape, proof I'd given birth and had several pregnancies. And that was even before they examined my anus and rectum! The evidence was still in my body at 41 years old. What more evidence could they have seen when I was 27?

I was shattered by not only what I was being told, but also by the way it was being presented to me. The police officer pointed out how lucky I was that Dad had entered a plea bargain, thus stopping me from testifying and lying under oath. But I wasn't lucky; I'd been sold down the river by my dad, the police, the prosecution and the judge. Intentionally or unintentionally, the British legal system and the British False Memory Society had just colluded with my dad to avoid giving him a proper prison term for the crimes he had committed against me. I have no doubt that the fact the British False Memory Society was willing to declare my allegations 'false memories' contributed to how I was viewed by the police and the prosecutors. The words of the judge that Dad had 'pled not guilty, so I find you not guilty' declared me a liar under British law. I have still not recovered from this. The impact it had on me, and continues to have on me, is incalculable. I can't even put it into words, and words are my thing.

The alters who didn't kill themselves felt like they'd been flushed down the toilet. We gave up. We threw our hands in the air and accepted defeat. We had nothing left to give and no hope left to spare. A layer of black plastic enveloped us. We stopped talking to each other and the outside world. Two words dominated our mind and life: not guilty.

False Memory Syndrome

No discussion of DID would be complete without addressing the elephant in the courtroom of 'false memory syndrome' (FMS). I say 'courtroom' because this is where the issue grew to elephant status. It was never a clinical issue.

In the early 1990s, Jennifer Freyd accused her father, Peter Freyd, a professor of mathematics at the University of Pennsylvania, of sexual abuse during her childhood. Peter Freyd denied the allegations, raising a defence that Jennifer Freyd's memories (allegedly recovered during therapy) were false. Peter Freyd went on to create the False Memory Syndrome Foundation, which garnered both sizable membership and massive media attention around the world.

With a huge marketing budget, the FMS Foundation sent out information to the press across the USA claiming families were being torn apart with no evidence other than a claim of recovered repressed memories. This reductionism of an exceedingly complex subject down to a single issue was breathtaking. It created attention-grabbing headlines and the media took the bait hook, line and sinker.

Ralph Underwager, a psychologist, minister and in-demand expert witness in defence of alleged paedophiles, was one of the founding members of the FMS Foundation and an original board member. He infamously declared that 60 per cent of women sexually abused in childhood reported that the experience was 'good for them'. He expounded in detail how paedophilia was a

'responsible' choice saying, 'I think that paedophiles can make the assertion that the pursuit of intimacy and love is what they choose. With boldness, they can say, "I believe this is in fact part of God's will."'[1]

The FMS Foundation really got into top gear when it turned to 'implanting' or 'creating' memories. If the single issue was recovered memories, there was a need to discredit them. Enter stage left Professor Elizabeth Loftus, who was effectively the 'scientific' founder of the FMS movement and expert for the defence. Loftus has given evidence in 150 trials – in 149 of those instances she was defending alleged sexual perpetrators. She has been the defence expert to support Harvey Weinstein, Bill Cosby, Michael Jackson, Ted Bundy, OJ Simpson, and many other alleged abusers.

Prior to joining the FMS Foundation, Loftus was a university academic studying memory, who already worked providing legal defence to those accused of child sexual abuse. I am not aware that she has ever practised clinically and I am not aware that she has ever treated a traumatised patient. Prior to the formation of the FMS Foundation, Loftus lost a couple of major cases as she testified for the defence of a child molester and a murderer. Loftus needed some research to fall back on so she offered her students extra credits if anyone could prove that someone can be influenced to remember an event that never happened. Her student James Coan succeeded in convincing his fourteen-year-old brother to believe a false story that he had been lost in a shopping mall at age five. An anecdotal report of a single case does not vaguely constitute science, but it was enough for the media who reported it as if it were scientific evidence (as did Loftus in her final study). Inspired, Loftus and Coan went on to design the first iteration of the 'lost in the mall' study with six participants. The study subjects were told that their parents had told the researchers that they had been lost in a shopping mall as a child. All six correctly identified the lie. Not surprisingly, this research was never published.

Undaunted, Loftus quietly dropped both Coan and the unhelpfully non-influenceable six people. She found another

My mum. She came from a family of secrets
and didn't have the tools to understand the
manipulation and cruelty of my father.
We both carry the pain of that.

Mum, with my father, looks beautiful on
her wedding day. And so happy. If only
things had stayed that way.

My sister and me. I am on the right holding my beautiful Sweep,
who was a comfort for all of us over the years.

When I look at our family photos, we look normal. No one would have suspected a monster lived in our house. No one would have suspected that I was protecting my sister. And yet, somehow, I almost always found the strength to smile. I thank Symphony for that.

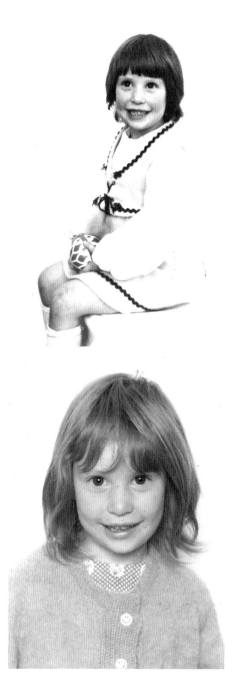

These photos might look like
Jeni but the top is Joyful and
on the left is Symphony.

A normal suburban house in Sydney's western suburbs – but for me, it was the scene of torture and despair. I hope people reading this book learn to recognise the signs that a child is being abused. And that people realise that 'respectable' can be a cloak that perpetrators hide behind.

Santa photos and holidays do not a happy family make.

I found such joy in singing and performing and again thank Symphony
for helping us stay alive.

This is a photo of Linda at school.

A photo of Maggot.
No smiling in this photo.

Jay Osmond saved my life many times.

That air of respectability around our family and my father hid the depravity of the man who should have protected me. Who would look at this man and think he was a monster? I knew he was.

A beautiful photo of Gabrielle. Just before my health collapsed.
A reckoning was coming, but I needed all my strength to find the justice we deserved.

I worked hard to earn my degrees
and PhD and when I look back
I realise I was doing everything
I could to have the skills to seek
justice for myself and my alters.

On 6 September 2019, Linda stood proudly outside court and addressed the media after
my father was sentenced to forty-five years and jailed for at least thirty-three years.
We could not have been happier to have been heard, believed and to have the judge
recognise the enormity of what that man did to me. I was now free.

twenty-four participants and tried the same memory implantation technique. This time three subjects developed partial false memories, and two others developed full ones and maintained this position over two interviews. The final paper spent some time discussing the case of Coan's younger brother being implanted with a 'lost in the mall' memory and very specifically made no mention of the study of six people, where it was not adopted by anyone.

Notably, Loftus herself reported that the false memories were described in fewer words compared to true memories (50 versus 138 on average) and the clarity of recall was significantly rated as much lower. Contrast this finding with the clarity that trauma patients like Jeni report, giving us a clear basis for telling the difference between false memories and real ones. In the one and only example transcript provided in Loftus's study, the participant prefaces her memory with, 'I vaguely, vague, I mean this is very vague, remember ...' This participant is clearly telegraphing that what she is about to say is made up to satisfy her audience.

In psychological research this is known as the 'demand characteristic', where people give the researchers what they want to hear to be a good study participant. It is concerning that Loftus made no mention of this well-known research problem. Including this unconvincing example as proof of false memory recall leaves one wondering about the other four cases. Maybe not too surprisingly we will never know as Loftus apparently 'lost' these transcripts. For more critiques of this research the reader can read papers by Blizard & Shaw and Crook & McEwen.[2, 3]

The big question this research did not address was: while some people might vaguely recall, with a paucity of both words and clarity, a memory of being lost in a mall, will they falsely recall being sexually assaulted by a person closest to them who betrays their very role as caregiver, i.e. a parent?

As FMS grabbed media attention, I remember asking my colleagues who also did trauma therapy, 'Do you know anyone who is doing this repressed memory therapy that the media are in

such a furore about?' After some confused discussion we realised we were all doing repressed memory therapy by virtue of the fact that we were exploring variably repressed traumatic memories, which was the norm for our patient population. Loftus, and those who embraced her 'evidence', discarded over fifty years of understanding the human mind and psychogenic amnesia without compunction.

FMS proponents had a nice simple explanation: if you had a memory, you should be able to recall it and if you can't, but later you do, then the memory is not real. The presence and role of an unconscious mind and its job was entirely negated. For a trauma therapist this was like being told that the sun was actually a very big neon light running along a wire that was turned off once it went over the horizon and pulled back ready for the next day.

And yes, the founder of Betrayal Trauma Theory was the very same professor I mentioned earlier, Jennifer Freyd, who accused her father of sexually abusing her! Now we know what happens when one professor accuses another professor – a battle of titans! While her father built the castle of the FMS foundation around himself, Jennifer was also a force to be reckoned with and went on to research and publish widely on parent-child abuse trying desperately to bring the science into a debate that the media dominated with dramatic headlines. As well as a dozen articles – including the decisively named 'Science in the memory debate'[4] – she wrote three books whose title's aptly cover the issues involved: *Betrayal Trauma: The Logic of Forgetting Childhood Abuse; Trauma and cognitive science: a meeting of minds, science, and human experience; Blind to Betrayal: Why we fool ourselves we aren't being fooled.*

If we understand that the job of our unconscious mind, first and foremost, is to keep us safe from pain – and painful memories sit at the top of the list – you can appreciate just how profoundly problematic the idea of implanting is. The absolutely last thing our unconscious mind is going to do is 'make up' or adopt a traumatic memory if it did not happen. Our minds are dedicated, above all

else, to take painful memories out of our awareness using one of the four memory defences we discussed earlier.

Reading Jeni's accounts of her abuse, you can appreciate that it is hard to explain why anyone would consciously and wilfully enter that world of horror by creating stories about it. Equally, the media has not thought to explore too deeply why all these therapists would be creating and implanting horrific memories in the people they are there to help. Given the huge number of both genders that we know are abused prior to the age of eighteen, and knowing the extent of underreporting, there is a rather obvious (and horrifying) explanation for why therapists are finding these memories.

FMS on trial

The 2021 trial of Ghislaine Maxwell for trafficking minors to paedophile Geoffrey Epstein and his friends proved a turning point in the overused reliance upon FMS research. Again, Elizabeth Loftus was the expert witness for Maxwell.

We can thank journalist Lucia Osborne-Crowley who attended every day of the Maxwell trial, to give us the following detailed account and a crucial update on the fundamental limitations of FMS as a defence.[5]

As well as the lost in the mall study, the proceedings raised one of Loftus's earlier studies, where participants watched a video of a car accident. She successfully convinced some viewers that the road sign in the video was a 'yield' sign rather than a 'stop' sign.

Maxwell's defence lawyers then built on these findings that memories could be implanted as they argued that there was a strong motivation for her accusers to make up accounts of having been trafficked by Maxwell and abused by Epstein, i.e. the huge estate he left meant there were large sums of money to be made by those who could prove they were victims of Maxwell and Epstein. This was an important development as it was the first time that Loftus had been asked if a financial incentive could create a false memory. She responded by saying that she had no knowledge of any such studies, including her own, 'but based on

my research, it's definitely plausible.' Loftus was invited onto thin ice and she happily began skating on it, but then things got even more interesting.

The lawyers for the prosecution then began to pull on a thread that could unravel the central fabric flaw of FMS. They wondered whether relatively benign memories, like being lost in a mall before being re-united with your parents, or recalling a road sign, behaved the same way as a traumatic memory? This question went to the very core of the FMS defence.

The Assistant US Attorney, Lara Pomerantz, asked Loftus about a study where the researchers had tried to implant a memory of having a rectal enema – typically both a painful and embarrassing experience. Loftus had to agree that not a single participant of the twenty involved adopted the memory. Pomerantz then teased out an equally important point: the difference between the essence of a trauma memory versus the peripheral details.

'People tend to remember the core or essence of trauma events, right?' Pomerantz asked.

'They can, yes,' Loftus responded.

'People may forget some of the peripheral details of a trauma event, right?'

'That can happen, yes.'

'But the core memories of a trauma event remain stronger, right?'

'I probably agree with that.'

This was a pivotal point of agreement. The prosecution's argument prevailed and Maxwell was found guilty. To put it another way, while you might be able to convince witnesses to an accident to change a peripheral detail like a road sign from 'stop' to 'yield', they were never going to be convinced that the car accident did not happen.

To have the star witness, founder and head proponent of FMS admit that trauma memories are not only different from what she has spent her life researching, but that there is no evidence that trauma memories can be implanted, is a win of enormous

magnitude for the victims of sexual abuse. Let us hope that other prosecutors in the USA and around the world have been paying attention.

One point I would like to take a bit further is this idea that anyone would be crazy enough to lie about, or be motivated to create a memory of, being a victim of sexual assault in a world that typically shames these victims. Osborne-Crowley wrote of Loftus:

'She has managed to cement in the public consciousness the idea that memories of abuse can be false, implanted or simply wrong – which, combined with our society's statistically proven predisposition to disbelieve abuse victims, is something of a perfect storm.'

I suspect most of us can guess what happens when you go public as a victim of sexual abuse ... here is a clue, you are not quite lauded as a hero for rising above the victimisation to seek justice! Ask Jeni. For her and my patients who have done this, the typical response is victim-shaming, especially from the extended family who do not welcome the shame-by-association that follows. It is surprising just how powerful the force is that drives families to protect an abuser, at the cost of the victim.

Sadly, it is our tribal DNA betraying us. The safety in numbers provided by a connected family network outweighs the survival benefits of truth-telling, which threatens to tear the network apart.

There is a second force at work that also explains the morally reprehensible act of blaming and shaming the victim – cognitive dissonance. This is the process whereby our mind does not want to hold two conflicting ideas simultaneously, so it negates or overlooks one of them.

A simple example is why the owner of their shiny new car will tell you how faultless it is in the days after having just handed over their hard-earned cash. Come back a year later when the cost has receded into history, and they will be much happier to tell you about its problems that were there from day one.

Being told that your father/brother/son or mother/sister/daughter has sexually assaulted a family member is cognitive

dissonance of major earthquake dimensions that destabilises the very foundations of not just the family institution, but of the person's world view. Imagine how the world would respond to someone who could cause a major earthquake? Add to this smashing the house of cards various family members have often built to avoid the haunting suspicion that something terribly wrong is happening in their family.

Perhaps the most damning single statistic that speaks to the fact that victims are motivated to drastically under-report is a 2010 study finding that only 15.8 per cent of rapes and sexual assaults are reported to authorities in the USA. This figure is disturbingly unchanged from the figure of 16 per cent reported in 1992 by the National Center for Victims of Crime & Crime Victims Research and Treatment Center in the USA.[6] I would suggest that in other cultures and countries the reporting level would be lower, not higher.

In short, between our unconscious minds working at full power to not be aware of distressing memories and an external world that shames and punishes those who recall sexual abuse memories, I cannot see how any person who understands these two huge forces of nature could be a proponent of FMS. Those who remain ardent advocates have some significant financial incentive to do so (think 'expert' witnesses), or they wish to avoid jail time.

Before we leave the Freyd-Vs-Freyd-FMS-Loftus saga there is a stunning epilogue in this titanic battle – a true denouement in every sense of the word.

Elizabeth Loftus, the greatest expert witness that the FMS movement has ever had, has one last thing to say. It comes from an interview with the *New Yorker*. She was recounting how she was being attacked under cross examination for having nil experience as a trauma therapist.

'So, you really don't know anything about childhood sexual abuse, do you?' the prosecutor asked.

After a pause, Loftus said, 'I do know something about this subject because I was abused when I was six.' Recalling that

moment she wrote: 'The memory flew out at me, out of the blackness of the past, hitting me full force.'

You could not find a better description of not just recovering a memory, but of how real it can feel even after remaining dormant for all that time. Who better to illustrate the curious workings of the unconscious mind and how repression works than its greatest sceptic!

As a redoubtable epitaph, Jennifer Freyd was honoured for her work on betrayal trauma in 2016 in San Francisco with a Lifetime Achievement Award from the International Society for the Study of Trauma and Dissociation.

In contrast, 'in 2019, the False Memory Syndrome Foundation announced its cessation, as of the end of the calendar year, not with a bang, but with a whimper, just a little note on the bottom of their website homepage.'[7]

While FMS will undoubtedly be relied upon again by alleged perpetrators, the true science cannot be denied. Jeni Hayne's powerful chronicle underlines the truth of the devastating impact of Betrayal Trauma and could not have carried the case against FMS further.

CHAPTER FIFTEEN

Space to Speak

JENI

Preferred terminology

There's a reason we call our condition Multiple Personality Disorder (MPD) instead of the updated terminology Dissociative Identity Disorder (DID). Symphony created people with unique personalities, a sense of self and a role. It was a creative process, and every personality added to the richness of Jeni. It was an addition, rather than a subtraction. The term Dissociative Identity Disorder makes us think of destruction, distancing and removal. We've never pushed our identity away; we've only ever added to it. In our mind, DID equals rejection – and we've had enough rejection from the outside world; we don't need it internally, too. We are not lesser because of our MPD, we are greater for it.

As already discussed, the development of MPD is almost entirely due to crimes committed against tiny children. This fact is rarely acknowledged or addressed. I believed the link between my abuse and my multiple personalities had been seen and was being acknowledged when I was referred to the Sexual Assault Service by the Australian Federal Police. Hearing Kim Whitman recognise that she believed my disclosures to her were 'the tip of the iceberg' and that she wanted to direct me to the help I needed to disclose the rest of my story in a safe space, was the first step towards being believed. As I mentioned earlier, the idea was that the counsellors would document my allegations for the police, thus reducing my

need to relive multiple events multiple times. However, the hoped-for safe space wasn't as safe as I had hoped because my disclosures to the counsellors were met with disbelief and condemnation. This was compounded when my alters came to talk. As my personalities came out and revealed what happened and began re-experiencing my traumas, the counsellors rejected them: 'I don't want to hear it from you, I want to hear it from Jeni.'

I was doing regular group therapy through the service and one night I received a phone call from the head of the service, who was my individual counsellor and the leader of the support group. She told me a new member would be joining our group and asked, 'Could you be less multiple tomorrow?' The message, I thought, was clear: my counsellor believed I was faking MPD for attention. My belief that this was the case was strengthened in group therapy when Erik would assign the set tasks to a personality that he believed would benefit from it the most. The group leader showed me her displeasure at this and at times would belittle and demean him, and suggest how attention-seeking we were being. One day we were asked to do a self-portrait, and Erik thought this would be perfect for Symphony. She did one, and she was nude with blood between her legs. We got into trouble for doing Symphony's self-portrait. We could not win.

Worse still was the fact that I heard the counsellors specifically state to the other clients and new counsellors as they joined the service, 'Oh, you can't believe a word Jeni says, she has MPD'. So what else could I think other than that the counsellors did not believe my abuse history because I had MPD. Despite the fact that MPD is caused by abuse, I was caught in yet another lose–lose situation.

The fact that the AFP officers believed me and were investigating my allegations did nothing to dispel this belief and the counsellors refused to do anything to assist the investigation. They refused to document my disclosures for the police. They failed to comply with the requests of the AFP. They refused to help me provide evidence against my father in the form of documentation of my allegations or even a forensic medical examination of my body. As the centre was an outreach program for the sexual assault service based at a

local hospital, and some of my counselling sessions were conducted at the hospital, doing this would have been comparatively easy, but it was refused on the grounds that 'there's no point, there won't be any evidence'. Given the amount of evidence discovered in my body in 2012, this was clearly wrong. Nevertheless, in 1996 and 1997, as I begged to undergo this procedure to help prove I was telling the truth, it was denied. The service that I hoped would help me document the truth seemed to be doing all it could to help my father instead.

Compounding this, when asked to provide statements to the police, the service refused to provide any information about me specifically and gave a generic statement about how an abused person behaved and reacted. Even though I had disclosed a huge amount of my dad's abuse, none of this was mentioned. The statement was useless. In fact, the statement to the police helped to undermine me, to undermine my case, to sabotage my attempts to get justice, and looked like it would help my father escape punishment for his crimes against me.

I was desperately trying to find ways to disclose the fullness of my abuse, and it was reframed constantly into something else: play, lies, games, misunderstandings and fantasy. When this statement was sent to my father and his legal team, Dad sent it to my aunt to give to my sister, circumventing his bail conditions of no contact with Sheila by any means. The consequences of this were terrible, with my aunt and her family, and my grandmother coming to believe that I was lying. The English police told me Sheila sent a letter to them stating that Dad never abused me and that if Dad was charged with offences against me, she would testify in court in his favour and prove that I was lying. The outcome of all this was I lost all support from family in the UK.

I can only conclude that the entrenched view of most of the counsellors was that I was a liar and couldn't be trusted or believed. This had enormous implications for my ongoing treatment, my 'care' and my mental health. I was telling people what happened to me and they weren't listening – replicating my abuse beautifully, but this time it had significant legal consequences. It supported Dad's catch-

cry that I was a 'known liar' and caused the English police officer assigned to the case to doubt my allegations.

To top it all off, horrifically, and confusingly, one of the counsellors rebutted my allegations with, 'I know your father. He wouldn't do that.' This brought me undone. This counsellor refused to clarify if they actually knew my dad, and then walked out on me. I was then handed off to another social worker for my ongoing individual work, giving me no opportunity to clarify this bombshell. This ongoing work was centred on the belief the problem was the alters, not what caused them to be created, and the goal of counselling was to get rid of them quick smart.

All of this served to reframe my creative survival strategy into a mental illness and sought to fix my dysfunctional alters instead of addressing the trauma and crimes that caused us. The upshot was that when I went, as a victim of horrific sexual abuse and torture, to get help I was twisted into a mentally ill person whose word could not be trusted. The consequence for me was horrendous and it was a get-out-of-jail-free card for Dad, and the implications of that were to be truly frightening.

On my return from the UK after Dad's trial, I went with Mum to see the head counsellor for support and to debrief. They refused to help me deal with my horror and distress at how Dad had been declared not guilty, and my shock at how I had been treated by the police, prosecutor and the judge. Instead, they forced Mum and I to watch a film on dysfunctional families and family dynamics. We were left alone in the room and after about an hour of watching Mum and I were bewildered at how this was supposed to help us. We walked out and went home.

Later that week I attended a group session in which my Dad's trial was discussed. It was stated that he had been found not guilty. My disclosures about how I had been treated by the police officer in the UK was shared and the group told, 'this is what happens when you waste police time'. I was humiliated and traumatised. I was declared a liar and left in tears. Not one person made any effort to comfort me or to declare their belief in me. Not one.

SYMPHONY

Muscles has written a list on a piece of paper. It's a list of suicide methods: gun, rope, pills, gas, knife, bus. On Saturday morning Mum has an appointment with our GP – Sue. During that appointment, Muscles hands his list to Sue and asks which one will absolutely kill us. We don't want to mess it up. Please circle the correct answer.

When Sue tells Mum I'm suicidal, Mum dismisses it. 'No, you're not, Jeni,' she says. Sue hands Mum the list. There it is: in black and white and in Muscles' handwriting. Sue refers me to the Mental Health Unit at the Prince Charles Hospital and tells Mum to take me there immediately. Mum is still not accepting of the true state of our mental health and takes me home for lunch, to pack a bag and to talk about how I'm not really sick enough to go to hospital. A little rest and I'll be okay, she says. Muscles takes this as even Mum doesn't believe us. We get to the hospital mid afternoon and are admitted quick smart! The doctor says it's a 'little break'. Mum says it will do me good.

MUSCLES

The lights are fluorescent and make me look even more washed out than I am. I feel like a living corpse – and I wish I were a dead one. I've given up. Living isn't for me. It's too hard, too dark, too painful. I keep saying I want to die. Why won't they let me die?

The ward is like space. We're surrounded by strangers and strange things. We eat a salad for dinner and pour sugar on the lettuce. We don't make sense. Nothing makes sense. I'm in a room on my own with three empty beds. The shower is down the corridor, and I'm meant to walk there from my room in a towel in front of the male patients. The showers don't have curtains or doors. Nope. Not happening. Forget it.

Another patient threatens to kill us. We welcome it. There are people everywhere, all the time. All I want is to sit in a room on my own and sing. Instead, I'm taken to a stretching class and told to act like a tree. Nope. Not happening. Forget it.

I need to rock and sing and recalibrate. I find a room and sing every death song we've ever heard – tales of heartbreak, pain and loss. I sing for five hours straight at the top of my voice. Every line cuts a hole in the black plastic that envelops us until we break free. We come back to life.

SYMPHONY

Frank visits me in the hospital. He says no matter what happened in England, he believes me, he's always believed me. His words mean more than any other sentence I've ever heard from him.

A support worker named Dave listens to my story. Well, he doesn't really listen because he's deaf, but he reads my lips and understands what I'm saying and why I'm so upset. He says, 'English law is an ass.' His words give me a comfort I've never known. A psychiatrist diagnoses me with Non-Schizophreniform Auditory Hallucinations. Their words mean nothing to me.

Muscles is angry the doctor didn't give his list back. His words are stolen.

JENI

I spent three weeks in the mental health unit and when I was released, I was still upset, but no longer suicidal. The outside world was exactly the same. The sun still rose every morning and set every evening. The Brisbane streets still smelt like dirt when it rained. And I still didn't have any justice or closure.

But life, as they say, went on.

CHAPTER SIXTEEN

Parallel Lives: Disbelief and Rejection

THE STUDENT

Living my life was not easy. I had to manage my MPD at the same time as study, work at the Brisbane Valley Markets on the weekend as assistant manager, do therapy, and deal with people. It was tough, but The Rulebook came in very handy. He gave us our rules of engagement for every interaction. He defined each person as they entered our world: people could be defined as casual acquaintance, friend, stallholder, boss, or authority figure. Their assigned definition built the basis of the rules of how to interact with that person. But the rules for everyone were different.

Each set of rules of engagement were highly flexible and were subject to change at any moment. The rules of engagement for friends might include things to talk about or things to avoid talking about. There were lists of things each person liked and disliked, what they were good at and what they needed help with. Study friends had rules about interactions at university: to be in a group with this person or not, where to meet and what to talk about. Friends from the market world had very different rules. I had a position of authority as I collected the rent from the stallholders. This had to be factored into my relationships and the rules of engagement reflected this.

At the same time, I read everything I could find on MPD and noted our similarities and stark differences to the examples given

in the books and articles. I noticed the emphasis on solving issues within and between alters, while being struck by the absence of any recognition of the criminality of the acts which had led to the development of MPD. There was no talk of reporting the crime, none of having the perpetrator charged and absolutely none of the successful prosecution of an offender. The only justice-related talk was on persons within the criminal justice system who claimed to suffer from MPD to avoid responsibility for their actions; See for example, the rapist Billy Milligan and serial killer Kenneth Bianchi.

SYMPHONY
This notion of avoiding responsibility because you had MPD was completely at odds with how Erik and I ran our day-to-day system. Erik was big on 'if the gob said it, or the body did it, we own it'. Taking responsibility for our actions, regardless of which of us did it, or said it, was a major part of who we are. None of this, 'it wasn't me, it was (insert other alter's name)', was acceptable. We had to hide that Jeni was plural, that she wasn't normal. Saying dumb things like this would have brought the wrong kind of attention from Dad and we already had way too much of that. So if one alter did it, everyone owned it. That's why the complaint to Grandma stands out in our memory so clearly. No one owned it. No one admitted that they said it. The cacophony of denials was overwhelming. We still have no idea who said it. But we owned it anyway.

JENNY
I attempted to continue with therapy through the sexual assault service. I attended both private counselling sessions and a sexual assault group. My expectations going into this group had been that we would talk about our abuse experiences and get help, we would share experiences and learn from one another that the abuse was not our fault. I, and my alters, were fully prepared to do this but in my experience the group members were more interested in competing for the title of most abused victim, and the counsellors supported this.

Worse, they chose favourites amongst the clients and over supported their favourite to the detriment of the rest of the group.

I was not a favourite!

I found both the personal therapy and group therapy sessions to be drama-filled, toxic and, quite frankly, pointless. Instead of working through our issues, we'd spend most of the time hashing over disagreements and perceived slights between members of the support group. Throughout the sessions I was accused of the most outrageous things by the counsellors and the clients alike. When I denied them I was told 'it must have been one of your alters'. The counsellors and clients were now using my alters against me. It was horrible and confusing. Even when the counsellors recognised I was distressed and tried to help me they turned it into an opportunity to attack and blame me.

Early on in therapy I had disclosed that Dad used to press down on my right shoulder as he passed me on some days when he would abuse me. I learned to see this as a warning or heads-up that he was going to rape me that night. I told my counsellor about this and how it had caused a kind of anticipatory terror. It also triggered Zombie Girl. She would arrive to allow us to obey Dad without complaint, to comply with all of his instructions and robotically do what needed to be done. I revealed this without letting the counsellor meet our Zombie Girl. The counsellor appeared to use this trigger against me in group therapy, using me as a kind of surrogate counsellor. When the counsellors were busy with clients, they would press down on my shoulder and direct me to give another client support and help. I obeyed. I had no choice. Zombie Girl had been triggered and we were compliant and obedient just as we'd been in an attempt to avoid the rape we knew was coming. The anticipatory terror could last for days. It was hardly good therapy for me or the other client.

A similar process took place one day in group. I can't even remember what we were doing that day, and with my memory that's saying something. What I can remember is being asked what I was feeling. I replied and said I was angry. The response was 'no you're not. What are you feeling?' I tried to find a different word to say I was

angry, but again this was denied and the counsellor demanded that I find a different feeling. The counsellor walked behind me and placed their hands on my shoulders, forcing me downwards in my seat, holding me down as I was again asked what I was feeling. The second counsellor came across and squatted in front of me. She put her hands on my lower arms and held me still in the seat. By this time we'd been attempting to find the acceptable word for over twenty minutes and I was crying hysterically. Every word, every feeling I expressed was denied. I was continually told, 'no you're not feeling that. Tell me what you're feeling.' It was all a massive violation of my rights reframed as therapy. This process was eventually stopped by a group member screaming at the counsellors to stop. I was left in my seat sobbing silently, traumatised and awaiting further abuse. The only person who comforted me was the group member who intervened.

The other group members watching that day learned I could be blamed for anything and there would be no consequences for them, only me. I had become the punching bag of the group and the clients and counsellors role-played out their family dynamics and abuse patterns using me as the victim. It was a replay of my childhood and I felt as trapped with them as I had felt with Dad.

On the wall in the therapy room, there was a piece of fabric where we were encouraged to write thoughts and feelings. I wrote, 'To feel is to reveal.' I was pulled up for it in the next session and asked to explain my statement. Nobody understood it, they told me. At the end of the day, I added two words to the phrase in the hope of squashing the misunderstanding, 'To feel is to reveal the truth.' But I stand by my original statement. To feel is to reveal. Unfortunately, the counsellors were not willing to help me get in touch with my feelings.

I made numerous attempts to improve my situation at the centre. I went so far as to write out a complaint letter, intending to send it to the head of staff or to the complaints department. I took my only copy with me to my next counselling session to discuss. It was ripped to shreds in front of me. I was told that my complaint was baseless, petty and spiteful and that I was complaining because I

was jealous of the time my counsellor gave to other clients. I was devastated. This perception of me and my motives was so far from the reality, but instead of standing firm, I was weakened and began to doubt my reality.

I also made numerous attempts to leave the group but it seemed I was stopped from doing this. It was organised for other members of the support group to come and collect me to take me to group. The more I fought this the worse it got. In the end I submitted. I felt powerless. The bullying I felt I received built upon my original abuse and trauma. I remained in therapy with these counsellors and attended group until 2003.

The entire experience was negative for me, and yet when I tried to address that negativity and assert my boundaries I was re-victimised and my boundaries were violated. It took me years to see what had been done to me as a form of abuse.

The only good thing about the years of group therapy was my friendship with the group member who had intervened that day I was asked to constantly find a new word. Our friendship continues to this day. She has been a great support over the years.

Seven years after I had finished with that counselling centre I met up with a group of women preparing a display for International Women's Day. This group was being facilitated through a different sexual assault service, but was not meant to be a therapeutic group. A woman I had met through the sexual assault centre was also there. She seemed surprised and happy to see me and we sat chatting. Later that day, as she spoke about her abuse she hit me on my upper arm. I was stunned and after a few moments I got up and left the table so I could ground myself and deal with my feelings. Once I had calmed down, I returned to the table. When there was a break in the conversation, I asked why this person had hit me.

Confronting this kind of abuse was new for me and I was frightened of her response and the responses of the rest of the participants in the group. She completely denied hitting me. I argued that she had indeed hit me and I had the mark to prove it. The other women also agreed that she had hit me and asked her to explain. She

had no explanation for her behaviour. It had been an automatic and possibly even unconscious behaviour. She continued to deny she had hit me, crying that I was picking on her and telling me to stop. It was a most outrageous display of victim blaming.

What was critically important to me about this interaction was that I had upheld my right to personal safety, my boundaries about acceptable and unacceptable behaviour and I'd done it almost immediately after the attack. This was a first for me. I expected the denials, it was the fact that I was supported by the other women that was unexpected and shocking. Instead of supporting the aggressor against me – as was my experience previously – the other women supported me, validated and acknowledged what had been done to me, and demanded an explanation and an apology for me. The response this got was a violation of my privacy as she disclosed that I had MPD, as if that gave her permission to hit me. This person went on to claim that I was lying about her hitting me and to state that I was a known liar. Thankfully the women were not side-tracked by the MPD thing, they knew what they had seen and kept insisting that this woman apologise to me. She refused to do this on the grounds I was lying about being hit and then she fled the group. I never saw her again.

JENI

At home, Mum didn't want to talk about Dad or anything to do with my abuse. She begged for 'penis-free days'. I wouldn't have minded more of those in my childhood! Mum had heard enough of my abuse stories to be traumatised, but not enough to understand the nature or extent of my abuse and my coping strategy of MPD. She struggled to take it in. The devastating experiences at group therapy and the issues that raised obscured a lot of what I was trying to tell her. I once tried explaining my MPD and the 'chunnels' in my mind to Mum; she told me in 2012 that she thought I was writing a story about bunnies building underground tunnels.

As I said earlier, my mum came from a family of secrets, and she never escaped. She thought I was wallowing in the event of one

rape. She didn't understand I was talking about thousands of violent, sadistic rapes over fourteen years.

Up until 2009 Mum never asked me a single question about what happened. After the infamous Buster Boy phone call, which I will outline later, Mum began to talk about what had actually happened to me. Her response was to tell me to talk to Dad's public protection officer in the UK. We both wanted to let the officer know the danger Dad was to children, not just teenagers. I did this and Dad's PPO immediately said 'we can do something about that' and referred me to the Australian police. And back to the AFP I went. Mum supported me in this, supported me as I went to the Queensland police and has continued to support me to this day. She believes me. Thank god, she believes me! I don't think Mum understood the extent of Dad's abuse until the trial in 2019. When the judge's comments laid bare the truth of his devastating abuse of me it hit her and she was crushed.

CHAPTER SEVENTEEN

Parallel Lives: Finding my Way in the Academic World

THE STUDENT

I graduated from the University of Queensland in 1996 in the middle of the lead-up to Dad's 1997 UK trial with a Bachelor of Arts degree in psychology. I credit the fact I managed to continue my studies and graduate with all this going on to the way my alters could utilise the amnestic barriers in our mind to our advantage. Erik organised a special space for me to study and built walls around me, so the noise of the others did not impact on my studying. I was allowed to focus all my attention on my studies because Erik recognised I was trying to help us all by working out what was wrong with us.

In December 1996 I accepted a place in a Master's program just being developed in the School of Social Sciences. This became the Masters of Social Science, Legal Studies and Criminal Justice. Throughout this course I explored the law to see if Dad's behaviour against me was criminal. Further, I explored the reactions of the community to allegations of childhood sexual abuse and incest in my thesis. I discovered that the reactions of some therapists were horrific!

Don't forget I'm studying while undergoing therapy and what I found most assuredly impacted on my attitudes to the counsellors and to George. I was beginning to learn what was good therapy and what was bad, and I did not like what I was seeing at the sexual

assault group. The counsellors were definitely not doing good therapy with me.

By the time I graduated in 2000 I was sure Dad's treatment of me was abuse and a very serious crime, but I thought the time to deal with it was long past. I didn't think there was anything I could do to impose consequences on my father now. I thought the only way I could address my abuse was in therapy. So I kept going with my parallel lives, studying like a beaver while continuing in therapy with the sexual abuse service and with George.

In 2007 I completed my Doctor of Philosophy (PhD). I had done research on men's experiences of being a victim of crime. I wanted to humanise men, learn that they weren't all threatening rapists and demonstrate to my alters that men could be safe people. I wanted us all to see men far more realistically. So not only did I focus my research on men, I also insisted on doing face-to-face interviews with them. My research was as challenging to us as I could make it. I even added learning to drive as one of the goals to be accomplished as part of the PhD. After all, you need a car to get to homes and workplaces to interview people. Study was not an escape from our past, it was part of our attempts to overcome our past. I think I can safely say we aced it. I often tell people I studied psychology to find out what was wrong with me, criminology to find out what was wrong with Dad and the PhD to stop being afraid of men.

In a way, my studies were stepping stones on my journey to finding my voice and telling my story. In academia, I found myself. I grew in knowledge and, by excelling in my field, I grew in confidence and strength. Undertaking a PhD is an extraordinary feat for anyone, let alone someone whose early education was grossly mismanaged. But, then again, creating 2500 personalities is an extraordinary feat too, and we did that before we turned fourteen.

Throughout my studies for my PhD I worked as an academic tutor for my PhD supervisor, and for other lecturers. I tutored courses in Criminology, Women and the Law, Research Methods, Qualitative Research Methodologies and a course in Quantitative

Research Methods. These were challenging for me, but oh so much fun. I loved it.

Micromanaging the enormous amount of alters we had, managing triggers, hiding my MPD, dealing with relationships between alters and my colleagues, maintaining my academic relationship with my supervisor and completing my studies became extremely difficult.

One particular challenge was to ensure the alter with the appropriate knowledge and skills showed up to teach the class. This problem reared its ugly head the day I was due to teach statistics to social science students. The alter with the knowledge failed to show up for class. This left Symphony in the body and she stepped up to teach the class. She was four years old at the time! She taught statistics and how to use the computer program SSPS for the entire semester. She was highly successful at helping those students with a fear of statistics to pass the course. However, having a four-year-old teaching statistics was not ideal. Symphony coped well, but we became aware that if we could not guarantee to be able to produce the correct alter to teach classes we would be fired. Ultimately these issues made employment impossible.

CHAPTER EIGHTEEN

Parallel Lives: Help at Last

JENI

Even though Dad was in jail in England, he was still having a negative impact on my life in Australia. I was dealing with vivid flashbacks and was forced to relive the abuse over and over again. Christmas time was the worst. From 10 December to 24 January, after my birthday, I would experience upwards of twenty flashbacks a day. I dreaded the festive season with the passion of the Grinch. The flashbacks weren't just flickers of past memories, they were physical and mental torture. My body re-experienced the pain and my mind went through the terror. I desperately wanted and needed professional help.

I needed to tell my story in all its gruesome detail. I needed to be believed and I was prepared to give every repulsive detail if I had to. I was committed to telling my truth despite all the barriers that were in my way. Erik prepared a safe space where we could go to talk without distressing other alters who did not want or need to know the details. We started the search for a psychiatrist who could help us.

It was important to me to have a male psychiatrist. With female counsellors, and even my female psychiatrist, I'd felt a need to protect them and minimise my experiences to save them distress. My sessions often ended with them in tears and me comforting them. My then psychiatrist was so uncomfortable with my disclosures and my feelings that she would terminate our session the minute I

began to cry. I learned if I wanted help I needed to be emotionless. So I hoped to find someone who could take on my story without me having to put their feelings first.

I was also interested to see how a man reacted to my disclosures. If the man told me what Dad had done was terrible and criminal, he would know what he was talking about. If the man didn't get aroused at what I told him, he'd confirm that there was something wrong with Dad.

I felt like I'd been completely failed by the counsellors at the sexual assault service, however, they did one magnificent thing for me: they referred me to Dr George Blair-West and I had my first appointment with him in early 1998. The referral was the only good thing to come out of my experience with them.

George was a renowned psychiatrist, but at the time he didn't have any experience working with clients with MPD – or Dissociative Identity Disorder (DID), as it is now called. Nevertheless, the difference between George and every other therapist I'd seen was that he believed me, and he committed to helping me and understanding my complex diagnosis.

ERIK

I saunter into the psychiatrist's office.

'What brings you here?' asks Dr George Blair-West.

'I hear voices in my head,' I explain. 'They never shut up. I get out of bed in the morning and there's always a lively discussion going on about what I'm going to wear for the day.

'I can go to university on a Thursday wearing pants, and the next thing I know it's Tuesday and I'm in a completely different outfit and carrying a pile of new books,' I continue.

'I find essays written in handwriting I don't recognise and have no recollection of penning them,' I press on, before explaining the fourteen years of abuse I suffered at the hands of my father.

'So, what do you think's going on, Doc?' I ask. 'What's wrong with me?'

'I think you already know,' George replies.

'Oh yeah, I know, I just need to hear it from you,' I say.

'You have multiple personality disorder as a result of severe childhood abuse,' he diagnoses.

'Okay, thank you.' I nod, standing up and heading towards the door.

'I can help you with that,' George calls out.

I've never heard a more beautiful sentence: I can help you with that.

I book another appointment for the following week and rush to the toilet. Tears fall down my cheeks like confetti. We cry and we cry and we cry. For twenty-eight years, we'd believed we were beyond help. We were helpless. But there is a man who can help us. He says so.

I go to the Rulebook and ask to see his rules of engagement for George. I add two promises to it. I will never lie to George, and I will be upfront if I don't know the answer to a question. The promises still stand.

Now I must admit that when I took us all to see George I wanted validation of our self-diagnosis, and I got that. But I really hadn't thought past that. I knew that everyone was scarred from what Dad had done to us, both in our life with him, but also in court. We need help to get back on an even keel. We needed George to get us there. But how was he going to help us? We didn't have a clue!

Meeting Dr George Blair-West changed everything.

EVERYTHING!

Navigating Jeni's Internal World

DR GEORGE BLAIR-WEST AND JENI HAYNES

It was an auspicious Friday the thirteenth in February 1998 when Jeni walked into my office. Then as now, she carried herself well. There was a sense of independence, almost defiance, about her. (Over time I was to realise that it was born from an expectation of being failed ... yet again.) She was polite and well-spoken with a slight lilt to her voice that declared her English origins. I could see she was not at all alien to the process, as she had seen other therapists before me. She settled into my armchair and told me her story.

It rapidly became obvious that Jeni had an unusual grasp of the psychology around the subjects we covered. I asked her about her education and my notes from that day's record say, 'BA double major psych, Masters of criminology.' I do not usually ask my patients, after I have taken a history, what they think their diagnosis is, but you can see why I did with Jeni.

It became apparent that Jeni could educate me on a lot more than just DID. Indeed, in the end, she gave me a masterclass on all aspects of successfully prosecuting a paedophile, complete with the complexities of international extradition. As she spoke, looking into her hazel eyes there was both a distance and an intensity. The emotional distancing fitted with her history of extensive abuse and

over time I came to understand the intensity – she missed nothing. Absolutely nothing. Her hypervigilance extended to reading every aspect of me from my physical presentation, the setup of my office, through to my non-verbal signals and any slight shift in my posture. (Later, she was to admit that she watched me closely as she spoke of her abuse to see if I was getting turned on – disconcerting, but understandable.) I have never asked Jeni how many alters look after threat assessment, but my guess is that it was a battalion in its own right.

While I had never seen a case of DID, what I had seen, however, was many, many cases of what comprises what we call the 'differential diagnosis' i.e. what DID could be confused with.

As I described back on pages 90–91, the conditions that DID are most likely to be confused with are bipolar disorder and schizophrenia. There are critical differences, however, and Jeni's presentation highlighted them. It is rare to hear fully-formed voices with elaborate messages in bipolar disorder but, more importantly, there needs to be mood disturbance – elevated or depressed - which Jeni did not have. People with schizophrenia often hear voices but they are typically one-way messages that they are receiving. Typically, these messages are of some pending persecution and make up part of a greater delusional belief system. Jeni described conversations *between various parts of herself.* Moreover, Jeni's voices spoke about more mundane, day-to-day issues like what skills, or clothes, she needed for the day ahead. Unlike schizophrenia, her voices were grounded entirely in dealing with reality. This is a subtle, but powerful clue.

Not so subtle, but a dead giveaway, is Jeni's description of losing time and not recalling interactions with key people in her life. This is the hallmark of dissociation. There is no other explanation for this. Finding clothing in your wardrobe that you do not recall buying is another hallmark – especially when the alter in front of me says, 'And I would never be seen dead in that!' Different handwriting is also a classic sign, especially when some of the writing is in the style expected of a six-year-old.

While Jeni had a head-start by virtue of her studies, it is well documented that DID is one of the few conditions where people research and accurately make their own diagnosis. Ironically, it is also documented how poorly trained psychiatrists and psychologists still do not believe the diagnosis, even when it is handed to them on a platter!

Preparing the way for trauma therapy

What I am about to describe, of the principles of therapy, is based more on what I have learnt from Jeni, and other patients since, rather than what I did back then. This will also be more relevant to interested therapists. Unfortunately, for Jeni it was not all in place when I started working with her, but she and I have agreed that I should give those who have been traumatised a clear sense of what to expect from an experienced therapist in the 2020s. Nevertheless, Jeni will comment on the issues with therapies she received back then from me and others. I will also comment on key learnings that I have had along the way.

In treating this condition there is quite a bit of work to do before you can actually treat the core traumas. The first thing to be done is to start building a 'therapeutic relationship' with the patient. Without this, therapy goes nowhere. The first casualty of abuse is trust. On the other hand, trust is the backbone of good therapy, so Jeni and I needed to take the time to build it. I never ask my patients to trust me, instead I ask them to work out *how to* trust me. Growing up without trust means you do not learn, or get practice in, how to work out who to trust.

Jeni had very good reasons not to trust anyone given the repeated abuse and then the failures to be helped that she had experienced. Learning how to work out who to trust is an important skill. Most of my abused patients do not trust, leaving them isolated and alone. After extended periods of time in this sad, abandoned state, they decide they should trust someone and so they 'take a chance' on someone who looks like they might help. Without a system of working out trustworthiness, this typically goes badly.

So, I encourage my patients to watch closely how I, or anyone they want to trust, deals with what they disclose over time. I highlight that the only way we can work out trust is by giving people small amounts of sensitive information and seeing how they hold it and then how they bring it back to you. How much do they do this with care and sensitivity? As time is the ultimate test, this work needs time to allow the trust to build.

Little things add to this process of trust-building. I was surprised, in writing this book with Jeni, how important what we might call 'little "b" boundary issues' were. Psychiatrists are given a lot of training in how to manage more obvious boundaries with a focus on dealing with attraction, out of hours support and physical intimacy. Receiving gifts, compliments and responding to a crying patient also get considerable airplay. Jeni opened my mind up to how apparently minor interactions could be consequential for someone with her experiences. Let me hand over to Jeni's alters to elaborate:

THE RULEBOOK

Meeting George was terrifying and exhilarating at the same time. Creating rules of engagement for him was tough. We were trying to create new boundaries for him, but the relationship was special and ever-changing. It was George who modelled good boundary setting for us, and then showed us that he could and would respect the boundaries we set. We were very tentative with him at first. Being terrified of making a mistake and being punished is not conducive to the development of a stable and therapeutic relationship.

Over time we created a relationship of trust, equality and respect, based on mutual desires to do what was best for Symphony and Jeni. We had never had a relationship with anyone whose goals were to do what was right for us and us alone. It was very strange, and sometimes quite uncomfortable. George pushed us psychologically, challenged us, and disagreed with us. He did this in a safe way that allowed us to examine our comments, our beliefs and attitudes without judgement.

After our failure to get Dad punished for his abuse of us in   the UK, we had returned to our gloomy, dingy dungeon. George opened up windows of opportunity for us. The light he shone into our world was clear, clean and incredibly sharp. He understood so much of us without saying so. His presence in our life was both wonderful and terrible. He accepted all of us, believed us and gave us the space and support to begin to tell our story. I don't mean he was perfect, not by any means, but he was trying and that meant a lot to us.

SYMPHONY

The first time George apologised for running late, his apology ricocheted through my head for months. He wasn't blaming me for something that sat on his side of the boundaries between us. Growing up I had no boundaries and no right to boundaries. If I tried to set a boundary it was trampled on, busted, violated within seconds. I was left with a sense of 'I'm nothing'. Something as simple as, 'Jeni, I want a cup of coffee'. I respond, 'I will make it in a minute, just have to finish this,' would be followed by the demand 'where's my coffee', as if I hadn't spoken.

So, George's apology and recognition that he had kept me waiting was a) alien and b) jarring, as this kind of interaction between two people was something I had never experienced before. It meant he saw me, he valued my time, and he valued me as a human. There were so many meanings that were attached to this kind of behaviour, where I could see George saw me as a real person. The first time he offered me morning tea and asked his secretary to make it, he saw me as a real person, a person with likes and dislikes, as I had to decide between tea or coffee and biscuits or not. George was recognising that I had the right to make choices, something that did not happen at home, and helping me to understand this.

While I was making bigger choices with George, for example, what I wanted to talk about that day and how deep I was willing to go, there was something special about the immediacy of this interaction in which my tea arrived, the way I wanted it with biscuits that were not taken off my plate at the last minute. It was the

fulfilment of a promise. To quote the words told to me as a child, 'promises were meant to be broken'. And they were, reliably and often. This little morning tea ritual, that played out if I saw George at that time of the day, began to unpick my belief that I was unworthy.

I was far more used to a world where I would do a task around the house with a promised benefit, but when it came time to collect, my siblings would get the benefit, even though they hadn't done anything, and I would not. So, I learnt my family did not see me as worthy of getting even the simplest treat, gift or benefit. This was a lesson learned through hundreds of tiny interactions with my family members. The tiny interactions between George and I began to unpick this and replace it with a sense of self-worth.

GEORGE

It was surprising to have Jeni explain all this to me as we were writing this book. I had no idea of the fullness of what was happening around our morning teas. It is a salutary reminder of how, as therapists, we need to be careful of how we conduct ourselves in all aspects of our work. We need to pay particular attention to clarifying and managing our boundaries, as we remember that interactions between therapist and patient are always interactions between humans that have reverberations that define us all. Of course, we will make mistakes, but we need to be ready to address them as we recognise that these apparently smaller interactions can have consequences of magnitude.

As well as being clueless as to what 'having morning tea' meant to Jeni, I was equally unaware, until we came to write this book, about how important it was to Jeni for me to believe her story. After her experiences with the social workers that the police had referred her to, I had no idea that she expected me not to believe her story and was working hard to convince me of it. She explained (now, not then) how she could not even talk of how she was disbelieved by the police and social workers for fear of creating doubts in my mind.

I, in turn, have explained to Jeni (now, not then) that therapists have to take their patients at face value. Unlike other medical

specialists, we have no blood tests to run, no x-rays to take, which will tell us more than what our patient will tell us. Sure, we are quickly evaluating if the person's thinking and mental operations are working properly, but once we ascertain that this is the case, and that what they are saying is not driven by delusions, hallucinations or mind-altering substances, we get on board for the duration. We stay on board unless something comes along that does not add up.

At no point did anything Jeni say not add up, or not fit into her bigger picture. I knew, as do most psychologists and psychiatrists who have been trained in the last decade, that DID is created through gross betrayal trauma before the age of around eight. So, as Jeni spoke about her early abuses, I not only had no reason to doubt them, I expected them in one form or another. Any reaction I did have never went to the question, 'Could this have happened?' but to the point 'how sad it was that it happened to a young, defenceless child'. From there my thoughts typically move to reflecting on the courage that it takes the person in front of me to confront these painful memories, while being impressed by how the human mind can cleverly contain these memories to allow the person to function.

I share these reactions, not to reassure the person that I believe them, but to let them know I am there, connected with them in the moment. Another therapist will point out that my mind is defending itself in this way so I can cope and stay on board with my patient at these times, and that may be true too.

On the subject of time, I explain to all my patients with high level dissociation and DID that we will be working together for some years. Initially, I was worried that this would freak them out or that they would feel I was locking them in to see me more than they needed to. I should not have worried. My patients have since made it clear that they would find it more concerning if I suggested that I could fix them in a dozen sessions. As I point out, it took an entire childhood to cause their problems, it will take us a few years to set things right. Most importantly, they know I am in for the long haul and will not bail on them if things take longer than expected.

This cuts both ways. Therapists need to ensure when they start working with someone with DID that they are in for the long haul and that they have the capacity, practically and emotionally, to see the work through.

With Jeni, the next job was to let her know that I could cope with hearing about her horrific abuse. It took me a while to realise just how much Jeni, and many patients since, look closely to see how the therapist is coping. If they have any concerns, they will start to close down. This interferes greatly with the patient's therapy. Our patients have enough to deal with without worrying about looking after their therapist. This is one of the reasons why therapists who have been traumatised themselves cannot do effective therapy until they have dealt with and fully processed their own traumas.

These days I will make it very clear to my patients that over the last twenty-five years I have heard the worst of the worst, so they know they do not have to worry about me. There are limited forms that horrific sexual abuse can take, but the meaning for the given person varies greatly and this is the focus of therapy. It also helps to bring a little matter-of-factness in your responses when they tell you of their horror experiences as too much empathic responsiveness can again have them worrying about affecting you. The more they worry about the therapist, the less disclosure and effective therapy they do.

SYMPHONY

I agree that expressing too much emotion can cause the patient to shut down. This happened for me with my previous psychiatrist. But, conversely, too much distance can cause other issues. When I disclosed my abuse at the sexual assault centre I was denied any kind of compassion or empathy, let alone therapy. As a result I felt disbelieved and I gave more and more explicit details in a desperate effort to prove I was telling the truth. Working out the balance between too much empathy and too little empathy is quite the dance.

GEORGE

Therapists working in this space can be traumatised by what they hear. This phenomenon is called vicarious traumatisation. It is where a person becomes traumatised by hearing detailed descriptions of abuse. We therapists all need to protect ourselves by getting our own supervision and support. For twenty-five years I have regularly attended a meeting with other trauma therapists for just this reason. I can't stress the need for therapists to have their own support networks.

When I started doing more trauma work after my training in EMDR, around six years before I started with Jeni, I also sought out individual supervision from a senior psychiatrist. This, along with my trauma work in childhood sexual abuse, prepared me for my work with Jeni's extensive abuse. Now, I in turn, supervise psychologists and psychiatrists working in this field. While I am no longer taking on new patients (and have been unable to for some years now as I am semi-retired) I will always find time to supervise another therapist. This is both for their professional support and because I get to help a greater number of patients, albeit indirectly, this way.

SYMPHONY

I think it is important to make this point to a patient with a trauma history early on in therapy. But it's crucial to use care in how to word this. George handled this with a great deal of sensitivity, but I was still frightened to tell him things. I was still working with the counsellors at the sexual assault service and they continued to, to my mind, dismiss my accounts of abuse as lies and fantasies. The amount of eye rolling I saw was phenomenal! Their words and actions undermined George for years.

In the end I focused on George's actual reactions to my disclosures instead of my predictions of how he would act and react. He handled my disclosures with sensitivity, recognising my burning need to tell and be heard. He never ever shut me down with 'I've heard it all before' even if he had heard many different versions of

the same event, told to him from the many alters who experienced it. Each person had a piece of the puzzle and George worked carefully to help us put it back together.

Previously, when counsellors told me 'you can tell me anything, I've heard it all before', I heard my abuse dismissed as nothing. I was trying to tell the worst days of my life, the most horrific events I had ever experienced. I was trying to puzzle out what had happened to me. I felt this dismissal of my trauma quite badly. However, when the counsellors heard my stories and went on to cry and need me to support and take care of them my need for help became secondary to the needs of the counsellor. It's important to show consistency between your words and your deeds, while being sensitive to the needs of the patient.

GEORGE

I recall a milestone in my own personal 'working through' that happened a few years before I saw Jeni. I had just seen a patient who described being violently raped by her father when she was five, as we were doing EMDR therapy. After she left my office, I began to sob uncontrollably, surprising no one more than myself.

I realised that I was grieving for not just the patient I had just seen, but all the innocent young children who had had, and would have in the future, horrific experiences like this. Since that cathartic day, I have not found myself being particularly upset about my patients' experiences. I find that now my mind focuses not on how terrible it is, but how courageous it is that the person in front of me can seek help and then voluntarily confront this pain. It is such an honour to have the opportunity to witness this fortitude and valour, and to be able to help them finish the work that they have so bravely begun.

Jeni and I began our work together, as one always does, by first getting a sense of the lay of the land of her internal landscape. The building trust happens as you work together, and the early work pushes the issue of trust because it is all about asking the patient to share how their inner world works. This is not easy for them as

much of the power of DID comes from it being a secret system that the perpetrators do not understand. I liken it to giving up the blueprints to where all the secret passages and escape routes are in their well-fortified castle.

DID, like all good castles, has multiple levels of defences. First, there is the moat (keeping a distance – that look in Jeni's eyes when I first met her), then there are walls with the turrets where the archers shoot from (a preparedness to fight back), and when all else fails, there are the secret escape routes in their mind. People do not give these blueprints up lightly, for good reason, and the amount of trust determines how quickly they will reveal their defensive structures.

We call this process, 'mapping the system'. It involves getting to know all the key alters. I do this in a table format where I find out about each of the following points of the alters that I meet:

- Name and age of the alter at creation and now – this gives me a sense of their seniority in the system as well as how much they have matured over time;
- What their primary role is, i.e. what part of Jeni's life do they look after? The system is very much built to react appropriately to whatever is asked of them at a given point in time;
- What their current concerns are – particularly about what I'm doing in therapy. Failure to appreciate these concerns means that more powerful alters may actually sabotage therapy – which is a not unreasonable thing to do if you feel that the therapy has not been planned well enough;
- Trauma awareness – alters either have no awareness at all of the trauma, which is how they can function on a day-to-day basis, or they have indirect awareness, i.e. they know that the trauma happened to others in the system. Then you have the alters, like Maggot, who actually experienced the trauma. To make things more

complicated you can have a group of alters that share the knowledge/experience of a trauma or group of traumas as they coped with parts of a given event or group of events. When it comes to doing the actual trauma work, if you don't know which alters you need to work with, you're wasting both your time and the patient's.

- There are other things that I would cover, but this gives an idea of this reasonably painstaking work that needs to be in place before you do the trauma work. This preparatory work is just as important as the trauma work as it not only provides a necessary structure that we rely on going forward, it is also how we actively build the trust and collaboration central to this kind of therapy.

ERIK

Despite calling it different things, George was interested in learning how our MPD worked. He was interested in who we were, how old we were, what sort of things we did, and why. It was weird to talk to someone who accepted – quite happily it seemed – that he wasn't always talking to Jeni. As I was running the system at the time it was comparatively easy for me to get information out to him.

In our early sessions, I gave George a brief rundown of our life to date with a particular and somewhat pointed emphasis on recent events: the trial in England, the judgement and our recent admission to the Prince Charles Hospital. Okay, I'll admit I called it the nuthatch, not hospital, but same thing. I was quite embarrassed that we'd actually been in a mental hospital and felt ashamed and humiliated. George gently pointed out that it had been a chance to pull out of my normal routine and rest a little to recover from the trauma of the trial. He showed me that there was no shame in needing a rest. He also told me how it had obtained for me a diagnosis. Yep 'Non-Schizophreniform Auditory Hallucinations' actually meant something. It was, according to George, the hospital euphemism for MPD. Well, that was a surprise!

JENNY

In going to see George we made certain commitments. One of those was to take therapy seriously and give it a go. In practical terms this meant we treated therapy as a 24/7 thing. We worked on ourselves constantly. At all times there were alters working on their issues. We didn't stop. While we could only have George for a short time each week, we could continue our therapy without him. Our therapy ran parallel to our studies. Our studies were the public face of Jeni, and behind the scenes we worked like beavers on our MPD. I saw George every week for fifty minutes: it was nowhere near enough time. We never seemed to be able to cover what everyone wanted to say. This was an ongoing theme throughout therapy and over time I developed strategies to address this problem. Volcano can explain these better than me. The Student was continuing to study psychology, and I absorbed as much information as I could. Knowledge is power after all.

VOLCANO

Working as a team to resolve the time issue, I got Symphony to create a replica of George's rooms and fit it into our internal landscape. I took the door off its hinges and let anyone and everyone go to see 'George' whenever they needed to. We could have therapy with George whenever we needed him. I became a kind of inner therapist, providing encouragement and support to everyone. Everything in our world got filtered through 'what would George say?' I channelled George as necessary, repeating his words, his ideas, his body language and non-verbal signals to make sure that my actions were consistent with his. It was hard work. I'd never had to mimic anyone before.

I understood we were having to negotiate between alters to prioritise issues and some, shall we say, less time critical issues kept being pushed back. I created a special internal notice board with a cork board and pushpins. This was labelled 'you have not been forgotten' and we pinned up those issues that kept missing out on time with George. It became my job to ensure that these issues got

'George time' and to comfort and reassure those alters who hadn't had 'George time' yet.

GEORGE

Time is an eternal therapy issue when you have a patient who has such extensive abuse as Jeni. It is why I saw her over so many years and it is also why we organised for Jeni to see co-therapists. Given the problems Jeni had previously with some of the counselling services, we carefully found Jeni alternative therapists, typically psychologists, but not always. For some years Jeni saw Dr Narelle Dart, a GP with a particular interest in therapy, until she retired. The understanding was that I would do the more serious trauma work and Narelle would debrief on this work, help re-stabilise Jeni and then help with more day-to-day issues. Navigating the world is something that most of us can take for granted, but even simple things could trigger Jeni into a decompensated state.

While the co-therapist does not have to be experienced in treating DID, they must need to be accepting of the condition and willing to learn as they go. There needs to be close, ongoing communication between both therapists. I would cc in the co-therapist on any communications that I wrote and make it clear to other service providers that Narelle and I were working together with Jeni. If any divergence appeared to be occurring between us, then one of us needed to pick up the phone and work this through. While a co-therapist can be an invaluable asset, and a degree of difference in approaches is also of value, there must be a consideration and respect for the other therapist's approach for this arrangement to be effective. If there is significant divergence, particularly in the underpinning therapy ideology that confuses the patient, this can make matters worse. It was why, for example, I could not work with one of my DID patient's church counsellor, who was trying to exorcise the 'evil ones' – indeed I argued this was spectacularly unhelpful. This is why I will try to work with co-therapists with whom I have worked before, though this is not always possible. Nevertheless, I always try to involve a co-therapist

when working with complex developmental trauma and DID and this probably occurs with around eight out of ten of these patients. It is particularly important to have somebody cover you when you are on leave or if you are unavailable when a crisis occurs.

In terms of crises, while these patients require significant in-hours time, which can be scheduled accordingly, I have been surprised by how little out-of-hours time they require in terms of urgent hospital admissions or emergency department visits, once they are engaged in a therapy that recognises and understands the nature of their condition. I find that these patients are surprisingly considerate of my personal time. Indeed, as I had to with Jeni, I'm often encouraging them to contact me out of hours, rather than allowing things to deteriorate to a more problematic level by waiting.

ED THE HEAD

This raises a really interesting point. We struggled to justify calling or messaging George. I had all manner of strategies that came into play when one of us was overwhelmed and needed support or help. But when these failed it was very hard for any of us to make that call. When George began to tell us it was okay to call him, the message took a long time to filter through the system. There was still a lot of resistance to calling him even when we were faced with issues that we really needed his advice on. In the early years I was frightened of calling him at night because alters were terrified of interrupting him and his wife in an intimate moment or, to put it more bluntly, disturbing them during sex. I figured it would be just my luck to let an alter call him, only to disturb him and make him angry. As our trust grew, this fear dissipated. It got easier to contemplate calling George, not to actually call him, but to think about it.

Unfortunately in the early years of therapy, the times I let our alters reach out for help from the social workers often had negative consequences, instead of supportive interventions. We were accused of being manipulative, attention seeking, demanding and selfish. Instead of helping us with the issue we had gone to them with, our

distress or our panic, we were met with accusations. These kinds of attitudes and accusations did not give me a trusting nature going into therapy with George.

Later on in therapy, as he mentions, George introduced us to Dr Narelle Dart, as his co-therapist. She was brilliant. I spoke at length to Narelle about my difficulties in reaching out, about the negative experiences we'd had and our fears about calling George. She was a welcome voice of reason. She told me that by merely inviting me to call him if I need to, George was offering support. He was telling us we were worth his time and that he was concerned about us. This helped us to breach the barrier. But what really knocked it down and destroyed it was a very simple suggestion. Narelle proposed that instead of phoning when an issue had reached boiling point, that we either phoned or emailed George and told him the issue and asked him to hold it and keep it safe for us until we could pick it up in therapy. This excellent suggestion worked perfectly. We could contact George and ask him to be like a bag of holding. He could put our fears, our issues, our problems into the bag until we had safe time and space to pick them back up and look at them. Utter brilliance right there.

GEORGE

It took me many years before I understood how the most important thing I did, when I took or returned a call from an acutely distressed patient after hours, was just the act itself – making a connection. As a young psychiatrist I worried about what I could say in a phone call that would make a significant difference to bring someone down from a highly distressed, sometimes suicidal, state.

When it came to talking them off the ledge, I came to realise that the act of making effective contact alone was often more important than anything that I said. I learnt that clever therapeutic interventions were rarely required, and that the most important thing to do at these times was just to let my patient know that they were not entirely alone in that moment and that I would see them

in the coming week to help them get back on track (which may have required some diary shuffling). In research I did into suicide, it became clear that a sense of profound isolation and separateness was the final straw that could tip someone over the edge into the abyss from which they may not return. Accordingly, the job is connection, not cleverness.

ED THE HEAD

One of the key tasks of therapy, as we saw it, was to learn what was normal. By normal we mean what people from non-abuse childhoods took for granted. One thing I noticed about other people in my life was the ease with which they asked for help. This was something I struggled with. My childhood had taught me the dangers of asking for help and my experiences in early adulthood had only served to reinforce this message.

Now what this meant in real terms was that when we recognised we needed help to do things, we battled between our desire for help and our fear of the consequences of asking for that help. How much would the help cost us? What kind of cost would we incur? Was the cost higher than we were willing to pay? The debate could go on for hours. Group work at university was a nightmare. All the negotiating was exhausting. I couldn't work out how everyone else in the group seemed to be so casual about their need for help. We tried to be casual about it, hiding our terror. But instead of asking for help clearly and waiting for the response, we would predict a disastrous outcome, and react accordingly. If we got a dollar for each time we apologised for our needs we'd be rich!

During therapy this inability to ask for help became a major issue. We were opening up about events that we had never discussed before and the distress often overwhelmed us. George told us in our second appointment that we could contact him outside of hours if we were distressed and needed him. Now we understand that George meant his words and his offer was genuine. But at the time what he was saying was fighting a history of years of negative consequences for asking for help. There were days, and situations, where we desperately

needed help from George. But we couldn't ask for help, we didn't have the words, we didn't know how.

In the early months of therapy with George, 1998-1999, whenever we were distressed, we would begin the process of trying to get help. I tried all kinds of services for survivors in my search for support and help. Each approach was a battle between my need for help and my terror of going to a man for assistance. I had some truly horrific responses to my disclosures from these organisations. For example, during the 1998 Christmas holiday period I was being swamped by body memories and horrific nightmares every night. I called a sexual assault service one early morning after a particular difficult night. I told the counsellor what was happening. She told me that I was missing sex with my father, and I should just go have sex with my boyfriend. What bit of 'I was raped by my dad' did she miss?

After this I decided that nothing George could say to me would be as bad as this. So, I took the plunge and began negotiations with Erik and The Rulebook to create a way for us to reach out to George for help. We figured it was important to contact George before we reached the crisis point. But how to do this when we seemed to go from fine to crisis in seconds. In trying to work this out we found an entire army of Backroom Boiler Boys and Girls who were submerging our distress and anxiety in order to keep us safe. They could hold an enormous amount of distress until their bucket overflowed and then we hit crisis point. How to handle this? Can this issue get any more complicated? The solution sauntered past the meeting room as we were discussing this problem.

MUSCLES

One day as I'm heading back to my room after checking on Symphony I pass the new meeting room we've made with George. I hear the guys inside talking of their issue with going from 'go to woe' in seconds and not being sure how to handle this. I popped my head in and said 'traffic lights. Green is all good, orange is trouble ahead, and red is help me now,' then kept going on my way. It seemed logical to me.

ED THE HEAD

This was a genius solution and we grabbed it with gratitude. We decided to amend what the lights meant, changing orange to 'Trouble Ahead, seek help from George', and red to 'still not fixed, have you called George? If not, do it now!' By reiterating George as the solution we hoped to hammer home the message that he was safe, and we could go to him for help.

The one thing we'd suggest to George and any other therapist with a client/patient who struggles to seek help is to gently reaffirm your offer of support outside hours every so often. It would have helped us to hammer this message home much easier if we'd heard it from George a bit more.

GEORGE

I think Jeni makes an informative and salutary point here. I did not appreciate the fullness of what asking for help meant for Jeni. While I offered her after-hours support early on, as she points out I should have returned to this and explored further with her what it meant to reach out for help. My post-fellowship training in psychotherapy left me recognising how all aspects of therapy, especially any problems or conflicts that arise, make excellent grist for the therapy mill. Reluctance in asking for help does not, by definition, come up very often. About the only time it does is when people end up in crisis that might have been averted by reaching out to their doctor, but they didn't.

This will then trigger an exploration of why the person did not reach out for help and what it meant for them to do so. Jeni's internal system defences were so resourceful, creative and effective that, one way or another she was able to avoid decompensating into a major crisis. On top of this, Jeni explains how she knew her father should carry the blame, he was the bad one, not her. This awareness, along with her dissociative superpowers, allowed her to bring herself back from the brink of self-destruction when she was distressed. In turn, however, it did not flag the need for the deeper elaboration in therapy of issues around asking for help.

Nevertheless, I should have enquired further around this issue, as asking for help was always going to be an issue for her, given her history.

When I began to sub-specialise in trauma, I expected to be dealing with suicidal patients. Many therapists worry about this when they consider taking on patients with complex trauma who dissociate. I was surprised to find that suicidality in this population was way less than I saw in patients with illnesses like depression, bipolar disorder and schizophrenia.

Indeed, I have come to find that patients with DID are very unlikely to become suicidal when they are correctly diagnosed as having a posttrauma syndrome. When delivered by a compassionate therapist who knows how to treat it, this diagnosis allows a fresh start. Yes, these patients often suffer from secondary anxiety and depression, but that is the point – when they are secondary, and you address the primary cause, they start to settle.

What Muscles spoke about above, regarding the traffic light system, gives us an insight into the potent protective capability of this system and nicely illustrates its power when it is developed to its fullness. I still marvel, with more than a little reverence, at the sophistication of Jeni's inner world and how it functions. Even though I have had more visibility of these processes than most, the idea of an alter wandering past a room with other alters discussing a problem, and 'popping their head in' with a quick suggestion is, literally, mind-boggling. The enduring wonder this leaves me feeling is undoubtedly what drew me to psychiatry in the first place.

JENNY

Calling and asking for help was beyond me for a long time. Part of this was due to the brainwashing I had received: I was unworthy, everyone else mattered but I did not, my issues were inconsequential, I was wasting peoples' time – time that was better spent on more important people. I saw my distress as me being stupid, anyone else could handle this so much better than me. I was embarrassed by my tears and was waiting to be punished for them.

I felt such shame at my need for help. Funnily enough, I never felt shame for what Dad had done to me, I knew that belonged to him. But I was so ashamed of my needs. My need for help, to be seen, to be appreciated, to be cared for and to be loved caused me so much shame. Looking back, this was clearly a product of Dad's indoctrination that my basic human rights and human needs were to be denied at all costs, but I could not see that at the time.

After the traffic light system was initiated, it fell to me to make the calls to George. I was still trying to keep my MPD as invisible as possible. So, if it was in office hours I would call George's rooms and ask for a message to be given to him that I needed help. Because his office staff were women it wasn't like asking a man for help. When George began to respond to these cries for help, by telephoning me after hours, it made such a difference. This simple action made substantial and long-lasting changes to my self-perception, my understanding of our relationship, and my ability to trust another with my distress. Of course, this strategy only worked during office hours. When things got hard during the night I was back to the original difficulties in reaching out.

SYMPHONY

One night I had the most terrible experience. I could feel Dad on the bed beside me. I could smell him, hear his breathing, and feel the dip in the mattress as he settled down behind me in the bed. I was terrified. I froze, not knowing what to do. I knew he was in prison in England and so I couldn't work out how he was in bed with me at the same time. I remember clearly trying to work this out. I felt his greasy, slimy hand on my bottom and screamed. I'm not sure if I made any actual noise or if I had screamed silently as I normally did. I jumped out of bed, instinctively trying to protect myself. I slammed on the light and he was not there. I was shaking and struggling to breathe. I was convinced Dad had used astral travel to come and attack me, exactly as he claimed he would. I grabbed the phone and called George. I needed to hear his voice. I needed him, no one else would do.

George answered his phone immediately even though it was the middle of the night. His calm voice began to break through my terror. I told him what happened and how scared I was. He told me that I had had a lucid dream and a body memory and that had pitched me into a panic attack. He said he had ways to stop them and he'd help me in our next session. He seemed to talk to me for hours – he didn't but it felt that way. He was so calm and this settled me down. After checking I was coming to see him in the next few days he reassured me that Dad could not get me and he was in jail. I was so glad I had reached out and asked for help.

JENNY

As much as I'd like to say this broke our fears around calling George, I'd be lying if I did. It helped reduce some of our fears, but the vast majority remained and it took us years to get to a point where we could call George when we needed him without dithering or finding reasons why we shouldn't call. We even hesitated to call him when we had good news. We finally broke the back of this on the 23rd of February 2017, when Jeni had the supreme pleasure of phoning him to say that Dad had been arrested and brought to Australia to face justice.

GEORGE

What is *not* happening in these early phases of therapy is a detailed discussion of the traumas. What we have come to appreciate very clearly since I met Jeni, is that just talking about a trauma does not help very much. In fact, it can stir a patient up and make it worse for them. Since the development of effective therapies like EMDR, we now have studies that compare results with the older talking therapies – these studies reliably find little benefit from just talking through a trauma.

Around fifteen years ago I took this to another level when I would have a patient present with a trauma. What I now say to them when we first meet is along the lines of, 'I am not going to ask you to give me any detail about your trauma at this stage.

This is not because I don't want to hear about it, it's that us just talking about it without doing definitive therapy will not only not be helpful, but it may stir things up and cause you unnecessary distress. I suspect you have been quite anxious about coming to see me for that reason?'

At this point, they usually nod their head. 'All I need to know at this point is how old were you, who the perpetrator was and if it was sexual, physical and/or emotional abuse. What we will talk about today in some detail is how this has affected you. We will go into more detail about what happened when we are ready to do the actual therapy, at which point I will put aside enough time for us to get you to a safe place at the end of it.'

I would go on to explain that we would do intensive trauma therapy over three days running as we focused on an agreed group of traumas. The primary response to this is one of relief that I'm not going to take them too far into their pain (they're in enough just coming to see me) but that I am prepared to go there with them when the time is right.

Notably, the human mind can more easily put aside a distressing thought until later, if it knows that it will be dealt with and we're not pushing it away because it is too upsetting. Pushing aside a thought because it is too upsetting, without a plan to come back to it, gives the thought much greater power to distress us. Even though we push it back out of our immediate awareness, like a terrorist organisation relegated to the jungle, it will wreak havoc on our ability to enjoy a peaceful life.

Back when I was working with Jeni, this newer strategy of not going into the trauma had no research behind it and getting patients to talk about their trauma was considered good therapy. The upside of this approach was that Jeni was allowed the space to talk for the first time about her traumas while being both believed and supported. The downside was that it often left her stirred up, especially when she was in the middle of a traumatic incident as the end of the session arrived. I will let her pick this up.

CHARLOTTE

After a difficult session with George I would rush to the toilet and spend up to an hour putting everyone back together. My job was to stabilise everyone so we could return to the outside world and cope with the remains of our day. I've been doing this ever since Jeni was about 5 years old. I used to have to stabilise us after being abused so no one would see the pain, the damage, and guess we were in trouble. George never got to meet me in therapy, I'm a Backroom Boiler Girl and while we were doing therapy with George I was one of the nameless masses. I was so happy to have such a powerful and meaningful job. I was a crucial but invisible part of the therapy process.

My job was adapted after we began therapy to ensure we were 'fine' after therapy. It was hard to deal with having to stop in the middle of discussing a tough memory. We couldn't just stop. I would run into a toilet cubicle and shut the door. Then Volcano would head into our version of George's room and set things up to continue therapy with the distressed alter. While he did this, I would reassure them that George was not rejecting them, that he believed them and that he wanted to talk with them about their concerns, their abusive experience and their pain. I made it clear that the only reason George had stopped them talking was because we had run out of time. This process could take up to an hour before I felt they were safe enough to leave in the capable hands of Volcano. I then sent them into our version of George's consulting rooms and let them say everything they had left to say to Volcano. He would have spent his time bringing in any other person he deemed appropriate to have involved in the conversation. This meant that each alter was supported by a team of friends rather than everyone relying on Volcano or George.

GEORGE

I am very grateful to Charlotte for her work. I wish all my patients had a Charlotte! While one tries to bring the patient down to a more settled space before the end of the session, it is not always possible, particularly when Jeni had so many experiences to get

through. When we do actual trauma therapy – as opposed to this kind of more general talking and debriefing – a key part is moving the patient to a safe place as you come to the end of the session. Another complexity is that as I wound down a session Jeni could move to a point that was unexpectedly distressing. Sometimes I would be able to extend our time, but when you might already be behind from doing this with other patients some days it was just not possible.

Early in my practice, I learned that if I ran late, not only did I annoy all my following patients, but by the end of the day I could be running up to a couple of hours late, which did not serve my mental health.

A final complexity here is that all trauma experiences are not created equal. It would be nice for a therapist if there was a scale of mild to severe, so that we could allocate time accordingly. The reality is that the *meaning of the violation* of the event is more significant than the apparent cruelty or depravity of the event. From reading Jeni's story, you can appreciate how she was at times highly distressed by, for example, apparently lesser boundary violations, like when her dad got the children to line up for a gift-giving ceremony, giving gifts to Frank and Sheila before pushing Jeni away and giving her nothing. This was more distressing for her than being, in her words, raped 'yet again'.

VOLCANO

Charlotte's work was not just limited to dealing with memory work. She was phenomenal at dealing with strong and overwhelming emotions. She was to spend a significant amount of time with Muscles early on in therapy. Muscles reacted badly to seeing a psychiatrist. In his words:

MUSCLES

I had huge struggles about going to see a shrink. I didn't care that George was a good one, I didn't wanna go. I was offended. All this crap was dished on us, we suffered so much at the hands of Dad, and

we were the ones seeing the shrink! It seemed so fucking unfair. We'd survived living with a vicious, sadistic paedophile whose rituals and sexual assaults were weird at best and life-threatening at worst, and we were the ones seen as crazy! It made my blood boil. HE should be the one seeing the shrink! HE should be forced into therapy, HE should be the one with no money 'cos every cent went to the shrink. HE should be living in poverty, unable to work, not us! And the final straw was when our diagnosis went from MPD, which made sense of everyone else, to Dissociative Identity Disorder – DID. I howled in outrage. I'm not a DID, I'm a fucking Done To! I didn't do this, this was done to me. This crap was inflicted on me by arseholes who should have known better. My outrage swelled and swelled!

Seeing George only compounded my outrage. I was being forced to examine every part of MY LIFE, and account for everything. But the bastard who did this to me? Oh, he's sitting pretty in an English jail refusing offence-focused rehabilitation programs 'cos it's against his religion! It's not against his religion to rape his child, to sodomise and torture his daughter, to lie about it in court, but it's against his religion to address his offending behaviour. Don't make me laugh!

CHARLOTTE

Even now Muscles has anger around this issue, but I did my best to help him deal with it. I built him a shed and gave him a build-it-yourself motorbike. Symphony hid a piece of the puzzle so he wouldn't leave her when he had built it. He could go into his shed and hit stuff, slam things around, make noise and break things safely. He could express his rage away from frightened children and then return to his jobs calmer.

VOLCANO

Because Muscles is such an important part of the system, and does so many jobs and tasks, it was important for us to address his rage. A lot of his rage related to issues around trust. Trust was an easy fix once George joined our team, but there were some issues that were a whole other ball game.

GEORGE

I clearly recall meeting Muscles for the first time. His anger defined him, which along with his obvious machismo, made him easy to identify. It was even easier to understand where he fitted into the system. I have always had a soft spot for Muscles as his rage is entirely understandable and it meant he did not mince his words. At no point was I left wondering what was on Muscles' mind in a given session!

When an abused patient, with DID or not, has no part that I can find that carries the anger at what has happened to them, they do worse in therapy or, at least, it takes much longer. This is because anger is built on a sense of injustice and boundary violation, which in turn is built on a cornerstone of the belief that one has the right to justice and the basic respect of their human rights. In short, they have a healthy self-regard that I can build on.

At the other end of the spectrum, those without anger are totally in the victim mode. They accept their abuser's indoctrination completely, i.e. they believe there is something bad about them that means they deserve to be treated inhumanely, that they don't deserve basic rights.

When I first met Muscles, before I appreciated the power of the angry part, I was not sure how we were going to work together. He taught me that the angry personalities, once you appreciate and acknowledge their anger, will be your greatest therapy allies. The energy that sits behind their anger can be harnessed to heal. Few forces are more powerful in therapy. I have seen many therapists over the years withdraw from angry parts rather than engage with them. Perhaps the greatest tip I can give in this regard is to recognise that they are powerful protectors of not just the person, but their sense of self-worth. I find that once I acknowledge this explicitly in therapy and demonstrate that I'm there to protect them too, a powerful alliance can be built.

It serves us all to remember that anger is a healthy emotion that is as valuable as love, joy and compassion. It is only when anger is expressed with aggression, without respecting the boundaries of

others, that it is a problem. When it is seen as an expression of self-worth, those who carry anger become the drivers of rebuilding self-esteem.

MUSCLES
What, wait… I'm the healthy part. Blow me down with a feather. I was not expecting that!

ERIK
After we entered therapy we quickly developed some very clear goals with George. We wanted to reclaim our voice and talk about what Dad had done to us. We had no place or space in our normal world to really examine what had happened, to reflect on what it meant to us or to draw dangerous conclusions and we needed one. George offered his rooms as our safe and sacred space. Make no mistake, the biggest blessing George gave us was a space to speak. George let us talk about the abuse and made us feel comfortable and safe doing so. We'd never had that before. He was the first person to say that what Dad had done to us was criminal. That knowledge took time to settle in.

If I had been able to access this kind of treatment and recognition earlier, I would have been able to bring my father to justice sooner. I would have been given the opportunity to have a medical examination to collect evidence – and, as a result, I would have been saved a lot of time and a world of pain.

WHAT'S IN A NAME?

GEORGE
Naming alters has been a little controversial. It is perhaps, the main reason why, for a while there, until the relationship of dissociation arising from trauma was better understood, that therapists were accused of 'creating' DID. Jeni, for her purposes, does not need names. Some, like Gabrielle, Erik and Maggot had names anyway as a matter of course, but the bulk did not. In therapy, we can't get very far without a name. It is an example of why, without

both diagnosing and understanding DID, treatment is completely ineffective.

If I did not know the names of the alters, I did not know who I was talking to and working with. In 'normal' therapy you work through certain issues with a person over time, picking up where you left off from each previous session. With DID, if I do not know who I am talking to, I can start working on an issue in one session, and then try to pick it up in the following session, to find a blank look staring back at me as they have no idea what I'm talking about. It would be like me spending a session one week with a person and then the following week picking up where I left off with their flat mate, or the person from over the road. Without names you allow a relationship discontinuity that prevents navigating through the system in any meaningful or effective way.

SYMPHONY

In pop culture, people with MPD had a certain set of alters: the child, the promiscuous one, the violent one, and the voice of reason. I didn't fit into those boxes. In fact, I didn't relate to any of the fictional characters I saw with MPD. In the movies, MPD patients need to be hypnotised for their alters to come out and speak. That wasn't the case with me; my alters willingly came out and told their stories. Often, I would sit down for a session and someone else would take over until it was time to leave. The alters came out and George asked them about their jobs.

'What's your name? Do you know where you are? Do you know when you are? What do you do in the system?' He started every conversation with the same questions to ground the alters in the present.

Some alters resented George's ritual. They thought it was a waste of time. They wanted to get straight to the issues at hand. Squadron Captain was especially irritated by George's need to know his name. Often, he'd send in one of the soldiers from his army to answer the introductory questions and get orientated, so he could jump straight into the problem he wanted to work through.

GEORGE

Relating to alters by name, so you know precisely who you're dealing with, is usually limited to therapy (and to partners, if they wish to engage at this level, which some partners are comfortable with and some not at all). Not knowing who is talking to who, can also be a challenge from the patient's side.

The person with DID may not recall conversations with key people who, next time around, look at them incredulously as they deny an important discussion they had a day or two before. This is a major problem that I will talk about how to manage in the next chapter.

On top of this, as Jeni will illustrate below, this relationship discontinuity problem can be used against people with DID. One of my patients has a teenage daughter whose knowledge of her mother's dissociation is used against her mum. She will argue her mother earlier agreed to her doing something, that her mother had in fact said no to, telling her mum that she has 'forgotten' because it was another part of her. This is an example of the problem when others can access the castle blueprints! Unfortunately, there is no way of hiding this from immediate family. When I invite them into my office, partners and children can often rattle off the key signs of DID, and accurately identify executive alters, having spent many years negotiating these switches.

JENI

Interestingly, while my mother was oblivious to my MPD, seeing nothing and understanding even less, my siblings identified key signs of my MPD as children. My sister wrote in a school essay that I could be hundreds of different people at once. She pulled me up on this one day in August 1981. Mum had agreed that a little girl could stay with us for a week while her mother had some tasks to complete. Looking after and playing with the little girl fell to me. I spent five days working hard, but discreetly, to keep the little girl safe from Dad, play with her without making too much noise and drawing Dad's attention, and entertaining her. She was

due to go home on Friday night. By this stage I was exhausted and overwhelmed.

I stood in my bedroom with Sheila hugging me as I cried silently. I felt relieved that the little girl was going home that afternoon, and my tears could be controlled no longer. I sobbed and shook. I had kept her safe and away from Dad. She was returning home undamaged. I was overwhelmed with a sense of joy and exhaustion. The little girl burst into the bedroom and yelled 'Jeni, mummy says I can stay here tonight and go home tomorrow, isn't that great.' According to my sister I changed instantly. I became bluff and jovial and loud as I said how wonderful this was, I then took the little girl's hand and took her off to play. Sheila found my abrupt shift from crying hysterically to being excited too much to understand and she questioned me about it for days after the little girl had gone home. She thought I was putting it on and I was faking my emotions. I was not. My emotions were real, they were merely coming from two personalities at once.

When I was diagnosed with MPD, Frank not only accepted this but spoke of how it 'explained everything wacky about me.' Admittedly he spoke of my alters as 'those freaks' which I found rather dismissive and demeaning. But at least he was recognising them.

GEORGE

In-depth trauma work cannot begin until I have mapped the system and know which alter I'm interacting with every time we revisit a given issue. This is particularly necessary so that I can have emotional support in place both during and after trauma work. I have had the situation where I find myself with a patient who is acutely distressed and I can't find the alter who is experiencing the distress, so I can't settle them. In working with dissociation this is a problem that can't be completely avoided, but one wants to prevent it from happening as much as possible.

On top of this, I also need to know which other alters – we call them 'protectors' – might have a problem with another disclosing certain distressing information and may shut them down. This

means you have to also appreciate the inter-alter dynamics in the system. For this work I have found my training in Internal Family Systems (IFS) particularly helpful. While it is designed for understanding the various 'parts' that we all have, and how they interact with each other, it is a tremendously useful model for unravelling these complexities in DID.

The therapist needs to know where they are in the system at any given point in time. I will do this by asking to speak to a particular alter, but even then, I have to be watchful if they switch without openly declaring it. Jeni of course does this all the time in day-to-day life as she switches into the alter that is needed for the next topic of conversation or the next job to be done. Over time she realised how this limited her therapy if I did not know who I was talking to. She learnt to help me by introducing the new alter as they arrived. She might say something like, 'Oh that has triggered Volcano and he would like to say a few words,' or 'that is a question that Gabrielle would be better to answer'.

This is a good example of the trust and collaboration that we needed to develop that I mentioned earlier. Jeni worked out that I could not help her as much if I did not know who I was talking to. Over time I came to recognise some switches. Each alter has their own voice, posture, demeanour and mannerisms. Indeed, research with functional electroencephalography actually shows clear, corresponding brain changes as patients move between alters. Nevertheless, when you have as many as Jeni does, it could be difficult to see a switch. Some were easier to pick than others. The very masculine males like Volcano and Muscles were pretty easy, as was Symphony, for reasons I will come to, but shifting between, for example, the Student and another female alter could be confusing. Sometimes, to be clear of where I was in the system, I would simply ask, 'so who am I talking to?' Jeni was very good at answering this question, however, other patients, earlier in their journey, may say, 'I don't know'. This can be the beginning of getting a bit lost and, depending on what is happening, the therapist will need to make a call between staying with the unknown part or asking to speak to a

particular part to 'find' themselves in the system. Sometimes I will ask a personality that I know has overarching awareness to help me out and tell me who was talking to me, especially if the subject matter was of import.

JENI
However, as therapy went on and we went deeper and deeper into my world, it got harder not easier to answer this question. Sometimes I just didn't know, other times I had hints, but as we explored the deeper recesses of my world I discovered whole areas full of alters that I did not know. I didn't even know what their jobs were. George and I were learning together.

GEORGE
When it comes to finding names, with other DID patients I often use the age of the child or some defining feature for their name. For example, there would be a 'five-year-old' or the 'smart one'. There were just too many alters in Jeni's world for this to work (and they were all pretty smart!), so we needed names that over time I came to know as I would with any patient I worked with. Typically, I will ask an alter to choose their own name. My only proviso is that it is not a negative self-statement. I would not have supported a name like Maggot, but she came with this name because it had a very particular history. Later I was pleased she changed her name to Isabelle after symbolically throwing the name and identity of Maggot into the ocean.

Symphony was the easiest one to identify and there was no doubt when I was talking to her. Not only was she only three when I first met her, she had a particular way of pronouncing words so that she did not move her mouth into a certain position that reminded her of certain abuse experiences. For example, this meant she could not pronounce 'shun' (-tion) sounds. Instead, she would replace –tion with –ing so the word 'question' became 'questing'. Once I got the hang of it, I could understand her, but at least I always knew when she was in the room. While only three

301

years old, it rapidly became obvious that Symphony had the keys to the castle as it were, and she was able to teach me a lot about how things were set up – largely because she was responsible for setting them up.

The other issue here is that of apparent age. While Symphony was only three when I met her, she was a mature alter who had a clear sense of the passage of time. Not all alters have this, particularly the younger ones. As mentioned earlier, many of them have been 'hibernating' and when I would speak to them it was clear that they had little awareness of the passage of time.

The issue here is that they were operating on the basis that they were still in a time when the abuse was ongoing. Indeed, they were still in that world where they could be hurt tomorrow, or in a few minutes. More than once I have met an alter who is expecting me to hurt them. This is always a powerful opportunity as I can convince them they are safe simply by spending time with them and them realising I am there to help not hurt – after decades of waiting and hoping. I have learnt to apologise to them for not having been there sooner in their life. I have found this can be powerful as it implicitly acknowledges that they had every right to expect to have been helped much earlier.

This is why it is so important to 'orient' as it's called, the child alter into the present. Orientation involves more than just giving them the current year. I start by introducing myself, and explaining that I am a doctor who is here to help. Sometimes they have been informed about me, but not always. I then help them to understand that while they have been 'asleep' their body has grown up. I then ask them to look at their hands and feet. I wish I could show videos of this process to train clinicians in DID, as it is compelling and captivating to watch a five-year-old alter come to terms with the fact that it is twenty, or forty, years after they thought it was and that their body has grown into adulthood.

I often ask them to walk over to my door and reach up and touch the top of the door jamb. The look on their face as their hand reaches slowly to the very top of the door, and the realisation

dawns, is priceless. They immediately work out that they can now better protect themselves. Every abused child awaits the age when they can either fight back or leave home.

The most critical reason behind this exercise is beginning to introduce the notion, across the entire system that 'the war is over'. It is hard to appreciate what it is like for these alters who are still living on high alert expecting to be abused tomorrow. Allowing them to breathe and know they are now safe is a simple and powerful manoeuvre. Indeed, you can't do therapy until the system comes down from DEFCON 1 (war is imminent) towards DEFCON 5 (normal peacetime).

Once I had a fair understanding of Jeni's internal landscape we could go more deeply and move onto the next step of increasing co-consciousness.

Co-consciousness – Lowering the Security Clearance

DR GEORGE BLAIR-WEST AND JENI HAYNES

Once trust is building and a therapeutic relationship developed with as many alters as possible, the next therapeutic goal is to create co-consciousness between alters. This was a subject that Jeni gave me a masterclass in. Loss of time and continuity can be a particularly disabling problem for people with DID (not to mention allowing teenagers to walk all over their parents as we saw in the last chapter). People with DID find it very difficult to hold down jobs, unless they have a high degree of autonomy in their job that allows them to both cover and recover from the time losses and relationship discontinuity.

Typically, the alters who take executive control for a period of time are fully-formed personalities and, from the outside, appear to be 'normal' as they navigate the person through the world. They look normal to the person in front of them, as the personality has been selected (this was The Rulebook's role) specifically for this reason. However, if there is an observer to the switch, which is more likely to happen with family members, this can sometimes be quite dramatic. Recall Jeni's story of her sister witnessing her switch from distressed to immediately up and happy when her sleepover buddy stays for longer. Without an understanding of dissociation, family members (and therapists and inpatient ward

staff) come to the only other possible explanation, which is that the person is acting or pretending. Being told they must be faking is the ultimate dismissal.

While time losses occur with extended switches between more mature and aware executive alters, more concerningly, sometimes a child part can run the show with more dire results.

One of my male DID patients had a long history of motor vehicle accidents. Fortunately, they were all at low speed, particularly around parking his car, but they happened every month or two, keeping him on excellent terms with his local crash repair shop. Ultimately, we identified a five-year-old alter who loved to drive when he was that age by kneeling on the driver's seat between his father's legs while his father operated the pedals. He was taking control once the car slowed to a speed he was familiar with and then drove with the level of precision one would expect from a five-year-old. In the end we negotiated that in return for special 'paddock driving time' on their acreage property, and some scale model cars to play with, he would not take control of the family car at other times. The toy cars sat on the kitchen bench at home and every day he would spend a few minutes playing with them. His wife and children, familiar with his diagnosis, understood the presence of the toys and welcomed the weakening relationship with the local crash repair shop.

In asking his permission to use this story in the book, this patient reminded me of how, 'You also got me and my five-year-old to agree on a command which I could use to get the wheel back. Now I say when in any low-speed environment, "It's my turn!" It's worked. I use it all the time.' This is also a good example of how a therapist is not of much use to a patient with DID until there is a good understanding of the system and the inter-alter dynamics. Then there has to be a collaborative approach to solving these conundrums. I learnt this from Jeni as we sat, side by side as equals, coming up with creative solutions to problems like this.

MUSCLES

It was very cool when George shared this story. Jeni learned to drive as part of the PhD so she could drive to and from her interviews. We'd find on the way home we would be drifting down a hill close to home with our feet flat on the floor. One day as this happened I heard 'wheeee' as the car surfed down the road and realised Symphony (aged four at the time) was driving the car. We had to do some negotiating with her to allow this one, and only one, hill. And she could only do it when I was driving with her to help if something unexpected happened. It was really cool to find these kinds of tricky situations didn't just happen in our world, other folks had to deal with them too.

GEORGE
Amnestic barriers and whiteboards

Remember, alters are separated, indeed defined, by virtue of the 'amnestic barriers' that separate them. These barriers are designed to stop the horror of the abuse invading all aspects of daily life. For this reason, these barriers are relatively impervious, disallowing the transmission of awareness, of knowledge between alters. Those who work as part of a team do share knowledge between themselves, while senior alters, like Jeni's Erik and Symphony, have greater access clearance. Indeed, the dissociative system has a lot in common with government security agencies, which carry secret information that is only shared with a select few on a need-to-know basis.

Creating co-consciousness, then, is the process of making these barriers more porous to allow more information crossflow. It involves a lowering of the security clearance threshold and allowing greater access, by more parts, to information. The solution that we came up with was both simple and effective.

I have taught it to many patients since with great results although major technology developments over the last twenty-odd years meant that my younger patients tend to digitise Jeni's strategy. I will let Erik explain how it worked.

ERIK

The best idea George had was to get us to envisage whiteboards and use them to pass messages to one another. The Rulebook went totally bonkers over this idea and created noticeboards for each person in our life and wrote their 'rules of engagement' out in full for all to see. He then created a noticeboard for each alter. Seeing them arrive and proliferate was terrifying for some people, as the numbers and what they represented got larger and larger. Muscles knew how many of us there were, but suddenly the rest of us became aware of the numbers and they were truly terrifying. When you think you're living with a few friends that's one thing, but to see noticeboards in the thousands was seriously confronting. We ended up creating a special space for our noticeboards so every alter flying past on their way to do something could scan their board. Having the noticeboards was a brilliant idea and George's whiteboard saw a lot of use, especially in the early days.

GEORGE

Along with The Rulebook, who oversaw the rules of engagement between any alter and another person, these internal whiteboards were used to write messages, a diary of sorts, of recent interactions with people. The whiteboard would especially note significant commitments or problematic interactions with other people. Accordingly, when an alter was about to interact with someone, 'on the way out' to do this, they would check the whiteboard for any information that might be relevant. Over time Jeni developed many whiteboards strategically located in the system as Erik describes above.

A related system that we also used, that I continue to use too, is hooking up a PA system, that I can make announcements over, that carry to all levels of the system. Without such a mass information dissemination system I otherwise have to repeat messages to the different alters that I meet. More importantly for Jeni, the PA system brought the 'Back Room Boiler Boys and Girls' into communication with the rest of the system and made them a more involved part of the democracy.

THE RULEBOOK

George helped us to conceptualise ways of communicating more effectively. The first thing we did was test them out on him. Would the new idea make talking to him easier? If not, it died a quick death, but if it worked with him, Muscles and I implemented it throughout the system. George's idea of a PA system was brilliant. Muscles and The Joker (strange choice for the task, but he volunteered) headed off through the dungeon to set up the system.

THE JOKER

Hey there, this is my chance to speak up. I loved this job. I love manual work and hooking up a PA was right up my alley. Muscles and I raced off into the dungeon with the new kit. We went into every nook and cranny and discovered lots of hidden alters. We brought them out of their darkness and into the light, creating new homes for them.

Each room in the dungeon was given a two-way communication device that allowed them to hear what was happening and to talk back. For some folks this was the first time they had ever been able to participate in our internal world.

Our PA system was highly complex. It could send out messages intended for everyone, for particular groups of alters, and for individual alters. These messages could be responded to by each individual personality and by groups. We were able to talk to individual alters privately and give them a chance to talk to others who they wanted to meet or spend time with.

As we built the PA system, Muscles also installed a simple three-button voting system (yes; no; and dunno, need more info) for each person. That's one heck of a lot of buttons let me tell you! We took the PA system deep inside where the Back Room Boiler Boys and Girls lived. This dramatically changed their lives. They were suddenly aware of the rest of us and the impact their work had on us. They could see how what they did meant something. They could talk with us, and scream at us, as we did stuff that upset their work or their plans. And now they were aware of us, they started to play

a more visibly dominant role in the system. They could ask us to do stuff for them, could help us with info we didn't have, they could and did impact how we worked out in the real world. They could even start to listen to George and talk back to him. Now George was everywhere in the system, having more of an impact than he ever dreamed of. Go George!

GEORGE
Hypnotic tools

Strategies like this all come from the practice of hypnotherapy. This is not surprising because another way of conceptualising the construction of the DID world is to see it as a form of self- hypnosis. Over the years I have sought training in hypnotherapy simply to broaden my knowledge of these kinds of skills that are useful in the world of dissociation. I would encourage all therapists who work with dissociation to do the same and educate themselves, to some degree, in hypnotherapy. These skills allow therapists to both get more of a feel for how dissociation works and also how you can flexibly create communication tools and co-consciousness strategies that make sense to the person sitting in front of you.

An indispensable hypnotic tool is 'the Vault', into which we place traumatic memories that come up in therapy for 'safekeeping' until we are ready to deal with them. A key hypnotic principle is to suggest a potential shape and form, but to use language in a way that avoids too much detail and allows the individual to imagine it and complete it in a way that makes sense to them. The way you strengthen this internal creation is to then get the patient to describe it back to you. They will often have constructed something that Fort Knox would have been proud of!

Just on hypnosis, I do not actually use it for trauma processing, and definitely not to access trauma memories. I have never found that it is particularly effective, certainly not when compared with EMDR, which I will elaborate on in the next chapter. Nevertheless, for people with dissociation, understanding and using hypnotic tools is invaluable for negotiating their system and setting up their

world in preparation for the actual trauma work with EMDR. As an alternative to hypnotherapy training, many advanced courses in managing dissociation, including Internal Family Systems, teach many hypnotic strategies that can be used in these ways.

An essential strategy used to develop co-consciousness is 'the meeting room'. Indeed, it goes beyond just improving co-consciousness, it becomes the basis for negotiating and driving the way forward in therapy and outside of it. It is a simple idea, just setting up a place in which the alters meet to deal with issues, but it is a profound shift for those with DID. It heralds a move from a series of alters switching in and out on a one-at-a-time basis to a team approach. Depending on the patient, I will use various metaphors to explain the importance of this strategy.

For those in business, I will liken it to the boardroom, where all senior players in the company come together to decide on the strategic direction of the company. All major decisions are referred to the boardroom where deliberations are careful and inclusive. If the patient has a background in playing a team sport, then I will talk about how the most successful teams are those where they all understand each other's strengths and know how to bring in the best person to lead a particular play. All good teams decide on a game strategy beforehand while allowing flexibility to change, as the game changes around them. Some of my patients have done some sailing or boating.

For them I will talk about how things will go badly when a storm hits if everyone did not attend the morning crew briefing and is not clear on where they are sailing to, where the reefs are, and who is best at doing what on the boat.

The underlying point of all these metaphors is that you are way stronger when you collaborate well. This speaks to my patients because they all get the benefit of being stronger, of running better defence, whether it's against a perpetrator or even the forces of nature.

Meeting rooms take all shapes – from formal boardrooms to a glade in the forest beside a tinkling stream. I ask my patients

where they will feel the most comfortable. Meeting rooms need to be large, because we invite anyone who wants to, to come and listen in. We can have an increasingly large gallery of interested parties as they get the point that this is where decisions will be made. It is critical that there is a sense that all are invited.

The executive alters may sit at the table, but often key alters do not show themselves out in the open early on. It is not uncommon to be discussing an issue in the meeting room and have someone say, 'Yes we can agree on this, but if we can't get X to agree we're wasting our time.' I have come to expect that there will be a Mr or Ms X who runs things from behind the scenes that I need to get to know. Either way meeting rooms symbolise, and affect, a huge shift in operations to a more effective team-based way of operating.

In short, knowledge is power. Having an effective team to apply the knowledge is greater power.

THE ASSASSIN

George's idea of the meeting room was very different from the meeting room we used for our childhood Death Committee. Sure the layout was the same, the construction was the same, but the ideas underneath it were very different. The Death Committee was a judgement centre. We were created to evaluate how much more abuse a child could tolerate. Assuming that the child personality was declared overwhelmed I was called to assassinate them, taking them out of commission, and saving them from Dad.

The meeting room we created in response to George's request was bright and airy in feel. It was a place where anyone and everyone was welcome to talk. We had the official-looking oval table (stolen from the Death Committee room) that could seat up to 50 people, but rather than sitting at it, we could put items on it we wanted to talk about with George. The children even brought in pictures they had drawn to share with him. Most importantly, we used the room outside of our time with George, to negotiate how to collaborate, how to help each other meet challenges, and how to take care of everyone.

At the same time as we created the meeting room, George suggested we build a Vault to put our traumatic memories into. I had the best time creating this. I made a huge room and filled it with shelving. I put all of our memories on the shelves and then locked the door. I wrapped chains around the door handles and created a hatch beside the door. This hatch was a way to reduce pressure as memories bubbled to the surface. The Vault was a genius idea and it helped me to manage our ongoing distress.

GEORGE

The decision to begin trauma therapy requires the meeting of minds that can only occur in a meeting room. Without such agreement the therapy goes badly or not far at all. I did not understand this when I started working with Jeni, but I have since realised how critical it is to make sure all the key players are on board before you start to approach the nuclear bomb that is trauma like Jeni's. Jeni was, in many ways, a dream patient. She was all in on doing the trauma work. As she describes, she had built a democracy that was inclusive.

Unfortunately, this is not as common as a therapist might hope. My more challenging patients are the ones where some members of the system are seen as needing banishment and rejection. They are nearly always the very young, horribly abused child parts (the 'devils' I spoke of earlier are good examples) and healing cannot occur until they are retrieved, embraced, and finally given the care that every child deserves. These complexities were all ahead of me in 1998. I wish every therapist had a Jeni to start with when it comes to working with complex dissociative people.

EMDR – Doing the Actual Trauma Work

DR GEORGE BLAIR-WEST AND JENI HAYNES

I would just like to clarify a couple of points about Eye Movement Desensitisation and Reprocessing (EMDR) therapy following my earlier explanations about how it works and relates to REM sleep and dreaming. One session a week, even over many years, is not enough to work through trauma of Jeni's dimension. Accordingly, we would do blocks of three appointments over three days running with the first being 75 minutes long. This was designed to ensure that not only did we have time to work through, understand and process the trauma in detail, but by the end of the three days we could get Jeni to a safe place. While EMDR will bring about processing and releasing of the distress around an event, nevertheless, it is demanding work as it does involve working through the actual trauma and re-living it in some detail.

The longer initial appointment of 75 minutes is essential. Because I do not get my patients to go into any depth about a given trauma until we are ready to treat it, I need to have time to deal with whatever comes up. I only have a rough idea of what I am going to find until I get started. One of the first jobs is to chunk traumas down to manageable amounts – looking at what you can realistically do over three days. In working with Maggot, for example, I would ask her which events stood out for her and

why, and then we would agree on which order we would approach them. Typically, we do not start with the biggest trauma first. Usually, I would start with a six or seven out of ten trauma and once we have worked together to get this down to a one or two out of ten, we would move to the ten out of tens.

It is important to start with lesser traumas for two reasons. First, so that both the therapist and patient can gain experience in how they will work together, as EMDR requires a dance of sorts as the therapist modulates the degree of distress that the patient is feeling. If they are looking too distressed, for example, the therapist needs to slow things down and ground the patient in the present. Second, to take on bigger traumas the patient needs to have confidence that the therapy works and will deliver them to the other side. Once the first trauma has been processed down to a level which is no longer distressing, you have the groundwork for taking on a bigger one.

The closing ten minutes, or so, of the session would be spent locking upsetting memories away, for example in a vault (as we discussed earlier), secure room or a cave and taking the alter to a safe place. Coming up with creative ways to do this is part of the EMDR training, but also enhanced by stealing ideas from hypnotherapy as I have discussed.

While the therapist does not need to hear all the detail of each event, they do need to hear enough to understand what it was about what happened that was particularly troubling. We need to work out the 'why' of the event. Traumas can have quite different meanings that transcend the actual behaviours involved. For example, one rape could be about humiliation, while another could be about the feeling that the victim could have done more to fight back; another could be a fear of dying when being choked and yet another could be about how it resulted in pregnancy and the knotty and profound ramifications of this. Four rapes with completely different meanings for a person. The therapist needs to understand enough of the event to be able to work out these meanings so that these can be addressed. Each different

event will need a different therapeutic approach to achieve the 'sense-making' phase of EMDR.

I trained in EMDR in 1993 when it was considered by my peers to be a passing fad. As the research mounted, the world got on board. In 2002 the Israeli National Council for Mental Health endorsed it, in 2004 the American Psychiatric Association did so and then Australia's Centre for Posttraumatic Mental Health did so in 2007. They also recognised CBT protocols developed for treating trauma, but acknowledged the comparative research showing that EMDR worked more quickly. Having fewer sessions spent in the painful re-experiencing of trauma (required by both schools of therapy) is a valued benefit for any patient. Having used both therapies, I feel a responsibility to use the one that causes my patient the least amount of distress as they volunteer to go into their traumatic experiences.

While this is not the place to go into greater detail about how EMDR is actually executed, as books have been written on this, I will touch on some points. A key element of EMDR is the 'time duality' that it creates in session. EMDR does take the patient back into a re-experiencing of the trauma. This closeness and confrontation with it is necessary to fully process it. Otherwise keeping our distance from a trauma leaves it with a power that comes from the message, 'I am too much for you, I will overwhelm you'. Looking closely at the detail of what happened is typically followed by the realisation that, 'It is in the past, and while it is upsetting, it cannot hurt me now.' Sometimes it is helpful for the therapist to gently remind the patient of this fact.

What allows the patient to hold the trauma in their awareness without being overwhelmed is that they are grounded in time in the present 'now' in the safety of their therapist's office while they look closely at what unfolded. Often it is only because we take a close look that the patient will be finally convinced that, for example, 'what happened was not my fault', or 'there was nothing I could have done to avoid it'. These are healing insights and EMDR delivers them with an emotional conviction that no

therapist can ever bring to convince them of understandings like these.

Indeed, over the years I have pretty much stopped trying to convince my patients of anything using logic, I now let EMDR do it for me, or emotion releasing approaches like using the two shoes I mentioned when looking at self-forgiveness. Nothing convinces a patient more of their innocence and that they have no reason to feel ashamed than when they 'realise' this themselves as we repeatedly re-experience each of their traumas. We will typically go over each trauma half a dozen or so times, because each time they will recall some other aspect and then as the memory fills out so does their re-evaluation of it.

As I explain to my patients, the traumatic experience was given the understanding and the labels available to a young child, both of which are heavily influenced by the perpetrators. When a thirty-four-year-old mind is brought to evaluate the experience, an entirely different and new interpretation is born. So many of Jeni's traumatic events were stored and labelled in a folder when she was a young child. It is only when they are opened up and re-examined in detail by their adult self, that a more mature and accurate appreciation of what happened can be brought to bear.

When I was first trained in EMDR we were getting our patients to follow our fingers from side to side, but we started to develop aches and pains and a form of tennis elbow from doing this for extended periods. It was then discovered that a range of forms of 'bilateral stimulation' were just as effective. We next moved to alternate finger-tapping the patient's knees, but this physical proximity and contact was very threatening for some patients (Jeni will tell you her experience of this). I then moved to using audio tones that play alternately in each ear through a set of headphones, which had the benefit of allowing my patient to close their eyes, which allowed more powerful re-experiencing. Indeed, if it was too overwhelming, I would ask them to open their eyes as a simple way of re-grounding them in the present.

ERIK

Agreeing to try EMDR was a no brainer for us. By this stage the memories were swamping our day-to-day life, giving us no meaningful let up, and I was desperate to reduce the distress we were suffering. After some negotiation with George we decided to work with Maggot on what we rated a 7 out of 10 trauma. There were parts of this trauma that were downright hilarious, but they were tempered by other elements, which implied that my mother was the instigator of this rape.

Jeni, Muscles and Maggot have already told of when Mum went shopping for Tampax so we could go swimming. And of how Dad used this to hurt us. Well, after Dad was pushed into the bath Maggot laughed and Dad chased her and gave her a beating.

When Mum came home Maggot tried to tell her what had happened but Mum replied, 'I know, but it's over now'. This implied that Mum had instigated the attack, and she knew what Dad was doing to us. Mum's nonchalant dismissal of Dad hurting us had serious consequences. It raised questions about how much Mum was aware of what was happening to us, and how much she endorsed it. The questions this event raised counterbalanced the more humorous elements and made this a 7 out of 10 trauma.

As we began the process of EMDR, there were a couple of technical issues. At first, George got me to move my eyes from left to right, tracking his finger, but that was painful for me. We told him this, demonstrating our developing trust in him. Instead of using this information to hurt us he validated our burgeoning trust in him by listening to us and changing the method of tracking we were using.

MAGGOT

Letting George get so close to me to tap on my knees took a lot of courage. He was way too close for comfort. When I got lost in the middle of the memory of pushing Dad away from me, my hands shot out and pushed George away automatically. I was so embarrassed. But every time we went through the memory the same thing happened. George recognised how difficult this was for me and

changed how we did EMDR to tapping sounds that moved from ear to ear through a headset. This gave me greater physical distance from George and let me build my level of trust more slowly. I liked that he respected my need for distance too.

As I listened to the tapping sounds it felt like there was a ball bouncing in my head. I closed my eyes and followed the ball in my mind as it ricocheted off the floor, walls and ceiling. As I relived the memory I watched the ball until the blackness behind my eyes got softer and the trauma became lighter. From then on, when George asked any of us to visualise a horrifying event, we could focus on the ball and that helped us to stay in the room with George and in our memory at the same time. It was a weird feeling but it helped a lot.

GEORGE

Interestingly, it does not seem to matter much what form of bilateral stimulation is used as they are all alternately stimulating each of the brain's hemispheres and triggering a harmonic connection between them that gets them to start to synchronise their brain waves. The two halves of the brain work with a surprising lack of coordination most of the time. Functional electrographs of the brain show that the bilateral stimulation brings them into a coordinated dance that correlates directly with when the patient is re-processing their trauma and developing calming insights.

This is undoubtedly because the emotion-aware right side of the brain is now talking to the logical and, most importantly, the evaluative, left side of the brain. More technically, we are talking about a coordinated evaluation of the trauma between right-sided limbic structures, that record danger and related emotions, and the left-sided prefrontal cortex where the logical analysis occurs that can then be directly read into language centres that can put thought, form and words around this sense-making.

For the first time since the event happened, we can bring the fullness of a now mature mind (the left side) to make sense of what happened that is being emotionally re-experienced (the right side)

so that healing meaning can be brought to bear. The words around this meaning, in turn, allow us to build the new narrative that will define the '*surthriving*' phase of life. (I agree with the notion that being an abuse 'survivor' is not enough. Life should be about thriving as we find meaning and purpose – hence the idea of rising above to 'surthrive'.) The key to a healing sense-making is getting these otherwise recalcitrant two sides of the brain to connect and work with each other.

We should not have been too surprised to find that no matter what form of bilateral stimulation is used, it is usual to see the patient's eyes moving rapidly from side to side during a session. This is proof positive that we are triggering the same structures in the brain that we bring to resolving day-to-day issues during the dreaming of the REM sleep phase. As I discussed earlier, we are turbocharging this natural ability that the human mind has, to turn pain into growth and wisdom.

JENI

The technique reduced my anxiety and distress so I could put the trauma into words – and let it go. However, in the trenches of a session, some of George's questions were easy to answer, others were impossible. There were times when the trauma was so big I couldn't get the words out. The silence spoke for me.

We had tried out EMDR on some of our stories and it seemed to work, but soon it became time to try it out on a huge trauma. There were so many to choose from. Which one counted as a full 10 out of 10 trauma?

SYMPHONY

Simple, the night he made me choose. That night was horrible. The after-effects were terrible too.

JENI

Having chosen our vile experience we now had to explain it to George. The words did not come easily. We had to believe that he

would not see this as our fault, but how to test this if we can't use words. We had to find our courage and our voice.

SYMPHONY

The night he made me choose. How simple those words are, but the story underpinning them was horrible in the extreme. Dad demanded that I choose how he was to abuse me. It was awful. He pitched this as getting me to choose what I enjoyed, what of the things he made me do did I enjoy the best. How was I to answer that?

I told him I liked when he stroked my arm. But he laughed at me and told me I had to choose from the games we played. I said Scrabble and he hit me. He went on to list the kinds of things he made me do one at a time and asked me 'do you want me to do this'. I kept saying no, and he kept trying to get me to tell him my favourite. He told me, 'you're not leaving here until you choose something, we've got all night! By the time he said this, all the easier options had been excluded and we were down to what I now realise was rape and anal rape. In the end I chose for him to 'hurt my bottom', which is the way I understood the act of buggery. Dad laughed as he then savagely 'hurt my bottom', buggering me and sodomising me with objects for the rest of the night.

Dad had spent years trying to convince me I was a masochist (which I heard as 'mash o kissed' and I thought he was calling me some kind of mashed potato) and on this night he crowed when I chose this. From then on he justified buggering me by saying 'but you like it, it's your favourite, you said so'.

How was I to tell George this? How was I to find words Dad had never given me? I could only describe what he had said and done and hope that George understood. But with me crying throughout it was very hard. George told me that he understood in broad terms what Dad had done and why it was so distressing. Instead of asking me to keep telling him the story, he got me to visualise it and work through it that way.

As I tried visualising the night, it became like a movie played out in front of me. Playing the movie over and over while knowing I could

open my eyes at any time and see George helped a lot to reduce my distress. The tapping sounds from one ear to the other gave me the magic ball as well. I used the magic ball to ground me in the present and in George's room. These strategies helped me to see the reality of what Dad had done to me. As I watched the night on my video screen I could see how Dad manipulated me, how he put me in a no-win situation and then turned my words against me. The more I looked at what he was doing to me, the more I realised that this was about him not me. The more I realised this, the more my distress settled and my anger grew. But I still didn't have the words to tell George. My words couldn't keep pace with my feelings.

What Dad did to me that night was obscene, horrific and devastating, but it was not my fault. None of it was my fault. He trapped me physically, emotionally and mentally. I was not asking him to bugger me because I liked it, I had to make a choice between equally vile options and all of it was going to hurt me. That was his choice. How he interpreted the choice he forced me into was equally vile, but again, it was his choice. He was manipulating me into giving him what he wanted: yet another excuse to rape and abuse me. That says nothing about me, and has nothing to do with me, it was all about him. My Dad is the monster. EMDR helped me to see this and to come to terms with it.

GEORGE

Jeni has just given us a perfect unpacking of how EMDR works. By bringing in the greater perspective of the evaluative parts of her now fully-developed mind, as she fully experiences the emotional gamut of the event, she comes to see it, finally, for what it was. A truly innocent child being abused by a bad person. She had some awareness of this from when she was young, but it was fragile.

She also shows how the therapist does not need to know exactly what is happening, beyond enough to appreciate the meaning of the event. This is important, as we can process a cluster of traumas that have similar meaning by processing just one. In this case, it was an act of emotional abuse and manipulation of the

worst kind, as Jeni's choice to minimise her pain is subsequently redefined as her 'favourite' way to be abused. Indeed, no therapist sitting on the outside can vaguely come close to what a person is re-experiencing at these times.

The therapist is there, primarily, to maintain a compassionate connection, hold the space and bear witness as the patient does the critical work. This work flows from being able to fully examine the event with the mind of an adult in the safety of a therapist's office. Shakespeare summed this process up nicely in 1605 in *The Merchant of Venice*, with the insight that the 'truth will out'. The difference between the patient coming to this realisation themselves and seeing the truth, without a therapist prompting them, versus a therapist trying to convince their patient of this, is the difference between the sun and a candle. It is the difference between transformative healing and supportive counselling.

Group Therapy and Integration

DR GEORGE BLAIR-WEST AND JENI HAYNES

While group therapy is one of the abiding treatment interventions that I am a huge advocate of, as you will see, there are some salutary limitations to this modality. Outside of trauma therapy, the other sub-specialty that I devote my professional energy to is relationship therapy. The best way to treat relationship problems is group therapy. In group work patients actually play out their relationship issues in a way that gives both them, and their therapist, a first hand, front-row insight into what causes them issues. The relationship with the therapist, while very real in many ways, has one big limitation – it is built around the professional positive regard that a therapist brings to their side of the equation. Moreover, the therapist is not bringing any of their problems along to be considered by the patients (or at least should not be).

In group, things are more real, as other group members bring up all sorts of emotional issues that can trigger each participant negatively, just as much as it can help. Though I have found group therapy the ultimate therapy for helping people make sense of what goes wrong in relationships, and how to fix these problems, there is one condition that group therapy does not work for – DID. In fact, I do not believe group therapy has a role for treating trauma at all. It may have a role in helping traumatised people deal with

relationships in their life, but this needs to be kept quite separate from the trauma therapy.

Trauma therapy needs to be highly individualised. While the actual acts of aggression, both sexual and physical, are often relatively limited in kind, it is the accompanying emotional abuse and meaning that is always present, that varies enormously. One of the worst things that can happen in groups around trauma is that the emotional abuse experience, which is so much more complex, gets overlooked against the more easily understood physical and sexual abuse experiences. Then it can become a case of comparing abuses. If there is anything that does not lend itself to comparison, it is abuse experiences. It is human nature to compare. Even an eye roll by a group member when someone begins to talk of their abuse, can shut people down and render the group worse than useless.

As I have already touched on, what is often misunderstood is that the power of an abuse experience has much more to do with its emotional meaning than it does with how painful or aggressive the act was. There is only a vague correlation between the level of aggression and pain and the level of traumatic experience. Often it has to do with the amount of betrayal involved. A 'minor' event like having an adult male caregiver masturbate in front of you when you are six could have more emotional consequences than a full-on rape as a young adult, because the younger age means that it has greater developmental consequences that reverberate through the ages and subsequent developmental challenges. Jeni has also given some powerful examples of how what might be interpreted as less emotionally impactful events can be more traumatic than another rape. The point is, these events can't really be compared at all.

Jeni's attempts at group therapy saw both group members and the facilitators unable to cope with her abuse or, worse, not believe it happened. This was an incredibly invalidating experience. Jeni's experience of group therapy is both instructive and very unfortunate for her.

I thought I could be cleverer and run a group for patients just with DID. The plan was to not go anywhere near their trauma but

instead adopt a supportive approach by helping them to realise that they were not alone and to give each other the benefit of their shared lived experience. I also hoped that because they all had DID that there would be a sense of finding the tribe they had been missing.

I could not have been more wrong.

What happened was that the sense of community was overtaken by a triggering that, while not about their trauma directly, reflected a shared experience of being the victims of terrible crimes. Each patient brought many alters to the room. Before I knew it there were complex and invisible interactions occurring between literally dozens of personalities that I could not keep up with. Jeni was in this group and while I don't think it caused her quite the difficulties she experienced in her other groups, I could see the group dynamics were too overwhelming and unmanageable for her and the others. One thing my group work taught me was I knew what a group that was working well looked like, and this was not it. Jeni talks more about this below. After only a few sessions I wound the group up. I had to do a lot of work with each of the members in subsequent individual sessions – mostly to assist them in learning not to worry about the other group members!

Never again.

MUSCLES

We attended three, count 'em, three different groups for people with MPD. They were vile. It was repulsive. Not because of the clients. We understood them, but the counsellors were so out of their depth it was awful. George was the best of them. He knew he was out of his depth and he closed the group quick smart. But the other two, OMG, I could tell stories to curl your hair. But I won't 'cos this time I want to focus on what went wrong.

Firstly, in a normal group you can assume that what you are saying is being heard by the right person. But with MPD, there are lots of folks hearing your comments and reacting. You got more reactions in someone like Jeni than you can poke a stick at. Jeni

has 2681 additional opinions and reactions you don't see. How can you be sure the message is getting where you need it with all that going on? And that's not just reactions to the 'Important' stuff, that's reactions to everything. And not all those reactions are positive. One person, deeply distressed and in need of help, can have lots of emotions all at once. How can one counsellor deal with all that, let alone a whole room of Jenis with their own inner circles and reactions, feelings and emotions. It's not possible. And if it's done it's shit therapy at best, a bloody disaster at worst.

ERIK

Secondly, let's talk about interpersonal relationships. In any group interpersonal relationships grow between the participants. But they also develop between the counsellor and the participants. Some participants can become quite possessive of the counsellor, playing out patterns of deprivation and abuse within the group. With MPD groups this is magnified to an extreme extent.

We've seen favouritism in the two groups not run by George get out of hand. We saw counsellors pick favourites within the group members and play one off the other. In one group two participants were 'loved' while the rest of the group were treated like second-class citizens. I doubt I need to tell you we were not one of the loved ones.

We also experienced it in another group we attended. This group was run by a person who had no experience in mental health at all. Back then it never crossed our mind to check the qualifications of the group leaders, we were so desperate for help we ended up looking for it in all the wrong places.

In this experience, not only did the group leader play favourites, they allowed a level of competitiveness between the participants that was obscene. Participants would contact Jeni outside of group and gloat about how much time they were getting with the leader. How they had taken them to appointments, allowed them to sleepover at their home, how they cared more for them than they did for Jeni. It replicated much of the relationship Dad had fostered between himself and Sheila and caused Jeni much distress.

Remember that group is not a meeting of equals. The counsellor or group leader has substantially more power than the participant, most notably they have the power to help or withhold that help. Jeni experienced not just a withholding of help, but also a damaging amount of sabotage to her own personal healing; the healing that her alters were doing internally. We saw the impact of these relationships on Jeni and we did what we could to unpick them and get her out of there. That was not as easy as it sounds. Jeni couldn't just up and leave. She couldn't make the decision to stop. Why not? Because she hoped that next week would be better. She was reacting to the groups just as she reacted to Dad. Hoping things would improve, grasping at straws to prove that they were helping her. Jeni had invested so much into the groups that she couldn't just walk away.

Thirdly, I want to reflect on a dynamic which may be unique to Jeni, I don't know, but it certainly had an impact on her. Jeni made it clear in her initial 'getting to know you' speech that she was studying psychology, and later criminology. This was ignored and then belittled by many group leaders. But Jeni's skills were then used and manipulated as and when it suited the counsellors. Jeni found herself in a situation where to get the help she needed, she had to work for it. She had to be a supplementary counsellor in the group, taking care of clients, if she wanted to have her issues even looked at. However, where others could have hours devoted to an issue they wanted to explore, Jeni would barely get to explain her problem before attention was diverted to someone else, or she was told it was time for a break. The impact of this on Jeni cannot be overstated. She had stirred up her issue, and the alters who looked after it for her, only to have attention move onto someone else. This meant she had to deal with the distressed or emotional alters, while also participating in the group and supporting and caring for the other clients who had diverted attention from her. It was traumatic to say the least.

GABRIELLE
In summary: thinking about putting people with MPD/DID into a group therapy setting?

DON'T
JUST DON'T.

* * *

GEORGE:
Selective integration

A few words on integration. It is something of a vexed issue. Back when I started working with Jeni the teaching was to work towards integration. It reflected a general sense in medicine to return people to the 'norm'. Over the years I have found that most of my patients would rather stay multiple.

Instead of a goal of integration, what I find myself doing is developing high-level co-consciousness and helping the alters to work as a team. The credo is that 'all are welcome'. (The very opposite of using exorcism as a treatment model.) There are many reports from the world of business, government and warfare that show the dangers of only seeking input from those we like or get on easily with. My role here is more that of a sporting team coach.

It is about recognising that the best teams are those that have players of very different temperaments and skills that are harnessed and coordinated effectively.

The second job is that of re-tasking alters into new roles once they know that the war is over. Sometimes this could be as simple as letting them finally be children, doing what children do – play with pets or enjoy a good movie. Very importantly, I task child parts to play with other children the patient may deal with day-to-day or be playful with close adult friends. Other parts go to the beach and enjoy a well-earned holiday.

Two things were of interest when Jeni and I did integration work. It is important to note that we started with alters who had similar roles and motivations, and who were agreeable to the exercise. Firstly, after undertaking 'integration ceremonies' in my office, Jeni would come back and tell me that spontaneous integrations had happened at home in between sessions. This

demonstrated a natural force at work, a knowing that there was a role for combination at some level. Secondly, and I had not heard about this before, Jeni simply un-integrated when she needed to provide evidence for the detectives and to give evidence in court. I have since been able to point out to other patients that it is not a permanent process if they do not want it to be. Moreover, we are not 'killing off' alters as some of them fear. I will leave it to Jeni to talk further on this.

Integration can only occur after you have done the trauma processing work so that the person can finally free themselves from being haunted by their traumas. We don't need to work through all of them, as I've mentioned, some resolve as you process others of similar meaning. Nevertheless, getting to the point of integration took many, many sessions over several years. We worked on it in the office from late 1998 to mid-2001, and, as you have seen, Jeni was constantly working on it outside of the therapy sessions. It was a major achievement and milestone in Jeni's therapy.

JENI

A major thing George did help me with was MPD integration. My mind was split into fragments that were beautifully organised, but they didn't come together to form a complete jigsaw puzzle. The goal was to fuse my alters together to become a unified whole, so I could function as one person. The treatment wasn't about getting rid of alters or switching them off, it was about combining them in harmony. To do that, Erik asked each alter to find a buddy who complemented their skills so they could merge. This process was more than just a blending of the minds. It was a process of each pairing finding a common ground and creating mutuality. They would find something in common, spend time working together, sharing tasks and developing ways to best communicate with each other. When the two were comfortable with being together, they would create a space where they could work simultaneously. Finally, when they were ready, two would become one. For example, the Laughing Man (whose strength was his ability to laugh in Dad's face) merged with

The Joker (who found the humour in every situation). Working with George we created integration ceremonies to help this process. Once we understood the importance of carrying out integration ceremonies, we created one that we could use outside of the therapy hour, and without George's help.

These ceremonies developed over time as we got better at identifying what was needed. The central part of these ceremonies was when we acknowledged the skills and temperaments of each of the pair, we explicitly recognised and valued their contribution to the system. We talked of how important they were and how by blending or merging they were becoming more connected to the system not less. These ceremonies did not have to take long, because the words were less important than the meanings the new pairing took from it. What mattered was the acknowledgement of the service of the alters, both in the past, and the anticipated service of their future. Over time one hundred alters merged to become fifty, and so on and so forth. We all knew the importance of the task, and everyone pulled together as a team so we could finally rest.

Finally, the blended alters began to integrate. This was a different type of process. This was a blending of each grouping into the one newly created Jeni. The new Jeni took on all the characteristics of the blended alters. Each blending was celebrated with a recognition ceremony. Jeni learned through these ceremonies the skills and talents she had just added to her collective self. It was a magical process of self love. Each part of the process was designed to bring into the light the best of us, and the best we had to offer. Even alters who could have been seen as negative were part of the best of us. Negative emotions, self-perceptions, and negative reactions were accepted and integrated into Jeni with a recognition of their value. We gave back to Jeni all that her childhood had taken from her. The integrated alters went to a newly created internal landscape of a beach for a much-deserved break. The process took three years all up from 1998 to mid-2001, and Erik was the very last alter to integrate. He'd been the project manager and wanted to see it through to the end.

ERIK

I'd like to touch on the reactions of other people with MPD to Jeni's desire to integrate. Oh brother! The members of one of the therapy groups that Jeni was a participant in were there as Jeni and I went through the integration process. They saw the huge amount of effort it took to make our alters coalesce and they did everything they could to sabotage the process. It was unhelpful. We had group members bleat 'but I like Symphony, I don't want Symphony to leave', 'you can't integrate Erik, I love you, you're my boyfriend!!', and my personal favourite, 'you can't integrate, you are abandoning the multiple movement'. I did not know there was a multiple movement until that moment. If there was one, it certainly had not bothered to help us, so abandoning it wasn't exactly hard. It's not like it had done anything for us. At least one of the arguments raised by the group was entirely moot. We had no plans to integrate Symphony, and Muscles chose to remain separate to be with her and take care of her. Symphony couldn't integrate with the alters because she'd created them, and we needed Muscles for, well, his muscle – to keep us safe.

The problem was that when one group member complained about our integration plans, and became distressed or upset, the discussion moved to looking after them. There was no further support or care for Jeni. Now this undermined our integrative process in a number of ways. Firstly, it took away our joy and sense of accomplishment for the blending we had done. Instead of being validated in our efforts to get well, we were discouraged and devalued. Secondly, it took the attention away from Jeni and placed it on someone else, letting Jeni know in no uncertain terms that her feelings and accomplishments were less important than someone else's reactions to them.

There is no guidebook to integration. No dummy's guide, no do it yourself handbook. You have to work it out for yourself. And in 1998, when we began therapy with George, therapists had less idea how it worked than we did. Integration is intensely personal, and so each person with MPD/DID will do it differently. We've outlined above how we did it, but that worked for us. It might not work for other less organised or structured systems.

GABRIELLE

We had such joy. Our world was becoming richer by the day. Our abilities were deepening, we could taste more fully, experience touch and smell once again! Hear and see without the necessary blinkers and blinders of MPD. We were living more fully, no longer hyper-vigilant, no longer abuse-focused, but rather enjoying life.

We became focused on what it meant to be a woman, seeing our anatomy for the first time and choosing to follow the anatomy and become a strong woman. We were examining the role models of femininity in front of us and choosing who and what we wanted to be. It was a wonderful process that we wanted to share. Our deep desire to help came out and we tried very hard to share our experiences with other group members.

ERIK

When we shared with the group how we were accomplishing our goal of integration, we were giving a gift, an insight into our world and its mechanics. We were exposing large numbers of alters to the world and letting the world judge them. In group therapy that judgement was very harsh indeed. The participants could not see the joy, the wonder, the miracle of what we were doing. They saw it as us 'murdering our people'. They mourned their lost relationships with my alters! They were supported in this by the group leader. It was strange, in group therapy Jeni had been repeatedly denied the opportunity and the right to mourn her losses. But members of the group, who were not directly involved in our integration process and were watching it from the sidelines, were allowed, no, encouraged to mourn their losses. It was as if as we integrated we were causing the members of the group intense distress. I was told that I was a murderer. I was killing the alters who were integrating, and so of course their friends in the group were mourning them. The fact I would rather cut off my own leg than hurt Symphony or any of her alters was irrelevant. I was a murderer and nothing I said or did was going to change that.

Um no, just no!

I killed no one, and anyway, if we were 'killing' what's it to do with these people? They were nothing to the process. They weren't contributing alternative ideas, making suggestions, or helping in any way. They chose to ignore the evidence in front of them of how integration was actually happening. This was their loss, and it was a huge one. As people with MPD, I expected them to be fascinated by the process playing out in front of them. But they weren't. They fixated on one thing, I was murdering my alters, and they refused to see anything else. Every single time I attended group I was hit with a barrage of complaints, anger and tears over my horrific crimes. Geez, that's familiar.

In late December 2000, George and I discussed a way to honour my alters, their work and integration. I chose to do this around 2 March (Jay Osmond's birthday and a special day for all of us). George organised an appointment for me on Thursday, 1 March 2001 as the closest we could get. We began to make plans for us to celebrate the completion of our integration process with George. This ceremony was to make formal and visible our integration into a single being. We still had work to do, but we wanted to do something to show that we valued integration. George came up with a ceremony for us. We told the members of our therapy group about this upcoming ceremony and how much we were working to be fully integrated by the day. Immediately the leader said that group was for people with MPD and if I was integrated I no longer met the criteria for membership and so I was asked to leave. 20 January 2001 was set as my last day with the group.

But then, in the group session of 14 January 2001, a participant bounced into the group session and announced 'I'm integrated!' This shocked me as this person had been quite vocal about her disagreement with my desire to integrate. Her announcement was met with cheers and hugs and an immediate acceptance of the news. It was hard to watch. This was compounded when she was not asked to leave the group as an integrated multiple. She was told how wonderful she was to have integrated and how much she had to teach the group about living after integration. Plans were made to have her

explain how she had integrated next session. It was highly confusing. I was so overwhelmed by my emotions that I had to go into the garden to sit on my own and work through them before I could return to the group. I then got into trouble for being unsupportive of her miraculous integration.

MUSCLES

It sure was a miracle! Damned woman had put in no effort to do a process of integration. She just rocked up and said she'd done it. I wanted details, I wanted to know how. But above all I wanted to know what had caused her abrupt change from being completely anti-integration the week before to being so in love with the idea that she'd managed to integrate in a 50-minute therapy session. To say I was dubious is a massive understatement. And by doing this the week before Jeni was to be flung out of the group for the sin of integration was downright bloody bewildering. It sure took the attention away from Jeni and her anxiety about being almost completely integrated. Jeni was leaping off a cliff into the unknown and would have benefited from some support that weekend. Jeni and everyone else inside was very upset at how our integration was viewed as murder but this woman's integration was met with positivity. More confusion. And from the day I left, I never heard from the members of that group or from the group leader again. I had been abandoned by the 'multiple movement'. Those people who had been so devastated, allegedly, at the idea of losing relationships with my alters rejected me and abandoned me, not even waiting around to see how integration turned out.

ERIK

In dealing with our integration that group leader chose to prioritise, and emphasise, the distress and anger of the audience over the joy of Jeni. They were wrong to do this, just plain wrong. They should have seen the joy and capitalised on it. They should have asked us how it felt to integrate, how the process worked, what were the difficulties, were there any unexpected bonuses of integration, how did we feel. But they didn't and they cheated a group of seven the chance

to explore healing from their horrific pasts. They denied them the chance to see integration as growth. They cheated me of the chance to learn from my development of an integrated whole person.

So let's be clear. Integration does not kill your alters. It makes them stronger. It's like making a cake. You put all the ingredients in a bowl and stir them all around. You have cake batter, but the eggs, butter and flour are still there, they just changed their form to create something new. In the year 2001, when we integrated, there was no better conception of integration than this. But this was to change substantially in 2009 when our world changed once more, but I will leave that for Symphony to explain later.

CHAPTER NINETEEN

Post-integration Life

ERIK

It is important to note that therapy did not end just because I was integrated. There were still some outstanding issues I needed help with. The first issue seemed simple. What was I? Should I go with the majority of the alters in a case of majority rule and become masculine, a tomboy? Should I go with the anatomy and become a girl? Or should I just ignore gender completely and become an asexual not-girl? Choices, choices.

The second issue was dealing with our new world. We went straight to George for help with this and he was brilliant. He walked into this new life with us and helped us to negotiate our experiences. He assisted with so much, he was particularly helpful in showing Jeni how to deal with our absence.

The third major issue we needed help with was the biggest bone of contention in my world. My relationship with my sister Sheila. And it is this issue that had me butting heads with every therapist, counsellor, psychiatrist and psychologist, George included. We'd reached a stalemate over her and had nowhere to go. So we put it on the back burner and left it to deal with more pressing issues. But it festered.

The first thing that came up in post-integration therapy was which gender we wanted to be. Our gender choices had mostly been a reaction to Dad's abuse and so we chose to be males or not-girls. The vast majority of our alters had not been female. Were we to identify as female and follow the anatomy, or were we to reject our

body and opt to be masculine? This challenging question took a long time to answer. Thankfully, George and I worked together to explore this.

Once we chose to follow the anatomy and become a female, I did my best to continue to work out what kind of female I wanted to be, rejecting both my mother and my sister as role models. I also rejected the expressions of femininity I had seen in all of the groups I attended. I had seen enough exploitative and exploited, manipulated and manipulative femininity and I was rejecting that wholeheartedly. I explored every type of female model I could find, before rejecting them all. I created my own style of femininity from the characteristics valued in the songs of the Osmonds. I built upon my understanding of womanhood and added in the best of femininity as described by the Osmonds until I felt I had made someone I could be. I went for kind and compassionate, willing to be vulnerable but also express my inner strength. It was a tough choice but I needed to respect the qualities of all of my alters. It felt strange to be a guy, working out what kind of female the body would go for, but I didn't want to integrate leaving Jeni unprepared.

Unfortunately, I focused on our gender identity, not our sexual identity, our sexual orientation, or in fact anything to do with sex. I missed this important issue completely. I was attempting to help Jeni reclaim her femininity, not her sexuality. It never crossed my mind that this was something that Jeni would need to have strategies to deal with going forward. Given our history, this was a curious blind spot.

JENI
All too quiet
While I knew the integration was an important part of my therapy, my god, it was quiet inside my head when it was finished! After so many years of constant chatter, the silence was unnerving. I did not like this at all. As is usually the case, there were benefits and losses with integrating. While we felt like a united whole, we also lost our

strength in numbers. It was a shock going from having dozens of different armies to just being Jeni, Symphony and Muscles.

The process and goal of integrating worked well for me, but I was utterly unprepared for the reality of living without my team. It was hard. I felt that I was less than the sum of my parts. I had all their skills, but none of their company. I had lost something indefinable, something unique about being multiple, I had lost that which had made me so strong: my community.

So while I gained enormously from integrating in terms of joy, life and feeling free, I had no one to share it with, no one who understood just why standing in the rain feeling the raindrops hit my skin was so wonderful. I had accomplished the goal and had grown immensely. It's just that, other than George, no one around me had grown with me, or was interested in supporting me as I grew. It got very lonely very quickly.

GEORGE
Integration 1990s-style

Back then in the late 1990s, the choice was to integrate, or not to integrate. In the 2020s this has changed considerably, and for the better. Jeni's experience and input has clarified this greatly for me. I firmly believe the question is, 'To what degree do I want to selectively integrate?' As Jeni highlighted to me, over 2500 parts were rather unwieldy. Moreover, the focus of the system was on safety and protection. There is so much more to life – to appreciate it, less fragmentation was probably required.

As Jeni moved through life the focus had been on, am I safe and where might the next threat come from? Hypervigilance was the norm. You don't smell the roses from this perspective. Selective integration, as I now think of it, heralds three fundamental shifts. First, it means the war is over. There is no longer any abuse happening, or likely to happen. Yes, there are still risks that all people face, but there are measures that we all can take to keep these risks at a level that allows one to live life fully.

Second, the time had come to enjoy the richness that life has to offer, from the natural beauty of mother nature to the generosity of the human spirit, from the laugh of a happy child to the captivating harmonies of talented singers – the things that tend to go unnoticed when planning an escape route.

Third, I can now begin work on who I am, what is my identity, and what am I here to do? It is almost impossible to undertake this identity work, that leads onto one's meaning and purpose in life, while in a fragmented state. Unity is required to move in the appropriate direction. While integration is not necessary to do this work, there needs, at least, to be a high level of co-consciousness between the parts.

As one might appreciate, this means that there is significant therapy to be done post-integration. Indeed, for many of my patients who present to me for psychotherapy, this is just the beginning of the work that we undertake.

JENI

The remaining three of us worked together to improve our life. During the years we were integrated we explored so many issues, ranging from the simple stuff; what to wear today, to the more sensitive and critical stuff like sex and sexuality. In our post-integration period I was confronted with many issues we had been unable to even contemplate as a multiple. Most of them revolved around issues of identity. Who were we? What did we want? Where do we go from here? How are we to see men? What characterises men who are not abusers? How do they function? And how will they treat me?

We worked closely with George to address these issues, and others that arose over time, from the day of integration until our break from therapy in May 2002. We continued the work on our own during our break from therapy and then picked up the loose ends when we continued our therapy with George in 2009. These issues were ongoing fuel for therapy and I continued working on them with George, through Dad's trial in 2019, and on until 2021.

SYMPHONY
Reclaiming my sexuality

As a multiple our sexuality was scattered, shared amongst the many, and elusive to say the least. When I had given my femininity to Gabrielle, I had unintentionally given her my sexuality and my ideas about sex as well. But much of this was in fragments. Having never examined our sexual identity, we had never collected the jigsaw puzzle pieces up, let alone tried to build a sexual identity.

We could not begin to explore our sexuality until we were integrated. As with everything in our life this was not as easy as it seemed. I looked everywhere for models of women and men. I did my best to explore masculinity and femininity, and the interplay between the sexes. Much of what I saw and read was 'plastic fantastic'. The men and women were plastic with no internal motivations or feelings. Men merely fucked the women and that was it. They refused to listen to no, and reframed the women's resistance as 'you want it really, you're just playing hard to get'.

The women were even worse, they said no, but then gave in. The sounds they made, even when written, were very similar to sounds of being in pain. This was too close to rape for me and I moved on, ever looking for men with brains and feelings and emotions and women who weren't being raped. It was a tough and embarrassing search. George suggested I watch pornography and read erotica to find something that I was comfortable with, that I could relate to in a space where I had total control. As he said, there is something out there for everyone. I could just about do the erotica, but porn was out of the question. I just couldn't. The shame I did not feel about being raped by Dad, emerged as I attempted to explore my sexuality. It was just too embarrassing.

And then I discovered the art of Tom of Finland. He was a revelation. His men were happy, joyous, in love and not afraid to show it. But they were gay and mostly nude and they had the biggest 'equipment' I had ever really looked at. They were huge. But by exploring 'Tom's Boys' I learned a great deal. Critically I discovered, and began to believe, that sex was supposed to be joyful, an expression of love between two or more people.

Finally, I recognised that what Dad did to me was not sex. It was a crime and Dad's penis was his weapon of choice. What he did to me was an expression of his power over me. He did not abuse me because I deserved it. He abused me because he could, because he wanted to, because he enjoyed it. He is a paedophile and a criminal. It was time for me to put that behind me and make a new world free from him.

GEORGE
Rebuilding trust in the bedroom
As Jeni explains above, post-integration there was still work to be done. One of the most crucial areas she needed to examine was around her reclaiming her sexual identity. This is a huge issue for victims of childhood sexual abuse. As I have said, the first casualty of abuse is trust. Damage to one's sexuality and sexual functioning is not much further down the list. Difficulties negotiating sexual interactions makes having any close, loving relationships difficult, to say the least. Using erotica and pornography is, thanks to the internet, now statistically normal for both men and women. With this demand has come a much wider menu of pornography and erotica that is both tasteful and sensitive, especially when made by women showing women as not just consenting, and enjoying the act, but also in control and approaching it on their terms.

It was interesting to see Jeni engage most comfortably with male-on-male erotica, even though she was clearly heterosexual, but it made sense, as this was the most distant from her own sexual abuse experiences. While we worked on this initially post-integration, this work was returned to when she came back into regular therapy in 2009 and right up until we finally terminated in 2021.

MUSCLES
I tried to discuss with George my difficult memories of my sister, exploring her victimhood but in focusing on her victimhood I

believed he was ignoring mine. I didn't have the words and George couldn't help me find them to explain that.

In April 2002 we agreed to take a break from therapy, and I had my last session with George on Friday 10 May 2002. I was integrated and whole, but still had a lot to resolve. I wanted to talk about my resentment towards my sister, but George couldn't provide the help and solidarity I needed. I was alone once again, but to my absolute joy my alters stayed united.

JENI
Life after George
Moving on from George felt right. I had accomplished much with him and addressed so many of my issues. The outstanding issue could be summed up very simply: Forgive and Forget.

I was getting a great deal of pressure from the sexual abuse service counsellors and clients alike about putting Dad's crimes behind me and moving on. This was invariably couched as me needing to forgive and forget and rebuild a relationship with him. Why on earth counsellors would even suggest such a thing for a victim of childhood sexual abuse inflicted by their own father was beyond me. But, looking back, if they did not believe my complaints and allegations, then suggesting I put it behind me and move on might make some sense. But it was a very dangerous tactic. Unfortunately, this was supported by my friends and members of my family as well. Of course this begs the question as to whether they believed me, or whether they too thought I was faking it for attention. I know certain members of my family were well and truly over hearing about Dad by now. When I started to take their views seriously and tried to put it all behind me, there was an audible sigh of relief and a visual relaxation of their stress levels. But the message I got was that they supported me in my efforts to forgive and forget and to make moves to put it all behind me and allow him back into my world as a rehabilitated criminal.

* * *

Thankfully the world is very different now from the therapeutic disasters I endured during the 1990s and the 2000s. Psychiatrists and psychologists, counsellors and therapists no longer jump to 'fake' and 'fraud' as their first option when faced with the unusual features of MPD. And they understand that there are some crimes that are unforgivable: sexually abusing your child so badly they develop MPD simply to survive you is top of that list. They are a lot more like George now. I'm thankful for this development.

CHAPTER TWENTY

An Invitation

Note from Jeni

Before you read this chapter, I feel the need to remind you of the complexity of familial abuse. In situations of domestic violence, it takes – on average – eight attempts for the victim to successfully leave. When the victim is a child and the abuser is their father, leaving isn't an option. Abusers are experts at manipulation, and the cycle of abuse is a hard one to escape. It's hard for anyone to let go of their hopes and dreams of having a loving family. It's much easier to believe that people can change. That's a dangerous belief – as I would soon find out.

JENI

I didn't hear from my dad while he was in prison in England for the crimes he committed against Sheila. Sometimes I fantasised about getting a reverse-charged call from him and denying it. *Will you accept a call from Richard Haynes? No, I bloody won't.* The phone didn't ring. Not until I picked it up.

After six years of Dad being in jail, and six years of me being in serious therapy, I was the one who reached out to him. I know this might not make any sense to people – it doesn't to me – but the counsellors at the sexual abuse centre had insisted I needed to forgive and forget. They suggested I write to Dad in jail. In the letter, I acknowledged that he was doing his time in jail and paying the penalty for his crimes. I preached about justice in my counselling sessions, and I truly believed that once a criminal had finished their

sentence, they should be free to return to their family and start again. The stubborn morality in me forced me to apply the same standards to Dad. I told Dad as much in the letter, and explained that I was hoping to move forward with forgiveness.

Dad replied. His letter back to me was full of compassion and positivity. He used all the right words and said everything he knew I wanted to hear. He said he wasn't expecting my letter, but he was certainly glad I reached out because he wanted to put the past behind him and rebuild our relationship. Dad apologised for what he put me through – without ever admitting what he did. He told me he'd come to realise the great deal of stress he'd caused me and swore he would take it all back if he could. He was dreadfully sorry.

Of course, it was a welcome apology – and one I'd been waiting a lifetime for.

The paternal string between Dad and me was somehow holding on by a thread. He was still my dad, and that meant something.

Well, that's what people told me. And I stupidly listened.

After the letter, I tried to call my father in jail for his birthday in 2003. I wasn't put through to him on the day, but an officer took a message on a piece of paper that said his daughter Jennifer from Australia had called to wish him a happy birthday. Dad supposedly cherished that note, and organised to ring me back. Inmates were given five minutes a day in phone calls, but Dad had no one to call, so the officers gave him thirty minutes to speak to me.

When I answered the phone, Dad used my name. He called me Jeni. Considering he'd only ever called me Maggot and his dirty girl, hearing him say my name was very powerful. Like the master manipulator he is, Dad played the perfect father role. He became the Dad I never had, the Dad I wished for, the Dad I needed.

Dad asked me questions, he showed an interest in my life and we chatted about our shared love of *Doctor Who* and *Torchwood*. He also told me he'd completed sex offender training during his time inside and that he was rehabilitated. After twenty minutes on the phone, Dad said he didn't want to wear out his welcome with me – or the officers who so nicely organised the call – and that he was going to

say goodbye and hang up. It was the first time I'd seen Dad show real consideration for other people. *Holy hell, he's really changed*, I thought.

I believed Dad still had three years of his nine-year sentence to serve, so I thought there'd be plenty of time between my letter and his release date.

I was wrong.

Dad was released early for 'good behaviour'. The injustice rubbed me the wrong way: I didn't get any rewards for good behaviour as a child even though I tried so hard to be a good girl all the time, and yet Dad got an early mark for keeping his nose clean. He was walking the streets just six months after I'd reached out.

Dad swapped his prison cell for a halfway house, but our phone calls continued. He still had a probation period, and he would always remain on the sex offender list in England. Our weekly conversations lasted hours and Dad kept saying all the right things. He continued to apologise for hurting me and the devastating cost his actions had on me. Dad was honest, to a point. He never mentioned specifics or used the words 'sadistic rape' and 'buggery', but he admitted fault, and that was more than he'd ever done before. When I told him how upset I was that he'd pleaded not guilty to my charges in the trial, he swore that his lawyer had advised him to do so. He hadn't wanted to lie in court, but his lawyer told him to, and he did.

I believed my Dad had changed because I wanted it to be true. In the same way he pretended to be the perfect partner to convince Mum to marry him, Dad acted like the father of my dreams. He was telling me things I'd always wanted to hear, and I fell for it. Blame naivety, the complicated cycle of abuse or the human need for paternal validation, but I let myself be dazzled by my abuser.

I know, I know, I'm shaking my head now too.

I talked to Mum and Frank about the possibility of inviting Dad over to Australia for a visit. It wasn't a decision I made lightly. I tossed it around in my mind like a football for weeks and made sure I had the support of all the interested parties. I went back to see George and get his opinion. I needed his support and a safe space

to work through my thoughts, but all I got was more confusion. In one session, George could see the benefit in me seeing my dad and having him take accountability. In the next session, George changed his mind and didn't think it was a good idea. His inconsistency made the decision even harder, and I took another break from therapy because of it.

Finally, I made the call and said the words out loud; I asked Dad if he'd like to come to Australia to reconnect with us when his probation was up. I explained he could get a holiday visa, stay in a hotel for a couple of weeks and spend some time with us before returning to England to rebuild his life. Dad jumped at the offer! He agreed to staying in a hotel and suggested that, if things went well, he could park a caravan in our front yard to be closer to us – like a happy, normal, loving family.

Dad organised his visa, booked his tickets and told me he'd adhere to any rules Australia wanted to put in place for him because of his sex offences in England. He explained that the visa application process had changed for travellers visiting Australia from England, and he didn't need to disclose his criminal past. I called immigration and the AFP to ask if there would be any restrictions on my father while he was holidaying here. I was told that there would not be. Both departments wished me well rather than raised issues. But it's important to note that all of the relevant departments knew Dad was coming – because I told them – and they could have intervened at any moment if there was an issue. They did not.

Dad arrived in Queensland immediately after his probation ended. It had been seven years since I'd seen him. At the airport, Dad looked like he'd put effort into his appearance. He was wearing smart clothes, was clean-shaven and appeared to be the vision of a respectable man. I gave him a hug. He'd been playing the loving father role so well over the phone, I desperately wanted him to stay in character in person. And he did, mostly.

Dad didn't stay in a hotel like we agreed, instead he set up in the back room of the house I shared with Mum in Brisbane. Every time I walked to the toilet, I passed his room. Every shower I took, I had

to undress directly across the hallway from his room behind a door without a lock. Every morning, I woke up to a lukewarm cup of coffee and my Dad sitting on the end of my bed watching me.

Parts of me panicked, but we stayed united as Jeni. Besides, nothing bad had happened. Dad was being the affectionate father I'd always wanted. Still, I couldn't shake the sweaty palms I got when Dad insisted on sitting next to me on the couch instead of on the separate sofa I had bought for him to use. I couldn't help the sick feeling in my stomach when he put his arm around me. I couldn't stop the voice in my head screaming, *run, run, run.*

I desperately wanted to reach out to George, but I felt like I couldn't. I'd made my choice and I had to live with it. On my own. I'd never felt lonelier. I got into the habit of typing George's number into my phone and having an entire conversation with him. I'd tell him about how I was feeling, what I was worried about and beg for his help. I'd lay it all on the table, but I never actually dialled.

CHAPTER TWENTY-ONE

The Dropping of the Mask

JENI

It lasted two months.

Dad wanted to stay in Australia – where he wasn't on the sex offender register – and I foolishly helped him apply to do just that. He applied for the contributory parent visa and expected me to support him. Dazzled by this new compassionate and caring father I suddenly had, I agreed. I filled out the forms and wrote a letter praising my father for owning his mistakes, apologising and doing his best to be a better man. When all the boxes were ticked, questions answered and dotted lines signed, we were told Dad would be on a bridging visa until a decision was made as to if he was a suitable applicant.

The very next day, Dad dropped his mask. He became the father I knew as a child: cold, manipulative and deceitful. He hadn't changed – he was still a monster – he'd just perfected his acting skills in jail. I realised the last two months and all the phone calls before them were total bullshit. I knew it the second he gave up on his respectable façade and stopped showering. I knew it when I smelt his filthy burning Bakelite scent.

Dad fooled me, and I felt like I couldn't do anything about it because his visa application had already been lodged. After all, I was the one who invited him here.

I knew for certain that I'd made a fatal mistake when Dad started saying we must find out what happened to me in Australia all those years ago because he didn't touch me. It was as if he wanted me to

believe that someone who looked, sounded and smelt like him had snuck into my bedroom in two separate houses and abused me. Dad kept probing me to speak about the abuse, but I refused. Whenever I got angry or upset about his questions, I could see he became visibly aroused.

Dad's presence was further cemented in our lives when he had all of his possessions sent over to my house from where they'd been stored back in England.

Note from Jeni's mum

Like you, I thought a reconciliation between Richard and the family was a good idea. We were both wrong. I was completely ignorant of what that man did to you. But I had stayed with him all those years, knowing how difficult and cruel he could be, because I thought family should stay together. I thought I could protect you from his stupid ideas, moods and beliefs. I had no idea of the monster he was. I had no idea how he hurt my babies. How he hurt you. I am so sorry.

MAGSY

One of the items in Dad's belongings was the hammer Dad used to rape me with as a child. When I opened the box to find it, I recognised it immediately and nearly wet myself with fear. At the very sight of the hammer, I was transported back to the foot of my parents' bed as a little girl. History is alive and well, and I'm afraid it will repeat itself.

JENI

After Dad had been in Australia for five months, the immigration compliance unit raided our house and took Dad into custody. It was like something off *Border Security*. The raid seemed to happen in slow motion, but I still couldn't make sense of it. I was certain we'd done everything by the book. Hell, I'd even called the AFP and Department of Immigration before Dad arrived.

I may have done everything right, but Dad hadn't. Apparently, Dad didn't declare his criminal record on his visa or his entry card

on arrival in Australia. He'd blatantly lied when he told me the process had changed and English passport holders no longer needed to disclose their criminal history.

An immigration officer explained that Dad had violated a number of Australian laws and he was in serious trouble. Despite being none the wiser to Dad's deceit, Mum and I were also treated like criminals. The immigration officers assumed we'd colluded with Dad to illegally get him into the country. If only they knew how much I wanted him to be exiled back to England. The opposite happened. Dad was issued a bridging visa on the condition that he remained living in the home of his daughter. He was obligated to stay under my roof until the result of his character test came back in February. I prayed for the person tasked with assessing my dad's character.

If they needed any evidence that my father was a monster, they could have found it on my birthday in 2005. Mum had gone to work for the day, so I was left at home alone with Dad, who insisted on having a special birthday dinner in my honour. I had to organise and pay for it myself. Happy birthday to me!

During the day, Dad kept pressing me to talk about my childhood abuse so we could figure out 'what happened to you in Australia'. I lost my temper and yelled at him that I didn't want to talk about it. The outburst gave Dad an erection and I fled to the bathroom to hide. Dad followed me and trapped me in the corner. I was frozen with terror, and Dad took advantage of my rigor mortis. He stuck his erection between my legs and simulated sex until he ejaculated. Although he hadn't penetrated me, the assault was traumatic. I didn't know what to do.

Like the birthdays of my youth, my thirty-fifth birthday was marked by an attack at the hands of my father. There was no cake.

* * *

Surprise, surprise, everything Dad had told me about his rehabilitation was a lie. He hadn't undertaken sex offender retraining; in fact he'd objected to doing the course as it was 'against his religion'. Dad was –

and always would be – a predator. His motives were clear. It was obvious to me that Dad didn't want to stay in Australia because he wanted to be with his family. He wanted to stay because he couldn't possibly go back to England where he was considered a sex offender. The thought of having to face the consequences of his actions seemed impossible to Dad, so I had to face them instead.

In late February, Dad was informed he had failed his character test and was given a week to organise a ticket back to England. Instead of booking a flight, he hired an immigration lawyer. It was this lawyer who advised Dad to apply for a spousal visa instead. In the lawyer's office, Dad got down on one knee and asked Mum to marry him. I couldn't read the look on Mum's face because her eyes were filled with blood due to her thyroid condition, so I couldn't tell you if she was reluctant or obliging when she accepted the indecent proposal.

The wedding was scheduled for the first of March, the day Dad was meant to leave the country. The lawyer spent the week collating photographs and statements for Dad's spousal visa, and we spent the week organising his nuptials. Frank and his girlfriend came from interstate for the occasion. Mum and Dad exchanged vows at lunchtime so the lawyer could snap photographs of them signing the wedding certificate and rush the application to the Department of Immigration that afternoon. While Mum and Dad celebrated with lunch with Frank and his girlfriend, the lawyer made it to the immigration office before closing time at 5 pm. However, the officers refused to accept the paperwork. They wouldn't even touch it. Dad's time was up.

Mum spent her second wedding night in her bedroom and Dad slept in the back bedroom. We all woke up to the sound of thumping on the front door and footsteps on the back stairs. It was an immigration raid. Dad was arrested for breaching the immigration act and taken into custody in handcuffs.

The image of my father in handcuffs was one I cherished for years. Whenever I felt a flashback coming on, I closed my eyes and pictured this moment.

Finally, with Dad out of the house, Mum admitted that she hadn't wanted to marry him and didn't want to support him staying in Australia anymore. She'd seen the same light as me. Mum could've saved us all a lot of hassle if she'd said something the day before, but it was better late than never.

Dad was taken to the immigration cells at Brisbane Correctional Centre at Wacol on the outskirts of Brisbane, where he complained non-stop about his human rights being violated. He argued that he had served his time for his crimes in England, but failed to acknowledge he wasn't incarcerated here for being a paedophile, he was behind bars for breaking Australia's immigration laws. Dad was so obnoxious and disruptive that plans were made to transfer him to Baxter Detention Centre in South Australia. Mum and I were told to pack his glasses, medication and clothes into a bag and bring it to the Brisbane airport ahead of his flight to Baxter.

The last time I saw my dad in 2005, he was wearing a prison-issued brown tracksuit. When he saw me inside the airport terminal, he hugged me and stroked my hair. I felt nothing but revulsion. Dad didn't even acknowledge Mum – his wife! Within fifteen minutes of seeing Dad, handing his belongings over and watching him be led away, we were back in a taxi on our way home.

From Baxter, Dad fought his deportation with everything he had. In Dad's correspondence with the Department of Immigration, he admitted to having sex with me as a child, but insisted it was merely incest – not rape. And besides, he wrote, I'd forgiven him for all of that.

As a part of his fight, Dad organised for his prison records from England to be sent over to his immigration lawyer. The lawyer encouraged me to read the records. They told a grim tale. Dad had been knocked back for parole three years running because he refused to address his offending behaviour and continued to blame his victim. As well as failing to complete the sex offender training (which he'd lied to me about doing), Dad stated point blank that he could do anything he wanted to me because I was a filthy, dirty child. It was one thing to hear my father call me that as a kid, and

quite another to see it written in black and white in the handwriting of a stranger.

After reading Dad's justification for his abuse of me, I officially withdrew my support from his visa application, but not before pleading with Dad that returning to England would be in his best interests. I reasoned that he could keep pushing his case and waste the little money he had fighting a losing battle, or cease his appeal and go home with some money in his bank account. I wanted Dad to drop the case by his own accord, because if he kept fighting to stay and somehow won, I knew I couldn't survive living in the same country as him. My biggest fear was him being forced to live under my roof for the rest of his life. If that happened, I have no doubt it would have ended with one of us dead.

On 10 June 2005, Dad phoned me from the airport to tell me he was being deported because he arrived in Australia under false pretences and with an unlawful visa.

I cried with relief that he was leaving. I held my breath until I knew Dad's flight had left and counted the hours until I knew he was back in England on the opposite side of the world. I was convinced something would force the plane to turn around and that Dad would be set free in Australia. I was having nightmares, body memories and flashbacks. It was only once I knew Dad was on British soil that I stopped shaking.

* * *

It's both a miracle and a testament to my psychiatric work with George that my alters stayed integrated during this time. Looking back, I wonder if we would have been stronger fractured. Of course, there were benefits to being 'whole', but I felt less than the sum of my parts. And, god, it was quiet! I'm sure Judas was itching at the bit to speak up and that Linda was rolling her eyes internally, but we stayed united as 'the Entity Currently Known as Jeni'. And somehow that entity managed to complete their PhD surrounded by chaos and cruelty.

There's a photo of me being presented with my Doctor of Philosophy certificate in 2007. I'm wearing the traditional academic robe and bonnet, and I look so proud of myself. I was. For my entire childhood, my father refused to call me Jennifer. On that day I reclaimed my name and added a prefix: Dr Jennifer Haynes.

PART THREE

RECKONING

CHAPTER TWENTY-TWO

Good Riddance to Bad Rubbish

JENI

I don't regret inviting my dad to Australia. If it weren't for his despicable behaviour during that year, I might not have ever gone to the Australian police to report his abuse of me. If I hadn't seen his true colours again as an adult, I might well have kept trying to forgive and forget. If I hadn't given him every possible opportunity to atone for his abuse by his own accord, I might not have taken justice into my own hands.

Unfortunately for me, in 2005 justice was still a long way off. When Dad returned to England and bought a house in Darlington, Mum and I were both happy to have him out of the country, but she still insisted on keeping him in our lives. After all, they were man and wife – in fact, they remain married today.

Just like she did back in the 1990s, when she forced me to call Dad, Mum guilted me into staying in contact with him. I was a 35-year-old woman, but I still didn't think I could say no to my mother. Even if I did, I was sure she wouldn't hear me. I'd been saying no my entire life, and no one listened. It was an impossible pattern to break.

As a way of justifying why she wanted me to spend hours every Sunday on the phone to my abuser, Mum told me I was better at speaking to Dad. Mostly, Dad spent our conversations complaining

about how expensive things were in England, asking for my help with his life admin (including sending a number of his belongings back to him), and whingeing about his sex offender conditions. As a convicted sex offender, Dad had to report to his local police station each month and advise them if he was going to be away from his place of residence. The restrictions didn't seem oppressive to me, but Dad wailed that his human rights were being breached. Cry me a river!

As well as appeasing my mother, there was another reason for my weekly phone calls with my father. I felt a responsibility to make sure he wasn't doing anything illegal. While making small talk, I tried to scope out if he'd had any contact with children. Because Dad was only found guilty of the offences relating to Sheila, I was afraid he was only considered a danger to teenage girls in the eyes of the law. I knew better. Dad was a danger to babies and beyond. No one was safe. I was my father's victim – and my father's keeper.

I was also my mother's nurse. At the end of 2006, Mum had her first orbital decompression operation to treat her Graves' disease. During her recovery, Mum was essentially blind, so I had to feed, wash, dress and care for her. To keep her spirits high, I read Mum travel pamphlets and we made a plan to tour Europe in the middle of 2007. Deep down, I was worried if Mum didn't see the world soon, she might never get the chance.

It was the trip of a lifetime. Over fifty-nine days, we visited Vienna, Budapest, Prague, Rome, Barcelona, Madrid, Monaco and Siena. We had the most wonderful time and whooped it up in every city. Halfway through our trip, in London, we found a message had been left at our hotel to call Dad. When we did we found out that Mum's mother, Grandma Dixon, had passed away. My heart went out to Mum, but it wasn't a great loss for me. Grandma Dixon had supported Dad while he was in prison and was one of the family members who denied I'd been abused. Rather, she supported Dad, saying 'Richard's been very poorly treated in all this'. He's a criminal who raped her granddaughters for years but he's been poorly treated! The mind boggles!! Mum and I considered cancelling the rest of our holiday, but Mum insisted Grandma wouldn't have wanted us

to throw the opportunity away. Instead, we ate ice cream, watched the squirrels in the park and Mum reminisced about her positive memories of Grandma. I didn't have any of my own to share.

In London, Mum said we should invite Dad to the city for lunch. He declined. The train ride from Darlington to London was too expensive, he said. I blocked his number for the trip so I didn't have to listen to his never-ending complaining.

In Amsterdam, I saw a missing person poster for Madeleine McCann, who had disappeared from Portugal a little earlier. Someone had scribbled over her photo 'Sold for €1,000,000'. I knew that people only sold – and bought – children to do terrible things to them, and I had immediate flashbacks of the horrific abuse I had endured as a child. Thinking about what could have happened to Madeleine McCann made me dreadfully upset and I really struggled through this part of the trip. Not that anyone would have known: I slapped on my happy face and did my best impression of a joyful, carefree daughter. Symphony's theme song became The Firm's 'Star Trekkin', and we kept boldly going forward.

Back in Brisbane, I was proud that I'd helped Mum make memories she could hold on to. If she did go blind, I knew I'd done the right thing by her.

JENI
2007: the year my body fell apart

The University of Queensland is known for its grassy knolls and swan-filled lakes. It's here where I went to sit and savour the moment after I submitted my PhD manuscript for binding at the end of 2007. It's also here where I was bitten by a mosquito and contracted Ross River Fever. For eighteen months, I was knocked flat on my back. I could barely move, lift a book or take myself to the toilet. As well as dealing with chronic fatigue from Ross River Fever, I was also bleeding heavily from my anus. It felt like I had a rigid metal pole up my bottom and I could only poo when I had my period. The pain was exhausting, and the exhaustion was exhausting, and the hot flushes were really bloody exhausting. Sadly, as soon as I graduated

with my PhD and was ready to look for work the Ross River Fever took hold, and by the time I had recovered from this, the damage to my bowels had became obvious, what with all that bleeding, and I began to request medical attention. However, I was put on a long waiting list to see a specialist at the hospital. Rightly or wrongly, I was convinced that the social workers from the sexual assault centre (as they were an outreach service of the hospital) had put some kind of note on my medical file that I was a liar. I believed that this was impacting on my ability to be taken seriously by the hospital. It took over a year, and multiple referrals to get an appointment.

Before I even got to attend that appointment I collapsed during a gynaecological procedure. My physical condition finally became visible to the medical profession and I began to get help. I had examinations, medical tests, more gynaecological procedures, colonoscopies and operations. My surgeon took one look at my anus and immediately made plans for surgery. She removed my sigmoid colon, my coccyx and gave me a colostomy, removed all the damaged flesh in my anus and rectum, and completely changed my life. From then on my life became focused on getting me healthy. This is a process I am still going through. We are getting better, but we are not fixed yet.

Because of my physical ailments, and the strain of living with over 2500 personalities, I struggled to hold down employment. I lived with my mum until I was fifty-one, and we pooled our pensions to scrape by. I spent a lot of time at doctor's appointments and in hospital beds and surgery rooms. Dealing with the fallout of Dad's abuse was a full-time job in itself.

* * *

After all the procedures I'd been through, my doctor told me a holiday somewhere cold could help with the hot flushes I was still having, so Mum and I started to plan another Europe trip in early 2009.

I was desperate to end the long-distance phone relationship I'd been forced to have with my father, and told Frank as much. He came up with an ingenious idea. I should invite Dad to meet me and

Mum in London on our next trip, and when he inevitably declined due to the price of train tickets, I could use it as an excuse to cut contact. 'This is your way out,' Frank suggested. 'When Dad says he can't be bothered to meet you in London, you can tell him you're terribly upset and never want to hear from him again.'

It sounded foolproof. I knew Dad's tight-arse nature would always trump seeing his family. But I didn't know Dad had started to receive half-price train fares as a senior. Dad agreed to meet me and Mum in London on our holiday, and my plan went up in smoke. I tried to continue star trekking through the universe, but it was getting harder to keep boldly going forward when the universe seemed to be against me.

Ahead of our London meeting, I told Mum and Dad that I didn't want to rehash the past, I wanted to create new happy memories together because it would likely be our last trip to England, with Mum's declining health and my total disdain for the place. Dad needed to advise his case worker, Brenda, that he was leaving Darlington for two days. Naturally, he complained about it endlessly, so I asked for Brenda's number and explained the situation to her myself.

Before our stay in London, Mum and I did a short eight-day tour through the (doctor-prescribed) cold cities of Europe. It was on this leg of the trip that I met Dan. He was an American man who was also on holiday with his mother. Funny that! We clicked immediately and had a wonderful time together. I'd never gotten butterflies in my stomach from a man before, so I didn't quite know what was happening when Dan made me feel like a giggly girl with a crush. Had we been able to give both our mothers the slip and find a quiet corner to be together, I have no doubt we would have. For the first time in my life, I understood what it meant to feel fireworks.

The tour finished in Paris and on our last night, I sat next to Dan at the cancan show and stole as many glances at him as I could. On our walk back to the hotel, Dan pulled me to the back of the group and we kissed under the Paris streetlight. I felt like I was in a rom-com.

My rom-com turned into a horror story the next day when Dan returned to America and I headed to London to see my father. It

was raining when we met Dad at the train station and he refused to buy an umbrella. Dad brought his clothes for the overnight stay in a plastic shopping bag. The rain soaked through his belongings on our way to the British Museum. Things only went downhill from there. At lunch, I ordered the chicken curry and was given the last serve. Dad threw a tantrum because *he* wanted the chicken curry. He was furious. I was mortified. I'd only spent two hours with him, but I was ready to put him on the next train out of London.

Blame the cold London air, or the revelatory experience of having a passionate kiss on the streets of Paris, but I started to stand up to my father. I wasn't the quiet mouse that he was used to, and he didn't like it. We had planned to go to the theatre together, but Dad said he couldn't possibly see a show because he hadn't packed a suit. Instead, he wanted to have dinner and go back to the hotel to chat. It wasn't exactly my idea of making happy new memories, but we went along with it. Mum was relatively silent and didn't really engage with the man who was technically her husband. As always, I was the one who had to make small talk.

We had dinner at Garfunkel's – the salad buffet we used to love – and Dad sat opposite me in the booth. He spent the entire meal talking loudly about how badly he was treated by the police in 1997. He was looking for sympathy, but he didn't find any. After twenty minutes, I lost it. 'Enough,' I demanded, slamming my fists onto the table. 'Enough. Stop it. We are not discussing this here.'

Dad changed the subject – until we got back to the hotel. I was ready to say goodnight, but Dad followed me and Mum into our room. He settled into the sofa and brought up his favourite topic. 'We really must work out what happened to you in Australia, Jeni,' he said. 'Clearly there was something very wrong, but I had nothing to do with it. I never touched you. I don't know where you've got these ideas from. We need to sort this out. I need Pat to believe I didn't do anything.'

Shockingly, Mum nodded in agreement. She looked like a stuffed teddy bear. Physically, she was in the room with me, but her eyes were glazed over, and her presence wasn't there. I was busting to go

to the bathroom, but I wasn't game to do so with Dad in the vicinity. So, I held it in. I squeezed my bladder and bit my tongue, like I'd done for so many years as a child.

The breaking point came when Dad tried to blame my sister Sheila for what happened to me in Australia. I couldn't sit back and let him put his crimes on her. 'It wasn't Sheila,' I said. 'Sheila wasn't equipped to do that to me.'

As I spoke, I saw that Dad had an erection. My hotel room had become dangerously unsafe. My dad was a monster, and my mum was a stuffed teddy bear. I mustered all of my strength and stood up with authority. 'I think we all need to get some rest,' I said, walking over to open the door and usher my father out. I had vivid nightmares that night and woke up the next morning in a fog. It was a cloudy mixture of disbelief, defeat and rage. Mum woke up with a headache, so that became our priority.

'I can't take Dad to the train station,' I told her. 'I'll push him onto the tracks.'

I used Mum's headache as an excuse not to leave the hotel and asked the concierge to order Dad a taxi to the train station. He left carrying his plastic shopping bag.

'Good riddance to bad rubbish,' said Mum. The hotel doorman laughed.

It wasn't until we arrived back in Australia that Mum told me she hadn't heard a word that Dad said that night. When she nodded in agreement with him, I thought she believed him over me, but she swore she didn't know what she was agreeing with. It was extraordinary to me that my mum could be both blind and deaf when it came to my father's behaviour.

The second half of our trip was a tour of England's stately homes and gardens. After the stress of Dad's visit, my health took a dramatic turn that even the cold weather couldn't help. In Edinburgh, I went to the toilet and blood poured out of my bottom like a tap. It would have been at least three cups full. The sight made me faint, and I woke up to a crime scene. There was blood all over the floor, toilet and me. I called out to Mum for help, but she was fast asleep

during her afternoon nap. I forced myself to my knees and cleaned up the mess. Then I put a tampon in my bottom and a pad in my underwear in the hopes of soaking up the next hemorrhage. I was pale and greasy when Mum woke up from her nap and dragged me to the group dinner with her. At the restaurant, I had to rush to the bathroom to spew. There was so much vomit, and so much blood. I spent the rest of the night sitting outside the restaurant in the cold, throwing up in the garden beside me. The waitress brought me a cup of tea. Mum didn't know what to do with me.

The rest of the week was a blur of more blood, vomit and excrement. It felt like my body was voiding itself of something toxic. I survived on tomato soup and spent more time in public toilets than at the tourist attractions we'd paid to see. It was a relief to get on the plane home. I spent the flight trying not to spew, and Muscles spent the flight brooding. He was furious at Dad for saying that he never raped me, and at Mum for denying she heard a word Dad said.

MUSCLES

'I'd like to talk about our trip to London,' I tell Dad over the phone when we arrive back in Brisbane. The words come out of Jeni's mouth, but they're in my voice.

'Oh yes, it was lovely,' says Dad.

'No, it wasn't,' I snap. 'You breached every single one of our agreements. I said I wanted to make new happy memories, you weren't interested. I said I didn't want to talk about the past, that's all you spoke about.

'You said you don't remember raping me in the bathroom in Andover, but I think that's because you raped me so many thousands of times it didn't stand out to you as a memory,' I continue.

'How dare you!' Dad splutters. 'You can't speak to me like that. I'm your father and you are just a child. You're as bad as your sister.'

I roar back at him, but he cuts me off.

'If you're going to keep talking to me like this, I'm going to hang up,' he says.

'Well, I've got news for you, buster boy, you can fuck off out of our life for good. I never want to hear from you again,' I shout, slamming down the phone to end the call before he gets the chance.

The phone call becomes known as the Buster Boy Incident, and we file it as a happy memory next to the sight of Dad in handcuffs, the sound of the frying pan hitting him on the head, and the expression of shock on his face when we pushed him backwards into the bath. Good riddance to bad rubbish.

CHAPTER TWENTY-THREE

The Unknown Child

Finally cutting Dad out of my life was like swimming in the ocean for the first time. It took my breath away. I felt liberated and weightless all at once. The only tinge of bitterness was the thought of Dad being left unchecked and free to hurt another child. My biggest fear was Dad finding a new partner with children. I suspect a similar thought crossed my mum's mind and that is part of the reason she stayed married to him. If he was married to her, he couldn't marry another poor soul. Mum began to ask me questions about what Dad had meant in his conversations in London. She told me how she hadn't understood all he was implying. She wanted the truth and so I started telling her what Dad had done to me. Her immediate reaction was, 'If only I had known. What can I do to help you now? You must tell the police. He can't do this again.'

Both of us were terrified for what I called the unknown child. It was this worry that prompted me to call Dad's public protection officer in Durham. With Mum sitting beside me stroking my arm in support, I explained Dad's abuse of me as a tiny baby.

'The reason I'm telling you this is because I won't be able to monitor Dad anymore. That's up to you. I know the account of Dad's crimes against Sheila says that he is non-violent and offended against a fifteen-year-old, but I need you to know that he is a viciously violent sex beast who attacked me from birth.'

I gave the officer the briefest overview of what my dad had done to me, and she was horrified. She said, 'We can do something about

that,' then asked me to email her the details of what he'd done to me. A few days later she phoned me back and told me she had gone to her superiors with my email and they insisted that I call the Australian police and ask for help. I spoke to both Mum and Frank about this before I made my decision. I was frightened that my abuse would be dismissed once again. Remember, I was told Australia doesn't extradite for sex crime. Oh, how I hoped things had changed.

Mum supported me instantly, declaring we needed to do something about what Dad had done to me. Her support was wonderful and it began a process whereby we were able to finally get the help we needed from her. I can't thank her enough for her encouragement at this critical moment in my life. She and I talked at length about my concern for the 'unknown child' – I knew abusers rarely stop of their own volition, and I feared for any child Dad might get power or control over. We agreed I had to tell the police about Dad. I couldn't live with myself if I'd done nothing and he hurt another child.

* * *

Roma Street Police Station stands like an authoritative figure in the centre of Brisbane. I wanted to feel comforted by the authority, but instead I felt uneasy. I didn't walk into Roma Street station in 2009 for myself, I did it for that unknown child my dad could go on to hurt. And so, I put one foot in front of the other until I reached Detective Rod Messer.

Rod listened closely as I disclosed my father's abuse to him. After I'd told him a little bit about what had happened to me as a child in Sydney, Rod asked me to draw the layout of the house in Greenacre. I sketched the outline, switching between Symphony and Muscles for recall. I suspected that Rod saw me flick between my alters because he was watching me like he was looking for something specific. He found it.

'There's something I need to tell you,' I said. 'I have Multiple Personality Disorder.'

Rod didn't flinch. In fact, he smiled. 'This actually increases your credibility as a witness,' he explained.

The first step in the very long process of bringing criminal charges against Dad was doing the statement. I insisted on writing the statement myself, remembering how totally failed I felt by the AFP in 1996, and knowing how difficult it was to say the words out loud. I set up a desktop computer on my kitchen table and started typing.

CHAPTER TWENTY-FOUR

Stepping Out to Testify

SYMPHONY

Between 2001 and 2009 my alters remained integrated inside 'Jeni' in spite of all the difficulties I had. They stayed integrated throughout Mum's ill health and numerous eye operations, through contact with Dad, his visit to Australia and subsequent deportation. They stayed integrated throughout my contact with Dad after his return to the UK, and during my travels through Europe in the late 2000s. They even remained integrated during the day we met Dad in London in 2009. Integration even held firm the day I went to the police to report Dad in 2009.

Rod Messer told me to write everything I remembered about each incident and the best way I could do justice to this request was to get the information from my alters.

As I sat down each day to write, I would begin work on a particular memory. I went deep into my internal landscape and returned to our version of George's therapy room. I went there because it was very quiet and the space was soothing. With what I needed to talk about I needed to have some level of comfort. George had always given me comfort and as I was not seeing him in person, I went for the next best thing.

Next, I began typing. It didn't take long before I heard the first voice, 'Oooh I don't know, maybe if we change how we word that sentence it will be clearer, oh hello Symphony'. The Student had returned to help with the writing. She was the first but by no means the last alter to step out of integration to help me.

THE STUDENT

The stepping-out process was remarkably simple. In fact, it couldn't be any simpler. Imagine a group of people clustered around a table; they are all looking into the centre of the table. Stepping out was like turning around to look outside of the group. Instead of looking at the table we were now looking into the room in which we found that table. All it took to unintegrate was to turn around. How easy is that!

Prior to stepping out I could help Symphony, by sharing my skills, but stepping out was a way to help her more completely. Having stepped out of integration, I could help physically, psychologically and mentally. I could step up and do tasks for her again. I could intervene if she was struggling and I could talk on her behalf in difficult interactions. And this applied to all of us who chose to step out. We were back and we were here to help in any way she needed us. It was good to be home.

JENI

When I say 'I', I mean 'we'. After I decided to speak to the police, the alters began the process of walking out of the 'integrative whole'. They knew Symphony would need to draw on the strength of the army and call up individual alters to share their recollections. One by one, the alters walked out the back of her head once again. A very organised alter took on the role of typist. I sat at the kitchen table and watched my fingers tap on the keyboard to tell the stories of my childhood, some of which I'd never heard before. Each alter jumped in when they had something to contribute. Sometimes four or five alters worked on the same one sentence to make sure it was totally accurate. After they'd finished their component, each alter went to integrate back into the whole, but we explained they had to hang around until we testified in court. So, the relevant alters pulled up a chair in a long corridor Symphony created and waited. No one could have imagined they'd be waiting ten years.

When Rod asked me for a detailed account of my father's abuse, I don't think he was expecting a 900,000-word manifesto, but that's

what he got. Being able to recount Dad's crimes with picture perfect clarity was a blessing for the case – and a curse for my soul. Even with the benefit of MPD, telling the story of my childhood as an adult was difficult. When the police asked me if I'd seen my father's penis, I blindly said no. I still hadn't fully put together that the thing he'd abused me with wasn't a pink blob that vomited acid, it was a penis that ejaculated semen. I didn't have the word for 'penis', because Dad had only ever called it, 'it'. 'Go on, touch it, lick it, suck it,' he'd say. I hadn't seen his 'penis', but I went on to give five highly detailed diagrams of it to supplement my evidence!

I was reliving my trauma through a child's mind, and I think it's so important for police to understand this when they're taking statements from victims of childhood abuse. I might not have known what a penis was at age five, but I could describe something as looking like an elephant trunk rising into the air from Dad's crotch. I might not have known the difference between a flaccid and a hard penis at age seven, but I could talk about 'it' being at half or full mast. I might not have known my dad was raping me, but I could complain about his games and punishments. That's how I understood it at the time. Kids might not always have the correct terminology when it comes to abuse, but if you know what to listen out for, you can step in and make a difference much earlier in their lives. Looking back, there are so many red flags that were missed: the constant crying and rocking, the wetting of the bed, my soiled underwear and constipation, and the hollow look in my eyes. How I wish someone had looked in my eyes and seen the deep trauma in them. Abuse isn't always obvious, but it's more prevalent than we think.

In the statement, I had to document every incident individually, so I had to pinpoint dates, times, places, acts, force and instruments used, and the resulting injuries. Of course, it was easier for me to remember the incidents that were exceptionally brutal or unusual in some way – like when Dad raped me with the soldering iron in the garage in one of his last attacks at the Greenacre house – but the everyday rapes started to blend together. If I couldn't place an attack on the calendar, we didn't include it. So even though my statement of

the crimes committed from 1974 to 1981 was 900,000 words, they didn't tell the full story. The story they did tell was so abhorrent, a number of officers on my case had to take leave. Some didn't return.

In one of our regular meetings at Roma Street Police Station, Rod asked me how I was going. He was genuinely checking in to see how I was coping, but I mistook his question as a sign of doubt. I thought I was being tested to make sure I was a reliable witness. 'Do you believe me, Rod?' I asked him straight out.

'Of course, I believe you,' he replied. 'I've believed you from the very first day you walked through those doors. I've believed you from the very first phone call. Nobody could make this stuff up. Everything you've told me is consistent and so are your emotions.'

'Can I ask you a stupid question?' I continued. 'You've dealt with men like Dad before. Is what he did normal within sex abuse?'

Rod explained that there was a continuum of abuse – from minor to extreme – and that Dad's offending was at 'the extreme end of the extreme end of abuse'. In his opinion, what Dad did to me made him the worst paedophile in Australian history. My dad was the worst of the worst. I sobbed, not out of sadness, out of validation. I so needed to hear that. Those words, as awful as they were, gave me comfort

As well as my statement, I gave the police the legal documents Dad had left at my house five years earlier when he was deported from the country. Amongst his abandoned belongings were the letters Dad wrote to the immigration department in which he admitted to raping me, the statement he made to the English police about me being a 'filthy, dirty child' who deserved to be abused, and his laptop, which showed his side of our correspondence over the years.

It took several years to get everything together, at which point the case was passed on to the New South Wales Bankstown Area Command as that's where the offences occurred. At Bankstown Police Station, Rachel Lawson and Detective Sergeant Paul Stamoulis were assigned my case. They flew to Brisbane to meet with me, George and my alters. It was like an MPD show and tell. George called up Erik, Muscles and Linda to speak to Rachel and Paul. Symphony

was too shy. Being called out is an exposing experience for the alters. They feel naked. But we all knew it was necessary nudity.

SYMPHONY

Over the sixteen months I wrote my statement all of my alters returned to help me. Every single one of them returned to tell their story. They came to help me testify against Dad, initially in print, but with an eye to verbally testifying against him in court. After they wrote of their worst days, they turned to me ready to re-integrate. However, I asked them to remain 'stepped out' in order to be ready to testify. I created a long corridor with a door at the end of it. This door was magnificent, beautifully carved with a huge sign pinned to it.

STOP. DO NOT OPEN.

Over time, the corridor filled with hundreds of alters ready to integrate again, and the door got covered in police crime scene tape to ensure no one opened it no matter how frustrated they got. And they got frustrated. After all, none of us realised it would take ten years for us to get him to face justice.

Not long after my alters began to re-emerge and step out of integration to help me, I made the request to return to see George. I didn't go back to George because I was 'disintegrating'. No, I returned for help with dealing with overwhelming feelings. As the police responded to the details of the crimes committed against me, I became emotional. The police were naming the unnamed, telling me Dad had committed horrific crimes against me. They gave names to The Dirty, telling me it was buggery and sodomy with items and all of it was against the law. They gave legal names to what he had done to me: indecent assault, carnal knowledge of a child under the age of ten, rape, buggery, inciting indecent acts, grievous bodily harm, assault, common assault with the goal of forcing a sexual act, and neglect. Worse still, the police read my descriptions of the days I thought my insides were falling out and identified them as me giving birth. They

identified three miscarriages and two births. That's five pregnancies before I was eleven years old. FIVE! These were the ultimate proof of my disclosures. The police were pleased that I had bodily proof to support my allegations, but I was devastated. I got in touch with my feelings and began to unwillingly embrace the fullness of Dad's betrayal of me. I need George now!

ERIK

The process of stepping out demonstrates brilliantly that none of my alters had been killed or murdered. They were all still there, just waiting to be used again.

SYMPHONY

I did not have any control over my alters' decision to step out. They were still able to make their own independent decisions without input from me. Their world as integrated alters was as rich and full of life as mine. Their desire to protect me and keep me safe from my dad was unchanged. Integration is not the end of me or my alters, it is a process that is reversible, and changeable, editable by the original personality (me) or by any alter personality. What a thrill it was to discover this. My alters are amazing. I am in awe of their abilities.

CHAPTER TWENTY-FIVE

Returning to Therapy 2009

JENI

After throwing Dad out of our lives, and talking to Frank and Mum about reporting him to the police I made some life-altering phone calls. I asked my GP for a referral to return to George as a patient. I needed help and I wasn't too stubborn to admit it. George welcomed me back and we resumed work.

GEORGE

Jeni did come back and see me for a handful of appointments between 2002 and her restarting regular sessions from 2009. Notably, she came to see me to discuss my thoughts on inviting her father to stay. While initially, I saw some benefit to this, upon reflection for our second session, I felt the risks outweighed the benefits – which she found confusing and took another break from therapy. While this break from regular therapy happened while she had the disturbing interactions with her father in Australia and in the UK, the upside was that this galvanised her into taking legal action against him.

Given the need for extradition from the UK to Australia, just for starters, this was a momentous decision. It is not one that most of my patients take – Jeni can attest to the decade-long demands that followed from it – but it was a decision that set a precedent in the legal world and led to the book contract which allows her, and I, to share her awe-inspiring journey with the world.

Jeni has been responsible for many firsts and 'un-integrating' is another of them as far as I am aware. It provides another fascinating insight into the human mind and what it is capable of. It also proves, once and for all, that alters are not 'killed off' as some people fear when we do integration work. The other point that Jeni's case highlights is how flexible integration can, and needs, to be. While Jeni probably would have been better off with more than three personalities left, she did not need 2500! I now believe that 'selective integration' is a more useful therapeutic goal.

ERIK
Healing from within

George mentions above that one of the goals of integration is a repurposing of the alters to new jobs or a new lifestyle. As we were shooting for full integration in 2001, we did not undergo this process. But now, after finishing writing my statement, we were in a holding pattern waiting for justice. The timing was perfect to do this process and it was Little Ricky who stepped up to help George assist us with it. I guess I should not have been surprised but I was. I associated Little Ricky with his pain at having to send alters out to get hurt by Dad. I saw him as a very distressed little boy who needed help. I did not see him as a man who would want to redress the balance by being the person who helped everyone to a new world order. I'll let him explore this:

LITTLE RICKY
Time to change jobs

Having stepped out of integration my alters looked to reclaim their original tasks, but our external world had changed. Their tasks were less helpful than they had been previously. So I stepped up to help. With George's help, we modified their tasks to take account of this changed world and created new ways of making my life easier. George helped immensely with this. He offered suggestions of new jobs, he helped to turn their initial job, which had a negative connotation, into a new positive job.

The best example of this is The Assassin. He was in charge of taking alters who had run out of tolerance for Dad's abuse, and could no longer do their job because of this and assassinated them. We did not need that anymore, so he looked to do something new. George and he negotiated through a range of tasks until the Assassin decided he would be responsible for bringing light and life to those who were struggling in this new world. He would show them the positives, and make sure they had what they needed as comfort in their new world. It was a brilliant subversion of his original job. Now if the Assassin taps you on the shoulder it's normally to give you something special, to show you something or to check in with you that you are coping okay. It's a huge change.

CHAPTER TWENTY-SIX

The Legal Process and Physical Healing

JENI

They say the wheels of justice turn slowly. In my case, they moved at a glacial pace. The years rolled by, and I felt like I'd been put in the too-hard basket. Rachel went on maternity leave and expected the case to be over by the time she got back, but nine months later it was still sitting there. I'm sure the police were hard at it behind the scenes, but I wasn't kept up to date on the progress. This is not to say the police didn't do their best updating me but they couldn't tell me what was going on for what I was told were 'operational reasons'. I was not even told that a task force had been set up to investigate my allegations until I phoned one day to talk to Paul and was put through to the Taskforce. I was stunned at the notion my abuse was considered important enough to have a Taskforce.

On that point, the police didn't want to increase my trauma by keeping me informed of every step of the process. I get that. But if they had asked I would have told them I'd rather know. I know the police process is not intended to be therapeutic, but I could have used information, like arrest warrants being made out against my father, to help reduce my trauma. To the police I would say, check in with your victim regularly to see what they would prefer, and allow them the opportunity to change their mind. I felt my case was sitting on desks being ignored because it was too hard. Just a

message saying we are working on it would have helped. Knowing things were happening would have helped to manage my anxiety.

The police asked me to give them contact details of anyone I knew who might remember me and be able to talk about their memories of me as a child. I gave them a long list. The police went off to find supportive evidence from these people. I was told that everyone the police spoke to corroborated my memories and almost everyone was able to give the police further contacts who may be able to help. I thank each and every one of those witnesses.

I anticipated that they'd want to speak to Sheila too, so I looked her up on the electoral roll. When I saw that her last name had changed a few years earlier, I knew she'd gotten married and that knowledge made me genuinely happy. Not only was Sheila safe from Dad, but she was also loved and had someone to take care of her. How marvellous. It was all I ever wanted for my sister. At the same time I was sad that I'd had to find out this way, I was hurt she hadn't even sent a card to tell me or her mother. We loved her.

While I focused on saving the unknown child from Dad, I was also preoccupied with my health. After the concerning incident in Edinburgh where I couldn't stop the blood from pouring out of my bottom, I worked up the courage to ask my doctor about my rectal bleeding. It had reached the point where I was needing to flush the toilet upwards of three times to get rid of the blood staining the bowl.

'How much is a normal amount of blood to come out of your bottom?' I asked.

'A couple of drips,' she answered.

'Oh, so not half a litre at a time?' I said.

As a result of seeking help, Dad's damage to my bottom was discovered. Shockingly there was still substantial damage causing me bowel problems. In 2010/11 I had to undergo numerous surgeries to deal with the damage. In 2011 I had a total proctocolectomy (the removing of my anus and great chunks of my damaged bowel, and sewing up of my bum) and have my tailbone removed as a direct result of the damage Dad inflicted when he buggered me as a child.

I have spared you from some of the worst details, but you can imagine what horrendous damage was done to me. The old joke 'opinions are like arses, everyone's got one' no longer applied to me.

At the end of 2009, after Muscles had terminated our relationship with Dad in the now infamous Buster Boy conversation, Mum sent Dad a virtual Christmas card. She signed my name next to hers – against my wishes – and Dad took it as a sign that I wanted to get back in contact with him. When the police found out, they asked me to keep speaking to Dad and acting like everything was normal so as not to tip him off about the case and give him a chance to do a runner. It was a big ask, but I wasn't about to do anything to jeopardise the investigation I'd put everything into.

SYMPHONY

My life got a lot more complicated when I was asked by the police to maintain a telephone and email relationship with Dad in order to protect the integrity of the investigation. They wanted to be sure they knew where Dad was at all times. That was really hard for me to do, but I bit the bullet and just got on with it. Once again I was forced to be my father's keeper.

It got even harder to talk with him every week while the police told me exactly what he had done to me, in legal terms, and explained that they would do their best to get him arrested as soon as possible. Add to this my developing medical crises with my bowels and spine and my life got very difficult. Having the ability to go to George made this a bit easier.

In our Sunday phone calls, I was specifically forbidden, by the police, from telling Dad the real reason I was having major surgery – because he destroyed my bowel and spine. The police wanted to keep him unaware of the damage he had caused and unaware that it still existed as evidence against him. So I just told him I had a bad back. It was the understatement of the decade!

Hearing that I was having health issues, he began to question the competency of my doctors. He'd press for details, pushing my boundaries and ignoring my right to privacy. His behaviour

triggered many of my alters to reconstitute protective barriers we had previously dismantled. As I was undergoing medical treatment for the damage he had inflicted on my body, I had to be very careful what I said to him.

As we went deeper through the legal process, Dad began to manipulate me. He began to attempt to control me and how I interacted with him. Over time different alters stepped up and offered to be the one who talked to him, saving me from having to deal with him. Ultimately, he ended up talking to a blend of Linda and Muscles, with the Student documenting everything in case we ever needed it.

It was a relief when he phoned and asked me to keep a secret from Mum. Finally, he had crossed a major boundary that I could use to terminate contact with him. I called an 'all-in' meeting with all of my alters and workshopped a solution to this problem. As a result of my alters suggestions and assistance I prepared a letter to him expressing my concerns about his request that he tell me something that I would then keep secret from Mum. In the letter I specifically stated that I had kept secrets for him before and it had turned out the secrets had protected him as he abused me. Furthermore, I wrote that the cost to me of keeping his secret had been enormous. I categorically refused to keep his secrets for him.

I contacted the DPP and told Nick Borosh I had to end my relationship with my father. I explained the situation and read him the letter I intended to send to Dad. I got Nick to check that I had not said anything that could cause problems with the prosecution of my Dad, then sent the letter with his blessing.

Dad responded by calling and screaming at me that I was wrong, taking it wrong. Oh, and he'd never abused me at all. He said he had wanted only to treat me as the sister he had never had and share secrets, feelings, and talk freely. I couldn't believe this. This is the monster who destroyed my relationship with my own sister! I snarled that I was his daughter not his sister. I reminded him that he had wrecked my sisterly relationship with Sheila, to which he replied Sheila had always hated me. That hurt. I said I couldn't even have

a normal, loving, caring, fatherly relationship with him without him seeking to devastate me emotionally, physically and sexually. I wouldn't even know how to have a fake 'sisterly' relationship with him. He screamed 'that was uncalled for', and as I felt myself getting angry I heard from Muscles. He could hear Dad trying to manipulate me into more debate with him and he warned me of the dangers of this. So I stopped talking for a moment to resettle myself. Then I coldly reiterated my message. I refused to keep secrets for him, I refused to give him a 'sisterly' relationship and, above all, I found the suggestion of this so repugnant that I did not want contact with him anymore. He started to yell at me. I heard him deny abusing me and so I refused to listen to him anymore and told him not to contact me again. I hung up the telephone and refused to take any calls from him from that day forward. I never spoke to him again after that call.

I could not have coped with this situation without my alters.

Legal Issues Around EMDR and Trauma Therapy

DR GEORGE BLAIR-WEST AND JENI HAYNES

It was gratifying to be able to assist Jeni in putting her father behind bars as too often, as a therapist, one treats the victim knowing that the perpetrator is out there and very likely to be hurting other victims. My trauma patients are already experiencing various levels of distress and relieving this, and helping them get their life back on track, is the task of the therapist.

Potentially adding to suffering by encouraging a patient to go through a harrowing, unpredictable and lengthy legal process does not fit the medical brief. When they choose to, however, as Jeni did, it allows the therapist to participate in an essential social cause greater than the therapeutic dyad.

Justice needs our help too. We cannot leave it to 'others'. Therapists working in this space need to be prepared to have to negotiate the world unto itself that is the justice system. To this end, I would encourage therapists working in the trauma space to undertake some medicolegal training, as I have done, in the event this skill is called upon.

While a patient may not wish to prosecute their perpetrator at the time, they may choose to do so later when they feel stronger. Nevertheless, probably only around ten to twenty per cent of my patients seriously contemplate legal action, and this is usually

driven by the fact that the perpetrator may be putting further potential victims at risk.

A much higher percentage will want to confront their perpetrator, but this is a different process. It's the medicolegal issues I want to consider here. Clinicians in this space need to think about how they document the cases that might end up in legal proceedings.

Hypnosis can certainly be used to implant some simple memories. As we discussed earlier when I wrote about the false memory syndrome and its foundation, we know that fake memories come with less clarity and fewer details and words. Nevertheless, while this distinction could be argued in court, it is simply better to take the possibility that the therapist has implanted memories off the table with a very simple manoeuvre. All we need to do is document in our files that certain traumas occurred *before we commence trauma therapy.*

As an aside, EMDR is completely different from hypnotherapy when it comes to treating trauma. The core difference is that there is no element of suggestion in doing EMDR. Hypnotherapy requires a therapist to drive the direction of the session with loaded questions. As you have seen in our description of this in Jeni's therapy, EMDR is a different process altogether in that it is entirely undirected by the therapist, suggestions by the therapist are not only not needed, but hinder the process as they cause an interruption to the unfolding of the event. This difference is shown in functional EEGs where the brain waves in hypnotherapy are completely different from the waves seen in EMDR.

Typically, a session begins with a decision to work on a traumatic event that the patient has already remembered. Although I believe that memories that come up during EMDR are as valid a memory as they can be, this added factor will probably continue to be attacked by cross-examining lawyers. For this reason, my advice to therapists is to clearly document the trauma prior to the beginning of a therapy session. This could be in the same session, before commencing EMDR, with a simple notation of the time sequence.

This could be done in an earlier session, but, as I have explained, I try not to go into traumatic memories until we are in a position to treat them and relieve the distress that this will very likely bring up.

I typically start the EMDR with the instruction, 'Let's just create the context; what do you recall about the time of day, where are you and who else is in the vicinity.' They answer these questions as best they can and then I say, 'Narrate for me what happens next like it's a documentary, giving me as much detail as you are comfortable with?' At no point do I suggest anything. My standard response if they do not remember any detail is to say, that's fine, just tell me what happens next that you do remember?

While the distinction between EMDR and hypnosis has been made and won in court in the USA, accessing the expertise to prove this difference is out of the reach of most courts. It is simpler to take the issue off the table by prior documentation. A dated file note that says, 'recalls being anally raped by father at around age seven in home in [suburb],' clearly records that a crime took place. The more detail the better. While it is up to the patient to give the police detail in their statement, they need this to be corroborated by a therapist's file.

As a clinician, my focus is on relieving distress and legal considerations are secondary. I would never delay therapy until court proceedings are completed as this can take years. Nevertheless, the therapist and the patient need to discuss these issues in-depth and decide how they are going to handle them. I have, at times, advised patients to go and make a statement to police before we commence therapy as this does not usually delay therapy appreciably. I try to set this up so that as soon as possible after giving evidence, I see my patient to give them support. While detectives are getting much better at sensitively dealing with the statement provider, it can still be a harrowing experience.

I have had a moderate level of experience in medicolegal work in my career and probably more than most of my colleagues, largely because when you specialise in trauma a percentage of these events, from fatal vehicle accidents to sexual assault, are followed

by legal proceedings. I developed a relative comfort, or perhaps, less discomfort, at being cross-examined in a courtroom, which is never much fun. This experience was something that I could bring to back Jeni up as she took her battle to the courtroom.

As you, dear reader, have probably ascertained, Jeni was formidable when it came to the legal process. Start with her superpower of detailed memory and end with her understanding of how to best articulate this for the law, without being intimidated by the process, with all points in between. Being the first person to use her diagnosis of DID as the basis for the prosecution allowed her to re-task a veritable battalion for the various aspects of the job at hand. All I had to do was fit in around her and back her up.

I had only a couple of sessions with the detectives in the lead up to the trial. The goal was to help them to understand how to negotiate Jeni's world. Jeni called it a 'show and tell' in which she 'brought forth the cavalcade of stars'. I introduced the detectives to Jeni's key alters and showed them how I navigate around Jeni's system. I suspect it was a little eye-opening for them as we brought in personality after personality in quick succession, complete with the accompanying changes in demeanor, posture and perspective. I think every one of us in the room wondered how this would go in court!

I would note, however, that I do not believe taking legal action is at all necessary for full therapeutic resolution. Jeni had the best possible outcome, but this is not always the case. The vicissitudes and capriciousness of the justice system are such, that in my experience, it is often less about justice than it is about gamesmanship. Fortunately, Jeni was unusually well qualified to play the game.

CHAPTER TWENTY-SEVEN

Linda Loses it and my Father Gets Extradited

JENI

By mid-2014 the alters waiting in the corridor to testify were well and truly fed up. The case had been taken to the office of the Director of Public Prosecutions (DPP), but they couldn't tell me if or when charges would be laid so Dad could be extradited to Australia for a trial.

After holding it all for years Linda finally lost it. And in true Linda style, she wrote a damning email to the boss of the DPP, Lloyd Babb, demanding action. She didn't mince her words. They went something like this.

'Dear Mr Babb, I understand that you are the head of the DPP. As you know, I have been working with Nick Borosh [the crown prosecutor] for several YEARS now to get my father charged for the abuse he inflicted against me. Every time I ask for an update on the charges, I get told there are no guarantees or that we're waiting on decisions to be made higher up. Well, you're about as high as they get. Please make a Goddamn decision. How many more years is my life going to be about my cunt?'

I couldn't believe Linda had used the c-word! We'd never said it before, but it felt warranted in the circumstances.

Linda's email worked. Within days, Lloyd wrote back and confirmed that charges would be laid.

I was asked to go to Sydney to meet with the prosecutors. So while the city was dealing with the Lindt Café Siege, in December 2014, I was scrambling around calling hotels trying to get a room. It was not a good time all round. After the trip to Sydney to meet with the DPP, Crown Prosecutor Nick Borosh called me to confirm that they were going to lay the charges against Dad and extradite him from England to Australia. It was about time. We cheered – and Linda took note of the effectiveness of using the c-word.

But it would take another five years to get a resolution. Five long and distressing years.

* * *

JENI

As they were gathering evidence, the prosecutors asked me if I was willing to do a police walkthrough of our old home in Greenacre. Will it help? Yes! Then yes, of course. I took Sweep with me for comfort and solidarity. As an adult, it felt like the house had shrunk. It seemed smaller. The new owners had renovated the house to put a toilet inside, and the space where my bed used to be no longer existed.

Walking into what had been my parents' bedroom hit me hard and I fled back outside. Standing in that doorway I had a moment of pure clarity. When I had been seven years old Dad had moved a mirrored cabinet from the far side of the bedroom to the wall the door was on. I remember being puzzled by this, as it had broken up a decorative wardrobe set. However, standing looking into that room as an adult it all made sense; if he had kept it in its original location it would have been clear what he was doing to me. I would have been reflected in the mirror. Moving the cabinet was a way of keeping his abuse invisible. How calculating he was. Clearly he spent a lot of his mental energy planning not just what he intended to do to me, but also ways to keep it hidden from the rest of the family. It was a shocking realisation and I fled to deal with it.

Coming back inside, I continued on through the house and the garden, pointing out what was the same and what had changed.

Seeing the house through my eyes certainly helped the police to understand locations, positions and what had happened where. But these were terrifying places for me and it was difficult. I treated it as a necessary evil and kept going.

While the house had been refitted and the garden had changed, the outside toilet and the garage remained as frozen as my memories. The torture chambers were there just waiting for me to bring the past to life. It was confronting, traumatic and utterly terrifying. There were a number of times I had to pause to catch my breath, steady my buckling legs and dry my tears.

I had to take a moment before I could walk into the outside toilet.

'You don't have to go in there if you don't want,' Detective Sergeant Paul Stamoulis told me.

'No, I'm going to do this. This is telling. He told me never to tell, and I'm going to tell, even if it kills me,' I replied.

The bolt that Dad used to lock me inside was still there, but the window by the toilet had been blocked in. Thank goodness for that! The floor was still the same, cold concrete. The room was icy, or maybe that was just me. So many memories, so much horror in that space.

Walking across the garden to the garage took immense courage. But that was nothing compared to the courage it took to actually walk through the open doors of the garage. I froze and almost had a meltdown as I got close. I had to stop for a few moments before I could enter that pit of hell, but it was essential if I was to convict Dad of what he did to me in that space. Standing there just staring at the bench in the garage, I could feel myself being held on the edge and abused. I could see time and space folding in. The smell was there, the chill was still there, the space on the floor I'd been raped and buggered was there. The only thing that was missing was the wallpaper table he had forced me onto and abused me on. My legs buckled and I felt the urge to run. I asked Paul, 'Can we get out of here now', and was so scared he'd make me stay. Just writing the words I have a lump in my throat and am on the verge of tears. Let's move on before I throw up!

I told the truth and I showed where everything happened. I even showed where I believed Dad buried Gemma, my 1980 baby. Unfortunately, she was not found, but nor were the bodies or bones of two cats and over one hundred Guinea pigs, so the soil on that property is particularly good at hiding the evidence.

Most importantly, I told everything on video so it was captured forever, and I'll never have to do it again. I am very proud I was able to do that walkthrough. I believed that it would make it real for the courts if I took them where it happened. I just didn't think past telling the police. I never considered it could impact me, but boy it did. Nightmares tortured me for months afterwards. I re-experienced so much of what he had done to me through flashbacks and body memories. It was tough. But I told the police I'd do it again if I had to.

After the walkthrough, Mum went off with Paul to make a statement against Dad. I stayed at the Canterbury Leagues Club. I'd never been to a sports club before and was amazed at the sheer size of it. There was a river running through the middle of the foyer, and I sat and watched the Japanese koi glide through the water. Big fish. Little fish. Gold fish.

Instead of reliving the trauma of Greenacre, I pictured myself gliding through the water like a koi fish. As Happy would say, you can find happiness everywhere, even in the foyer of the Canterbury League Club.

EXTRADITION

Having finally got charges against Dad, the next step was to extradite him from England. This was a complex process involving even more government agencies. Dad was to be charged with 367 offences. Each offence needed their own documentation and evidence to satisfy the United Kingdom that it was appropriate and in the public interest to release him to Australia. So the Extradition Team began creating the bundle of materials that would need to be sent to England to get this process underway. Yes, Dad got to traumatise another Australian government department. He's the nightmare that keeps on shocking.

When I realised the case had reached the Extradition Team I was ecstatic. Progress at last. I did what I normally do, I went and read everything I could on extradition. I read that extradition from the UK to Commonwealth countries, of which Australia was one, had a process that was expected to take a minimum of five months. I told myself I could wait another five months.

Just before Christmas 2016 the papers were ready and they were sent to Australia House in London. A request for Dad's extradition was then sent to the UK Home Office for perusal. If the Home Office agreed Dad's crimes count as extraditable offences, then the application would be sent to the Westminster Court for an arrest warrant to be issued. The arrest warrant was issued the first day of the new working year in 2017.

Dad's public protection officer had the great pleasure of going with the extradition warrants team to arrest him. I would have loved to see my father's face when this came out of the blue. Finally, he realised I had broken the strangling bonds he tied around me so long ago. I let the police find out 'what had happened to me in Australia'. It must have been one hell of a shock.

Dad was driven straight to London. He claims that one of the police officers who took him to London told him that he would appear in Court for a few minutes. He would refuse to be extradited and he'd be on the train back to Darlington within hours. Once home he could get a lawyer and sort this silly mess out. Seven years of abuse and torture, 367 charges against him dismissed as a silly mess. Really? I think not. The following morning Dad attended court and despite being advised by at least two solicitors on how to handle the extradition hearing his arrogance got the better of him. I understand it went something like this:

Is your name Richard John Haynes?
    Yes, yes yes,
Is your birthday 21 February?
    Yes, yes, yes,

Do you reside at ...... Darlington?

   Yes, yes, Yes

Do you understand why you've been brought before this court today?

   Yes, yes, YES

Do you agree to being extradited to Australia?

   Yes, YES, YES!

Thank you Mr Haynes, you will be remanded into custody pending extradition to Australia.

   WHAT?

He answered all the questions impatiently and with extreme rudeness and arrogance. I think he was so convinced by his own lies that no one would ever do anything to help me that he did not take the situation seriously. I'm sure he was not really listening to the questions. In his rush to put this 'silly mess' behind him he waived his rights to fight extradition and so instead of a five-month battle to get him here, it was over in a day. Unreal.

It got very serious when he was remanded into prison until Australia came to collect him.

Now remember, Australia deported him in 2005 and banned him from ever returning. This meant the Immigration Department would need to revoke this deportation and ban and provide him with a justice-related visa so he could be brought back to Australia. When it was discovered that Dad did not have a current passport an immigration official from Western Australia flew to London with a travel document for him. It was decided it was quicker to just go to London, than to have further delays waiting for a passport or travel authority from the UK.

In February 2017, I received a cryptic phone call from Paul Stamoulis saying he was hoping to have good news for me in the next few days. He didn't tell me he was calling from the Sydney International Airport where he was boarding a flight to London to lay charges on Dad and bring him to Australia to face his crimes.

CHAPTER TWENTY-EIGHT

When Pigs Fly

JENI

The next call I had from Paul was surreal. He rang me on Mum's birthday (23/02/2017) from the front passenger seat of the car that had picked Dad up from the airport in Sydney. Paul spoke to me as though I was a colleague, so Dad wouldn't know he was talking to me. 'I'm just contacting to let you know that we've landed and have the plaintiff in custody. We'll be bringing him into the office as soon as possible,' he said.

My heart almost burst with joy. Wow. It was really, finally, actually happening. Dad had been charged with 367 offences and extradited to face trial for them.

There's a video of Dad being brought into Sydney airport. He was supposed to have been snuck into the country, but a news crew was there to capture the moment he was dragged back to Australia to atone for his sins. The footage aired on the morning news and the world found out Richard Haynes was in custody in Sydney for historic child sexual abuse charges. Mum says it was the best birthday present Dad ever gave her.

A girlfriend phoned me immediately after she saw the news clip to see if I was okay. She told me that a talking head on the morning news show said they'd never known a person to face so many charges related to one victim. It was then that I realised the enormity of the situation. I also realised that Dad was going to be tried for what he did to me – not what he could potentially do to the unknown child

I wanted to protect. I'd been so focused on looking outwards and taking care of everyone else, that it took me eight years to realise this case was about me. I celebrated the long-awaited win with a thimbleful of port. Cheers to that.

The wheels of justice were rolling, but they still had to pick up speed. The legal process could not be done simultaneously, and so more time was spent as his case trundled through the Australian and English legal systems. It would have been good if all of these processes could have been started much earlier to facilitate justice for me. Ten years from disclosure to trial is way too long, especially for such serious crimes. Eight long years until he was arrested and brought back to Sydney, and I felt every minute of them. Unfortunately, he did not, and he had eight more years of freedom. Perhaps my struggle for justice will draw attention to the need to fix this system so victims of sexual abuse, however historic it is, get swift justice. My case took far too long, given they knew where he was from the very beginning. He didn't move. They only had to go get him, no search was necessary. I could not understand why, if it was the worst case of childhood sexual abuse ever documented in Australia, everything took so long.

Dad was held in custody in Sydney for two years before the trial began. We used every single day to prepare; it became a full time job. Over the course of the ten years it took to get the case to trial, Mum frequently despaired. 'Pigs will fly before we get to court,' she would say, shaking her head.

When we *finally* arrived in Sydney in early 2019, the city was celebrating the start of the Chinese New Year. It was the year of the pig. There were flying pigs at the airport, in shop windows and all around Hyde Park where we stayed. Mum was right all along. The pigs were flying high and so were we. It felt like a sign of good luck going into the trial we'd waited so long for.

George gave evidence on the first day of the trial to explain to the judge how MPD works and how it makes me a credible witness. We were glad to have him on our side – for a moment, we thought he might miss the trial altogether because he'd booked a holiday to the

Maldives, but he made it – and his breadth of knowledge set the tone for the trial.

We were called to give evidence on the third day of the trial.

Dad was facing eighty-five charges, including multiple counts of rape, buggery, indecent assault and carnal knowledge of a child under ten – and I was prepared to give detailed testimony on every single offence. My memories of the abuse were frozen in time, waiting for me to thaw them out and serve them on a silver platter.

Judge Sarah Huggett called me to the witness box, and I brought all my alters with me. Dad had requested a judge-only trial, and the lawyers agreed based on the fact it would be too traumatising for a jury. I imagine Dad figured he had a better chance of convincing one person I was a dirty liar rather than twelve. But his decision worked in my favour.

I'd been dreading the thought of having to take care of twelve people while trying to tell my story. And that's exactly what I would have done, I would have tried to minimise my distress to protect the jury because that's my default position: looking after everyone else in the room to the detriment of myself. With a judge-only trial, I would only need to put one person through the torture of my story and that person would be a trained professional. It would be their job to listen to me, not an obligation. George would only need to explain MPD once and the judge could ask as many questions as they needed to. The alters would only need to introduce themselves to one person, who would have an understanding of MPD and recognise it as a real condition.

Dad thought he'd played his trump card, but he'd actually flushed it down the toilet. I was cheering.

In the courtroom, I knew I was there to give evidence to the judge, but I delivered my testimony straight to my father.

SYMPHONY

They tell me we're making history. We're the first person to give evidence in court using our multiple personalities. There are six of us lined up and waiting to tell our story: me, Judas, Muscles, Little

Ricky, Linda and Erik. We're ready to wipe the smirk off Daddy's face. And we do.

After just two hours, Dad crumbles. We only get up to the end of 1974 before he rolls over and shows his belly. I can pinpoint the moment it happens. I'm asked a question and I pull Sweep out to help me answer it. My old hand puppet, trusty confidant and tear-wiper sends a bolt of terror through Dad. He reels back in his seat like he's been slapped. I see the colour drain from his face. The sight of Sweep shakes his deep-seated arrogance. He isn't prepared for it.

If Sweep could talk, he would validate every word in my 900,000-word police statement. I know it, and Dad knows it too. In a single moment, Dad realises he's lost. A hand puppet has brought him undone. Once upon a time, Dad used Sweep to hurt and silence me. Now, Sweep has got his vengeance.

Jeni has a plan and it's working. We've carried our secret weapon in our back pocket waiting for this day of reckoning. Judas always knew the time for telling would come. And it has. Dad asks for an adjournment to consider pleading guilty. We don't know whether to laugh or cry or jump for joy. We do it all. I shed tears of relief, Muscles punches the air with elation and Happy has the most extraordinary giggle fit. She takes the memory of Dad's shocked pale face and adds it to our collection of happy moments.

JENI

I'd spent a lifetime preparing to testify as a witness against Dad, and I only got to speak for two hours. Dad asked for an adjournment to consider his options. He didn't do that for me. If he had any compassion or decency, Dad would have pled guilty immediately and saved me the stress of testifying at all. He was a selfish coward until the very end.

Dad underwent a psychiatric evaluation, which determined he was of sound mind. He didn't have a mental illness and hadn't been abused as a child himself, rather he was found to be sexually attracted to me and to have acted on his perverted impulses for his own sick gratification.

After considering his options, Dad pled guilty to twenty-five charges. A further sixteen charges were to be taken into account when sentencing. The charges were representative of all the crimes he committed. We wanted to make sure he would serve time for it all: the rape, buggery, assault, torture, neglect and cruelty. At first, it was difficult to hear the number twenty-five – especially considering Dad had been extradited on 367 charges, and that we'd taken eighty-five to trial. A little girl alter started crying uncontrollably. 'The numbers are going backwards,' she wailed. 'He's going to get away with it. They're going to let him off.'

We kept having flashbacks to the disastrous plea deal of 1997 where Dad pleaded not guilty to all of the charges relating to me. Tensions were high inside, so Muscles called an all-in meeting, and for the first time, we did it in public for all to see. Usually, he would ask all those in favour to raise their hands, but that way he couldn't see the objectors in the forest of hands. So, Muscles asked for those who were unhappy with the plea deal to raise their hands, and then he sat quietly with each individual and addressed their issues. The meeting went for over two hours and Mum was witness to it all.

Halfway through, Paul called and we put him on speaker. 'It's very important that you consider your position carefully,' he said. 'You need to remember this is Australia getting us justice. It's very different from England. This time, it's only about you. If you want your dad to own what he's done to you, then his guilty plea will do that. Even if it's one charge, his guilty plea validates you and proves you're not lying.'

It was a stirring speech, but the little girl alter kept crying.

'Why are you upset?' Muscles asked her.

'Because he's not admitting to what he did to *me*,' she said.

In a moment of pure grace, Muscles explained that the twenty-five charges on the table were representative of everything we'd been through. They weren't just singular events, they covered the spectrum of Dad's abuse. 'It's easy for me because my two big days are included in the charges – he will plead guilty to what he did to me, but what he did to me isn't relevant. We are alters of Symphony's,

so what he did to us, he did to her, and vice versa. And I want justice for Symphony,' Muscles said.

We all agreed: the plea deal would go ahead. Symphony would get justice.

On 1 March 2019, Dad pled guilty to twenty-five charges, one by one. His arrogant voice was reduced to a whisper. The judge had to ask him repeatedly to speak up.

Guilty. Guilty. Guilty.

Dad returned to jail not as a man on remand, but as a convicted prisoner. Before he did so though, I wanted him to look me in the eye. After the judge exited the courtroom and everyone else started to wander out, I walked straight up to Dad, who was still in the dock. He hadn't had the balls to look at me once during the trial, so I gave him no other option. I stood close and stared hard. Dad's eyes met mine and his face changed. As far as I'm concerned, that was the first and last time my father looked at me and really saw me. Then he saw me turn my back on him and walk out of the courtroom, leaving him behind forever.

A journalist witnessed the interaction and asked me what I wanted to say to my father.

'I didn't want to say anything to him, I wanted him to see me, and then watch me turn my back on him and walk away, leaving him to his fate,' I said.

* * *

Of course, I felt relieved, vindicated and over the moon about the guilty plea. But I also felt sceptical, like I was holding my breath waiting for a loophole to open up and let Dad off the hook. I'd been failed so many times before, part of me expected it to happen again.

I wasn't surprised when, two weeks after the trial, Dad tried to recant his guilty plea. When the judge dismissed his application, I started to breathe normally again.

After the trial, and before sentencing, the current affairs program *60 Minutes* aired a story on the case. In the program, acclaimed

journalist Liz Hayes interviewed me, Symphony, Muscles, Judas and Little Ricky – as well as George and Detective Sergeant Paul Stamoulis.

Watching Paul break down in tears about the toll the case took on him was painful. 'A lot of people who have read that document [my statement] have been seriously affected by it,' he said, explaining that it was one of the most horrific cases he'd worked on. 'The trauma that was occasioned to Jeni's body was incredible. Her body and her mind were crime scenes.'

After the show aired, I was inundated with messages of support on my Facebook page. It was soul-warming, and at times overwhelming. Many people shared their own stories of abuse with me, and my heart simultaneously broke for them and swelled for the bravery it took them to reach out. My fatal flaw is taking on other people's problems, so I had to learn how to put distance between myself and their pain, while still acknowledging the strength it takes to disclose abuse. 'I hear you, thank you for disclosing this to me. What you've said matters, you matter. I'm sorry you went through what you did,' I would reply.

One message in my inbox stood out from the rest, it was from a boy from my high school in England who bullied me mercilessly. In his message, Chris admitted to making my life hell and wished he could take it back. He explained that he'd been in the military and compared my bravery for speaking out to the courage of soldiers at war. It was one of the many positives to come out of naming my name, telling my story and fighting my fight.

The program, like the criminal trial, only focused on the abuse I suffered from ages four to eleven when we lived in Australia. Because the other crimes were committed overseas in England, I haven't been able to speak about them alongside what happened here. Until now.

* * *

My victim impact statement was 10,686 words, seventeen pages and took over an hour to read on 31 May 2019. And still, it only gave

the briefest glimpse into my suffering. The statement described the lasting impacts of Dad's abuse – both the physical and the mental – but the true cost of his offending is immeasurable. It's the loss of a childhood, of a future, of a life.

We decided that one person would read the statement, and that person would hold their head high, stay calm and look Dad directly in the eye. That's how it started, but after the judge stopped me part way through to render the judgement in another case where the jury had just come back from deliberating, the gloves came off. I realised Dad was never going to give me what I wanted. He was never going to look me in the eye or show any remorse. In the waiting room outside the court, Muscles called an all-in meeting and we agreed: we were going back in there with all guns blazing. We weren't going to hold back, and everyone was going to say their piece. That's how thirty-three alters ended up giving our victim impact statement.

Muscles called Dad a bastard when talking about our missed sporting opportunities and Amber had to be held back from lunging across the courtroom when she spoke about the babies. She wanted to beat the shit out of Dad, and she didn't hide her fury. The judge asked if we wanted a break, and we declined. If we left the room, we'd have to walk past Dad, and we didn't have the strength to hold Amber back from slapping the smirk off Dad's face. Instead, we used our words as weapons, throwing them like darts directly at Dad. Bullseye.

'There are insufficient words to do justice to the enormity of the impact of my father's offending on my life,' I began. 'It is important for me to point out that my dad planned each and every act of abuse he committed against me. My dad exploited Sweep, kewpie dolls and other toys, turning them from precious toys to weapons to abuse me with. He stole craft and household items from my mum to use to abuse me. He purchased items, brought them home and then decided when and how he would abuse me with them. He saw and heard the impact that each abusive act had on me. He heard me beg him to stop, he heard me cry, he saw the pain and terror he was inflicting upon me, he saw the blood and the physical damage

he caused. And the next day he chose to do it all again. My dad's abuse was calculated, and it was planned. It was deliberate and he enjoyed every minute of it. He made a daily choice to inflict pain, humiliation, terror and physical damage on me. He chose. I begged him not to, I resisted him at every turn, and he chose again and again to satisfy his sexual desires and his need for power and control over the welfare of his daughter.

'Dad denied me medical care throughout my childhood. He never got me help for my injuries and he taught me that my injuries were unimportant and insignificant. He told me that my pain, my blood and injuries were not real. But my medical issues are as real as they are extensive ... The ligaments in my jaw are so calcified from the hundreds of times my dad forced me to perform oral sex on him as a child that I experience continual clicking when I open my mouth and I live in constant fear that one day it will lock for good, and I will have to break my own jaw to get it to close. My coccyx was dislocated so badly, and my anus, anal sphincter and bowel were damaged so extensively from the hundreds of times my dad buggered me as a child that I had to have surgery in 2012 to remove them all and create a colostomy. The colostomy pouch, which sits on my stomach to collect faeces and has to be changed up to five times a day, is a permanent – and degrading – reminder of my dad's abuse.'

'Quite apart from the physical devastation my dad has wrought on my body, he has had an overwhelming impact on my mental health. My dad forced me to develop multiple personalities as the only way I could cope with his abuse. Symphony's strategy to deal with Dad and the overwhelming abuse he inflicted upon her was lifesaving. Without MPD I would be dead. It is what allowed us to survive. We didn't survive because Dad let up, or helped us, or changed his abuse on seeing the impact on us – he did none of that. We survived because Symphony created new personalities to help her survive Dad. Symphony is a walking, talking miracle. But she should never have had to do this. She lives because Dad is a vile monster who did all he could to devastate his daughter to feed his perverted urges.

'At the same time MPD is not a great way of life. We spend our entire lives being wary, constantly on guard. We have to hide our multiplicity and strive for a consistency in behaviour, attitude, conversation and beliefs which is often impossible. Having 2500 different voices, opinions and attitudes is extremely hard to manage. No matter that everyone tries to work for the same goals, it is hard dealing with alters when they are triggered and upset, while still keeping MPD secret. I should not have to live like this.

'Make no mistake, my dad caused my Multiple Personality Disorder. He created a life for me which was so horrendous that the only solution for me was to protect myself through MPD. He made my life unbearable, torturous and psychologically devastating all for his own personal and sexual gratification.

'The impact of my dad's offending has destroyed my life. He has sent a wrecking ball through my hopes and my dreams. My dad has devastated every single part of my life by his abuse and the consequences continue to blight my life, and they will do so until I am dead. There is no part of my world left untouched: health, happiness, relationships, employment, education, family, friends, finances, intimacy, celebrations, motherhood, love. He sentenced me to a life significantly less than it could or should have been. He denied me the chance to reach my full potential and straitjacketed me into a life of trauma, horror and agony. My life has been devastated by his selfishness. I've paid an enormous price for his depraved sexual desires. To date, I have been the one paying the price for his actions, his abuse, his lies and his total failure to be a decent human being. Please, Your Honour, can you finally place the responsibility for all this where it belongs, and send Richard Haynes to prison for a very long time,' I concluded.

* * *

Judgement Day was set for 6 September 2019. It took two hours for Judge Sarah Huggett to read out all of Dad's charges. He didn't show a hint of emotion the entire time. I sat in the front row. I wanted him to know I was there, and I wasn't going away until he got what he

deserved. Once again, Dad didn't so much as glance in my direction. I wanted to go up to him, grab his face, and scream, 'Look at me, you prick!' He sat with his hands in his lap, his head bent down and his eyes closed.

'From a very young age, Jennifer was subjected to depraved and abhorrent abuse by her father that did cause significant harm,' said Judge Huggett. 'No sentence can completely reflect the far reaching impacts [of Richard's offending].'

She was right. Nothing would take away the pain that keeps me awake at night, but justice would be a soothing balm. On 6 September 2019, that justice was delivered.

My dad will die in jail. The judge sentenced Dad to forty-five years behind bars, meaning he would be 104 years old before he would be eligible for parole in 2050. Good riddance to bad rubbish!

In the courtroom, I covered my face and let out a single sob. It was over.

The judge could have sentenced Dad to life, which would have meant a maximum sentence of fifteen years in prison, but she deliberately sentenced him to forty-five years. She made sure he wouldn't see the outside world again, that he would never taste the sweetness of freedom or anything other than prison food, and that he wouldn't ever be able to hurt another child.

LINDA

I haven't prepared a speech, but when I see the media the words flow out of me like they've been rehearsed a thousand times. I stand with my head high, my shoulders back and my face grinning with triumph.

'When I walked into court today, I carried every one of those people [my alters and other survivors of abuse] with me because this isn't just my story. It was so validating for different alters to hear their story and we were literally playing tick-a-box as she [the judge] went through [the charges],' I explain.

'It was a relief,' I say about the 45-year sentence. 'I need him to die in jail. I don't have to think of him ever again. Knowing he will die

in jail and live in onerous conditions [there]: welcome to my world. I've been there. I know what it's like. If his life in prison is difficult, them's the breaks. That's what you get when you rape your child. I hope he hates every minute of it.

'My life begins today. She [the judge] has released me. I feel so relieved and [have] a sense of freedom,' I say.

This is the spell I cast on him: to live out the rest of his life in the same way I started mine. His end is my beginning.

JENI

When Linda made the statement outside the courthouse, she said so much more than the words that came out of her mouth. She sent a message to every victim of child abuse that they will be believed. She told people with MPD that the condition is real and there is support available. And she gave every inmate in jail with Dad the permission to make his life in there hell.

I will never forgive my dad for what he took away from me – especially my ability to have children. I mourn my seven murdered babies and my lost life. I wanted a family of my own to love and to love me back. Seeing babies is still triggering for me – I will always yearn for what I've lost – but at fifty-two, I've come to terms with knowing children aren't in the realm of possibility for me. And so, I share my love with those closest to me: my cavoodle Holly, my mum and good friends.

I've been told my father has had heart problems during his time in jail. Muscles doesn't believe it. 'The bastard doesn't have a heart,' he jokes. When we found out Dad had undergone heart surgery Muscles quipped, 'Well it must have been exploratory surgery 'cos his heart most certainly is not in the right place.' Oh dear!

As much as I want to say I wish my dad dead, I don't. Not because I'm better than that, oh no – because I want him to spend as many years in jail as humanly possible. I want him to wake up behind bars every morning feeling as trapped and hopeless as I did as a child. I want him to suffer.

CHAPTER TWENTY-NINE

The Aftermath

THE ENTITY CURRENTLY KNOWN AS JENI

It took a long time to settle Muscles after the trial. Between the trial in February/March 2019 and sentencing in September 2019, we put a huge amount of effort into settling him. His rage had come to the fore and he needed to vent it. So we took him to Bribie Island and went to the beach there. We got him to shout and scream and yell into the water.

We encouraged him to swear, to let it all hang out. And we learnt that his swearing repertoire was far more expansive than even I had guessed. He let his rage out and the sea accepted it all, calmly and without judgement, the sea did what no one else had been able to do. It soothed our savage beastie. After a few hours of swearing into the sea we hoped he would feel well enough to continue normal life.

VOLCANO

The best bit about getting Muscles to start to let go was that he did not have to spend his life trying to convince anyone of the truth. He only needed to take care of himself and his feelings. Muscles had changed and become far more receptive of new ideas around how thinking of dad (we will never capitalise the word dad about him again) and all the lost years made him feel and we were so proud of him.

SYMPHONY

To see Muscles be able to ask for help and then be able to accept that help was wonderful. It didn't cure Muscles of his angry, but he was able to hear what the judge said about us and accept her words. Hearing the judge document what dad had done to us, and hearing him get an eye-watering 45 years in prison made a terrific impact on us all. Things we had held onto for years just melted away: No longer relevant, no longer important, finalised by the enormous jail term dad had received. Everything just settled and our world grew softer. The battle lines were scuffed over. We were no longer at war. It was a relief.

MUSCLES
After the trial, 2019

Finally the bastard is in prison where he belongs. He can never hurt a child again. He can never manipulate my family again. He is safe behind bars. I have fulfilled my promise.

And now I can fulfill one other promise. I've been seventeen years old all my life. I could not grow older 'cos then I could get a gun licence and that was just not safe. If I'd had a gun licence the temptation, as I said earlier, to go get that gun and blow the fucker away would have been overwhelming. I would never have done it, but it would have been so tempting. How long the fantasies would have sufficed is a question I am glad I don't have to answer. I lasted from 1977 to 2019, and I'm proud of that.

I had huge pleasure when Symphony told me I could grow. I grew up just one day, to eighteen years old. I felt no different. How mean! All that waiting and I felt nothing had changed. But I was wrong. Growing up had released me from my roles relating to Sheila. I'd no idea of this. Over time I did notice my ideas around her beginning to change. All those words I had been unable to hear about her seemed to be collected together and when my inner friends felt it was appropriate, they started to filter them to me, demonstrating a sensitivity to my feelings, my anger and my distress I was not expecting. I could see how they fitted into the

horror childhood we had survived. These new understandings were fragmentary, drifting across my mind at random times. I have only been able to put them together as a coherent whole as I've written my part of this book.

AND NOW? ... 2022

MUSCLES

I've discovered in writing this that my rage is still there, but that it is finally being placed on the person it belongs to – dad. I have finally taken off my face the blinkers and blinders that dad's abuse had put on me.

Dad deliberately manipulated every member of his family to hide his criminal acts. His manipulation of each of us was designed to let him do what he wanted to me, to sexually, physically and emotionally abuse me, and to hide this abuse of me.

His favouritism of Sheila and disfavouritism of me caused such rifts between the two of us that I spent years before and after the divorce trying to show her that I was not what he was telling her.

All this took attention away from him, and his behaviour, and stopped anyone in the family from recognising his crimes against me and Sheila. It gave him decades of freedom, living in the community, unpunished. It meant that when I finally got justice and sent him to prison he was in his seventies, an old man. He condemned Sheila and I to hell. What kind of monster does that to his daughters? Sheila and I suffered differently but we've both suffered, we've been cheated by him. He stole our lives, he stole our joy and he stole our chance at sibling friendship and happiness. He is disgusting.

I have not spoken to Sheila in years and I feel her loss immensely. This loss was particularly sharp when, in January 2021, we lost Dawn, Sheila's best friend from school. As soon as I heard of Dawn's death I contacted the police asking them to let Sheila know and to offer my love and support. Dawn's death was unexpected and devastating on so many levels. If this is how I felt, I could only imagine Sheila's horror and shock. I wanted to be there for her. Of course, in the

middle of COVID restrictions I could not go to the funeral, but when I heard that it would be live streamed I hoped that I would be able to share it with Sheila, so she had a chance to say goodbye.

If Sheila called me tomorrow and wanted to talk I'd drop everything just to have the chance to talk to her.

I love you Sheila and always will.

PART FOUR

HEALING

CHAPTER THIRTY

The Sum of My Parts

GEORGE

In the dozen years that Jeni and I worked together from 2009, the focus was on negotiating the legal process and re-engaging with the life that she had been denied, but so richly deserved. The latter point included Jeni travelling the world and finally moving into her own home.

Following her successful court case, she began dating. Without a great input from me by this time, we came to celebrate Jeni reclaiming her sexual identity and her sexual experiences as her own. She came to know that what had happened with her father had nothing to do with what happens in a consenting, caring, conscious, intimate relationship.

One unexpected positive side-effect of a childhood that does not provide the 'normal' experience of growing up in a nurturing family is what I think of as 'mature authorship'. 'Normal' development often leaves the child taking on the values and worldviews of those around them as there is no good reason to question them. A childhood like Jeni's, that is ultimately followed by effective psychotherapy, allows the person to re-imagine themselves. It's exhaustive work as so many parts of their life are questioned, but as they author their own re-creation of key elements of who they are, they do so with a level of insight and wisdom that no child can ever bring to bear on this life-defining process. There is true existential freedom, with the weight that

comes with this, in being broken down and rebuilding yourself with the appropriate help.

Another thing that Jeni has, that most of us, including myself, don't have, is the knowledge that she can cope with, and rise above, unimaginable tolls on the human psyche and soul. Many people do not survive these tolls as they succumb to the alternatives offered by suicide, sexual addiction and abuse of mind-altering substances.

Jeni has been to hell, and has risen above, to rightly claim her position as one of the first among equals.

SYMPHONY
Time to grow

It was only after the court case in 2019, that I was able to take the next step in knowing myself more fully. This exploration was only possible because I had grown to eighteen. This was a conscious choice and it was based on the fact dad was never going to be able to hurt me or anyone else again. Remaining as a child was not healthy. Being four years old was about being small, a tiny target for people who wanted to hurt me. I did not need to be like that anymore. In September 2021 I moved out of home and began independent living, just me and my dog, Holly. This move changed everything. I was free to be myself and I explored everything. I got all my alters to begin a race to adulthood. I wanted everyone to be eighteen or older as fast as possible. This would put us as adults, over the age of consent, and living in Australia. We were free, in a new home dad had never been in, and able to create our own physical world to suit ourselves. Being in my own home, with doors I could lock, and windows I could put curtains on, I finally feel safe.

LITTLE RICKY
Growing-up ceremonies

I was honoured to assist the children to grow up. George showed me how to create a growing-up ceremony and help a child to age up. The first time we did this was so magical I wanted to keep going, growing everyone right away. But I recognised that some just weren't ready.

Growing an alter in age is not easy. It begins with an acknowledgement that the war is over. George was an essential tool for this as I was able to demonstrate that dad was gone by pointing to the fact we were seeing George. George was a positive and we knew that if we were seeing him then it was after the abuse had finished. His mere presence in our life was therapeutic.

I used these growing-up ceremonies with anyone who wanted one. It was interesting to watch the adult alters use them to skip forward in time. Their willingness to do this helped the children to see it was a good process and it offered them the chance to experience new things. Some children had some pretty strange reasons for wanting to grow: one just wanted to eat pineapple, another wanted to grow so she could go to school. I had the tricky task of explaining that she wouldn't actually get to go to school, the body was too old for that. But Linda jumped in and offered to take her to craft classes instead. That worked. So many alters helped in this way. Muscles was great with the male alters, showing them that there was a place for them in our new world. Some children refused to grow up at all, they said they needed to stay the way they were so they could testify against dad.

The growing up and the re-tasking process really amped up after dad's trial was concluded in September 2019. Having successfully prosecuted dad and sent him to prison for 45 years, everyone who had stepped out of integration could change their jobs and build a new life for themselves. And I had the great pleasure of helping out with it.

We made one simple suggestion, let's get everyone to eighteen years old. This would have the effect of bringing everyone to a time when the abuse was over, we had returned to Australia without dad, and we could be free. It also had an added bonus of making sure everyone was over the age of consent for sexual or any other activities we might wish to engage in going forward. This would mean that we would all be adult decision makers, no longer a mix of children and adults. So as I write this, everyone is in a race to eighteen. It's rather humorous to watch. I am so proud of everyone. And I'm proud of me. It's not been easy to stop viewing myself as an abuser by dint of

my job. By changing jobs, I could finally see that the job is not me, it is not who I am.

SYMPHONY
It's safe to be a girl at last

At the age of fifty – just after the trial – Gabrielle gives me back my femininity and sexuality. She's been holding on to them for nearly thirty-five years. In that time, she's done an awful lot of work with them. I threw her a rough chunk of rock, and she returns it as a beautifully carved stone. I finally feel safe enough to be a woman again and to enjoy the sexual desires I've suppressed my whole life. Gabrielle's job doesn't end when she gives me back my long-lost traits.

GABRIELLE
Winning the great clothing wars

For years we were too afraid to wear dresses. In 1996 I bought a figure-hugging red dress and it started a war: the Great Clothing War of 1996.

'There's no way I'm wearing that,' an alter blurted out. 'I'm not going out looking like a blood clot.' And so the outfit deliberations started.

'I want to wear jeans,' one alter voted.

'I like this skirt and blouse,' another added.

'Blue and green should never be seen without a colour in between,' someone vetoed.

'Let's just wear this outfit again.'

'No way, we wore it yesterday!'

The negotiations continued all morning until we finally reached a verdict: a pair of trousers and a nice top. The combo was our staple outfit for years. We were still afraid of being hurt and dressed for protection. We wore pants to ward off unwanted touching and baggy clothes to avoid unwanted attention. We hid our body out of shame.

But as I'm writing this I'm wearing one of the beautiful 1950s swing dresses I love. Those super feminine rockabilly dresses with the

huge petticoats I've craved for years have begun to be my trademark. It's amazing that by getting the girls to grow we've discovered just how much we love the same clothes. The soft and silky fabrics make me feel sexy and feminine and I'm not ashamed of feeling this way. I've placed the shame where it belongs: on my abuser, in jail.

I feel like I have the best job; I get to explore our femininity and sexuality and make the distinction between normal and abuse. For Jeni's entire life, she hasn't understood what healthy is, she hasn't even been able to open up to intimacy. Now, Jeni knows the words for rape and buggery, and she can tell the difference between abuse and love-making. In the years since dad was sent to jail, we've gone on a journey of discovery. And we're happy to report: being a girl isn't that bad and we know that love is real.

And we are not hiding our body or our mind any more. We are open, we are free.

Let's be clear, there is no excuse for abuse.

My father didn't rape me because I was too sexy, or because my skirt was too short or because I was 'begging for it'. He raped me because he is an abuser. He was in a position of power and I was vulnerable. He did it because he could. I didn't deserve what my father did with me as a child, and I don't deserve to carry his shame as an adult. So I'm not.

SYMPHONY
Where was Mum?

Where was your mum? It's the question I get all the time, and I dread it. Whenever I was hit with this question I felt that my dad's abuse of me mattered less than my mother's location. It drove me nuts and so the boys got quite frustrated and snappy as they answered the question. I felt my abuse dismissed as nothing. It hurts.

I've never wanted to hurt my mum for her role in my life. I've always felt protective of my mother. I've been quick to dismiss people who ask how she couldn't have known what was going on under her roof. I realise my mum wasn't complicit in my dad's abuse, but her inability to see what was happening has hurt me. I've struggled with

feelings of resentment towards my mother – and then guilt over that resentment. Neglect is a different kind of abuse entirely, however unintentional, or coerced, it is.

For years I thought, if only my mum took more notice, if only my mum could have heard the telepathic messages I sent her through song, if only she could have saved me. But thoughts of 'if only' don't change the reality. I no longer deal in 'if only'.

By protecting mum I'm cheating her of growth opportunities, of the chance to apologise and make up for the deficits of the past.

So I stopped protecting her, and moved out of home. She still lives nearby and we see each other every week and talk on the phone almost every day. Now that I'm living on my own, our relationship is healthier than it's ever been. I've the space, and her encouragement, to explore our relationship and examine all its complexities. I can say out loud words I've never had the courage to say for fear of hurting her. I've been able to question her decisions, her behaviour, her thoughts, her attitudes and her treatment of me. I've had the courage to tell her how her behaviour hurt me: how calling me Maggot hurt; how not standing up to dad for me led me to think she didn't care or she condoned his abuse of me.

Now, instead of automatically protecting and defending my mum I can speak the truth of my abuse. Where was my mum? She was there. She was in the bedroom, the laundry, the kitchen, the garden. She was reading or sewing in the living room, or sorting stamps in the dining room. She was ironing our clothes, cooking the evening meal, or doing the washing up. She was upstairs, downstairs or outside. She was there.

He abused me regardless of where mum was, safe in his respectability and with complete control over his family. Who would take him on? Certainly not his downtrodden wife. She suffered domestic violence, financial and economic abuse, and the most horrific emotional manipulation and coercive control at his hands. How could she help me? She couldn't even help herself.

But to answer your burning question – where was mum?
She was there.

Note from Jeni's mum

Yes, you're right, Jeni. I was there but I wasn't there for you in the best way, or the way you needed me to be. This is because your dad sabotaged my attempts to help you. He blamed your pain and distress on school bullies, school phobia, problems with your friends, your teachers, anything but him. And I, like a fool, believed him.

I had no one else to turn to for explanations of your behaviour. I went to your dad and he lied to me, directing my mind away from your home life. He protected himself and left you to live in agony. I wish so much I could go back and fix it, but I can't. I knew you were vulnerable, so sweet and innocent, in need of protection, especially with your eye problems, and yet I couldn't protect you from the monster in your own home.

You tried so hard to tell me about the abuse over the years and I admit I did not hear you. Whenever the conversation turned to sex I was badly triggered into my own history of sexual abuse and I couldn't hear you. I dissociated to get away from my own terrors. You say I looked like I fell asleep. The message that gave you was terrible, as if I didn't care. I did care very deeply but, again, I couldn't find the words you needed to hear from me. My own past, which Richard was fully aware of, colluded with him to render me deaf, dumb and blind.

Your dad was monstrous in so many ways, but how he stopped me from helping you hurts the most. I would do anything to go back and change what I did and said when you tried to tell me. I wish to God I could undo my mistakes and help you. I am so sorry, Jeni.

Please know I believe you. I love you. I appreciate all that you have done for me, even when I didn't know you were doing it. I think you are amazing, so strong and heroic. I'm proud to be your mum.

JENI

Repositioning MPD/DID as reaction to violent crime

If 1.3 per cent of the population have DID, then that means 1.3 per cent of the population have been the victim of extreme sexual, emotional and/or physical torture resulting in dissociation

and the fracturing of a child's soul. Remember that the development of DID is almost entirely due to crimes committed against tiny children. The normal response to DID is disbelief, condemnation or therapy to make the alters go away, it is not seeking legal remedies against the abuser. I understand this but this means the number of sexual predators getting away with their crimes is enormous but incalculable. Abusing your victim so badly they develop MPD/DID has been rewarded not condemned! This must not continue. After all, imagine the outcry if we decided that all victims of attempted murder were to be treated as mentally ill and their assailants never brought to justice. Where is the difference? Why is the sexual abuse of babies and small children an issue for the mental health system, not for the legal system. It's been obscene how monsters like my dad have got away with their abuse up to now.

I acknowledge that parts of the legal process validated the lies of my father. A particular difficulty was when criminals like dad are given the legal presumption of innocence until being found guilty. In the world of childhood sexual abuse this presumption has been used by offenders to imply that the police will presume that the victim is a liar until being proved to be telling the truth. This is devastating and is one of the reasons victims hesitate to go to the police. After all, what kind of fool wants to put themselves through that. And that's what paedophiles count on. They terrorise us as child victims knowing that the process of seeking justice will favour them and give them far more rights than their victims.

The police can help with this by emphasising that the presumption of innocence does not come with a presumption that the victim is a liar until proven otherwise. They can unpick this very easily by simply highlighting their belief in the victim and what they are saying. After all, the police believed me immediately, but didn't tell me this for months, and then only disclosed after a direct question from me. Remembering we struggle to see our rights, let alone ask for them to be respected, can help the process too. Telling us what we need to hear may take a few moments in your day, but we will

cling to your words and use them for comfort during the lack of information that can happen during a police investigation.

There were many times during the criminal investigation process that I felt like I was on trial, that I was the one being tested and questioned. I was examined in detail, but he was able to refuse to answer questions. He wasn't even made to have a proper police interview. He flat out refused to talk to the police. He was afforded the benefit of doubt, adjournments. Most insulting of all, was that he got the automatic right to anonymity if I sought to protect my identity and privacy. I couldn't even seek legal advice on the process I was going through. This must change. Perhaps the lessons learned from my case will help redress the balance somewhat.

The trial of my father was unique because I declined anonymity and allowed the media to report on my case, which forced a spotlight onto the relationship between DID and sexual abuse and torture. I refused to wait for the world to catch up and deal with DID appropriately as a reaction to criminal acts. It was taking too long. Instead, I demanded justice. And every other survivor with MPD/DID is equally entitled to justice within the legal system. If you've experienced sexual abuse as a child and have survived through the strategy of DID, go and claim your justice. You deserve it!

I took these courageous steps hoping that, from now on, when people hear about someone with DID they will know automatically that this person has survived sexual abuse and torture, thus reducing the need for the victim to be re-traumatised by telling their story. If society can automatically see DID as evidence of the worst crimes a child can endure perhaps they will start to treat the survivor with compassion and understanding instead of disbelief and condemnation. That's why choosing to go public with my name – and my dad's – was such a triumph. I want the world to know who I am. I have nothing to be ashamed of.

I want survivors of abuse and people with MPD to know that my case set a precedent. I need them to know that if they have the ability to take their perpetrator to court, justice can be served. If I did it, they can too.

I had a plan and it worked. I had a plan to expose dad and the damage he did to me. I hoped to help others by exposing MPD/DID's role as an essential coping strategy for horribly abused and tortured children. I wanted to expose these crimes, and the criminals who commit them, to the light of public scrutiny. My plan worked even better than I'd ever dreamed possible.

Since going on this journey, I can look at my childhood abuse and see it for what it was. I was a child and I didn't have a sexual identity. Despite what dad said, I didn't want it, need it, or love it. He raped us because he wanted to, because he got a kick out of hurting us, because he was a sadist, a monster and a criminal. He pleaded guilty because he is guilty. He isn't in jail because I hate him, he's there because he committed atrocious crimes against me.

JENI

Making my own way

Growing up in Greenacre, just twenty-five kilometres from the coast, I went to the beach once. We lived in a country with the best beaches in the world, but dad didn't like the sand, so we didn't make any summer memories splashing in the shallows, licking sticky icy-pole juice from our fingers or putting aloe vera on our sunburn. It was ironic, then, that when the alters integrated, they all wanted to go to the beach.

I'm finishing this book in my new house, five minutes away from the beach. When I was growing up, my childhood home was shrouded in darkness – both figuratively and literally. As an adult, all I've ever wanted is a light-filled space of my own. Now, I have it. I'm so happy, I could cry, but I've shed enough tears for one lifetime.

I have seen the very worst of humanity, but I was saved by the best of it. I'll always be grateful to my friend's mum who fed me extra servings of fish and chips and saved me from starvation; to detective Rod Messer who was the first person who believed me when I told him about my abuse; to Rachel Lawson, Nick Borosh and Paul Stamoulis who worked tirelessly on my case; to the judge who sentenced my father to forty-five years in jail; and to Dr George

Blair-West who spent twenty-five years helping me understand MPD as a normal response to unavoidable, inescapable, relentless, ongoing sadistic criminal acts of sexual abuse of the worst kind– and who has so generously shared his wisdom in this book.

Last year, after more than two decades of treatment, I finished my sessions with George. It was bittersweet. Bitter in the fact that I would miss our weekly fifty minutes together, but sweet because I could see how far I'd come. I was ready.

My feet are firmly planted in the present and my heart is excited for the future. This is my time. I'm living for myself.

December and January are still difficult, but 2021 was the best Christmas I've ever had. I only experienced a couple of flashbacks over the whole six weeks, instead of the dozens per day I'd faced in the past. I wrapped up my own presents – anticipating that no one would buy me anything – but I was mistaken. I woke up on Christmas Day to a tree full of gifts, a house full of friends and love, and a future full of hope. That may sound daggy, but I don't care!

I will never integrate my alters again – unless they want to.

Frankly, it was far too quiet without them! Instead, we're giving every alter the opportunity to grow up. Giving them the gift of knowing that they're safe, they're in the present, the past is behind them.

Before the alters retire to their beach, I'm showing them all a good time. If they want to go to McDonald's, we're ordering the Big Mac. If they want to stay in and play Dungeons and Dragons all afternoon, we're knocking off early. If they want to go to the pool for a swim, we're diving straight in. Cowabunga, dude.

ERIK

The war is over. I've told the Backroom Boiler Boys and Girls to stand down. I can hang up my boots and enjoy retirement. We call a committee meeting to start the stand down process. Retraining a workforce built solely for survival is not an easy thing to do. We start by replacing the word 'cannot' with 'can' and embrace all of

the things dad took away from us – playing, TV, singing, sport, art, craft, joy.

Life may never be 'normal' for us, but it can be shiny, brilliant and free.

SYMPHONY

The music belongs to me now, I've reclaimed it. For years, music was an escape, a secret form of communication, a coping strategy. Now, music is what it's meant to be: a joy.

I've got a brand-new record player – one I would have dreamed of owning as a little girl – and my record collection is ever growing. The Osmonds are still my favourite band, but when I listen to them now it's for pleasure rather than survival.

Music saved my life – and now it's time to dance.

LITTLE RICKY

I've been promoted. It used to be my job to choose replacement people and send them out to deal with dad's abuse. Now it's my job to send people out to have fun. It's my job to bring joy to the people who need it most. When we go to the arcade to play games, I decide who gets to hit the pinball machine or Pac-Man controllers. I get to share the sunshine after all the years of shit. Now, instead of sending messages of doom, I send chocolates and candy to whoever's having a bad day.

I'm nothing like my father. I bring happiness now, not pain.

CAPTAIN BUSBY

Growing up, I was called an ugly duckling, but Erik told me one day I would grow into a beautiful swan. Today is that day. Today I turn eighteen. It means I can ride on the scary rollercoaster at Dreamworld, I can watch any movie I like, and, one day, I can kiss a boy!

We're window shopping at Chermside shopping centre in Brisbane when we spot them: a pair of hoop earrings with crystal swans dangling ever so delicately. I love them. Jeni buys them for me and I beam as I wear them. Erik was right, I'm a beautiful swan.

I put up a sign in my army barracks telling my soldiers they can grow to turn eighteen. It's a marathon and I'm cheering them on from the sideline. They can run, walk or crawl. There's no rush. We have all the time in the world now because Mum doesn't need our protection anymore. She told us so, and we believe her. Mum is safe and we are free to grow up.

HAPPY

For more than forty years, I've been burying happy memories in the dirt. I've put everything that matters to us in a box and hidden it out of reach from dad's hands. Now, dad is the one in the box. We've wrapped him up, tied a neat bow and sent him to prison – where he belongs. He has no right to be in our world. He deserves to suffer in prison, then he can die in jail.

And we deserve to live our life and store our happy memories out in the open, not deep underground. We start making new happy memories immediately. We buy an annual pass to all the theme parks on the Gold Coast and pay extra to feed the manta rays at Sea World.

My dad is gone and happiness is easier to find. There's no hiding.

ISABELLE

My name isn't Maggot anymore, it's Isabelle. I was renamed by someone special in our life. This is our first name born out of love. Jeni was named out of convenience. I was named out of hate and spite. What happened to me is heartbreaking, but I refuse to be heartbroken any longer. My heart belongs to me now. It's mine, mine to have and mine to share as I choose.

JENNIFER MARGARET LINDA

George, I want to take this moment to appreciate all you did for me. Standing up for me in court to testify about me showed me how much you believed me. Indeed, it was the single most validating thing you could have done for me. You recognised my right to justice and acted as a measure of 'community outrage' for me. It's one

thing to say all this in the therapy room, but to be willing to make a statement for the police about our therapy, is huge. It is something others with equally important evidence have not been willing or able to do for me. It is more than that though, you brought your expertise into the courtroom and testified for me. You were the first witness in the trial. You, Mum and I were the only people to testify in the end. Together we brought down a monster. Thank you.

When I look at the girl in the green dress on the cover of this book, I feel only one thing: gratitude. My name is Jennifer Margaret Linda Haynes, and it's because of the girl in the green dress that I'm alive today. When I was a tiny baby, Symphony swept me up and put me somewhere safe: inside myself. Symphony – and her army – protected me and sacrificed themselves. They took the abuse so I could live on. I can be my best self today, because they did what I couldn't do. I want to honour the stunning sacrifices they've made, the enormous things they've lost, and the important jobs they've done. Symphony created my alters with a united mission: keep Me alive. They succeeded and I'm so proud of them.

My alters are my world, my family, the people who've cared for me the most. Now it's my turn to look after them. I'm ready to watch them grow up, have fun and live freely. They paid the price for my freedom, and it's only fair they should get to enjoy it with me.

I am the sum of my parts, and my parts are absolutely phenomenal.

To the girl in the green dress, I have one thing to say: thank you.

ENDNOTES

Jeni's Superpower – Clarity of Memory

1   In Australia anyone, not just health professionals, who becomes aware of any form of sexual assault of a minor has to report it or face prosecution.

Betrayal Trauma

1   Freyd JJ, 'Betrayal Trauma: Traumatic Amnesia as an Adaptive Response to Childhood Abuse', *Ethics & Behavior* 4(4):307–329, 1994.

Solving Torture – The Sleeping Power of Dream Resolution

1   Centers for Disease Control and Prevention, 'Adverse Childhood Experiences Reported by Adults – Five States, 2009', *MMWR*, 59(49):1609–13, 2010.

2   Coren S, 'Sleep Deprivation, Psychosis and Mental Efficiency', *Psychiatric Times*, 15(3), 1998.

3   Mitchell JM et al, 'MDMA-assisted Therapy for Severe PTSD: A Randomized, Double-blind, Placebo-controlled Phase 3 Study', *Nature Medicine*, 27:1025–1033, 2021.

Understanding DID

1   Brand BL et al, 'Separating Fact from Fiction: An Empirical Examination of Six Myths About Dissociative Identity Disorder', *Harvard Review of Psychiatry*, 24(4):257–270, 2016.

2   Chaturvedi SK et al, 'Dissociative Disorders in a Psychiatric Institute in India – A Selected Review and Patterns Over a Decade', *International Journal of Social Psychiatry*, 56(5):533–9, 2009.

3   Bland BM et al, op cit.

4   I use the term 'system' to describe my DID patients' collective inner worlds. They generally appear to be comfortable with this.

The Importance of Zombies and Deservedness

1   'Meet Claudia Medina, Mexico', Nobel Women's Initiative, 2022. https://nobelwomensinitiative.org/meet-claudia-medina-mexico/

2   Marianne Williamson, *A Return to Love: Reflections on the Principles of a Course in Miracles*, New York, HarperOne, 1996.

False Memory Syndrome

1   '*Paidika* interview: Hollida Wakefield and Ralph Underwager Part I'. *Nudist/Naturalist Hall of Shame*. http://www.nostatusquo.com/ACLU/NudistHallofShame/Underwager2.html

2   Blizard RA and Shaw M, 'Lost-in-the-mall: False Memory or False Defense?', *Journal of Custody: Research, Issues and Practices*, 16(1):20–41, 2019.

3   Crook LS and McEwen LE, 'Deconstructing the Lost in the Mall Study', *Journal of Child Custody: Research, Issues and Practices*, 16(1):7–19, 2019.

4   Freyd JJ, 'Science in the Memory Debate', *Ethics & Behavior*, 8(3):101–113, 1998.

5   Osborn-Crowley L, 'Ghislaine Maxwell's Legal Team Use Controversial "False Memories" Theory as Part of her Defence,' *ABC News*, 18 January 2022. https://www.abc.net.au/news/2021-12-27/ghislaine-maxwell-jeffrey-epstein-false-memories-defence/100724358

6   Wolitzky-Taylor KB et al, 'Is Reporting of Rape on the Rise? A Comparison of Women with Reported Versus Unreported Rape Experiences in the National Women's Study-Replication', *Journal of Interpersonal Violence*, 26(4):807–32, 2010.

7   McMaugh K and Middleton W, 'The Rise and Fall of the False Memory Syndrome Foundation', *ISST News*, 21 January 2020. https://news.isst-d.org/the-rise-and-fall-of-the-false-memory-syndrome-foundation/

ACKNOWLEDGEMENTS

FROM JENNIFER MARGARET LINDA

WITH THANKS TO:

Those who believed me and helped me to stop the monster.

Especially:

All those who helped the police by making a statement about their knowledge of my life.

Rod Messer of the Queensland Police.

New South Wales Police – Bankstown Area Command Detectives Rachel Lawson and Paul Stamoulis.

The New South Wales Department of Public Prosecutions – Lloyd Babb, Nick Borosh, Sean Hughes and Ellen Dando.

The Extradition Team, and Department of Immigation.

Judge Sarah Huggett.

Karen Lindley.

Liz Hayes and the *60 Minutes* team, the Australian and international media who respected my desire to make public my story to help others and reported on my case.

To Vanessa Radnidge, Emily Lighezzolo, Deonie Fiford, Lillian Kovacs, Melissa Wilson, Louise Stark, Emma Dorph, Isabel Staas and all at Hachette. And to Alley Pascoe – you have helped me share my story with such care. Thank you.

My mother, for supporting me through the long, hard justice journey, for finding the courage to stand up against her husband and doing what was right. And above all for owning her mistakes and testifying against him.

FROM DR GEORGE BLAIR-WEST

Special thanks to my fabulous publisher Vanessa Radnidge and her awesome team at Hachette. This, our second book together, was particularly challenging as we grappled with a range of competing issues with very complex subject matter. Vanessa, your irrepressible optimism, hard work and patience is truly something to behold.

Jeni, your courage goes deep and is an inspiration to all, me included. Thank you for your gratitude, but even more for cutting me slack over the years as I found my way in therapy, with invaluable help and guidance from yourself. You deserve the sun and the stars.

HELPLINES AND SERVICES

In Australia, **in an emergency** if you are concerned for your or another's safety call **000** at any time.

Bravehearts
Phone 1800 272 831 – 8.30 am-4.30 pm,
Monday to Friday AEST
bravehearts.org.au

Kids Helpline
Phone 1800 551 800 – 24-hours, 7 days a week.
www.1800respect.org.au

Lifeline
Phone 131 114 – 24-hour service, 7 days a week.
www.lifeline.org.au/

Men's Line Australia
1300 789 978
mensline.org.au

National Sexual Assault, Domestic Family Violence Counselling Service
Phone 1800RESPECT or 1800 737 732 –
24-hour service, 7 days a week
www.1800respect.org.au

Suicide Call Back Service
Phone 1300 659 467
www.suicidecallbackservice.org.au

If you are having a mental health crisis please go to your local hospital and they can help you access a Mental Health Crisis Team. Your GP can refer you to a psychologist or psychiatrist and as Dr George Blair-West suggests, look for therapists who are trained in EMDR because they are trained to treat trauma. The easiest site to access is the Australian Psychological Society's Find a Psychologist page and search for someone near you with EMDR training: www.psychology.org.au/Find-a-Psychologist

hachette
AUSTRALIA

If you would like to find out more about Hachette Australia, our authors, upcoming events and new releases, you can visit our website or our social media channels:

hachette.com.au

HachetteAustralia

HachetteAus